TRANSACTIONS

OF THE

AMERICAN PHILOSOPHICAL SOCIETY

HELD AT PHILADELPHIA
FOR PROMOTING USEFUL KNOWLEDGE

NEW SERIES—VOLUME 66, PART 4
1976

THE BOURGEOIS DEMOCRATS OF WEIMAR GERMANY

To

ANNE MARIE

Copyright © 1976 by The American Philosophical Society

Library of Congress Catalog
Card Number 76-3198
International Standard Book Number 0-87169-664-9
US ISSN 0065-9746

ACKNOWLEDGMENTS

Grants from the Committee on Research and Creative Work of the University of Colorado made completion of this work possible. Also important was a grant from the American Philosophical Society which, while made for another project, nevertheless allowed me to go to Germany in 1973 and thus to basically complete research for this work even as I was primarily concerned with working on this other project.

The staffs of the Preussischer Geheimes Staatsarchiv in Berlin, the Institut für Zeitgeschichte in Munich, and the Bundesarchiv in Koblenz were all extremely courteous and very helpful. What the Heussarchiv of Stuttgart lacked in size was more than adequately compensated for by the helpfulness and unfailing courtesy of its staff. As always, the secretarial staff of the Department of History of the University of Colorado displayed extraordinary patience and sangfroid in dealing with the author and his seemingly endless list of requests.

My friend and colleague, Professor David Gross, was of great assistance to me. Insightful and encouraging, his presence was of very great importance indeed. Tributes to spouses often smack of the bromidic. However, in this case, I can say with complete frankness that if my wife, Anne Marie, had not provided support and encouragement, this work never would have been completed. For this most singular of reasons, it is dedicated to her.

Robert A. Pois

Boulder, Colorado
1975

THE BOURGEOIS DEMOCRATS OF WEIMAR GERMANY

Robert A. Pois

CONTENTS

	PAGE
Introduction	5
I. The Weimar Democrat before the Weimar Republic	8
II. The Democrats and the Weimar Constitution	15
III. State and republic: from constitution to the death of Ebert	29
IV. State and republic, 1925 to 1930: the last attempts to defend parliamentary republicanism	51
V. The Weimar Democrats turn toward political romanticism. The formation of the *Staatspartei* and the background of this action	70
VI. The German Democrats and the Jews	79
VII. The Democratic reaction to Nazism	87
VIII. Two examples of Democratic rejection of republicanism	100
IX. Conclusions	107
Bibliography	113
Index	115

INTRODUCTION

A valid approach to understanding Nazism is that of attempting to place this phenomenon within the broader framework of Western history in general and German history in particular. Numerous authors—Peter Viereck, George L. Mosse, Fritz Stern, Ralf Dahrendorff, and Karl Dietrich Bracher among others (some of these, admittedly, are of the "liberal" persuasion)—have attempted to do this and, on the whole, their efforts have been both noble and successful. However, yet another way of approaching that admittedly somewhat singular phenomenon of Nazism is the "indirect" approach, i.e., one which does not focus upon Nazism itself, but rather upon other movements or individuals which co-existed, at least for a while, with National Socialism and its adherents. It is, admittedly, more exciting and, at times, morbidly fascinating, to focus upon the Nazis themselves and the doctrines to which they at least formally adhered. However, we must admit, at the same time, that most Germans were not Nazi in temperament or in inclination. Thus, to understand the place of Nazism in German history and, above all, why it was so successful and why it met with so little real resistance, it behooves the historian to consider the attitudes and actions of non-Nazi Germans. For only by attempting to discover the ideational make-up of the non-Nazi German can we discover in turn what it was that allowed the Nazis to rise to and to hold power.

I have chosen to investigate the Weimar-period Democrats, i.e., members of the German Democratic party (DDP), the one bourgeois political party committed to the Weimar Republic. This will be in no way, shape or form a "party history." Rather, what I will be doing is investigating the political and social attitudes of bourgeois Democrats during the Weimar period.

I will be attempting to point out a very substantial reason for the success of Nazism—or at least for the lack of resistance to Nazism—through an examination of some of the attitudes expressed by Germany's Weimar-period Democrats and the party which supposedly stood for democratic republicanism. The reader will be able to discern elements of statism, political romanticism, and anti-Semitism within the republican-democratic camp itself. It is not the intention of this author to prove that such individuals as Friedrich Naumann, Friedrich Meinecke, Gertrud Bäumer, Max Weber, and Erich Koch-Weser or, for that matter, the German Democratic party itself were covertly or overtly "racist," much less Nazi. Perhaps as indicated above, enough attention has been focused exclusively upon Nazism itself and upon its own roots and development. Rather, we shall be concerned with examining both the reactions of republicans under stress and those attitudes too deeply impressed upon German political thinking to be expunged by the stroke of a pen. The story told by this work will be that of either the questioning of or, in some cases, the outright rejection of political pluralism and toleration by the best that bourgeois Germany had to offer during the Weimar period.

Naturally, one cannot gainsay the fact that many historians think that the collapse of the Weimar Republic was in large measure due to the chaos of political parties. If one accepts this view *in toto,* then one can easily reach the conclusion that some, if not all, of the anti-pluralistic views displayed by such people as Naumann, Meinecke, Bäumer, *et al.* were justified. Each of these individuals and, as we shall see, the German Democratic party itself evidenced a strong suspicion of parliamentarianism and political parties. They continually called upon the German people to rise above party and faction and commit themselves to the national interest. If one considers this seemingly heroic attitude in an unreflecting manner, it might well appear that Germany's Weimar Democrats had put a collective finger upon the greatest ill of Germany in the 1920's: divisiveness. However, if one takes a somewhat broader view of things, it becomes all too apparent that the very concern for *überparteilichkeit* and attacks upon parliamentarianism were both indicative of an attitude which had to be pernicious to the existence of any parliamentary system. For the irony of German political life during the Weimar period was simply this: that, with the exception of such self-confessed parties of class interest such as the *Wirtschaftspartei,* every party of the bourgeoisie claimed to be above politics and the crass activities of political parties. In a word, all professed allegiance to a state which, more often than not, was considered to be not merely above day-to-day politics, but above the republic as well.

It is of immense significance that one of the major criticisms which was hurled against Nazism by many of Weimar's most dedicated supporters was not that it was a vile movement of irrational racism, but that it was divisive, setting one element of the hallowed *Volk* against the other. This is not meant to imply that many bourgeois defenders of the Republic were not shocked by the extreme anti-Semitism evidenced by the movement. We shall see evidence of this as well. However, as the republic and its supporters came under more sustained attack, many democrats urged that the new republican state increase its rootedness in the collective *Volk* by making itself less "dependent" on one prominent element of support, German Jewry. Anti-parliamentarianism, anti-Semitism, and a suspicion of party activities had been ensconced within the Democratic party from the time of its formation, and many of those prominent in the party voiced such views rather early in the history of the Weimar Republic. However, they truly blossomed as Germany's democrats saw the republic slide inexorably to its doom. If one assumes that political pluralism and toleration are good, then there can be little doubt that those supposed defenders of these doctrines who sniped at them were wrong. Nevertheless, we must acknowledge that they felt compelled to do so in the name of political realism. No bourgeois party which adhered to seemingly pallid doctrines of pluralism and religious toleration—at least of the Jews—could have survived in the unhappy Weimar period. To the same degree as the republic itself had become dependent on the anti-republican army, the preservation of a formal republicanism had become dependent upon a gradual swing towards the right; in effect, upon a disavowal of those characteristics vital for the existence of a pluralistic society. Perhaps the one major criticism that we can make of the harassed republicans of Weimar is that, for many of them, such a disavowal was not terribly painful.

While the author wishes to reiterate that this work is not intended to be, in any way, shape, or form, a substantive party history, but rather a study of attitudes, definitions of several of the terms utilized in this study should be given.

Parteivorstand. The powerful Executive Committee of the party. It exercised effective party leadership and was, in effect, the official representative of the party. The committee consisted of members from the various voting districts (*Wahlkreise*) throughout Germany, in direct proportion to the number of Reichstag delegates drawn from each respective district.

Parteiausschuss. This organization was composed of about one hundred individuals representing every element within the party. It was supposed to work in close conjunction with the *Parteivorstand;* but, in fact had little real power of its own.

Parteitag. The yearly meeting of the party in which the program of the party was to be established and party leaders selected. It was supposedly the most important organ of the party, and all leaders of the party were responsible to it.

The more important individuals relating directly to the German Democratic party and mentioned in this study are:

Gertrud Bäumer (1873–1954). A noted German feminist and literary critic. After Friedrich Naumann's death in 1919, co-editor of *Die Hilfe,* Naumann's old journal and, during the Weimar period, the leading literary organ of the German Democratic party. She was ministerial adviser to the minister of interior between 1919 and 1933.

Hermann Dietrich (1879–1954). *Reichminister* of finance and vice-chancellor between 1930 and 1932. After November, 1930, leader of the *Staatspartei.*

Anton Erkelenz (1878–1945). Co-editor of *Die Hilfe* (with Bäumer). He had been active in liberal trade unions, the Hirsch-Duncker movement, and served as a DDP delegate in the Reichstag. After 1930, he left the newly formed *Staatspartei* and joined the Social Democrats.

Ernst Feder (1881–1964). A noted author and, between 1919 and 1931, a political editor on the *Berliner Tageblatt,* one of the leading liberal newspapers in Germany. He was extremely active in the German Democratic party until it became the *Staatspartei* in 1930. He was of Jewish ancestry.

Otto Gessler (1875–1955). Active in DDP politics until 1927, when he left the party. He served as *Reichswehrminister* between 1920 and 1928.

Conrad Haussmann (1857–1922). An attorney by profession, Haussmann was one of the best-known authorities on constitutional law in Germany and, with Hugo Preuss, played a singular role in the writing of the Weimar Constitution. A member of the Reichstag since 1890, he had been an active fighter for parliamentary reform before the establishment of the German Democratic party.

Theodor Heuss (1884–1963). Noted publicist and prominent member of Naumann's circle before the First World War. He was an extremely important DDP (later, of course, a *Staatspartei*) delegate in the Reichstag between 1924 and 1928 and between 1930 and 1933. First president of the *Bundesrepublik* after World War II.

Erich Koch-Weser (1875–1944). Mayor of Kassel, 1913–1919. Chairman of the DDP, later the *Staatspartei,* between 1924 and 1930. He was minister of the interior between 1919 and 1921 and minister of justice between 1928 and 1929. Was of half-Jewish ancestry.

Wilhelm Külz (1875–1948). Mayor of Bückeburg between 1904 and 1912 and mayor of Zittau in 1912. He became mayor of Dresden in 1923 and was minister of the interior in 1926 and 1927 (in the second Luther and third Marx cabinets). Was active in DDP politics.

Hermann Luppe (1874–1945). Was mayor of Frankfurt am Main in 1913 and mayor of Nürnberg between 1913 and 1933. Was active in DDP politics. Killed in an air raid on Kiel in 1945.

Artur Mahraun (1890–1950). Was the *Hochmeister* of the right-wing *Jungdeutsche Orden*, the group with which Koch-Weser sought an ill-conceived alliance in 1930.

Friedrich Meinecke (1862–1954). Noted German historian of the Historicist school, he contributed much to the ideological overtones of the DDP.

Friedrich Naumann (1860–1919). Before the First World War, Naumann had been very active in the Progressive party. He was concerned with achieving an integration of all Germans, including the working class, into the state and hence put forth a doctrine of "national socialism" (his own "National Social Union," founded in the 1890's, was disbanded in 1903). Between November, 1918, and August, 1919, was first leader of the DDP. Even after his death, his influence was probably the single most important one upon the party.

Friedrich von Payer (1847–1931). Before the war, von Payer had been active in Württemberg politics and, in 1906, had played a prominent role in constitutional reform in that state. During the last two years of the war, he served in the position of vice-chancellor. Was prominent in Democratic politics until the mid-1920's.

Carl Petersen (1868–1933). Leader of the DDP after Naumann's death. He remained at this post until 1924, when he became mayor of Hamburg. Remained an important figure on the *Parteivorstand* (executive committee) until the forced disbanding of the *Staatspartei* in 1933.

Hugo Preuss (1860–1925). Wrote the original draft of the Weimar Constitution and active in the DDP until his death. Was of Jewish ancestry.

Ludwig Quidde (1858–1941). Distinguished Roman historian and pacifist, he left the German Democratic party in 1930, after it had fused with the *Jungdeutsche Orden* to become the *Staatspartei* and helped to establish the *Radikaldemokratische Partei* which was of no electoral significance whatsoever. He died in self-imposed exile in Geneva.

Walther Rathenau (1867–1922). Head of one of Germany's largest electrical concerns, the AEG (established by his father, Emil Rathenau). Rathenau was responsible for the establishment of the War Raw Materials Board (*Kriegsrohstoffabteilung*) during the First World War. In 1921 and 1922 was first minister of reconstruction and then foreign minister in the cabinet of the Centrist Dr. Joseph Wirth. Was active in DDP activities. Assassinated by the right-wing and anti-Semitic *Organization Consul* on June 24, 1922. Was of Jewish ancestry.

Hjalmar Horace Greeley Schacht (1877–1970). Banker by trade, he played a prominent role in the ending of the great German inflation of 1923 through the creation of the *Rentenmark*. Between 1923 and 1930, he was Reich currency minister on several occasions and, after 1933, he was president of the Reichsbank and later, minister of economics. He was one of the first to join the German Democratic party in 1919, but left it in 1926, feeling that it had drawn too close to the Social Democrats.

Eugen Schiffer (1860–1954). Before the war, Schiffer had been active in the left wing of the National Liberal party. Was vice chancellor and minister of justice in 1919–1920, and a member of the DDP until 1924. Was of Jewish ancestry.

Ernst Scholz (1874–1932). Was active in the right wing of the German People's party (DVP) and often opposed Stresemann. Between 1923 and 1929, he was chairman of the DVP Reichstag delegation and after Stresemann's death, he headed the party and was responsible for pushing it towards the right.

Walter Schücking (1875–1935). Distinguished professor of law, he was prominent in determining the foreign-policy positions of the German Democratic party. He was also active in the National Constitutional Assembly in 1919 and was a member of the German delegation to the Versailles Peace Conference.

Gustav Stolper (1888–1947). Noted economist and active in formulating economic policies of the DDP. Was of Jewish ancestry.

Gustav Stresemann (1878–1929). Founded the German People's party (DVP) in 1918 and headed it until his death in 1929. Was chancellor between August and November, 1923, and foreign minister until his death.

Ernst Troeltsch (1865–1922). Distinguished historian and, for a while, devoted to the Historicist school, he was also known for his writings on theological problems and issues. Was fairly active in Democratic politics until his death in 1922.

August Weber (1871–1961). Prominent banker. Was active in the National Liberal party before World War I. Reichstag delegate 1907–1912. He was with the Ministry of Economics in 1923, and, in 1929, was Chairman of the DDP Reichstag fraction. Because of his marriage to a Jewish woman, he was forced into exile in 1939.

Max Weber (1864–1920). World-famous sociologist and political theorist, he was one of the first nationally known figures to join the DDP. He served on the *Parteiausschuss* between 1919 and 1920.

Theodor Wolff (1868–1943). Between 1906 and 1933, he was chief editor of the *Berliner Tageblatt*. He was one of the founders of the DDP during the week of November 10–November 17, 1918, and in fact drew up the party manifesto. He left the party in 1926 over the controversy surrounding the *Schund und Schmutzgesetz*. Died in the Oranienburg concentration camp in 1943. Was of Jewish ancestry.

I. THE WEIMAR DEMOCRAT BEFORE THE WEIMAR REPUBLIC

The oft-mocked naïveté of Germany's 1848 liberals, which often has been overemphasized, most certainly had been expunged by the turn of the century. Eugen Richter might well have been still holding forth with myopic vigor for constitutionalism, but he had become an object of scorn for most of Germany's liberals, who had long since attained a reconciliation of power and *Kultur*.[1] His own Progressive party itself was torn with dissension. On the one hand there stood Richter himself, determined to preserve the party as a bastion of constitutionalism and free enterprise; on the other hand, there were such liberals as Conrad Haussmann and Friedrich von Payer who, under the influence of Friedrich Naumann (to be discussed below) were determined to make the Progressive party into a vehicle for that interesting variety of national socialism that had been espoused by Naumann since the mid-1890's. Eugen Richter died in 1906 and, only four years later, there arose a new Progressive party based upon Naumann-determined principles. At the same time, there was developing a considerable dichotomy between the right and left wings of the National Liberal party, one which was in large measure due to the influence of Hermann Fischer, an individual who was also interested in Naumann's efforts to wed *Volk* to state. Basically, Naumann, and those who thought along similar lines, believed that a reform of the Prussian voting system, i.e., an abrogation of the three-class voting system, had to be put into effect, that more power had to be given to the Reichstag and the powers of Prussian *Junkertum* limited—all of this dictated not by social conscience, although this had a role to be sure, but by needs of state. While Richter and liberals of his ilk had seen the state as representing some sort of threat to constitutional development, the "new" liberal *á la* Naumann, viewed the state in more positive terms. Success in foreign policy and imperial ventures would assure the ultimate happiness of inhabitants of the state as well as its *Kultur*. However, to allow the state maximum ability to exercise a commanding role in foreign affairs, integration of the entire *Volk* into it was necessary. State and *Volk* could and should become one; the unspoken dichotomy between state and *Kultur* and, as Richter saw it, between state and freedom, did not exist.

The last two decades of the nineteenth century and the first decade of the twentieth witnessed the emergence of a form of German liberalism which gave happy testimony to the ability of Germany's intelligentsia to fuse power and *Kultur* for the benefit of the state. Here, one need only to consider the names of Friedrich Naumann, Max Weber, and Friedrich Meinecke, all of whom called upon the so recently unified German state to provide for that internal unity so necessary for sustained programs of external expansion. What the brilliant, racist-tinged Treitschke and monocled hysterics such as General Friedrich von Bernhardi shouted out, more cool-headed devotees of the power state such as Naumann expressed in a quieter fashion: the unified German state must assume a place in the sun commensurate with its national potential. To achieve this end, a truly mass power state would have to be created. The mass armies and warfare of the future necessitated a fusion of *Demokratie und Kaisertum,* of democracy and empire. The socialist scales had to be dropped from the eyes of the masses, and they had to be brought to the state. The state could no longer be a pallid reflection of agrarian *Junkertum*. Rather, it had to become an industrialized behemoth, supported by the unwavering allegiance not only of clergymen, businessmen, and *Junker,* but of those who stoked its furnaces and mined its coal.

Such thinking was concretely embodied in the writings of Friedrich Naumann as well as in his short-lived National Social Union. Pastor Naumann, at one time a romantic compatriot of the anti-Semitic Pastor Adolf Stöcker,[2] had forsaken the latter's astringent romanticism and in the decades immediately before World War I had become an almost hallowed prophet of the power state. This state, in a self-consciously casuistic fashion, was to provide for the social needs of its citizens, the better in order to use their collective energies for the fulfillment of foreign-policy goals. "If," Naumann warned, "Germany wants to assume its great role, it will need to clothe itself in new garments to that purpose. The old Prussian clothes are too stiff for that."[3]

Germany's military future was dependent upon the degree to which she was able to wed the masses to the state.[4] Naumann was not alone in these speculations. Friedrich Meinecke who, as it turned out, would be the last representative of the doctrine of Historicism,

---

[1] Two works are of particular importance in discussing this problem: Leonard Krieger, *The German Idea of Freedom* (New York, 1975), and Ralf Dahrendorf, *Society and Democracy in Germany* (New York, 1967).

[2] For a discussion of Naumann's involvement with Pastor Stöcker, see George L. Mosse, *The Crisis of German Ideology* (New York, 1964), pp. 193–194. Also, Theodor Heuss, *Friedrich Naumann, der Mann, das Werk, die Zeit* (Berlin, 1937), 40–41.

[3] Friedrich Naumann, *Demokratie und Kaisertum* (Third enlarged edition, Berlin, 1904), p. 214.

[4] *Ibid.,* p. 202.

lent intellectual and moral support to Naumann although, as he confessed in his *Erinnerungen,* he remained too much of a "Biedermeier" ever to have much of an appreciation for the industrial age.[5] Max Weber, while skeptical as to the political maturity of Germany's bourgeoisie, and tending to view the proletariat's ability to indulge in power politics with contempt, augmented Naumann's demands with some more stringent ones of his own. In a May, 1895, speech at Freiburg, Weber remarked, "It is dangerous and incompatible with the national interest, when an economically declining class holds political domination in its hands."[6] Weber was of course attacking ossified *Junkertum.* He complemented this attack with a somewhat less than clarion call for economic reform and social justice, emphasizing that reform of any kind was not designed to meet the needs and interest of any one class, but rather to serve ". . . the enduring power-political interests of the Nation."[7] While Weber retained a considerable degree of skepticism in regard to Germany's masses, both he and Naumann were striving towards much the same goal: strengthening of the German power state through basing it upon mass support. Theodor Heuss, in his *Preludes to Life,* recalls that as a young man he

devoured *Demokratie und Kaisertum* and found a new vindication of democracy based not on internal political considerations, sentiment, or a spirit of opposition, but on a realistic appraisal of the interests of the State; and the Kaiser was no longer looked upon as the personal representative of a dynasty, but as an institution of national political leadership.[8]

As mentioned above Naumann's National Social *Verein* was somewhat short-lived. However, the ideals which were supposedly concretized in the party were definitely not and, after a new, revivified Progressive party was founded in 1910 under Naumann's leadership, it served as a convenient vehicle for them. Moreover, many left-wing National Liberals, e.g., Meinecke and Eugen Schiffer, found themselves either agreeing with Naumann or coming to approximately the same conclusions all on their own. In Zittau, *Oberbürgermeister* of Bückeburg Wilhelm Külz, later to be prominent in the German Democratic party, took the occasion in 1911 to point out how true liberalism worked for the unified fatherland and eschewed class politics.[9]

In 1912 Walther Rathenau, then head of the AEG, one of Germany's largest electrical firms, and later to be head of Germany's wartime Raw Materials Board, foreign minister in the Wirth government, and prominent member of the German Democratic party, suggested to Bethmann-Hollweg, German Reich chancellor, that Germany move in the direction of establishing a central European customs union.[10] That such a union would be dominated by and would benefit Germany was presupposed. Such a suggestion did not constitute a machiavellian intrusion into an otherwise humanitarian/pacifist soul. For Rathenau considered himself to be above all else German, and he shared the concern of all liberals that Germany's foreign-policy goals not be threatened by a lack of mass participation in the state.[11] In many ways, Germany's pre-World War One liberals were as romantic as their *Paulskirche* ancestors had been; but theirs had now become a romanticism of iron.

There was little reason why things should have been any different. After all, the educated bourgeoisie, the *Bildungsbürgertum,* had cut its intellectual teeth on philosophical and historical doctrines that saw power itself as something spiritual. Perhaps of greatest importance in this regard were the writings of Leopold von Ranke, who steadfastly maintained that nations demonstrated what spirit they had when confronting or actually fighting other nations.[12] A merciful and just God might well have been the ultimate arbiter of history; however, in an imperfect world, nation-states had to be laws unto themselves. Of course, Ranke himself was a political conservative, spiritually more at home in a traditionally monarchical environment.[13] He would hardly have felt comfortable in the company of such liberals as Naumann, Weber, or Heuss. Obviously, he would have been pleased with Meinecke's—at that time, at least—almost slavish adherence to his own ideas on power and the state; but, most certainly Meinecke would have appeared to him as something of a backslider in the field of politics. Nevertheless, it is of the utmost significance that, not only German historiography, but Germany's most enlightened liberals, accepted the Rankean view of the state and of its mission.

Perhaps the most important consequence which stemmed from this acceptance was the liberal tendency to view internal policy as being subordinate to external policy. This had been a basic precept of the Rankean approach, one which stemmed quite logically from his view that states revealed whatever "moral energies" they possessed only in conflict with other states.[14] After all, if such were the case, then the most important

---

[5] Friedrich Meinecke, *Erinnerungen, Vol. II Strassburg, Freiburg, Berlin 1901–1919* (Stuttgart, 1949), pp. 261–262.

[6] Max Weber, *Gesammelte Politische Schriften* (2nd enlarged edition), newly edited by Johannes Winckelmann (Tübingen 1958), p. 19.

[7] *Ibid.,* p. 18.

[8] Theodor Heuss, *Preludes to Life, Early Memoirs,* translated from the German by Michael Bullock (London, 1955), p. 113.

[9] Bundesarchiv, Koblenz, Nachlass Külz, Nr. 56, Reden in Meeran. Bückeburg und Zittau, 1911–1933, 1941–1943, 3.

[10] Fritz Fischer, *Germany's Aims in the First World War* (New York, 1967), pp. 10–11.

[11] Rathenau's most famous work on this theme was his *Zur Kritik der Zeit,* of 1912.

[12] For an excellent discussion of this see George G. Iggers, *The German Conception of History* (Middletown, Conn., 1968), pp. 78–84.

[13] *Ibid.,* pp. 87–88.

[14] Leopold von Ranke, *Politische Gespräch,* Introduction by Friedrich Meinecke (München, 1924 ed.), p. 37.

questions for a state would be ones of foreign policy in general and warfare in particular. All of this was quite logical, but it boded ill for the future of German social reform. Only an avowedly class party, the Social Democrats, who felt themselves compelled to pay at least lip-service to the Erfurt Synthesis of 1891, could serve as a whole-hearted exponent of social reform for its own sake. The class which in Western lands had traditionally served as a vehicle for republican aspirations, the bourgeoisie, was hardly in the position to do so in Germany. Either, as in the case of many National Liberals, it had sacrificed constitutional and social reform upon the altar of extreme nationalism or, as in the case of many left-wing National Liberals such as Meinecke and Progressives such as Naumann, its efforts at constitutional and social reform were simple exercises in political casuistry. Internal reform for its own sake was hardly a concern for Germany's *Bildungsbürgertum* before the war. Indeed, virtually all of the burden of such a struggle was placed upon the backs of the Social Democrats. In the eyes of many, this led to disastrous results for the party in particular, and for the nation in general.[15]

The attitude of Germany's left-wing liberals before the war is perhaps best summed up in a statement by Naumann in his much-acclaimed *Demokratie und Kaisertum* of 1900: "External policy is, in its collective course of development, yet more important and fraught with more serious consequences than the inner."[16] Such a statement, which could well have come out of Ranke's *Politische Gespräch*, points out with admirable clarity the role which was assigned internal policy by Germany's liberals. One could well argue that, in view of the prewar impotence of the Reichstag and the even then obvious growing confrontation between Germany and Great Britain, it would have been unrealistic for people such as Naumann to have imagined that internal reforms could ever have taken precedence over the more pressing needs dictated by the grim possibility of war. However, this habit of elevating foreign policy over internal policy, and seeing the latter as in effect serving those purposes dictated by "imperial" concerns was a difficult one to break. Furthermore, by seeing social, economic, or political reforms as serving a neo-Rankean reason of state, Germany's prewar liberals were in effect making them expendable. What would occur, say, if one drew the conclusion that constitutional reforms, republicanism, or alteration of the existing class structure would not serve the interests of state; or worse, threatened the interests of state? While this never really became much of an issue before and during the war, the Weimar period would see no end to this sort of lugubrious speculation.

The tendency to view the state in a collective manner also had rather interesting consequences insofar as the prewar liberal view of politics and political parties was concerned. In *Demokratie und Kaisertum*, Naumann did indicate that he saw an important role both for the "parliament" (Reichstag) and for political parties. "The task of democracy cannot be anything else other than the construction of parliamentary majorities on the German left."[17] Parties and party activities, Naumann suggested, were part of the democratic growth process anyway. However, these were not really the parties of political pluralism. The strengthening of the democratic parties was necessary in order to prevent Germany's industrialists from aligning themselves with the conservatives, a moribund group whose archaic interests could hardly serve those more important interests of state.[18] Furthermore, Naumann made the somewhat interesting observation that, in his view, constitutionalism *per se* was merely a form of "compromise," while monarchy and democracy represented principles.[19] With amazing dexterity, Naumann had succeeded in divorcing the interests of Germany's democrats from admittedly needed constitutional reforms. Such an attitude represented a necessary appendage to Naumann's tendency to view the state in functional terms, a tendency which was reflected in his claim that *Kaisertum*, the new "industrial aristocracy" and democracy were really just different aspects of one and the same thing. Democracy was, after all, merely the majority principle; the industrial aristocracy the economic form of the nation, while the Kaiser provided for national unity, in effect serving as the "dictator of the new industry."[20] While Naumann was adamant in his belief that the old monarchical structure was not catholic enough in its abilities and interests to function alone in a world of mass armies and heroic imperialism, it was of immense significance that, in *Demokratie und Kaisertum*, he saw the Kaiser as being far more realistic and progressive than the Reichstag. After all, Wilhelm II seemed to be far more sensitive to German needs for power, e.g., the necessity of building a strong navy, than many of the more precious Reichstag delegates. It was he, and not they, who was pointing the way to the future.[21] Somewhat stiffly, Naumann suggested that the Kaiser would be more sensitive to the "sighing ... moaning of the working masses" when the masses began to be more concerned with Germany's power position in the world.[22] Thus, for Naumann, politics, parties, and even democracy itself were simply means to the end of furthering interests of state. Unlike others of approximately his political position, he never launched extensive attacks on the parliamentary system or upon pluralism. How-

---

[15] For a fine analysis of this problem, see A. J. Ryder, *The German Revolution of 1919* (Cambridge, 1967), esp. pp. 12–13.
[16] Naumann, *op. cit.*, pp. 178.
[17] *Ibid.*, p. 43.
[18] *Ibid.*, p. 95.
[19] *Ibid.*, p. 45.
[20] *Ibid.*, pp. 180–181.
[21] *Ibid.*, pp. 187–189.
[22] *Ibid.*, p. 219.

ever, there could be little doubt that Naumann's view of internal policy, political parties, and democracy was tinctured by what he believed to be were *Real*-political considerations. As Heuss points out in a 1960 speech entitled, "Friedrich Naumann und die deutsche Demokratie," Naumann did not see anything magical about the monarchy and was often critical of it.[23] However, the state which was embodied in the person of the emperor was, if not magical, then at least an entity which was somewhat more than the sum of its parts.

Naturally, this view of political parties which saw them as necessary, but of secondary interest when juxtaposed against interests of state, was not limited to Naumann. Friedrich Meinecke, who took an active if somewhat limited role in National Liberal party activities, once stated in a 1911 letter to Georg von Below that, as far as he was concerned, both conservative and liberal elements were necessary in national life. However, as for himself, the primary objective of his participation in political life was "to once more make 'Conservative' useful."[24] Party pressures, Meinecke thought, "cannot be dispensed with," although he felt himself to be free from party pressures of any kind. The conservatism which Meinecke was hoping to make useful once again, was none other than that variety which had been historically reflected in political dualism; parties and political life on one side, the state on the other. Party pressures, in Meinecke's eyes, were necessary. However, they were not necessary in order to advance the interests of a particular class or even a particular set of interests, but, as he put it in an earlier letter, to "lead the masses" onto national paths.[25]

It is also important to realize that for individuals such as Naumann and Meinecke, political Catholicism, in the form of the Centre party, represented a palpable threat to the state unity which was so desired.[26] Meinecke, particularly, was irked that the Conservatives had chosen to leave the Bülow bloc over the issue of tax reform and thus aligned themselves with the Centrists.[27]

It would not be much of an exaggeration to state that the pre-World War One "democrat" saw his task as being substantially the winning of an anti-national, Marxist-oriented working class and a potentially ultramontane Catholic population to the state. It is of extreme significance that such democrats either explicitly or implicitly assumed that the state was somehow embodied in the left-wing bourgeoisie, i.e., in themselves. It was in part this assumption which led them to believe that any sign of party clashing was inimical to the state interest. It was with considerable pride that Heuss pointed out that Friedrich Naumann's paper, the *Freisinnige Zeitung,* was "outside the sphere of party politics."[28] Such a tendency was at least partially responsible for the somewhat curious attitude, to Western liberal eyes, toward political parties that we have seen maintained on the part of Germany's "democratic" elements, *viz.* political parties ought not to be divisive but should, in some way, represent, or be made to represent, the national interest. In view of the tasks which Naumann and others saw before them—strengthening Germany's interests abroad, bringing the masses to the state, creating a state sensitive to mass needs while yet conscious of imperial needs—it is not surprising that they saw their political "party" (left-wing National Liberal and Progressive) as embodying the very essence of state-interest itself. While such a point of view was certainly not illogical, it did raise a problem insofar as the republican conception of politics was concerned. First of all, we must see that the democrats were unconsciously or, in some cases (e.g., Meinecke's), consciously adhering to the Rankean maxim that politics ought best to be confined to the area of foreign and power politics. Internal politics were seen in a contributory or supportive role. Secondly, we must also see that political parties were conceived of as being, in reality, *Staatsparteien,* parties which were supposed somehow to advance the interests of the German state. Naumann, among others, saw even his own party as being somewhat provisional in nature. The real purpose of pre-1914 political activities was to provide for a political unity "which extends from Bassermann to Bebel"; in other words, from the National Liberals all the way over to the Social Democrats.[29] Such a party would hardly have been a "political" party in the Western European use of the term, inasmuch as it would have quite simply embraced everything which Naumann and his colleagues considered to be coextensive with the state. Of course, one could not gainsay the fact that such a party would have stood for needed social and constitutional reforms, as did the Progressive party and the left wing of the National Democratic party. However, these would have been reforms dictated by demands of state policy. For example Gustav Stresemann, who, while evidencing considerable interest in Naumann's national-socialist schemes, did not come out for constitutional

---

[23] Theodor Heuss, *Friedrich Naumann und die deutsche Demokratie* (Wiesbaden, 1960), pp. 22–28.
[24] Friedrich Meinecke, *Ausgewählter Briefwechsel,* ed. Ludwig Dehio (Stuttgart, 1962), p. 35.
[25] Friedrich Meinecke, *Politische Schriften und Reden,* ed. George Kotowski (Darmstadt, 1958), p. 53.
[26] On Naumann's fear of ultramontane influences, see *Demokratie und Kaisertum,* p. 132. On Meinecke's, see the *Strassburger Post,* N. 31, *Erste Morganausgabe,* 10, January, 1912, in Preussisches Geheimes Staatsarchiv, Berlin, Kulturbesitz Rep. 92, Nachlass Meinecke, Nr. 91.
[27] Meinecke, *Politische Schriften und Reden, op. cit.*

[28] Heuss, *Preludes to Life, op. cit.,* p. 160.
[29] *Schriftenreihe der Friedrich Naumann Stiftung um Politik und Zeitgeschichte,* ed. Paul Luchtenberg & Walter Erse, Bd. 10, *Geschichte des deutschen Liberalismus,* p. 92. The most complete study of efforts to construct such a coalition is Beverly Heckart, *From Bassermann to Bebel. The Grand Bloc's Quest For Reform In The Kaiserreich, 1900–1914* (New Haven and London, 1974).

reforms until late in the war did not feel uncomfortable being snugly ensconsed in the left wing of the National Liberal party.[30]

The attitude of the prewar democrats towards the "Jewish Question" was certainly a progressive one in a Germany which had seen a marked rise in openly espoused anti-Semitism during the 1880's and 1890's up to the First World War.[31] Friedrich Naumann pointed out that, in blaming all the agonies of the industrial age upon the Jews, Conservatives and formal anti-Semites were really ignoring the fundamental realities of industrialism, as well as the necessity of Germany's becoming a strong, industrial state.[32] Throughout Heuss's memoirs, we can observe a strong reaction against vulgar anti-Semitism, and Friedrich Meinecke, in his *Erinnerungen*, points out that racial anti-Semitism made little impression upon him or upon those in the circles in which he moved.[33] The prewar writings of the German democrats seem to reveal that, for many of them, anti-Semitism was beside the point, and the Progressive party indeed attracted the support of a good many German Jews. It is also obvious, however, that, in a nation in which various varieties of intellectual and social (to say nothing of racist) anti-Semitism were taken as a matter of course, it was impossible that even democrats could have avoided coming into contact with anti-Semitic doctrines, or, in some cases, being influenced by them. As seen above, even Friedrich Naumann had been able to join with Pastor Stöcker in founding the anti-Semitic League of German Students in 1881. Friedrich Meinecke, in his *Erinnerungen*, confessed to being a "rugged anti-Semite" in the days of his youth,[34] while in a political essay of the Weimar period, he mentions how he greeted the Tivoli Program (1892) of the Conservative party, because it called for "class reconciliation" and the general alleviation of class tensions.[35] The fact that the Conservatives hoped that such a reconciliation could be bought at the price of German Jewry—against whose "decomposing influences" the Program took a strong stand—seems not to have made much of an impression upon Meinecke, either in 1892 or later. In his own *Erinnerungen, 1905–1933,* Theodor Heuss made the extremely candid observation that, although he knew many Jews, such as Rabbi Kohn of Berlin, the "development of the sociological structure in Germany had made it impossible ever to be really close to many Jews."[36]

Such isolated incidents and statements certainly do not point to the existence of systematically racist doctrines among Germany's prewar democrats. However, they do seem to be indicative of a fairly strongly embedded social anti-Semitism, one which made it well-nigh impossible for even a German democrat to see the Jews as being as German as themselves. Often a German Jew, e.g., Walther Rathenau, had to go to the most extreme lengths possible in order to prove himself to be German and, for individuals like Meinecke, only conversion itself would suffice.[37] Before the war, the existence of social anti-Semitism, or at least the tendency to see Jews and Germans as being somehow "different" from one another, was not terribly important in the history of German democracy. However, during the Weimar period, when the Weimar Republic and the party which stood four-square for it, the German Democratic party, were to come under attack for being dependent upon Jewish interests, such tendencies would become of considerable importance, and openly anti-Semitic remarks not unusual in the writings of Heuss, Meinecke, Koch-Weser, Gessler, and other luminaries of Germany's left-wing *Bürgertum*. For this class of individuals, crude, racist anti-Semitism was disgusting and often beside the point. Moreover, it would be preferable to have the Jews, as well as the workers and Catholics, on the side of the state. However, it appears that during the Weimar period even Germany's democrats considered the Jews perhaps more expendable than other German citizens. Certainly the circumstances surrounding the metamorphosis of the Democratic party into the *Staatspartei* in 1930, as well as attitudes displayed by the several prominent democrats mentioned above, would bear this out.

The reaction of German democrats to the First World War was both expected and understandable, and we shall dwell upon it only briefly. All of them proclaimed joyful adherence to the German war effort. Meinecke rejoiced that August 4, 1914, saw a unified fatherland; that the Social Democrats were not going to "desert" it.[38] Throughout the war, Meinecke adhered to Naumann's principles of social reform plus *Realpolitik*. He rejected the annexationist demands of the *Vaterlandspartei* as unrealistic while holding onto what he considered to be realistic territorial demands

---

[30] Henry Asby Turner, Jr., *Stresemann and the Politics of the Weimar Republic* (Princeton, 1963), pp. 7-8.

[31] The best single work on this phenomenon is Peter C. Pulzer's *The Rise of Political Anti-Semitism In Germany and Austria* (New York, 1964). It is well to point out, though, that by 1912, formal anti-Semitic *parties* were pretty much finished. See Richard S. Levy, *The Downfall of The Anti-Semitic Political Parties In Imperial Germany* (New Haven and London, 1975).

[32] Naumann, *Demokratie und Kaisertum, op. cit.,* p. 106.

[33] As an example of Heuss's reaction against anti-Semitism see his *Preludes to Life,* where he describes an incident that occurred during a visit to Cologne: "We turned at random down a side street, were angered by an anti-Semitic bookshop, and manifested our views by eating a hearty meal at a Jewish hotel" (p. 85). On Meinecke's reminiscences see *Erinnerungen* 2: pp. 27-30.

[34] Meinecke, *Erinnerungen* 2: p. 27.

[35] *Politische Schriften, op. cit.,* p. 369.

[36] Theodor Heuss, *Erinnerungen* 1905–1933 (Tübingen, 1963): p, 186.

[37] See Meinecke's *Erinnerungen* 2, where he tells how social intercourse with Walter Lenal became easier once the latter had converted to Christianity.

[38] *Ibid.,* p. 137.

in Europe.³⁹ In various essays, he called called upon the German state to recognize the efforts made by proletarians on its behalf and to implement those social reforms necessary if Germany were to be able to have that integrated state so necessary in an age of mass warfare.⁴⁰ Rathenau, from his position as head of the War Materials Board, continued to espouse his previously formulated notions of *Mitteleuropa,* while the master Naumann himself came out with a work of that name in 1915. Naumann also saw the war as a final justification of previous Progressive policies. Now that the German masses had proven themselves in battle, their sacrifices would have to be recognized. Progressive "trust" in the capabilities of the German common people, as opposed to that lack of trust revealed by the Conservatives before the war, had been vindicated.⁴¹ The war simply represented an acceleration of the earlier activities of the German democrats. Now, however, things had become a bit more desperate due to it. "[There can be] no war without the unity of the two great forces of Democracy and Empire," Naumann had written.⁴² While now, at least as Naumann saw it, greater things than voting rights were at stake, the government had to learn "to think national and to draw the whole *Volk* to it." ⁴³ Yet, Naumann was able to accept, at least "for the duration," the virtual ending of political life within Germany. For him, the suspension of political activities (at least those which called the government into question) that had been more or less agreed upon by all political parties on the almost hallowed day of August 4, 1914 (the so-called *Burgfrieden*) was "a national necessity." ⁴⁴ At the same time, as seen above, he was adamant that the government, which was now more or less being "left in peace" for the sake of a unified war effort, recognize that some sort of reform was necessary; if not during the war, then at least after it.

Naumann, Meinecke, and the other figures who would become important in the German Democratic party after the war, were united on one important point; *viz.,* that successful prosecution of the war effort had to be linked to internal reform. In this regard, we can consider Klaus Schwabe's division of Germany's World War I academics into those interested solely in external expansion, "the Imperialists," and those interested in internal reform, "the Naumannites." ⁴⁵ While this is interesting in a heuristic sense, we must bear in mind the fact that Naumann's "group" certainly never disavowed the pursuit of imperial aims of one sort or another. Meinecke, as pointed out above, never gave up the notion of realistic war gains while Naumann's work, *Mitteleuropa,* which came out in 1915, if not imperialistic, was at the very least calling for German economic and military predominance in Central Europe.⁴⁶ Even Theodor Wolff, the cosmopolitan liberal who edited the *Berliner Tageblatt,* maintained that Germany had legitimate claims in Eastern Europe, particularly inasmuch as Tsarist Russia had been, as he saw it, primarily responsible for the outbreak of the war.⁴⁷ For virtually all of the left-wing liberals who later would be associated with Democratic politics during the post-World War I period, that astringent dictum of *Demokratie und Kaisertum*—internal reform to assure a strong foreign policy—pretty well summarized their attitudes towards domestic policies. The ghost of Leopold von Ranke was as yet too palpable an entity to yield to exorcism. But then there were few who were as yet spiritually disposed to attempt it.

For whatever motives, however, the left-wing liberals were in favor of reforms within Germany. Moreover, they were sensitive to the notion, arising particularly from *Vaterlandspartei* circles, that a victorious war would serve the purpose of binding the German masses ever closer to the throne, and thus obviate the need of any substantive reform whatsoever. In a June 8, 1917, article in the *Berliner Tageblatt,* Theodor Wolff lashed out at such an attitude:

But, we should not say and write that, beyond these goals, the continuation of the war is necessary in order to suppress democracy. One should not say this of that democracy which bears [so] heavy [a] burden in the land, and not of that democracy which lies in the trenches.⁴⁸

To be sure, Wolff, Theodor Heuss, Hugo Preuss, and others stood more for the hallowed Hardenberg dictum, "Democratic principle in a monarchical government," and were thus more constitutional monarchist than republican.⁴⁹ However, at least these soon-to-be "Democrats" seemed to be more aware than most of their liberal colleagues of the necessity of constitutional

---

³⁹ On this issue, see *Politische Schriften und Reden* and his "Fur Welche Güter zog Deutschland 1914 sein Schwert?" in the *Schutzengraben Bücher,* No. 115 (Berlin, 1918). Fritz Fischer, in his *Germany's Aims in the First World War,* also discusses Meinecke's views on annexations. See pp. 172–173, 276, 460. Another discussion is provided by Robert A. Pois's article "Friedrich Meinecke and Eastern Europe" in the September, 1967, issue of the *East European Quarterly* (pp. 249–260).
⁴⁰ As examples of this, see "Fur Welch Güter zog Deutschland 1914 sein Schwert?" and *Die Deutsche Erhebung von 1914* (Stuttgart, 1918), p. 13.
⁴¹ Friedrich Naumann, "Es lebe das Volk!" in *Die Hilfe,* Nr. 25, 20 June, 1918: p. 288.
⁴² Heuss, *Friedrich Naumann: der Mann, das Werk, die Zeit, op. cit.,* p. 353.
⁴³ *Ibid.*
⁴⁴ *Ibid.,* p. 359.

⁴⁵ Klaus Schwabe, *Wissenschaft und Kriegsmoral, Die deutschen Hochschullehrer und die politischen Grundfragen des Ersten Weltkrieges* (Göttingen, Zürich, Frankfurt, 1969), pp. 13.
⁴⁶ Fritz Fischer, *Germany's Aims in the First World War,* is still the best source on this. See especially pp. 247–256.
⁴⁷ Gotthart Schwarz, *Theodor Wolff und das Berliner Tageblatt* (Tübingen, 1968), pp. 46–47.
⁴⁸ *Ibid.* pp. 49–50.
⁴⁹ *Ibid,* pp. 57–58.

and voting reform for its own sake.[50] This was something that statist Meinecke and national socialist Naumann never fully appreciated. Indeed, it is doubtful that Meinecke ever had any real understanding of so non-Rankean a conception. Naumann, Meinecke, Max Weber, and, from time to time, even Theodor Wolff as well, belonged to a group whose attitude towards the relationship between internal reform and foreign policy can best be described as "Rankean"; viz. as mentioned above, they saw domestic reform as necessary in order to strengthen foreign policy.

The views of this group were summed up best by Max Weber in several articles which he wrote in 1917. On July 19, 1917, the Reichstag passed its famous "peace resolution." To be sure, this resolution called for a peace which, in large measure, would benefit the Fatherland. However, the very fact that continuation of the war, even with American entry into it, could be questioned infuriated the super-patriots of the *Vaterlandspartei*. Left-wing National Liberals, Progressives, Catholic Centrists, and Social Democrats had united in voting for this resolution, and Weber felt constrained to come to the defense of such unwonted political activity on the part of a German parliament. In an article of September 20, 1917, entitled "Vaterland und Vaterlandspartei," he launched a bitter attack on the *Vaterlandspartei* declaring that reactionary demagogues of their stripe had been responsible for the disastrous course of German foreign policy before and during the war, a policy that had led to Germany's almost total isolation.[51] Again, the point which Weber was making was one shared by a good many of Germany's later "Democrats," viz., that *Realpolitik* called for the restructuring of German political life; this, to allow Germany to participate more fully in a modern world of mass political emotionalism and imperialistic foreign policy. In an essay of December, 1917 (portions of which first appeared in the November, 1917, issue of *Die Hilfe*), Weber pressed his point a bit further. Now, he suggested, the central questions about which Germans must concern themselves were those of parliamentarianization and democratization. The most dangerous consequence of the war (for all the participants, and not just Germany) was the tying together of a mass emotionalism to an actual or potential military dictatorship. Particularly in Germany, where the military caste, i.e., the aristocracy, had no political tradition whatsoever, the results of such a fusion could only be disastrous.[52]

What was needed was the creation of a true "parliamentary leadership," one which could control, or at least redirect, the raw emotionalism of the masses.[53] Only that mass leadership provided by "responsible politicians" could end that irresponsible leadership provided in times of stress by "opportunistic demagogues."[54] The choice for Germany was plain: either a bureaucratic authoritarian state with sham-parliamentarianism and a restless and dissatisfied citizenry, or a state in which all citizens would participate. "However, in this respect, a *Herrenvolk*—and only such can and, above all, should conduct '*Weltpolitik*'—has no choice."[55] As Schwarz points out, it is fairly obvious that, for Weber, humanitarian motives were not in the forefront in his call for parliamentary democracy. Power politics, i.e., the ability of Germany to conduct a responsible imperial policy, was primary for him, just as it was for Naumann and Meinecke.[56] However, it is important to note that neither Meinecke nor, at least at this point, Naumann went so far as Weber did when he called for parliamentary democracy. Voting reform in Prussia was necessary in order to allow for a greater participation of the *Volk* in the state. Nevertheless, the application of parliamentary government, after some sort of foreign model, would have had dangerous consequences in the eyes of most Naumannites, and even Troeltsch, who was one of the very few left-wing liberals who chose to emphasize the primacy of internal over external politics, was in agreement here.[57]

What united all those liberals of the Naumann persuasion was a fear of irrationality in foreign affairs. Emotionalism and the mindless archetyping of "enemies" was, generally speaking, anathema to them. In his *Erinnerungen: 1905–1933*, Theodor Heuss mentions how disturbed he was to discover that an intellectual of the stature of Werner Sombart could oversimplify the relationships and contrasts between Great Britain and Germany as being those between "shopkeepers and heroes" (*Händler und Helden*).[58] Alas, if some of these soon-to-be "Democrats" could have gazed into the dreary postwar future, they might well have been appalled at the emotionalism and anti-political statism that slumbered restively within their breasts. At best, the left-liberal calls for reform had been in large measure casuistic. Defeat would transform casuistry into idealism.

When it did come, defeat brought about little breastbeating on the parts of Germany's democrats. Instead, they chose to emphasize what they considered to be imperfections in the German state as it had developed up to that time. In an essay in *Die Hilfe*, November

---

[50] Klaus Schwabe points out that, of those "Naumannite" academics considered by him, only Preuss, supported by Ernst Troeltsch and Gerhard Anschütz, was really interested in constitutional reform for the sake of reform, and not merely as a device to allow for a stronger foreign policy. See Schwabe, op. cit., p. 133.

[51] Max Weber, *Gesammelte Politische Schriften, op. cit.,* p. 220.

[52] Ibid., "Wahlrecht und Demokratie," p. 270.

[53] Ibid., p. 275.
[54] Ibid.
[55] Ibid., p. 279.
[56] Schwarz, op. cit., pp. 68–69.
[57] Schwabe, op. cit., p. 143.
[58] Heuss, *Erinnerungen, op. cit.,* pp. 207–208.

21, 1918, Friedrich Naumann maintained that the blame in large measure rested upon Wilhelm II who had failed to follow the good advice proffered by Bethmann-Hollweg, but had instead allowed himself to be captured by military extremists.[59] The German army, particularly its officer corps, had remained too old-fashioned. *Volk* had been imperfectly wedded to the state, and now liberalism had best become completely democratic if Germany were to be protected against events such as had happened in Russia, and if liberalism were to prevent itself from becoming even more reactionary.[60] Naumann's reaction was a typical one for German democrats. Rathenau, Meinecke, and a host of others chose to view the military disaster of 1918 as stemming from certain grievous errors in foreign policy, but also, from the incomplete amalgamation of *Staat* and *Volk*.[61] In a word, those who would soon attempt to sublimate despair into renewed political activity saw the war as essentially proving their point, *viz.*, that a wedding of the German masses to the state combined with rational foreign policy was the only way in which the state could be assured of its existence in a world of industrialized molochs, each intent upon gouging out its own place in the sun.

Much the same attitude was evidenced by Ernst Troeltsch, in his *Spektator-Briefe* essay entitled "The Old State and in Termination of the War" ("Der alte Staat und der Kriegsausgang"). In this essay, Troeltsch placed the blame for disaster squarely upon the shoulders of the old ruling class. It was they who had failed to respond to the needs generated by a "radicalizing mass war" by instituting general reforms. Rather, they had chosen to place their faith in an illusive all-out victory.[62] In this regard, Troeltsch said, the vast majority of the German bourgeoisie was just as culpable as the general staff. With considerable perspicacity, he pointed out that that "militarism" which had pervaded the German state, was not merely reflected in the concern for a strong army. Rather, *German* militarism "was perhaps a political institution."[63] As such, it was the concretization of class rule in Germany. The classes to which Troeltsch seemed to be referring were the aristocracy and the bourgeoisie. Now, the old militarism was dead and the classes from which it had come and, wittingly or unwittingly, had provided support for it, had been thoroughly discredited. What was there to be done?

Salvation can come only through the principles of pure democracy, following reform and further development of those laws and institutions which still exist; [reform] which, at first, was rejected by the ruling class and then made impossible by the revolution.[64]

Despite his rather pessimistic outlook, Troeltsch chose to place his faith in the "majority principle of pure democracy" and in a national assembly.[65]

While, as we have seen, Troeltsch had recognized the necessity of internal reform, there is a note of despair in this article, a feeling that, somehow, too many chances had been lost and too many opportunities ignored for there to be any real solution to the woes of a Germany in collapse. As we shall see, this feeling was shared, or would be shared, by other Democrats. Yet, Troeltsch was able to summon up enough intellectual *sang-froid* to join a "new party" which, in November, 1918, was in the process of formation.

The German Democratic party, founded on November 22, 1918, in Nürnberg, was to be the inheritor of prewar democratic speculation. The individuals of whom the party would be composed were almost painfully aware that the mantle of an unwonted, and in part, unwanted, republicanism had fallen upon their shoulders. The era of political despair was about to begin.

II. THE DEMOCRATS AND THE WEIMAR CONSTITUTION

The responses of German liberals to defeat and the downfall of the monarchy seemed to be disparate in the extreme. On the one hand, one could observe the reactions of many National Liberals, e.g., Stresemann, who sought to hide their reluctance to accept republicanism behind the façade of *Volk*. The result of this was the transformation of the old National Liberal party into the "new" German People's party (*Deutsche Volks Partei,* or DVP).[1] On the other hand, one could observe the reactions of those individuals we have considered before, the liberals of Naumann's stripe who, accepting the downfall of the monarchy as irreversible, attempted to construct a party which would serve the state by confirming republican principles. The result of these efforts was the formation of the German Democratic party. This took place in several

---

[59] Naumann, "Wie es Kam" in *Die Hilfe,* Nr. 47, 21 November, 1918: p. 557.
[60] *Ibid.*
[61] As an example of this, see Meinecke's *Nach der Revolution* (München, 1919), esp. p. 38.
[62] Ernst Troeltsch, *Spektator-Briefe: Aüfsatze über die deutsche Revolution und die Weltpolitik 1918/1922* (reprint, Tübingen, 1924, Darmstadt, 1969), pp. 1–2.
[63] *Ibid.,* p. 4.
[64] *Ibid.,* pp. 11–12.
[65] *Ibid.,* p. 12.
[1] The machinations between Stresemann and those who were to form the new German Democratic party do not concern us here. At any rate, they have been adequately covered in Henry Ashby Turner, *Stresemann and the Politics of the Weimar Republic* (Princeton, 1963) and by Wolfgang Hartenstein in his *Die Anfänge der Deutschen Volkspartei: 1918–1920* (Düsseldorf, 1962). It is of interest to note, though, that Friedrich Naumann, who was to become the first leader of the Democratic party, was initially in contact with both those National Liberals who would go over to the German People's party and with those National Liberals and Progressives who already were inclined to the Democratic party and, like many in both camps, he at first had hoped for a fusion of the two groups. See Hartenstein, pp. 14–17.

stages. First of all, on November 10, 1918, there occurred a meeting of six professional people at the home of Theodor Wolff, editor of the *Berliner Tageblatt*. These six gentlemen then issued a "Call for the Establishment of a Democratic Party" on November 16, 1918: "We wish the union of all those elements, men and women, who are not today submerged in indolence, but who recognize the newly emerging facts and want to assure their opportunity for cooperation. What must come out of such a union is a great Democratic party for the unified Reich." [2]

At the time, there was not much of a program envisioned, and it would seem that the party was then mainly concerned with protecting the nation from the chaos of economic experimentation and Bolshevist doctrines.[3] (As mentioned, the party was formally founded in Nürnberg on November 22, 1918). In its first election call (*Wahlanruf*) of December 5, 1918, the party came out strongly against the disturbances created by the Spartacists and against "political strikes and senseless wage demands." [4] Such "internal splintering" within Germany itself had to be ended if external threats, such as that posed by the Poles in regards to the eastern territories, were to be met successfully. The *Wahlanruf* also called for the foundation of a German republic, one based upon recognition of the equality of all citizens before the law (regardless of class or sex), freedom of religion with the concurrent separation of church and state and a more or less *laissez faire* approach in economics, while recognizing that the interests of the whole took precedence. The party was adamant in claiming that, unlike the purely class-bound Social Democrats, it was sympathetic to the plight of the small tradesman and artisan.[5] During the period of the provisional government, the newly formed Democratic party was almost deliberately general insofar as goals were concerned. Indeed, as Theodor Wolff, editor of the *Berliner Tageblatt*, pointed out, the reason why it at first picked up such a wide variety of adherents—even the super-capitalist Hjalmar Schacht was able to join it with a supposedly clear conscience—was precisely because its goals, outside of preserving the German state against external and internal disorders, were so nebulous. Wolff himself claimed that the party would prove too attractive "to all elements of German society." [6] However, with the exception of such political sports as Schacht, the party essentially attracted the same type of individual as had the old Progressive party (or left-wing National Liberals) before the war. One need only peruse a list of its leading personalities—Theodor Heuss, Hugo Preuss, Friedrich Naumann, Max Weber, Alfred Weber, Friedrich Meinecke, Walther Rathenau, and Theodor Wolff himself—in order to be aware of this fact. As can be seen from its early pronouncements, the party, and those who supported it, saw preservation of the German state as the first duty of its citizenry. Of particular interest here, though, is the previously quoted statement which emphasized the importance of internal order for the purpose of preventing foreign depredations, e.g., those of the Poles. While somewhat subtle, this was a sign of a general, Naumann-like tendency of subordinating internal to external policy, one which was to characterize the positions both of the German Democratic party and many of its more prominent members throughout the Weimar period.

Indeed, if one considers the ideological tenor of the German Democratic party, as well as the role which it hoped that it would play in Germany's future, one can only come to the conclusion that this party was in many ways the party of Friedrich Naumann. To be sure, there were differing interests represented within the party ranks from the beginning. Hermann Fischer and the *Hansa Bund* must be considered in this regard. The *Hansa Bund* was essentially a self-consciously bourgeois interest group which represented business concerns in northern Germany. Hermann Fischer, its most well-known representative, had been, as we have seen, part of the left wing of the National Liberals before the First World War and, as such, had been drawn to some of Naumann's social imperial schemes. However, Fischer in particular and the group as a whole tended to be more national than social as well as remaining committed to a sort of *laissez faire* approach to economics. They were characterized by a more or less consistent opposition to the statism embodied in the overall approach of the German Democratic party. The apparently "anti-statist" elements of the party were strengthened by a large number of south Germans who were prominent in the party, e.g., Theodor Heuss, Friedrich von Payer, Ludwig Haas, and Hermann Dietrich, individuals who retained something of a suspicion of centralized state authority in the face of the more baldly statist conceptions of Naumann. Some Democrats, such as Eugen Schiffer and Hjalmar Schacht, were interested less in establishing a *Volksstaat* than in preserving an almost antiquated prewar order in the face of left-wing threats. However, for virtually all of those who gathered around the DDP standard, there can be little doubt that the overriding consideration was that of national unity with the establishing of some sort of bridge between bourgeoisie and proletariat being of utmost importance in the creation of this unity. Of course, as time passed, Democratic concern for being a "bridge" between bourgeoisie and proletariat did become hard to take for many of the more selfconsciously bourgeois members of the party, e.g., Schiffer and Schacht. Never-

---

[2] Felix Saloman *Die deutschen Parteiprogramme, Volume III* (Leipzig, 1926), p. 16.
[3] *Ibid.*, p. 18.
[4] *Ibid.*, p. 47.
[5] *Ibid.*, pp. 47-48.
[6] Theodor Wolff, *Through Two Decades*, trans. E. W. Dickes (London, 1936), p. 142.

theless, the goals of Friedrich Naumann—the creation of the strong *Volksstaat,* the amelioration of the class struggle, and the conciliation of all elements of the *Volk* in the interest of state unity—did remain as the guiding standards for the German Democratic party, despite occasional clashing between the various interests and/or ideologies that were to be found in the ranks of the DDP.

At the same time, moreover, it was obvious that, at least at the beginning, there were substantial spiritual differences between those ensconsed in the new Democratic party and those who were later to form the German People's party under the leadership of Stresemann. The former spoke of "the spirit of a new age, of a new beginning and of the decline of old principles," while the latter group condemned the *"Illusion-politik"* of the *Berliner Tageblatt,* one of the chief sources of support for the new party, and maintained a decidedly cooler attitude towards that new age which the democrats seemed to be welcoming with such enthusiasm.[7]

In another, very concrete way, the Democratic party, or at least some of its more prominent members, seemed to be welcoming the post-Wilhelmian era with enthusiasm: the party, or at least some of its members, virtually wrote the Weimar constitution. It is one of the ironies of Weimar Germany that a party which would be described by 1927 as being a "bowling club" for precocious dandies possessed of an abundance of grey matter provided the talent which in fact was largely responsible for establishing the governmental framework for Germany's first experiment in democratic republicanism. It is, of course, yet another irony that, on November 15, 1918, the Jew, Hugo Preuss, was designated by the then ruling Council of People's Commissars, to be minister of interior and, in that capacity, to begin work on a constitution.

Hugo Preuss was a believer in that gossamar phantasm of German political history, the *Einheitsstaat* (unified state). His beliefs were given substantive expression in the draft that was completed on January 3, 1919, and was revealed for all to see on January 20. In many ways, there would be a great resemblance between Preuss's version and that eventually approved by the National Assembly on July 31, 1919. However, Preuss's original version did undergo certain modifications.

The constitution of January 3, 1919, was a relatively brief work, consisting of only seventy-five paragraphs. The document was divided into four major parts: (1) *Reich* and the German Free States, (2) the *Grundrechte* ("Basic Law," or "Bill of Rights") of the German people, (3) the Reichstag, (4) the Reichstag and the Reich government. Preuss envisioned a bicameral Reichstag, which would consist of a *Volkshaus,* elected directly by the people for a five-year term and a *Staatenhaus,* which would be elected from the respective legislatures (*Landtagen*) of the states comprising the unified German Reich. Its term was also envisioned as being five years. There would be a president, elected directly by the people for a seven-year term. He would have great powers. He could, with approval of the Reichstag, declare a state of siege in any territory that was, or seemed to be, unable to preserve order. It was his prerogative to summon or to close parliament. The voting age was set at twenty-one (this later would be changed to twenty, and, in the elections of January 19, 1919, all citizens over twenty years old were eligible to vote) and there was to be universal suffrage.

What Preuss envisioned was the balancing off of a strong president against a strong Reichstag. If there seemed to be any "losers" in this scheme, it was obvious to all that these were the states (*Länder*). Under the old Bismarckian constitution, the states comprising the empire were possessed of great powers. This was reflected, on the national level, in the *Bundesrat*. This upper house of the Reichstag really was nothing but a sort of megaphone for imperial opinion. Representatives of the *Länder* governments comprised it but, because of her territorial and demographic preponderance, Prussia dominated the *Länder*. Nevertheless, the fact that there was a *Bundesrat,* furthermore one that could effectively squelch any proposal or program coming up from the almost helpless Reichstag, seemed to underscore the almost aggressively federal character of Bismarck's empire while, at the same time of course, allowing a unitary imperial rule to exist by default. This unified and, to a large extent, unfettered imperial rule might well drag Germany into crises or even wars. However, within their own antediluvian bailiwicks, the individual *Länder* exercised considerable authority. The schools, commerce, communication, and, most important of all, taxation rested in their hands. The organic *Volksstaat* of Fichte and Hegel might well have been enshrined in an atmosphere of heady idealism and powder smoke; but, in prosaic everyday political life, Bismarck's state had been a federal one.

The lack of unity had been responsible for accentuating the almost unimaginably primitive nature of German political and, to some extent, cultural, life. Prussia could elect delegates to its *Landtag* on the basis of the Three Class Voting System of 1850. Mecklenburg governed itself, or at least existed, under a "constitution" that had been first introduced in 1775. At the same time there was no unified educational system whatsoever, and denominationally oriented schools predominated at the primary and secondary levels. Of course, there was no really powerful national elective body that could push reform upon the *Länder* or, for that matter, upon the government, which both constitutionally and in practice seemed unable to do any-

---

[7] Hartenstein, *op. cit.,* pp. 36–37.

thing but create "alarums and excursions" and, of course, declare war.

In speaking of Bismarck's "unification" of Germany, one often assumes that the Iron Chancellor in fact had created a sort of modern, centralized police state. Imperial Germany might well have been a police state in many ways and certainly the helplessness of the Reichstag *vis-à-vis* the government, or the latter's ability to embark upon a *Kulturkampf* or, perhaps more pointedly, an anti-Socialist crusade, would certainly lend credence to such a view. However, this "police state" was hardly a centralized one.

It was against this somewhat strange creation of Bismarck, i.e., the authoritarian federal state, that the liberals mentioned in the previous chapter—those liberals who would become important in the German Democratic party—lifted intellectual lances before the First World War. As we have seen, they did so in order to strengthen this state, i.e., by turning the somewhat archaic authoritarian state bequeathed them gratuitously into a stronger, more unified *Volksstaat*. Preuss was part of this German liberal tradition and his constitutional proposal of January 3, 1919, must be seen in this context. As Preuss put it:

The primary and decisive political life form for the German people is not the being of the individual states, in either their monarchical or in their republican form[s]; much more [is it] the being of the German *Volk* itself as an historically given political unity.[8]

Of course, Preuss, in assuming that there was "an historically given political unity" of the German people was begging the same question as had the earlier romantic and/or statist thinkers that have characterized the history of German political speculation. In this regard, important aspects of his liberalism were shared by Friedrich Naumann, Friedrich Meinecke, and other seminal "liberals" of pre-Hitler Germany.

On January 25 and 26, 1919, Preuss met with representatives of the *Länder* governments. His schemes for the *Einheitsstaat* came under strong attack, particularly from the Prussian representatives and from Kurt Eisner of Bavaria who, as is well known, was engaged in some free-lance attempts at state-building of his own.[9] The upshot of all of this was the creation of, at first, a provisional "State Committee" (*Staatenausschuss*) and then a *Reichsrat* with broadened powers for the states, as well as Preuss's unhappy realization that particularism was still too strong for the *Einheitsstaat* to be realized at that time.[10] Between the end of January, 1919, and the beginning of February, Preuss's constitution underwent various minor changes, besides the more important one mentioned above. However, the other major changes it would undergo would occur at the hands of the National Assembly and the special constitutional committee set up by it in March, 1919. It is to this assembly that we must now turn.

On January 19, 1919, all German men and women over the age of twenty went to the polls. For the new German Democratic party, the results must have been very encouraging indeed. The Democratic party obtained 5,641,800 of the votes cast, or 18.6 per cent. This sufficed to make it the third strongest party in the assembly (behind the Majority Socialists and Center party, in that order) and to give them 75 out of the 423 deputies elected to this assembly.[11] Electorally speaking, of course, the German Democratic party would have little to rejoice about from this time on; but, for now, the party, with its large number of jurists, political theorists, and ideologues, was in an excellent position to exert a tremendous influence (beside that which had been already exercised by party-colleague Preuss) upon the making of the constitution.

On February 6, 1919, the National Assembly met for the first time in Weimar. On February 11, Friedrich Ebert was elected by a vote of 277 to 102 to be Reich president. Friedrich Naumann addressed the assembly on February 13, 1919. In this speech, some of the traditional left-wing liberal views were combined with a rather grim look at foreign affairs. There had to be, Naumann said, a final union of bourgeois and working-class interests in order for Germany to present a unified front to the outside world and to allay working-class suspicions that the revolution of 1918 had been betrayed.[12] Now the SPD and the German Democratic party were working together to "undertake responsibility for leadership," Naumann went on, with somewhat muted enthusiasm, and this signified recognition of the fact that "We have no castes and no classes anymore; we are one people."[13] The Socialists had to learn to accept individualism while, on the other hand, the bourgeoisie would have to learn to accept the emergence of a socialist, at least in part, *Volksstaat*.

Then, Naumann went on to make some extremely revealing statements. First of all, he condemned those who still dreamt of the return of the monarchy. This, Naumann suggested, was impossible and, even if it were possible, would only lead to the threat of civil war. The monarchy had proven its weakness by not surviving the war and by not providing the unity necessary to fight a mass war, a unity that had been possessed by the democratic peoples.[14] A "national

---

[8] Wilhelm Ziegler, *Die deutsche Nationalversammlung 1919/1920 und ihr Verfassungswerk* (Berlin, 1932), pp. 94–95.
[9] *Ibid.*, p. 102. Friedrich Stämpfer, *Die Vierzehn Jahre der Ersten Deutschen Republik* (Hamburg, 1947), p. 133.
[10] Ziegler, *op. cit.*, p. 104.
[11] Koppel S. Pinson, *Modern Germany: Its History and Civilization* (New York, 1965), p. 574.
[12] *Verhandlungen der verfassunggebenden deutschen Nationalversammlung. Stenographische Berichte*, **326**, 55A (Berlin, 1919), hereafter cited as VVDN.
[13] *Ibid.*, 55C.
[14] *Ibid.*, 56C.

fate" had dictated that a republic was to be formed; however, even before the war, Germany had been on its way towards greater democratization. A feeling of "state-citizenship" was abroad in August, 1914; this being evidenced in the feeling of national unity that had swept over Germany at that time.[15] After a brief review of the rather dismal foreign situation, one in which he, with some justification, saw Germany threatened by Poles, Czechs, the French, and Wilson's seeming perfidy regarding the previously hallowed Fourteen Points, Naumann went on to call for the establishment of a new form of socialism: "A socialism, not in the party-dogmatic sense; but as a moral duty and common life-expression [Lebenshaftbarkeit] of the whole Volk."[16]

This address is of immense importance in gaining an understanding of the mentality of the German Democrats as they faced the awesome and, as things would turn out, thankless task of creating a constitution. First of all, we must recognize that Naumann's basic concern was that of national unity. He was calling for that same state of class reconciliation that he had before the war. A Germany unified to face the monstrous pressures that would be brought to bear against her from the outside—this was Naumann's essential message. Only now, such issues as colonialism and/or Mitteleuropa seemed poignantly beside the point. Germany was threatened with annihilation and stringent measures had to be implemented in order to prevent this from occurring. Yet, the measures which Naumann thought desirable of implementation were essentially those for which he had stood before the war and it is of great significance that Naumann, in this address, emphasized that "national fate" was responsible for the emergence of the republic. This attitude of "fated republicanism" is one that will characterize the German Democrats, or at least an amazingly large number of them, throughout the fourteen-year tenure of the republic. Also important to note, is Naumann's use of the term "state citizen." What is implied here, of course, is not that more or less self-sufficient and independent individual extolled by the eudemonics of Western political liberalism. The "state-citizen" of Naumann was one who could share equally in contributing to the support of the whole as this was embodied in the state, and his wistful backward glance at the heroic "August days" of 1914 is quite indicative of this notion. Despite Naumann's public efforts to see the Constitutional Assembly as a potential step in the direction of a higher unity, the political romantic in him was disappointed by the seemingly prosaic character of this assembly. In his eyes, the proceedings at Weimar "lack the mystique of the birth of a state."[17]

What distressed Naumann, of course, were the mundane political bickering and party politics that seemed to be tarnishing if not obstructing, the emergence of that unified Volksstaat, that, for so long, had been the Fata Morgana of Germany's liberal bourgeois intelligentsia. In her Heimatchronik, Naumann's somewhat more romantic colleague, Gertrud Bäumer, who, like himself, was a Democratic delegate to the assembly, recorded her disgust with the "pure party-political tendencies" exhibited during the assembly debates.[18] The bourgeois liberals, true to their statist heritage, were demonstrating a rather non-pluralistic fear of interest and/or ideological clashing. Given the nature of Germany's political parties, perhaps some of this fear was justified. Nonetheless, this tendency towards the "non-partisan," or "non-political" point of view was one that had to hamstring republicanism, or at the very least, the emergence of republican attitudes, even before the Weimar Republic got off the ground.

Certainly conditions in and around 1919 Germany could only have encouraged such a tendency. This was reflected in a February 19, 1919, address of Democratic delegate Falk. With dismay, he pointed to the efforts that were being made in the Rhineland (efforts largely encouraged by the French, of course) to bring about secession of this vital area from the Fatherland, as well as to the "arrogance" (Übermut) of the Poles who were threatening German territory in the East.[19] It was because Germany was now "so humbled and bled" and so threatened by outside powers that it was "compelled to place itself on the foundation of the republic."[20] "Republic as the lesser of evils," an attitude evidenced by Naumann in his speech of February 13, was being displayed in Falk's address as well.

During the course of his address, Falk did take time to respond to DVP attacks on the German Democratic party. These attacks could be amalgamated into one: that the German Democratic party, by virtue of its being democratic, had abandoned the tenets of political liberalism (this issue of "democracy vs. liberalism" will become an important one for the German Democratic party itself as time goes on). Implied in the DVP attacks was the idea that the DDP, through overemphasis upon "democracy," was drawing too close to the Social Democrats for comfort, at least insofar as the comfort of the middle class was concerned. Falk responded to these attacks by asserting that the DDP and SPD were merely working together and, he added somewhat acidly, the relationship between the two parties was perhaps not as close a one as that which existed between the DVP and the out-and-out reactionary DNVP.[21] Nonetheless, Falk went on to state, there was "no more room for the old liberal-

---

[15] Ibid., 56D–57B.
[16] Ibid., 60C.
[17] Theodor Heuss, Friedrich Naumann: Der Mann, das Werk, die Zeit (Hamburg, 1968), p. 488.

[18] Bäumer, Heimatchronik entry of February 18, 1919, quoted in Ziegler, op. cit., p. 48.
[19] VVDN, op. cit., 190D–192C.
[20] Ibid., 194B.
[21] Ibid., 194D.

ism today." [22] That old liberalism had been a somewhat negative phenomenon anyway, concerned as it was with establishing a sort of protection for the individual against a central government. The new liberalism, which was democratic in orientation, had to function to assure that all could enter into national life. It was in this context that Falk reiterated a theme that had been placed into prominence by Naumann and others of his stripe before and during the war: the theme of "spirit of reconciliation." [23] Again, we can detect, without undue strain, that emphasis upon national unity which, owing to political and cultural conditioning, had become probably the most singular characteristic of the left-wing German bourgeois intelligentsia. It was reflective both of statism and that political romanticism which found resonance in a speech of Gertrud Bäumer, which she delivered to the assembly on February 21, 1919. After first of all tendering a warm "word of thanks to the army" for services nobly performed, she lauded that "idealism" which she saw as having characterized the late German war effort. Bäumer went on to define this "idealism" as follows: "The consciousness that the whole is more than the individual." [24] At the same time, of course, she was careful to point out that she and the party she represented were in favor of preserving private property, while furthering the interests of this "whole."

Again, besides pleas for school reform, increased child welfare and so on, Bäumer issued the usual Democratic clarion-call for the state of class conciliation. In this regard, she underscored the necessity for a democratization of labor relationships, for employees as well as for the traditional working class.[25] Most important of all, Bäumer declared, was "the reconstruction of our middle class." [26] At the same time, however, she was adamant in declaring that class struggle had to be overcome. All classes, while perhaps remaining classes, had to participate in the building-up of the German nation. "Class struggle is not really socialism," Bäumer declared. "class struggle is the application of social thought in the interests of one portion of the population. We of the Democratic party do not want to stand upon the ground of class interest. . . ." [27] Bäumer rounded out her speech with calls for "liberated women" to work with the men in constructing a new Germany, the establishment of a special national office on woman labor, the establishment of Germany as a true "*Kulturstaat*," and for the women of all nations to demand an end to the crippling hunger blockade of Germany as well as the return of German prisoners.[28]

The important speeches of Naumann, Falk, and Bäumer show most clearly the position of the German Democratic party with regard to the major issue of the day: the establishment of a republican form of government for Germany. The position which stands out most clearly is that of viewing the republic as being a stepping-stone to a higher unity, i.e., the state of class conciliation. What the Democrats really wanted, of course, was the creation of a national socialist republic, similar to if not almost identical with the national social constitutional monarchy espoused by the prewar Progressives (or at least those around Naumann). The call for the emergence of the true "state citizen," the demand that people rise above "class and political interest," and finally the desire that Germany unify herself at home in order to present a unified front to the outside world—these had been and would continue to be the tenets of bourgeois left-wing liberalism. From time to time, concessions would be made to pluralistic interests of course, and the DDP would remain a distinctly bourgeois party. However, it always would view itself as in some way being a true *Staatspartei,* providing a political bridge between bourgeois and proletarian interests, a gentle yet powerful solvent for the class struggle. Statism, the traditional *alter ego* of German liberalism, would remain such even as the prewar left-wing "liberals" became postwar "democrats."

On February 24, 1919, Hugo Preuss made an introductory address on the constitution. Somewhat petulantly (no doubt with his January meetings with the *Länder* representatives in mind), he pointed out that many of the problems involving the constitution were legacies of the past, e.g., the question of division of powers between the centralized Reich government and the *Länder.*[29] Preuss also made a very strong attack upon the apolitical tradition of Germany's past, particularly as this very tradition had been embodied in Weimar. Political freedom was essential and, in turn, it would be this political freedom that would open the door to social reform.[30]

At the same time, Preuss was careful to point out that, in title at least, the German nation would remain a "Reich" rather than be transformed into a "republic." The term "Reich," Preuss maintained, was too strongly rooted in the German past and the concept of German unity too inextricably intertwined with it for this most singular of terms to be expunged with the stroke of a pen.[31] However, Preuss announced, a change in the colors of the national flag was being suggested. Previously, in his earlier constitutional draft, Preuss had skirted the delicate flag issue. Under the influence of the Austrian representative to his earlier constitutional committee, Ludo M. Hartmann, Preuss had opted for a black/red/gold flag to re-

[22] *Ibid.,* 195A.
[23] *Ibid.,* 196B.
[24] *Ibid.,* 271A–272B.
[25] *Ibid.,* 273C.
[26] *Ibid.,* 273D.
[27] *Ibid.,* 275A.
[28] *Ibid.,* 275C–276B.
[29] *Ibid.,* 284D.
[30] *Ibid.,* 285A.
[31] *Ibid.,* 285C.

place the old black/white/red imperial flag. Such a flag might make Austria's eventual *Anschluss* with Germany somewhat easier, in that the old imperial flag had overtones of Prussian predominance associated with it. Because of associations with the old *Burschenschaft* and the spirit of 1848, the new black/red/gold flag had a certain "value of feeling" (*Gefühlswert*).[32] Preuss suggested that Germany might well, in the constitution, make some sort of arrangement for entry into a "League of Nations" (*Völkerbund*). However, overtures should be made only if the League were itself "democratic," i.e., not oppressive in its relationship to Germany.[33]

The seminal issue of church/school relations had not yet been settled owing to the intransigence of several of the *Länder*. The problem of the relationship of Prussia to a unified Reich had yet to be worked out. Obviously disgruntled, Preuss remarked that the *Einheitsstaat* was not to be expected in the immediate future.[34] He then devoted some time to explaining the mechanism involved in amending the constitution, and the rather limited role that he assigned to plebiscite and referendum (they were to be put into effect only if the inhabitants of a given *Land* wanted to amalgamate with another territorial unit or in any other way alter the composition of their *Land*, and only when called for by the Reichstag and the Reich president himself). The president, Preuss maintained, ought to possess considerably more than ceremonial importance. Indeed, he existed as a counter-balance to the Reichstag, a figure who was the "personal head" of the German people.[35] Thus, just as the Reichstag was to be elected directly by the people (for a three-year term; Preuss had modified his earlier position on the legislative period for this body; the Assembly would change the term from three to four years), so ought the president be elected directly by the people; furthermore, since he was the head of all of the German people, for a seven- rather than a three-year term.

Like his German Democratic colleagues, Preuss had come out for a strong, centralized state. In fact, on this point, one which, incidentally, separated the Democrats from their SPD coalition partners, virtually all Democrats were united. The day following Preuss's speech, February 25, an article written by Max Weber, entitled "Der Reichspräsident," appeared in the *Berliner Börsenzeitung*. While Weber did not mention Preuss or the German Democratic party, his essay evidenced essential agreement with them except on one particular point. Weber did think that a Reich president was necessary to provide a palpable leader of the *Volk in toto* as well as the opportunity for people to participate in selecting leadership. This last, Weber thought, could well lead to changes within the German political parties themselves.[36] Most Democrats implicitly agreed with Weber on these points. Weber's other primary reason for desiring a strong president was to facilitate those measures of socialization which the former thought would be necessary, if not particularly desirable.[37] Friedrich Meinecke, who, it might be said, was ensconced in the right wing of the German Democratic party, vigorously disagreed with Weber on this point. If the bourgeoisie suspected that a strong central government in the form of a president—favored by Meinecke, statist that he was—would push socialization, it might well seek refuge in a weak central authority, "and, in particular, in the parliamentary system."[38] As time went on, of course, the issue of "socialization," to any substantial degree, would become a moot point even for the SPD, to say nothing of the Democrats. Nevertheless, it would appear that, despite some grumbling about Preuss's rather dry presentation of it (Gertrud Bäumer complained that his speech was "prosaic and more tactically clever than soaring and historically grand"),[39] most Democrats agreed with the major thrust of his address, i.e., the need for Germany to advance in the direction of the *Einheitsstaat*.

At any rate, Preuss's speech touched off a four-day debate centered on the two most prominent issues, centralized or federal state, and monarchical or republican government form. Erich Koch, who would soon serve on the twenty-eight-man constitutional committee selected from the assembly delegates, took the floor on February 28, 1919, and made a strong and well-reasoned defense of centralization on the one hand, and republicanism on the other. The state of Bismarck, he said, had not been an ideal one. Rather it was merely what "was attainable at that time."[40] However, Bismarck had failed to provide unity for the Reich, and this lack of unity had proved to be fatal to the monarchy in recent days. If there had been a unified Reich, Koch maintained, it "certainly would have been possible to avoid the revolution and to proceed on the path of evolution."[41] In the West, Koch continued, people submitted willingly to elected leaders who were responsible, in the final analysis, to them. In Germany, the emperor and the chancellor had been responsible to no one, and the forlorn Reichstag had had to fight for whatever feeble powers it could ob-

---

[32] *Ibid.*, 285D.
[33] *Ibid.*, 286A–286B.
[34] *Ibid.*, 288A.
[35] *Ibid.*, 289A–291C.
[36] Max Weber, *Gesammelte Politische Schriften* (2nd enlarged ed., newly edited by Johannes Winckelmann, Tübingen, 1958), p. 487.
[37] *Ibid.*, p. 486.
[38] Friedrich Meinecke, *Politische Schriften*, edited by Georg Kotowski (Darmstadt, 1958), p. 297. This problem is also discussed in Robert A. Pois's *Friedrich Meinecke and German Politics in the Twentieth Century* (Berkeley and Los Angeles, 1972), p. 89.
[39] Bäumer, quoted in Ziegler, *op. cit.*, p. 109.
[40] VVDN, *op. cit.*, 390B.
[41] *Ibid.*, 390C.

tain.[42] Yet, Koch implied, there seemed to be less unity in Germany than in the Western camp. In a curious, backhanded sort of way, he seemed to be giving some credence to the notion, already fairly prominent, that German lack of unity at home had contributed to defeat in the field. While this was certainly not the same as accusing various nefarious elements of stabbing the German army in the back (the *Dolchstosslegende*) it can hardly be said to have served as an effective counter to it.

Koch indicated that the German Democrats were not entirely opposed to the Socialists and, to jeers emanating from the right side of the house, he declared, "But just as little as you want to rob the people of the belief in socialism, to the same small degree do you want to rob them of the belief in democracy."[43] Furthermore, Koch added—and in perhaps the most forthright manner he ever would ever put it—"The best form of expression for democracy is parliamentarianism."[44]

Koch called for a strong president, indicating that perhaps "a new German word" would be desirable for that figure designed to rise above parliamentary quarreling "and, in the hour of peril to constitute a counter-balance to parliamentary routine."[45] Like Preuss, Koch was concerned that a strong legislative power be counter-balanced by a strong executive. After making further demands for what he called the "decentralized *Einheitsstaat*" and for widened state authority in German public life, Koch went on to declare that the Reichstag "will always remain the parliament of German unity."[46]

Koch's address was a strong effort in the direction of defending parliamentary government. However, there was a rather curious aspect to it, one that brings to mind a problem that has been well summarized by Gotthart Schwarz in his *Theodor Wolff und das Berliner Tageblatt*. The problem involved, of course, is one that we have touched upon earlier: the role of parliamentary and political activities in national life as seen by Germany's left-wing "liberals." As Schwarz points out, in contrast to the English view, which saw parliament as being a sort of "battlefield" of interest groups, the German liberal notion of parliament saw it as bringing together disparate groups and individuals in order "to discover and to formulate an abstract super-individual general will."[47] In other words, parliamentarianism existed in order best to serve "the general well-being of the state." It would be most inaccurate to maintain that Erich Koch and many other members of the German Democratic party had no view at all of what constituted political pluralism (although one might well argue that individuals of Meinecke's stripe never really had such a view). However, what pluralistic notions they did have were greatly enfeebled by an overriding statism, which, on the one hand, was an historically conditioned reaction to Germany's seemingly perpetual inability to unify herself, and, on the other, was a doctrine which, if believed in by virtually every political group outside of the SPD, had to guarantee that this unity could be obtained only at the expense of parliamentary democracy itself.

As mentioned before, there most certainly was more than adequate reason for the Democrats, among a great many others, to be super-sensitive to questions of unity in 1919. Besides such internal brouhahas as the Spartacist troubles and the chaos in Bavaria, Germany was being assailed along all of her frontiers. On March 5, 1919, Dr. Alfred Hermann, the Democratic party delegate from Posen, made a speech about the Polish assault against German territories (or at least as seen by most Germans) in the East. Somewhat perceptively Dr. Hermann warned that Polish seizure of German lands could lead to the development of a powerful *irredentism* within Germany, out of which "a new world conflagration" could grow.[48] The Democratic delegate called the attention of the assembly to the fact that the Poles had undertaken systematic persecution of the Jews, killing over a thousand of them in Lemberg alone. Angrily and, at least seen through Clio's eyes, a bit self-righteously, Dr. Hermann declared that Germans would never want to live in a land "where *Unkultur* overwhelms us."[49] Strongly suggested, of course, was the notion that atrocities of the nature of those committed by the bestial Poles could never occur in a nation of *Kulturmenschen*.

As far as Germany's internal life was concerned, the German Democratic solution remained basically the same: the *Einheitsstaat* (with those concessions necessary to mollify regional interests) and unity of all the *Volk*, i.e., class conciliation. This attitude was clearly manifest on March 7, 1919, in a speech of Bernhard Dernburg (he had been German colonial minister before the First World War), in which the call for a "community of labor" (*Arbeitsgemeinschaft*) was voiced.[50] Class distrust had to be overcome, Dernburg said, and, at the same time, a thorough-going socialization of the means of production was quite out of the question. Possibly, he thought, a few industries such as the coal or other energy-related ones could be socialized.[51] However, Dernburg made this concession grudgingly and it was obvious that, in the call for a "community of labor" and for the overcoming of class distrust, if not hostility, his "socialism" was more of the national socialist variety *à la* Naumann than of

---

[42] *Ibid.*, 391B.
[43] *Ibid.*, 391D.
[44] *Ibid.*, 392B.
[45] *Ibid.*, 393B.
[46] *Ibid.*, 395C.
[47] Gotthart Schwarz, *Theodor Wolff und das Berliner Tageblatt* (Tübingen, 1968), p. 62.

[48] VVDN, *op. cit.*, 519A.
[49] *Ibid.*, 532B.
[50] *Ibid.*, 561A.
[51] *Ibid.*, 561C.

any other. Anton Erkelenz, perhaps the most "radical" of the German Democrats (he was of working-class origins and, before the war, had been active in the liberal Hirsch-Duncker trade union movement), made a speech on much the same theme the following day. In this address, he made about the same point as had Dernburg. However, he did remark that he was able to understand why many workers had followed the Spartacists. This was due, Erkelenz said, to working-class dismay with that lack of social conviction (*Gesinnung*) that seemed still to characterize the state.[52] More clearly defined right-to-work laws and greater limitations upon monopolies would be of use here, Erkelenz maintained. Classes would continue to exist in the new, democratic state, he thought, but there was no reason why the prewar class struggles and antagonisms had to endure.[53]

Throughout all of these speeches, the Democratic call for unity stands out as being the most singular of left-wing liberal objectives. Erkelenz, in his call for a more substantive social conviction, might well have been a bit more sensitive to the needs of the German workers as a class (indeed, as we shall see, he will leave the German Democratic party in 1930, when it becomes the *Staatspartei,* and go over to the SPD). However, even he was, in reality, calling for that same variey of state-directed class conciliation as had Naumann, Bäumer, Dernburg, and many others.

As various and sundry Democrats proclaimed what they felt to be the needs and dangers confronting the German state, and proposed measures to answer the one and confront the other, several of their colleagues were playing important roles on the twenty-eight-member constitutional committee. This committee, which was established at the end of Februray, 1919, was given the task of going over the government's, i.e. Preuss's, draft of the constitution, and of modifying it where they saw fit to do so. There were five members of the German Democratic party on this committee: Dr. Bruno Ablass, Conrad Haussmann, Erich Koch, Dr. Friedrich Naumann, and Dr. George Zöphel. The role of these Democrats in the creation of the Weimar Constitution was to be great indeed. The questions considered by this committee ranged from such issues as the role of plebiscite and referendum in the new state, all the way over to more emotional ones such as that concerning the colors of the new flag, and even the name with which the parliamentary democracy was to be dubbed. At first, Naumann seemed to be the embodiment of all that was reasonable. In fact, his party colleague Koch felt that he was being just a bit too reasonable, at least insofar as the vagaries of world opinion were concerned, when the former suggested that the term *Reich* be replaced by *Bund. Reich,* in foreign lands, implied "empire." Hence, thought Naumann, the term *Deutsches Reich* would conjure up all sorts of unhappy images for sensitive foreigners. Perhaps *Deutscher Bund* would be a preferable phrase.[54] Naumann's suggestion was rejected, as was one of Dr. Oskar Cohn, the Independent Socialist representative to the committee, that the new state be entitled *Deutsche Republik*. Perhaps taking a cue from the original creator of the constitution, Hugo Preuss, the committee decided to stick with *Deutsches Reich.* From March 6 to March 18, 1919, the committee was concerned mainly with the question of Reich versus *Länder* powers, with Koch standing out as a strong defender of unitary Reich power. In this regard, at least, things seemed to be moving in the direction envisioned by Preuss, i.e., the *Einheitsstaat.* As Koch put it:

the arrangements as they have been arrived at here signify an essential advantage for the Reich because, in this way, the Reich is given the opportunity to work where it must in the interests of Reich unity....[55]

The new constitution gave the *Länder* rights to direct their own respective economies, their schools, churches, cultural life, welfare, and so on. To the state went all others including, as time would reveal, powers of taxation and finance that went far beyond those held by so-called Imperial Germany.

On March 18, 1919, Friedrich Naumann's "reasonableness" (if not, in the eyes of some, his reason) seemed to enter the valley of the shadow. For on that day he, as Theodor Heuss put it, "surprised" his colleagues on the constitutional committee by presenting them with his model for a *Grundrechte* ("basic law" or "bill of rights") for the German people, a proposal which was then submitted to rigorous scrutiny beginning March 31.[56] A "bill of rights," as seen by Preuss, was something that flowed organically out of the other primary concerns of the constitution. It was to be fairly limited, concerning itself with such things as equality before the law, freedom of religion, and so on. It was, further, to be general, lucid, and, above all, brief. Such, in fact, had been Preuss's original *Grundrechte.*[57] Naumann's version was anything but this. It was "a catechism," as Koch remarked with hurtful cynicism, when, on July 11, 1919, a much-modified *Grundrechte* came up for debate in the assembly.[58] Preuss, who, as Heuss points out, was possessed of a somewhat nonphilosophical turn of mind, viewed extended *Grundrechte* as downright dangerous. In his view, the problems involved in creating

---

[52] *Ibid.,* 613C.
[53] *Ibid.,* 614A.
[54] Ziegler, *op. cit.,* p. 113.
[55] *Ibid.,* pp. 116–117.
[56] Heuss, *op. cit.,* p. 497.
[57] For an interesting comparison of Preuss's version of January 3, 1919, and the final version, whose greater thoroughness and complexity was due largely to Naumann's influence, see Ziegler, *op. cit.,* pp. 326 ff.
[58] VVDN, *op. cit.,* 1501D.

such a chimera had helped to shatter the Frankfurt Assembly in 1848/1849.[59] Naumann's more-than-comprehensive proposal did little to allay the fears of Preuss and Koch.

Upon reading it, one discovers that Koch was probably in error when he referred to it as a "catechism"; "quagmire" would probably have been a better word. Naumann envisioned his *Grundrechte* as taking up thirteen articles in the constitution (articles 28 to 40, inclusive). In many respects, his proposal sounded very much like what Preuss had in mind; Naumann also concerned himself with the equality of all Germans before the law (article 28), the uniformity of voting laws throughout the Reich (article 29), freedom of religion and separation of church and state (article 31), more uniformity in the schools and education for all (article 32), and so on. However, throughout the work, vaguely quaint aphorisms emerge with almost Nietzschean suddenness. In article 29, for example, the reader's eye is caught by the phrase "The Fatherland stands above party." "A free path for the qualified!" somewhat shatters the dignity of article 32, while "Forests remain preserved" and "Cattle-breeding will be promoted," somehow manage to do the same for Article 34, which is concerned with farming and the overall use of the land.[60] Article 35 is one of the most interesting portions of the *Grundrechte*, for here Naumann seemed to be justifying the existence of workers' councils, workers' and employees' committees and syndicates, as well as that of "a German occupational parliament" which "would accomplish preliminary work for the Reich political government."[61] At the same time, however, Naumann was careful not to alienate those who lived in dire fear of proletarianization, i.e., the *Mittelstand* and small businessmen. They had "just as great a right to exist as large industry and state enterprise[s]."[62] Further articles dealt with the necessity of maintaining commerce, taxes, the equal participation of workers, employees, and bureaucrats in the state and, finally, the necessity of extending courtesy to foreigners residing within Germany. Just to be sure, however, that Germans did not forget themselves in a sudden (and probably unprecedented) concern for the rights and comforts of foreigners, Naumann concluded this article (number 39) with "Deutschland, Deutschland über alles, über alles in der Welt!"[63] Article 40, which concerns war, peace, and foreign policy, was ended with the following sentence: "We respect all peoples who respect us."[64]

Upon perusing this seemingly impetuous excursion into political romanticism and outright national pathos, one is tempted to say, "What noble a mind is here overthrown," and to describe the work as stemming from the brain of a patriot totally unhinged by the German disaster of 1918. Yet, this would not be the wisest course of action; for, in many ways, the almost pathetic *Grundrechte* proposal of Friedrich Naumann (some of which, at least, did find its way into the constitution) can be seen as really summarizing the attitudes, not only of Naumann, but of many of his party comrades, whether or not they took this particular work of his seriously. For here we see, in thirteen articles, the fundamental dream of all of Germany's left-wing liberals: the completely unified *Volksstaat*, that almost mystical state of "class conciliation." A Fatherland, one which, of course, "stood above party" would both serve and be served by a people united within itself, each class snugly ensconced within its own niche, content at having discovered its worth in the *Volksgemeinschaft*. Stripped of its romantic palaver, Naumann's "program," as embodied in the *Grundrechte*, was none other than the more tough-minded one of *Demokratie und Kaisertum*, i.e., of his pre-World War I national socialism. Only now, a World War and German military disaster had intervened, and, as in so many cases, cool, self-confident machiavellism had yielded at least in part to political romanticism.[65] Nevertheless, that fervent desire somehow to provide for all of the German people, to be the party of everybody and hence, no party at all, was and would remain a prominent, if not the prominent, driving force of the German Democratic party as a whole. This was concretely represented in the proceedings of the assembly where, on March 26, 1919, i.e., even before Naumann's *Grundrechte* was being seriously debated, Delegate Hermann of the Democratic party came out in favor of a special bill to protect artisans and shopkeepers. With some passion, Hermann pointed to the enormous sacrifices made by this group of people during the war, and to its fears of large-scale industry and socialism.[66] In trying to represent the fears of a "traditional" middle class threatened by large-scale industry on the one hand and proletarianization on the other, Hermann nevertheless was not viewing this class as a "special interest" whose concerns had to "confront" those of other classes or interests. Indeed, he thought, there was a way out of the impasse in the form of a special "Chamber of Artisans" (*Handwerkskammer*) which could be set up to assist in integrating this threatened group into the nation.[67] Depending upon how one wished to view this scheme, it could be described either as conciliation through syndicalism or through corporatism. Again, the eagerness to avoid

---

[59] Heuss, *op. cit.*, p. 498.
[60] Friedrich Naumann, *Werke*, ed. by Theodor Schieder, 3 (ed. by Wilhelm J. Mommsen, Köln/Opladen, 1966): pp. 574–576.
[61] *Ibid.*, p. 577.
[62] *Ibid.*
[63] *Ibid.*, p. 578.
[64] *Ibid.*, p. 579.

[65] As an example of this, see Friedrich Meinecke, *Nach der Revolution* (München, 1919). Also, the discussion of this in Pois, *op. cit.*, especially pp. 42–43, and 94–95.
[66] VVDN, *op. cit.*, 810A–811A.
[67] *Ibid.*, 812D.

"interest politics" stands out most prominently here, as well as a very Naumannesque concern to avoid political in-fighting of any kind. Friedrich Naumann's own, pathetic *Grundrechte* was merely an emotion-tinged apotheosis of that syncretic aspect of German liberalism that traditionally had stood against those aspects of political pluralism—recognition of interest groups, interest-oriented political parties, and so forth—which, hypothetically at least, had been central to Western European and Anglo-Saxon liberalism.

Of course, Friedrich Naumann's role on the constitutional committee was an important one, apart from his rather unhappy excursion into political abnegation. Along with Max Quarck of the Social Democrats, he worked out a compromise on the religious issue which proved to be satisfying to the Catholic Center party and conservative Protestants, *viz.,* that all churches were to be viewed as "public corporations" and thus to be allowed to tax their members.[68] The issue of a unified school system was a more vexed one, however, and even a serious attempt to work this out would have to wait until the final days of the constituent assembly. However, in a statement viewed by some as being disturbingly prophetic, Naumann came out strongly against that system of proportional representation favored by Preuss and other Democrats. In a speech of April 4, 1919, he remarked, "The consequence of the proportional voting system is the impossibility of the system of parliamentary government."[69] Whether or not most of the woes of the Weimar Republic can be traced back to the system of proportional representation must remain, at least for now, a moot point. What is important to note, however, is Naumann's obvious concern that parliamentary government succeed, even though what he conceived parliamentary government to be was no doubt quite different from the historical models proffered during the history of Western political thought and practice.

Indeed, it would appear that, at least on the constitutional committee, the greatest opposition to a sysstem of so-called "pure parliamentarianism" came from Erich Koch, who was able to push through motions that greatly strengthened the roles that plebiscite and referendum were to play in the Weimar Constitution. In this, he joined forces with the Social Democrats who exhibited an almost pathetic unawareness that such devices could be quite effectively utilized by the radical right as well as by the radical left and that, indeed, they had been historically associated with Napoleon I and with his nephew, Napoleon III. Preuss himself attacked these developments. People, especially German people, had to be educated in parliamentarianism, he declared. "You make its working illusory," he warned, "if you hang the Damoclean Sword of pure democracy over the parliamentary system."[70] In his suspicions concerning the roles of plebiscite and referendum, Preuss was echoed by Theodor Wolff. "Just because German parliamentarianism is still young," he remarked, "it does not have to be childish."[71] From the beginning, then, those Democrats most concerned with the creation of the Weimar Constitution were divided over the issue of just how "pure" Germany's new parliamentarianism ought to be. As we shall see, Democratic confidence in this, for Germany, so strange a foreign import, will wane over the years. Of course, they hardly will be unique in this regard.

There was one issue that lay heavily upon the thoughts and barely suppressed emotions of all those involved in the proceedings of the constitutional committee and the constituent assembly. This was, of course, the question of the peace treaty. On May 7, 1919, at the Trianon Palace near Versailles, the German peace delegation was presented with the Allied terms. A so-called "Peace Committee" (*Friedensauschuss*) had been in existence since the middle of April and, of the thirty-two members, 5 were Democrats, *viz.,* Conrad Haussmann, Bernard Falk, Dr. Alfred Hermann, Dr. Ludwig Quidde, and Hartmann Freiherr von Richthofen, and possible Allied sternness had been the subject of much discussion, not only for the committee, but for the assembly as well. However, the actual contents of the Allied peace proposal, as well as the tone in which they were expressed, came as a profound shock to Germans of every political persuasion. Theodor Wolff, who usually had an Enlightenment-conditioned contempt for appeals to raw emotion, unwittingly gave credence to the "stab-in-the-back" myth, when he declared in a rather paranoid manner, that Germany's failure to obtain decent terms from the Allies was due to the stupidity of a coalition of "intriguers, squabblers, pompous asses, and muddle-heads."[72] Among those individuals and groups singled out for attack by Wolff were the Independent Socialists (USPD) and the hapless Matthias Erzberger.

On May 12, 1919, the constituent assembly met in Berlin, rather than Weimar, in a symbolic gesture of national unity. There, in the Neuer Aula hall of the University of Berlin, under the stern gaze of Johann Gottlieb Fichte—a gigantic portrait of him "addressing the German nation" graced, or at least decorated, the hall—one delegate after another rose to attack the proposed peace treaty. Conrad Haussmann, who had been involved with work on the constitutional committee, delivered a strong attack on the treaty. With obvious satisfaction, he quoted Philip Snowden of Great Britain, who had declared, "'This peace is treason against democracy and against England's fallen.'"[73] The

---

[68] Ziegler, *op. cit.,* p. 126. See also, Heuss, *op. cit.,* pp. 510-511.
[69] Ziegler, *Ibid.,* p. 130.
[70] *Ibid.,* p. 133.
[71] Schwarz, *op. cit.,* p. 111.
[72] *Ibid.,* p. 121.
[73] VVDN, *op. cit.,* 1091C.

proposed peace, Haussmann claimed, was a continuation of the war "by other means" and, if implemented, would constitute a step in the direction of American domination over Europe.[74] The German people hated war, opposed militarism, and were willing to admit to past wrongs, Haussmann said. However, they were unwilling to be wronged by treaty, and the one produced by the Allies was unacceptable.[75] A very interesting attack on the treaty was made by Ludwig Quidde, the most prominent pacifist member of the German Democratic party. Pacifist though he was, Quidde declared, he was opposed to "peace at any price."[76] This treaty made a meaningful League of Nations impossible, Quidde proclaimed, inasmuch as its implementation would lead to the pronounced development of a strong "German Irredenta."[77] With some accuracy, Quidde went on to charge that the treaty was an act of revenge. The Allies were attempting to punish the German people for the sins of a government which no longer existed, and an international investigation commission was needed to determine the real causes of the war.[78] Quidde blamed a "war psychosis" for the vengeful nature of the treaty.[79] Almost every Democrat associated with the constituent assembly was unconditionally opposed to accepting the treaty, although Friedrich von Payer and Hugo Preuss were a bit more cautious in this regard.[80] Von Payer headed the Democratic party delegation to the assembly, and so his voice presumably carried some weight. However, by the time the assembly gathered, on June 22, 1919, either to accept or reject the treaty, his party had withdrawn from the government along, of course, with Philip Scheidemann himself, in protest against the Versailles *Diktat*. At any rate, von Payer was one of six Democrats who voted with the majority of delegates to accept the treaty. The vote was 237 for acceptance to 138 for rejection of the treaty, while, as mentioned above, all but 6 of the German Democratic party voted against acceptance. Most of the Democratic delegation withheld their vote on a second one expressing confidence in the new government, headed by Scheidemann's Social Democratic colleague Otto Bauer. On June 23, 1919, Eugen Schiffer, speaking for the Democratic party, declared that neither he nor the majority of his party which had voted against acceptance questioned the motives or the patriotism of those who had voted for acceptance.[81]

The vote of the German Democrats on acceptance of the Versailles Treaty points out with considerable clarity the rather awkward position of the party, particularly *vis-à-vis* their Social Democratic partners. The Social Democrats, with certain prominent exceptions such as Philip Scheidemann, Otto Landsberg, and Wolfgang Heine, could vote for acceptance of the treaty and not have second thoughts above betraying their constituents or the class principles for which the party supposedly stood. At least according to the Erfurt Synthesis of 1891, the SPD was a class party, not a national party and, if this formula had been more honored in the breach than in the observance, it was still one that could serve as a fairly convenient rationalization for supporting actions which could be viewed, in the cataract-clouded eye of public opinion, as being counter to the "national-interest," if not treasonable. The Democrats, on the other hand, evidencing admirable ideological *largesse*, claimed not to be representing any class in particular, but rather the nation in general. Of course, in all countries not merely Germany, it has been the bourgeoisie which, traditionally, has chosen to deny, if not the existence of classes (although in the United States, this particular bit of socio-political whimsy has been expressed fairly often), then at least the validity of representing class interests. Statism, in either its national socialist or corporatist form, has been a product of bourgeois ideologists who, either out of fear of or disinterest in the "class struggle," have striven for that "national unity" in which the interests of their class would remain untarnished by dispute or disruption. As bourgeois nationalists, for such they remained, even after World War I, the "left-wing liberals" of the German Democratic party had to vote against acceptance of the treaty and thus represent the wishes of the class from which virtually all of them stemmed (with the notable exception of individuals such as Anton Erkelenz); this, despite their claims that they represented no class at all, but rather—and this in keeping with over one hundred years of German bourgeois political speculation—a mythical *Volksgemeinschaft*. The irony of this, as we shall soon discover, is that the German Democrats will slide inexorably to political oblivion because of their involvement, however qualified at times, in the formulation of a parliamentary constitution and because Germany's bourgeoisie, under the pressures of economic crises and ideological enticements, will move ever farther to the right, even as the German Democrats will try frantically to keep pace.

As another example of the rather interesting position in which the Democrats found themselves during the constitutional period, we can consider the emotional flag issue. As we have seen earlier, Preuss had thought that the colors black-red-gold ought to replace the old imperial colors, which were black-white-red. Particularly if Austria were to enter into *Anschluss* with Germany, such should be the case. However, Preuss's Democratic colleagues were divided on this issue and, as to be expected, concerning an issue of

---

[74] *Ibid.*, 1091C-D.
[75] *Ibid.*, 1093C-D.
[76] *Ibid.*, 1108A.
[77] *Ibid.*, 1108B.
[78] *Ibid.*, 1109B.
[79] *Ibid.*, 1109C.
[80] Schwarz, *op. cit.*, p. 123.
[81] Ziegler, *op. cit.*, p. 86.

this nature, emotion played a rather strong role. Naumann, for example, had been originally for the black-red-gold colors because of possible Austrian *Anschluss*. However, after the receipt of the Versailles conditions in May, 1919, his position altered. Now, as an act of defiance against the insufferable Allies, he reversed himself. The old imperial colors were not to be deserted.[82] Koch agreed with him. It would be almost cowardly, he thought, "to strike the old banner at a time of critical need for the Fatherland."[83] With Naumann absent, however, the Democratic members of the constitutional committee, (with the exception of Koch) voted for the black-red-gold colors and, by the rather narrow margin of fifteen to eleven, the committee as a whole selected these over the old imperial colors. There was a compromise appended to this, however; a compromise in which a Democratic member of the constitutional committee, Ablass, played an important role. The old, imperial colors were to be kept as the flag of the merchant marine, while a black-red-gold jack (*Gösch*) was to adorn the upper corner.[84]

When the flag issue came up before the entire National Assembly, however, on July 2, 1919, during the second reading of the constitution, the majority of the German Democratic fraction, Naumann among them and voting as a delegate, supported a DVP resolution calling for retention of the old flag. Dr. Petersen, in speaking for the majority of his colleagues, declared that the old flag symbolized the achievements of the German people as a whole and was a sign of hope to all German-speaking peoples who, through injustice and persecution, had been separated from the Fatherland.[85] Ludwig Quidde, presented a fractional "minority report," in which he posed that liberalism, and those desires of South Germans, symbolized by the black-red-gold colors against those forces symbolized by the imperial flag. He also added that the new colors could be seen as symbolic of the reconciliation of class antagonisms between bourgeoisie and proletariat.[86] The DVP resolution was defeated 190 to 110, and Germany's new flag was the black-red-gold of the old *Burschenschaft* and of the shattered dream of 1848. Again, and perhaps in this case more understandably, since any flag tends more to represent heart (and sometimes spleen) rather than mind, the issue of primary importance for the Democrats was national unity; for the majority, it would seem, national unity in the face of foreign oppression. However, even for pacifist-liberal Quidde, the theme of unity, particularly that unity that emerged from class-reconciliation was pretty much at the heart of the issue. Insofar as the Democrats were concerned, it had merely come to pass that unity plus imperial memory had won out over unity plus conciliation and/or *Anschluss*. Although, when viewed from any sort of rational perspective, the flag issue was a minor one in the troubled course of German constitutional history, it, perhaps more than any other, can serve as an index to that confused amalgam of idealism, nostalgia, and defiance that constituted the emotional *Gestalt* of a large number of Weimar-period bourgeois Democrats.

For many of the German Democrats, the constitutional issue of greatest importance was that of parity between parliamentarianism and other agencies of government. We have seen this earlier in the discussion of the plebiscite and referendum issues. This was also apparent in regard to the question of Article 48 (Article 58 in Preuss's original draft), the famous (or infamous) "police-power" article which provided for presidential lifting of certain constitutional rights in case of obvious and palpable danger to public order. As Preuss originally had it, the *Reichspräsidant* had immediately to obtain the consent of the Reichstag as well as that of the entire Reich ministry in order to carry out his "emergency decrees." If such were denied to him, the decrees would have to be lifted. During the course of the constitutional committee's deliberations, it was decided that the president should "immediately notify the Reichstag" of his actions and, "on demand of the Reichstag, annul the measures."[87] It is obvious that such a change indicated a shift of power, at least in this case, from parliamentary to executive control. During the course of the debate over the proposed changes in content and emphasis of Article 48, which took place on July 30, 1919, during the third reading of the constitution by the National Assembly, Dr. Ludwig Haas of the German Democratic party defended this course of action, indicating that the effectiveness of implementing such decrees would be undercut if too many special devices and regulations were placed in the president's path.[88] Perhaps surprisingly, Preuss made little real objection to this change, indicating that the change in emphasis suggested (and actually accepted) was more of "a matter of taste" than anything else.[89] The changes in Article 48, changes which were due largely to objections raised by Democrat Haas against Preuss's original version, when taken together with the significant emphases that Democrat Koch chose to place upon plebiscite and referendum, are indicative of the Democrats' concern that problems of divisiveness and party politics, which they tended to associate with parliamentarianism, be overcome through a tying together of a strong executive power with so-called "direct democracy." Certainly, this is to some degree understandable and, in defending his call for a strong president, Preuss dis-

---

[82] Heuss, *op. cit.*, p. 496.
[83] Ziegler, *op. cit.*, p. 146.
[84] *Ibid.*, p. 147.
[85] VVDN, *op. cit.*, 1231A-C.
[86] *Ibid.*, 1235C-D.
[87] Ziegler, *op. cit.*, pp. 159, 306.
[88] VVDN, *op. cit.*, 2111D.
[89] *Ibid.*, 2112D.

played an almost grim perspicacity in describing what would happen if Germany were to be deprived of one: "Then you will see very soon that the plebiscite will scream for a saviour and Führer who embodies in his person the active strengths of the people."[90] Yet, the, at least to some degree, anti-parliamentary attitudes of many Democrats, as exemplified by such people as Meinecke and, among the delegates, by Koch, point to a very profound problem, one which would plague the German Democrats right up to 1933: the quest for state unity, as exemplified by appeals for such things as so-called "direct democracy" versus parliamentary government that has been considered, at least in the West, the *sine qua non* of responsible democratic government.

This problem was put into sharp focus during the debates of July 2, 1919, when Conrad Hausmann and Erich Koch both spoke in defense of that constitution which was taking shape in the hands of the constitutional committee. Haussmann spoke up in defense of proposed article 130 (part of the *Grundrechte*) which stated the following: "All state citizens are obliged, according to the measure of the law, to perform personal service for the state and the community."[91] (This did go into the final draft of the constitution as article 133.) "Every German," Haussmann enthused, "without limiting his personal freedom, has the ethical duty to utilize his spiritual and physical strengths in a manner required for the good of the whole."[92] Egotistical motives would be overcome, or at least greatly strictured, by so noble an ethical injunction as that prescribed in the constitution. With the allowances that were being made for direct participation of the *Volk* in the life of the state, i.e., those provided by plebiscite and referendum, a constitution had been created of which even the great Fichte would have been proud. "Fichte would agree with us, if we contemporary Germans formulated, 'The state must be filled with *Volksgeist*; the *Volk* must be filled with *Staatsgeist*.' "[93] This, of course, leads one to ask whether, in Democratic minds (to say nothing of some of the others), the state existed to serve the people, moreover, a people divided into interest groups of various forms, or whether these groups existed as prism rays of an assumed national whole, into which they would blend with joyful cries. Naturally, as Schwarz points out, the latter was the case. Pluralism, while recognized, really had not been accepted by the German Democrats who felt themselves to have been invested with the sacred task of achieving the *Einheitsstaat*.[94]

This anti-pluralistic, or at least apluralistic attitude was reflected in Koch's address of the same day. First of all, he admitted that, like many other liberal Germans, he would have preferred a constitutional monarchy to anything else. "Speaking for myself, and also for our entire party, I already have declared on several occasions that we have not become republicans on principle."[95] The monarchy had failed to recognize the need for such things as voting reform and thus, of necessity, a new government form had to arise from the ashes of national disaster. Koch, indicating that his position towards parliamentarianism had shifted somewhat since his speech of February 28, then took issue with Hans Delbrück who, conservative though he was (he was a member of the DNVP) had suggested that there were too many reservations (*Kautelen*) against parliamentary government in the constitution. "I am a confirmed democrat," Koch said, "however, I am not convinced that democracy and parliamentarianism are totally congruous with each other."[96] By the time Koch made this speech, he had grudgingly accepted the new black-red-gold flag. Now, he declared, the flag was a symbol of *Grossdeutsch* unity after all, as well as being a symbol, as Quidde had suggested earlier, of the reconciliation between bourgeoisie and proletariat.[97]

Several things emerge from Koch's address. First of all, we can again see that attitude of grudging acceptance of the republic and of parliamentary government as being quite prominent in Koch's political outlook. We can also see, and this of course is directly related to the above, the notion of "direct democracy," e.g., direct participation of the people in the state, as being equally as prominent an element in Koch's thinking. In a nation with virtually no parliamentary tradition whatsoever, this was a rather questionable if not almost dangerous position to take. However, we must point out again that such a position becomes readily understandable if we bear in mind the fact that, for the Democrats, the question of the unified *Volksstaat* was the crucial one in 1919, much as it had been for the left-wing liberals before the First World War. Positive, as well as negative, attitudes flowed from this, of course. Probably, one of the most important of the former was the Democrats' "saving" of the non-denominational school as being the usual and accepted form of school for all of Germany. This was done on July 31, 1919, the very day on which the constitution was ratified, by Eugen Schiffer who, speaking on behalf of the Democratic party, declared

---

[90] Ziegler, *op. cit.*, p. 170.
[91] VVDN, *op. cit.*, 1202D.
[92] *Ibid.*, 1203A.
[93] *Ibid.*, 1204C.
[94] Of course, the notion of sacrificing oneself for larger "interests of state" or the so-called "national interest" is not merely a German one and, in recent years, this call has been repeated with increasing frequency in the United States. President Kennedy's oft-praised and usually totally misunderstood inaugural cry, "Ask not what your country can do for you, but what you can do for your country," was certainly an example of this.
[95] *Op. cit.*, 1220B.
[96] *Ibid.*, 1221C.
[97] *Ibid.*, 1235C.

that the non-denominational school ought not even to be considered in the new constitution, thus pointing out that, in the eyes of the state, religious-affiliated schools and private schools, which were mentioned in this document, were given recognition by the constitution. On the other hand, a non-denominational school, presumably a step in the direction of a unified educational system, was accepted by the constitution as given, and not recognized as being merely equal to the other forms.[98]

However, taking that marvelous, retrospective overview provided by the telescope of historical hindsight, we must recognize that the search for the unified state, no matter how understandable if not justifiable this was, really served to enfeeble the republican-parliamentary impulse of the German Democrats. For, even as the Democrats were playing an incredibly important role in the formulation of the Weimar Constitution (a role for which they would be despised by increasing numbers of the bourgeoisie they in fact represented), their own attitudes regarding parliamentarianism and republicanism were mixed. Theirs was not the naïve liberalism of an Eugen Richter or the practical pluralism of the Western liberals. They viewed the constitution emerging in Weimar as both a testimony to and a product of the developing *Volksstaat,* that grandiose achievement which, up to then had eluded all attempts, Bismarck's included, to attain it. On July 31, 1919, by a vote of 262 to 75, the Weimar Constitution was accepted. Only the reactionary DNVP, the conservative DVP and the radical left-wing USPD voted against it. The German Democratic party, of course, voted with the majority. Yet, as the Democrats attempted to rejoice in their rather tight-fitting republican raiments, they were perhaps unaware of the possibility that, as time passed, that statism which, for most, was *rationale* for the parliamentary republicanism embodied in the Weimar Constitution might well prove to be an ever more alluring enticement, particularly as pluralism became more and more identified with anarchy. Indeed, as the Weimar Republic went from crisis to crisis, the German Democratic party was more and more willing, if not eager, to testify to the statist and romantic heritage of so many of its most prominent members. Thus, it is to a consideration of these phenomena that we must now turn.

III. STATE AND REPUBLIC: FROM CONSTITUTION TO THE DEATH OF EBERT

From early 1919 to the time that a formal Democratic program emerged in December of that year, the party membership engaged in merry debates over various constitutional and party issues.

One of the issues which proved to be most vexing was the position bourgeois liberalism should take vis-à-vis the Social Democratic party. As we have seen earlier, the German Democratic party viewed itself as being "above class and special interest." Yet, from the beginning, it was apparent that so grandiose a conception was not necessarily congruent with political and social realities. At the January 7, 1919, meeting of the party *Vorstand,* the question of combining electoral lists with the SPD or with the DVP came up for the first time. During the course of a somewhat involved discussion, the self-consciously bourgeois nature of at least some members of the party became immediately apparent. Hermann Fischer, one of the leaders of the *Hansa Bund,* declared that, while the DDP had to be careful not to alienate the SPD by drawing too close to the conservative DVP, any sort of alliance with the SPD, to say nothing of combining electoral lists was out of the question.[1] While the committee took a general stand against list-combining either with the SPD or with the bourgeois parties of the right, DVP and DNVP, the thought of combining even with the anti-Semitic and reactionary DNVP in Polish-threatened Ostmark had crossed the minds of several of the members of the committee.[2] In many ways, as we have seen in the preceding chapter, the question of national unity was uppermost in the minds of Germany's Democrats.

The disturbing position of Germany's liberal Democrats. *viz.,* a party of national unity and class-conciliation which was, nevertheless, a bourgeois party (national unity being itself, of course, a bourgeois political ideal), was brought out in several further meetings of the *Vorstand.* In the April meeting, for example, Fischer again cautioned the committee that the DDP could not allow itself to become simply a *Mitläufer* ("Accompanier") of the Social Democrats.[3] While certainly none on the *Vorstand* would have been in favor of such a position, at least at this point, people such as Anton Erkelenz had been more inclined towards active cooperation between the DDP and SPD. The question of whether the DDP ought to be a party of national unity or a party of national unity plus being a more or less self-consciously bourgeois party was one that would haunt Democratic circles throughout the Weimar period.

One of the other issues that also was of interest was that of the Constitution itself. Since so many Democrats were involved in work on the Constitution, it is not surprising that what they envisioned in articles and speeches bore a striking resemblance to the actual product of Weimar. In this regard, Friedrich Cauer wrote a somewhat prophetic article which appeared in the February 1, 1919, issue of *Das Demokratische Deutschland.* In this article, Dr. Cauer made the point

---

[98] *Ibid.,* 2164B.

[1] Bundesarchiv, Koblenz, R45 III/15, Sitzungen des Hauptvorstandes der DDP Schriftwechsel und Protokolle, 20.
[2] *Ibid.,* 13, 20–21.
[3] *Ibid.,* 100.

that Germany was in danger of falling into divisiveness. The way out of this dilemma would be the creation of a "strong and unified state power." Such a creation would not have to be inimical to democracy; indeed, the Western democracies had had such powers during the war.[4] If necessary, Prussia itself ought to be divided up, as Preuss had suggested, for the sake of overriding German unity. A strong Reichstag was necessary. However, a strong president would also be necessary, in order to provide for a unity around one person, and to push through whatever socialization as would be necessary.[5] The Reich government would have to have power and it would have to be unafraid to use it if required to do so. The same notion was espoused in a later article in the same journal, this one written by Theodor Heuss. Here, Heuss called for a strong president, to be selected by the people as done in the United States. This was necessary, Heuss maintained, "to make certain that his power is strongly anchored, independent from parliamentary currents and considerations."[6] Those problems which would be posed by proportional representation—an issue with which Dr. Cauer also had been concerned—was another reason for the existence of a strong presidency.[7] The fact that a party colleague, Dr. Hugo Preuss, was intimately concerned with writing the Weimar Constitution was in large measure responsible for the interesting coincidence of the Constitution's bearing a remarkable resemblance to that hypothetical one suggested by many members of the young Democratic party.

Die Hilfe, Naumann's old mouthpiece, became an organ of democratic propaganda. A not uncommon sort of suggestion, one which was, as we have seen, in keeping with the modern German democratic tradition, was that the party avoid becoming a class party. Heinrich Gerland in an article entitled "Demokratische, nicht 'bürgerliche' Politik," which appeared in the February 13, 1919, issue of *Die Hilfe*, drew the usual comparison between the Democratic party and the Social Democratic party, claiming that, while the former organization derived its essence from interest policies, i.e., from representing the interests of the proletarian class, the new Democratic party should be and was above such interest policies.[8]

The economic program was also the object of some consideration, and Dr. Rudolf Oeser proposed that the party support a program of land settlement. Issues of social justice and national security were involved in his suggestion that big, uneconomical estates be divided up to provide for "farming village after farming village up to the Russian frontier."[9] Insofar as industry was concerned, Anton Erkelenz's article of April 3, 1919, in *Die Hilfe* set the tone. Certain industries, such as those concerned with gas, water, and electricity, ought to be transformed into national monopolies, with any profits accruing to the entire *Volk*.[10] Otherwise, private enterprise ought to remain inasmuch as bureaucracy and state ownership of property created more problems than it solved.[11] Erkelenz did differentiate between the actual property of a firm (*Betrieb*), its governing, and the division of yield, indicating that, while property should remain in the hands of private individuals, some share for workers and employees in direction of the firms and a more equitable share in profits ought to be provided.[12] Certainly, Erkelenz suggested, a unified working law should finally be created and he offered the hope that the future League of Nations would provide for international labor laws.[13]

What the Democratic party considered to be important in education was the formation of a unified educational system. This demand for an *Einheitsschule* would become an important point in the Democratic program, and one of the earliest commentaries on it was contained in a pamphlet by Paul Sommer entitled "Das deutschdemokratische Schulprogram." After making the usual demands for freedom of research and teaching, he emphasized that the main goal of the democratic school program would be the development of "intellectual efficiency and ethical character building of youth on German *völkisch* foundations."[14] All schools ought to be state schools and all teachers should be state officials. The unified school, *Einheitsschule*, was an absolute necessity.

In the journals of the Democratic party and in pamphlet form, a program was taking shape. It was a program which emphasized national unity and spiritual elevation of the *Volk*. Democratic republicanism was also involved, but this was seen as a means toward the end of national unity and spiritual betterment. Much as Wilhelm von Humboldt and Johann Gottlieb Fichte had proposed, the German Democrats saw the state as fulfilling a definite moral and educative purpose.

The first congress of the German Democratic party took place in Berlin, from July 19 until July 22, 1919.

---

[4] Preussisches Geheimes Staatsarchiv, Berlin, Hauptabteilung XII-III, Dr. Friedrich Cauer, "Die Reichsverfassung," in: *Das demokratische Deutschland,* 1 Jahr, Nr. 8, 1 February, 1919: p. 172.

[5] *Ibid.*, p. 173.

[6] Preussisches Geheimes Staatsarchiv, Theodor Heuss "Der Reichspräsident," in: *Das demokratische Deutschland,* 1 Jahr, Nr. 10, 15 February, 1919: p. 218.

[7] *Ibid.*

[8] Heinrich Gerland, "Demokratische Nicht, 'bürgerliche' politik," in: *Die Hilfe,* Nr. 7, 13 February, 1919: pp. 78-79.

[9] Preussisches Geheimes Staatsarchiv Hauptabteilung XII-III, Dr. Rudolf Oeser, "Demokratie und Landswirtschaft," in: *Das demokratische Deutschland,* 1 Jahr, Nr. 12, 1 March, 1919: p. 227.

[10] Anton Erkelenz, "Gemeinwirtschaft und Deutsche demokratische Partei," in: *Die Hilfe,* Nr. 14, 3 April, 1919: p. 169.

[11] *Ibid.*, p. 168.

[12] *Ibid.*, p. 169.

[13] *Ibid.*

[14] Preusiches Geheimes Staatsarchiv, Hauptabteilung XII-III, *Das demokratische Schulprogramm,* von Paul Sommer (Berlin, 1919), pp. 15-16.

Here, many of the concerns and problems that had plagued Germany's liberal Democrats came to the surface. On the one hand, Otto Fischbeck, Prussian trades minister, declared with some vigor that the German Democratic party, standing on the new, republican "state form" had to represent the will of the entire *Volk*.[15] In this he was strongly supported by Koch, *Parteitag* chairman, who maintained that the future would be decided by that party drawn from all classes of the *Volk*.[16] On the other hand, Otto Nuschke, while criticizing Stresemann and the DVP as reactionary, declared that the party had to be against combining electoral lists with the SPD because, in order to protect "bourgeois/democratic interests," an SPD majority had to be prevented.[17] Nuschke's position was supported by Dr. Carl Petersen, head of the Assembly fraction, who declared that while the DDP had been "duty-bound" to vote for a May 1 holiday, in order to seek out ties between proletarian and bourgeois interests, the council system that had developed in Germany (*Rätesystem*) was non-democratic and called for class domination. The issue, he suggested, was that between democracy on the one hand and class domination of the proletariat on the other.[18] While all Democrats agreed that the new German Democratic party had to have social concerns, the fact that this new party was and would remain bourgeois in outlook and character could not be expunged through the admittedly soul-stirring cry for national unity. The class nature of the party was clearly evident in a July 20 address by Dr. Köhler of Berlin. The DDP, he declared, had to draw a line between itself and the SPD. "Freedom of the economy" was of utmost importance.[19]

In a later address, Dr. Richard Frankfurter obfuscated the issue a bit by declaring that there was no real political difference between the SPD and the DDP. The difference lay in the fields of economics and culture. To be sure, the old capitalism was dead (which capitalism he was referring to is not so easy to discern). He also agreed with Gertrud Bäumer that "Our first task is the reconciliation between the working class and the rest of the *Volk*."[20] However, private enterprise still had to be preserved. At the same time, Frankfurter declared that Germany was a republic and that, if this republic were threatened, the party would stand with the Social Democrats, "On this side of the barricades!"[21] What Frankfurter was coming out for was a sort of socially conscious republic, one in which private enterprise would be preserved nonetheless. The fact that economic and cultural differences could find resonance in the field of politics seems to have escaped him. What also seemed to escape him (as it did many Democrats) was the strong possibility that the working classes might well be more concerned with having their interests represented either by the SPD or the Communists than by a party dedicated to a functional state of class conciliation. Dr. Frankfurter, perhaps without his knowing it, was holding forth as that almost archetypal variety of German bourgeois who, consciously or unconsciously, sought to veil his own class background and interests behind the phrase of national unity.

As another example of this, we can consider the address of Dr. Robert Kauffmann of Berlin. The whole economy, he declared, had to be elevated. The only way to do this was through private enterprise and individual initiative. To be sure, an investigating commission had to have the power to decide which branches of the economy ought to remain in private hands, and which ought to be nationalized. But this had to be done with extreme caution.[22] The commanding principle of the economic order ought to be "political, economic and ethical equality of all Germans."[23] Furthermore, Kauffmann declared that he was in favor of Anton Erkelenz's oft-mentioned factory council (*Bebriebsrat*) proposal as a means to the end of overcoming the class struggle. However, it was obvious that Kauffmann was speaking as a member of the bourgeoisie, a liberal bourgeois to be sure, but bourgeois nevertheless.

In this regard, Hermann Fischer was probably one of the more forthright members of the German Democratic party. In his speech of July 22, he remarked that the economic program of the DDP, bourgeois yet ostensibly sympathetic to the same interests as were being served by the SPD, was confusing. It held out false hopes for the working class, he said. Moreover, in seeming tacitly to ignore entrepreneurial interests (even though the DDP was a bourgeois party), the new party was putting itself in an awkward position. If the DDP continued on its present course regarding economic policy, Fischer warned, it would be trusted by none.[24] This perspicacious observation was one which would prove to be most accurate as time went on.

Another question of no mean importance which arose during the course of the first party congress of the DDP was that of the party's attitude regarding Versailles and its subsequent withdrawal from the government. On the very first day of the congress, Count Bernstorff, formerly the ambassador to the United States, declared that, inasmuch as Germany was in no position to continue the war against the Allies, the treaty had to be accepted. A peaceful fight for equality

---

[15] *Bericht über die Verhandlungen des 1. Parteitage der Deutschen Demokratischen Partei abgehalten in Berlin vom 19. bis 22. July, 1919* (Berlin, 1919), p. 5.
[16] *Ibid.*, p. 7.
[17] *Ibid.*, pp. 11–13.
[18] *Ibid.*, pp. 20–31.
[19] *Ibid.*, p. 82.
[20] *Ibid.*, pp. 170–172.
[21] *Ibid.*, p. 176.

[22] *Ibid.*, pp. 200–201.
[23] *Ibid.*, p. 202.
[24] *Ibid.*, p. 225.

and justice could come later.[25] Hartman Freiherr von Richtofen agreed with Bernstorff. The treaty had to be signed. It would have been most irresponsible for the government not to do so. Furthermore, he declared, the DDP should have remained in the government.[26] Richthofen's remarks constituted a slap in the face for Naumann, first chairman of the party, who had been in the forefront of the majority of the DDP opposed to Versailles and in favor of withdrawing from the government in protest. Naumann, obviously stung by Richthofen's remarks, replied that what the latter had said went beyond the bounds of the party day. A party day, he declared, ought to be concerned with "world historical and great questions."[27] Moreover, Naumann said, it was necessary to take a broader view of things. He could understand the feelings of those who had signed under the pressures of the moment; but how would things look in the future? Obviously if one was not in favor of signing the treaty, one had to leave the government (as had the SPD leadership itself).[28] It was in this context that a most interesting issue arose, that of the relationship between the liberal "Berlin press," by and large republican in sympathies (and in large measure Jewish-owned) and the party. George Gothein, speaking in defense of Naumann, declared that the DDP had to leave the government. Furthermore, he said that the well-publicized attitude of the liberal bourgeois press "broke our back" insofar as any attempt to convince the Allies that Germans as a whole were opposed to signing was concerned. Here, there sounded the *Zuruf*: "die Berliner Presse!"[29] Through declaring that refusal to sign would be just a pose or a gesture, the press had done much to force the hand of the government. This tension between liberal bourgeois republicanism and the press which supposedly supported it was one that would remain prominent throughout the Weimar period. The fact that a substantial portion of the press was in Jewish hands would not help the party—or at least many of its members—to preserve a tolerant attitude either towards the press or towards the Jews as a group. In regard to the "Jewish Question" (*sic*), it would seem that the party's official attitude was best summed up by Dr. Petersen. To be sure, he said, in a speech of July 21, there were many radical Jews in Germany. However, unlike Germany's hide-bound and bigoted conservatives, Democrats would not question the loyalty of those Jews who were not radical. This had to be done in the interests of "freedom, humanity and justice."[30]

Declarations in favor of a three-year voting period (to be over-turned in the constitutional assembly, as we have seen) a unified educational system, an enlightened foreign policy, the *Einheitsstaat* and, as to be expected, a state of social justice (but not socialism) rounded out the general program of the DDP. The official program would not emerge until December, 1919, but the outlines were visible in July. Also visible in July (and, indeed, earlier) was a most perplexing problem, one that would eat into the very vitals of bourgeois republicanism: how could a bourgeois party really claim to represent all interests of the *Volk?* Or, more pointedly, how could a class party claim to be "non-class"? As Fischer so clearly realized, a party that declared itself to be neither bourgeois (although it obviously was) nor proletariat (which it obviously was not), but which claimed that it really represented everybody, would end up being trusted by none. At the same time, however, this search for that fantasy of German political history, national unity, would be, in the end, responsible for the DDP's rejection of republicanism, just as virtually every other political party or interest group in Germany (with the ironic exception of the SPD) would also seek to abandon republican confusion for the more comforting and traditional security offered by the "state above party interest."

As mentioned above, a formal program for the Democratic party did not appear until December, 1919, five months after the death of its founder, Friedrich Naumann (the party was now headed by Carl Petersen, who would resign to be mayor of Hamburg in 1924). At first blush, the party seemed to stand upon completely republican foundations; indeed, the first paragraph of the program vowed defense and furtherance of the Weimar Republic.[31] On the question of "internal policy," the party proclaimed that "The German Republic must be a *Volksstaat* and absolutely . . . a *Rechtsstaat.*" "We are striving," the Democrats proclaimed, "for the unity of the Reich, however, with the consideration of preserving the unique characters of the German tribes (*Stämme*)."[32] There was a mildly *völkisch* aspect to the Democratic internal program, inasmuch as it called for law to "be developed in a *volkstümlich fashion.*"[33] But this would find but little amplification in future party pronouncements, at least during the early years of the republic. The party also came out in favor of military reform, i.e., a national militia system with universal service to take the place of the old army.

Understandably, the Democrats called for a strong foreign policy, with emphasis upon the revision of the Versailles and St. Germain peace treaties. Self-consciously taking a page from President Woodrow Wilson's book, the Democrats stated: "We will never de-

---

[25] *Ibid.*, p. 42.
[26] *Ibid.*, pp. 58–61.
[27] *Ibid.*, p. 64.
[28] *Ibid.*, pp. 64–66.
[29] *Ibid.*, p. 86.
[30] *Ibid.*, p. 140.

[31] Wolfgang Treue, *Deutsche Parteiprogramme, 1861–1954* (Tübingen, 1954), p. 122.
[32] *Ibid.*
[33] *Ibid.*

part from the principle of self-determination of peoples and, based upon this principle, we are striving for the amalgamation of all the German tribes."[34] Obviously, the party was referring to an eventual *Anschluss* with Austria; but its concern with the fate of German-speaking peoples did not stop with this.

A primary goal of German policy is close alliance with and protection of the *Auslandsdeutschen*. It is a national duty to help *Volksgenossen* under foreign domination to preserve their *Volkstum;* but also we consider it as a political commandment to respect the national minorities in Germany.[35]

It came as no surprise to anyone that the Democratic party, being in large measure a party of intellectuals, should have been concerned with education. In Section II (*Kultur*), it came out for a goal that would remain constant all during the Weimar Period: that of establishing a uniform educational system for all of Germany: the *Einheitsschule*. German youth, the party maintained, was dependent upon education for character building and physical reliance. The party proposed that German children be required to attend school until they were fourteen years old, and be required to study (*Lernplichtig*) until the age of eighteen. However, it was unfortunate that the German people "suffer from social, political, and religious divisions" and that these divisions were reflected in the multivariegated educational structure of the country.[36] The solution to this would be the creation of an *Einheitsschule* "which simultaneously embraces all elements of the nation," thereby securing "its endangered unity."[37] Such a school, of an obviously non-confessional nature, would actually be preferable to formally religious schools in that all students would be "made familiar with the history and essence of religion," and this would be done apart from the opinions and prejudices of parents and teachers.

The party platform agreed that, by and large, German *Kultur* ought best to be left alone by the state. However, "the state can at no time deny its strong protection to threatened *Volk*-morality."[38] This statement seemed to be justifying censorship and, as we shall see, various members of the party were to take protection of *Volk*-morality rather seriously from time to time.

Church and state were to be separated and the rights of all sects protected. The state should not support one religion or sect to the exclusion of all others, for "The crowning of the *Kulturstaat* subsists in the development of inner freedom in questions of *Weltanschauung* and religion."[39]

As regarded the economy (*Volkswirtschaft*), the German Democratic party declared itself to be a "party of work" with its goal being "the state of social justice."[40] However, lest anyone draw the unhappy conclusion that any form of socialism was being preached, the program was most careful to come out against nationalization because of the "deadly bureaucratization of the economy and concurrent lessening of its profit" associated with state ownership of the means of production.[41] Essentially, at least in the field of economics, the program came out for the watchdog state of Wilhelm von Humboldt. It was against monopolies and injurious economic practices. It stood for the individual entrepreneur, worker, or farmer, and was against monopolization of the land and land speculation. Questions of economics were not the only ones involved here, and the program betrayed the romantic views of its writers when it gave the following as an added reason for individual land ownership. "Thus will the soil of the homeland (*heimische Boden*) make possible for many German people a free, natural and useful existence and secure the health of the *Volk* and the nourishment of the whole."[42] As we have seen, even more nationalistic motives played a role in the party's demand for a strong program of land settlement. The program called for taxes on property and inheritance in order to help equalize opportunities and, in a somewhat romantic rebellion against the forces of modern industrialization, it stated the following: "The division of labor threatened to rob work completely of its soul. Therefore, hand work and small trade must be advanced and protected."[43] The program encouraged entrepreneurs to introduce more joy into labor as a "factor of production." "Thus should the democratic state of social justice establish the dignity of man in the economy."[44] Like the prewar Naumannites, the Weimar Democrats were determined to avoid somehow the problems of class struggle. Theirs was to be a state of reconciliation.

The program of the German Democratic party was a striking one indeed, particularly inasmuch as it seemed to promise all things to all people. For the *Kulturmensch,* there was emphasis upon the *Kulturstaat* and upon education; for the farmer, there was the offer of land; for the worker, joy in his work; for the entrepreneur, the protection of private property; for the democrat, adherence to the democratic constitution; for the nationalist, a strong foreign policy. There were even a few bits of gratuitous romanticism to titillate the romantic.

As amorphous as the party program seemed to be, it is important to bear in mind one salient fact: the German Democratic party was attempting, rather self-consciously, to become a mass political party, one that could embrace proletariat and bourgeoisie in a synthesis

---

[34] *Ibid.*, p. 123.
[35] *Ibid.*
[36] *Ibid.*
[37] *Ibid.*
[38] *Ibid.*, p. 124.
[39] *Ibid.*
[40] *Ibid.*, p. 125.
[41] *Ibid.*
[42] *Ibid.*
[43] *Ibid.*, p. 126.
[44] *Ibid.*

vital for the construction and maintenance of a true *Volksstaat*. There was, of course, a certain irony in this. As we have said before, the DDP was, after all, a bourgeois political party, one in which members of the business community, e.g., those in the *Hansa Bund*, as well as more worker-oriented individuals such as Anton Erkelenz could feel at home, at least for a while. The clash between the party's assumed role as constituting a step towards the *Volksgemeinschaft* and the palpable interests of much of its overwhelmingly bourgeois membership would create difficulties for this party as time went on.[45] Nevertheless, the party's avowed support of republicanism as well as the general nature of its program seemed to make it unique. Yet, was it?

In a letter of 1920, Walther Rathenau complained that the Democratic party had remained stuck upon the old road of prewar Progressivism.[46] At first glance, such an accusation would appear to have been somewhat ill founded. After all, the German Democratic party was a republican party, if nothing else, and certainly the old Progressives were not that. However, it is obvious that Rathenau's remarks were quite perceptive indeed. The old Progressives had stood for national unity plus strong foreign policy. For what did the new party stand? One need not have been terribly perceptive to have seen that the new party stood for much the same thing. Defeat in war had made the collection of idealists who drew up the platform a bit more sensitive to the realm of the spirit. Otherwise, though, the resemblance between the new party and prewar Naumannism was considerable and all the more remarkable considering that which had occurred in between. As we shall be able to see more concretely when we examine the writings of various democratic individuals, the party and many of those who belonged to it had a very strong conviction that their organization was a true *Staatspartei*, i.e., the party which represented if it did not actually embody the interests of state. As we have seen, such indeed was the view that prewar followers of Naumann somewhat immodestly appropriated to themselves.

Both the party program and the earlier statements of policy vowed commitment to the republican form of government and to the Weimar Constitution within which such a form had been rooted. However, it is important to note that, with the exception of relatively few, e.g., Anton Erkelenz—an individual often condemned as "doctrinaire" by his contemporaries—most of Germany's Democrats became republicans out of a sense of political necessity. Their own feelings regarding such things as political parties, republicanism, and toleration were often somewhat different from those views expressed in the Democratic platform and/or rationalized as the party goals. In a significant article of October 5, 1919, in the Democratic journal *Das Demokratische Deutschland*, Wilhelm Külz, now Oberbürgermeister of Zittau, made the following remark:

The compelling logic of historical facts does not allow us to pose the question of whether we want to recognize a democratic republic; but we must accept it whether we want to or not.[47]

The task of the party was to form a free *Volksstaat* and to prove whether it (the party) would "prove itself capable of continuously filling this state form with living contents."[48] As in the case of the prewar democrats, one is tempted to pose the question: What would happen if "the compelling logic of historical facts" brought one to the conclusion that republicanism no longer had a role to play in German political life, or that political pluralism itself was dangerous or invalid in Germany? What would happen if one drew the conclusion that the republican state form was too amorphous a body to allow for its being filled with living contents? As we shall see, while the German Democratic party itself officially remained committed to republicanism and the Weimar Constitution—at least up until 1930—many of its members began answering these questions in ways which were not exactly conducive to republican proselytizing.

To be sure, those who made up the new German Democratic party were committed, at least on paper, to republicanism. This was certainly more than many members of the German People's party were willing to do. Throughout the formative months of this party, the most that it was willing to do was to accept, in a most grudging manner, the historical "fact" of the republic.[49] Furthermore, while the German Democratic party saw, as one of its primary tasks, that of "building bridges between the bourgeoisie and the workers," the German People's party saw itself as being a distinctly bourgeois party, dedicated to the preservation of bourgeois interests against the Social Democratic threat.[50]

When the German People's party met at Leipzig in October, 1919, in order to formulate a program, it did not take a stand "upon the foundations of the Weimar constitution" as had the Democratic party, but merely said, in point three of its program, that it would work within "the present state form" in order to "reconstruct the Reich."[51] However, almost from the beginning, individual democrats evidenced grave reservations about the republicanism to which the German Democratic party was supposedly dedicated.

---

[45] For a fine discussion of this problem see Ernst Portner, "Der Ansatz zur Demokratischen Massenpartei im Deutschen Linksliberalismus," in: *Vierteljahrshefte für Zeitgeschichte*, p. 13. Jhg., 2. Heft, April, 1965: pp. 156–157.

[46] Walter Rathenau, *Politische Briefe* (Dresden, 1929), p. 216.

[47] Preussiches Geheimes Staatsarchiv, Hauptabteilung XII-III, "Der demokratische Staatsgedanke," by Wilhelm Külz, in: *Das demokratische Deutschland*, 1 Jahrg., Nr. 43, 5 Oktober, 1919: pp. 984–985.

[48] *Ibid.*, pp. 984–985.

[49] Wolfgang Hartenstein, *Die Anfänge der deutschen Volkspartei: 1918–1920* (Düsseldorf, 1962), pp. 48–49.

[50] *Ibid.*, pp. 50–51.

[51] Treue, *op. cit.*, p. 114.

One of the earliest and most sustained critiques of both the Democratic party and the state which it was to represent emerged from the pen of Walther Rathenau. As seen above, he felt that the Democratic party had become mired in the old Progressive program. On June 23, 1919, in a letter to Peter Hammes, he expressed extreme disappointment that the party was not putting forth a "strong social policy."[52] Almost before the nascent republic got off the ground, Rathenau was expressing suspicion as to the abilities and motives of one of the three major sources of its support, the Social Democrats. In the letter to Hammes he remarked:

What I fear is that they do not have the insight to develop further and that they will make themselves completely dependent upon the masses in their conscious striving after electoral majorities and political successes of the moment.[53]

In words reminiscent of Max Weber, Rathenau pointed to the powerlessness of the Social Democrats.

By itself, the party has developed only bourgeois business and compromise. Internally, it trembled before its goal, the revolution; indeed, it trembled before the simple rudimentaries of power, before majorities, parliamentarianism and republic. When power came it stood helpless.[54]

In extreme bitterness, Rathenau proclaimed that the German republicans had "tired of parliaments before we knew parliamentarianism."[55] However, his own critique was hardly written from a parliamentary or even republican point of view. Rathenau was calling for an overthrow of party politics and for freedom of action for the state.

... our party being so deeply immersed in beer table and clique foolishness, in the cult of local powers, tavern orators and public phrase-mongering that, in general, national elections, conducted over many year intervals by party machines, must bring to light assemblies which stand far beneath the level of European parliaments. Such houses and their attendant ministers cannot be trusted with the fate of the land ... the councils, the workers, and soldiers councils have accomplished more and shown more initiative than the German parliament has done in fifty years.[56]

Perhaps what Rathenau had to say was in part true. However, his own attitude towards the state was haunted by that all-pervasive dualism which saw it as being somehow above mundane issues of day-to-day freedom, indeed, even of public participation in its life. As he put it in an article in September, 1919:

The less free the fundamental institutions of state, the more lackadaisical and continuously arbitrary will it be in daily life. Various despotic arrangements from time to time fulfill themselves in the paradox of a certain daily freedom, be it in the press of *Volk*-life or in banal transitory forms. Common natures satisfy themselves with this freedom, particularly if it is also commercial, because to them fundamental things are of no consequence and because they prefer the shallow satiation of trade and business.[57]

In view of the weaknesses of the old German Reichstag such statements cannot be viewed with surprise. However, his fundamental distrust of political democracy put his role as a democrat under a cloud and, as we shall see, his criticisms of German republicanism would become ever more biting as time went on.

Rathenau's suspicions of parliamentary republicanism were echoed by Friedrich Meinecke who, in his 1919 work, *Nach der Revolution,* displayed an almost startling bitterness towards the German masses, at times accusing them of moral and spiritual cowardice because they were unwilling to see the war through to a successful conclusion.[58] However, Meinecke remarked in a political essay, he had become "a *Vernunftsrepublikaner,*" even if *Herz* had remained with the monarchy.[59] As such, he wrote numerous political essays calling upon the German people to accept the republican government "as the one form which divides us the least," while concurrently demanding that a strong presidency be established to provide for an institution that would be "independent from the changes of parliamentary majorities."[60] Certainly such an attitude is understandable and, under the circumstances, it was perhaps correct. However, an examination of Meinecke's motives for supporting republicanism reveals an attitude which was hardly sympathetic to this particular form of rule. In a letter to his wife, dated October 5, 1918, Meinecke remarked that, with the German government about to ask Wilson for an armistice, the end was near and

... there is ... nothing left for us to do than to become democratic in order to preserve the Reich and national unity. And, if we are successful in reconstructing ourselves democratically, without revolutionary distress and under constant maintenance of state authority, we will be satisfied.[61]

---

[52] Walther Rathenau, *Schriften* (edited and introduced by Arnold Harttung, Gunter Jenne, Max Ruland, Eberhard Schneider) (Berlin, 1965), p. 310.
[53] *Ibid.*, p. 311.
[54] *Ibid.* (from "Die Revolution des Guterausgleichs 1919"), p. 312.
[55] *Ibid.*, p. 313.
[56] *Ibid.*

[57] *Ibid.* ("Der Wahre politische Fehler" Sept., 1919), p. 314.
[58] Friedrich Meinecke, *Nach der Revolution* (München, 1919), p. 36. It is of some interest to note that many of the reasons, given by Meinecke in *Nach der Revolution,* for the collapse of Germany in World War I, were paralleled by those offered by Stresemann; viz., the cleft between officers and men in the German army, failures in diplomacy, and lack of identification of the people with its government. See *Nach der Revolution,* pp. 18–32, and Hartenstein, p. 62.
[59] Friedrich Meinecke, *Politische Schriften und Reden,* ed. Georg Kotowski (Darmstadt, 1958), p. 281.
[60] *Ibid.*, p. 288.
[61] Friedrich Meinecke, *Ausgewählter Briefwechsel,* ed. Ludwig Dehio, (Stuttgart, 1962), pp. 94–95.

Meinecke went on to say that a great deal of "conservative ballast" would have to be cast overboard; however, his attitude towards the republican form of government is quite clear: it was merely a form necessary "to preserve the Reich and national unity." Meinecke himself who, at one point, suggested that what Germany really needed was a "substitute Imperium" (*Ersatzkaisertum*) was hardly sympathetic to the new republic. Like Rathenau, he was immensely suspicious of the Social Democrats and their ability to function in positions of authority. "No state could rule for long," he maintained, "on the basis provided by the protaganists of the left, with their Jewish sentimental-soft ideas. . . ."[62] One needed iron as well as brains. However, in an age in which "the hero is abandoned and there remains only the shop-keeper!" one could expect little. *Vernunft* had dictated that Meinecke move to the Democratic camp. In this, he represented a not inconsiderable percentage of Germany's *Bildungsbürgertum,* which saw the state itself above and beyond transitory forms dictated by the fortunes of war. If the state could best be served in another fashion, the republican government would be sacrificed.

The Meineckes and the Rathenaus were not unusual phenomena in the period 1918/1919. Even Friedrich Naumann himself who, until his death in August, 1919, had always stood for increasing the power of the Reichstag and for parliamentary participation for the liberal bourgeoisie. could bemoan the "creeping-in of parliamentarianism" in November, 1918, and see it as a sign of divisiveness;[63] and Max Weber, who, as late as 1917 had called for a strengthening of parliament, had turned, by 1919, to that quasi-mystical sort of Führer speculation with which he is often associated. To be sure, Weber was merely seeing things as they were when he claimed, in his famous essay, "Politik als Beruf," that, in an age of mass democracy and mass parties, programs are created not really by parliamentary fractions but by the parties themselves.[64] Furthermore, Weber stood out against any sort of political romanticism in his famous division between what he called "ethics of conscience" (*Gesinnungsethik*) and "ethics of responsibility" (*Verantwortungsethik*); presumably, one could not have one without the other, and by bringing the two together, Weber was self-consciously setting himself in opposition to any sort of political romanticism.[65] However, Weber's thoughts on the matter of mass democracy led him to the conclusion that the old rule of *Honoratiorenkreisen* and of parliamentarians was ended.[66] Whether or not parliamentarians had ever really "ruled" in Germany was somewhat doubtful. However, Weber dilated, the choice in Germany now was between "Führer democracy with a 'machine' or leaderless democracy, which means the rule of 'professional politicians' without profession, without the inner, charismatic qualities which smooth the way to the Führer."[67] Parliamentary rule, something which had once been of great importance for Weber, had yielded to a sort of *Real*-political Führer who rooted himself in the body of the *Volk* through plebiscite. As C. Wright Mills and others have pointed out, it would be extremely specious to attempt to link Weber to Nazism through the conception of the Führer.[68] To begin with, Weber was no racist, and whatever *völkisch* desires that might have slumbered within him were pretty well hidden indeed. However, there can be little doubt that Weber remained a statist all of his life and that parliamentarianism became of little importance to him as Wilhelmine Germany yielded to republican Germany. While Weber felt no qualms about abandoning the monarchy, others in the Democratic ranks—such as Meinecke—did, and it was of great significance that the Democratic minister of defense who succeeded Gustav Noske after the Kapp *Putsch* of 1920, the Bavarian Otto Gessler, remained monarchist in sympathies; indeed, not merely to the Hohenzollern, but even to the Wittelsbach dynasty![69] In brief, it was extremely significant that, although the Democratic party as a whole, and many individual Democrats such as Anton Erkelenz and to a degree Theodor Heuss, remained formally committed to a parliamentary order, other members of the party, as early as the tumultuous 1918/1919 period, accepted the republic either in a most grudging fashion or as a means, perhaps a very temporary means, of preserving the state. The 1920's would see both the development of previously inchoate rumblings against parliamentarianism and party politics, and the simple playing-out of forces which had already manifested themselves during the constitutional period. For a suspicion of political parties, of "interest-bound" parliamentarianism and a concurrent tendency to strive for organic unity were not qualities which came out in response to crises, although these could and did act as catalysts, but rather, they were ideas which had become central in the political *Anschauungen* of many democrats.

The Democratic concern to appear as a party "above class and interest group" was soon put to a rather palpable test. On January 18, 1920, the second and final reading of the "Factory Council Law" (*Betriebsrätegesetz*) took place. This law was designed to provide a voice for workers and employees in the form

---

[62] Friedrich Meinecke, Vol. II, *Erinnerungen, Strassburg, Freiburg Berlin 1901–1919* (Stuttgart, 1949), p. 27.

[63] Friedrich Naumann, "Die deutsche Einheit," in: *Die Hilfe*, Nr. 48, 28 November, 1918: p. 569.

[64] Weber, *Gesammelte Politische Schriften*, p. 520.

[65] *Ibid.*, pp. 539–547.

[66] *Ibid.*

[67] *Ibid.*, p. 532.

[68] H. H. Gerth and C. Wright Mills, *From Max Weber: Essays in Sociology* (New York, 1958), p. 43.

[69] Otto Gessler, *Reichswehrpolitik in der Weimarer Zeit* (Stuttgart, 1958). See the excerpt from Gessler's letter of February 6, 1955, to Crown Prince Rupprecht (p. 518).

of "Factory Councils," modeled in part after the old Russian Soviet. Provision for just such a law had been made in Article 165 of the Weimar Constitution, i.e., in the *Grundrechte* portion of this document. As can be seen, this idea was congruent with Naumann's notion that class conciliation could and should be striven for, this to avoid class conflict, if not class war. However, despite the fact that a Democrat, Naumann, was to some extent responsible for this law, the bourgeois character of the party reared its head. Several aspects of it disturbed many Democrats. Most prominent here were three provisions: (1) that the management make its books available to the councils on an annual basis, (2) that members of the councils could serve on supervisory boards, and (3) that members of the councils could participate in hiring and firing of workers and employees.[70] Throughout the late summer and fall of 1919, Democratic opposition to the law was obvious. However, by the time that the law came up for its second reading on January 13, 1920, some of this had been dissipated. As was to be expected, the radical Independent Socialists and Communists did not think that the law went far enough. A mass demonstration greeted the Assembly delegates as they filed into the Reichstag building to vote, and the latter were often physically threatened and spat upon.

Under these disturbing conditions, the law bill was read. Unfortunately, as debate raged over it, the throng of demonstrators around the building grew somewhat restive. Thinking that the Reichstag was about to be stormed, police and army machine gunners, apparently favoring the Roman *dictum* that the best defense was a strong attack, opened fire, killing 42 and wounding 105.[71] The German radical left had demonstrated its usual propensity to gather large numbers of supporters together in one place, only to have them mowed down. During the final debate on January 18, 1920, Anton Erkelenz—as we have seen, the most "left-wing" of the German Democrats—made an eloquent speech in defense of the law. Labor relationships could not be what they were before the war, Erkelenz declared. Furthermore, the general "despiritualization" of labor that had taken place in the course of the development of modern industry had to be, if not overcome, then at least counter-balanced.[72] The law according to Erkelenz was not a "political concession to the streets." Furthermore, in England even Conservatives had come out in favor of such a law. But, Erkelenz added with a sarcasm worthy of Max Weber, the English Conservative had "a better political nose" than his German counterpart.[73] Everyone, even the DNVP, agreed that workers had to be given some sense of participation in industry; and this law was a way to provide for this. Erkelenz then quoted the late Friedrich Naumann. Employers had to concern themselves with their "human raw materials" as well as with their natural or mineral raw materials. What was at stake here, Erkelenz declared, was the spirit, the soul, of man. The law was really calling for a new working class, as well as for a new type of management.[74] Finally (and significantly), Erkelenz remarked that Bismarck himself would have gone along with it.[75] After further debate, the law was passed, 215 to 63, with one abstention. The Democratic fraction was split.

As for the German Democrats, what the "Factory Council Law" imbroglio revealed about their party was that its claim to represent the entire German people put it in an awkward, if not untenable, position. On the one hand, "radicals" such as Erkelenz could interpret this to suggest that the party stand for a strong "democratization" of the economy. Such a "democratization" would necessitate the implementation of measures which could only have disturbed, if not actually have frightened, the bourgeoisie (the DVP, DNVP joined with the USPD in voting against the law). On the other hand, the party as a whole could not have been terribly enthusiastic about such a law, and there was a core of Democratic opposition around the figures of Georg Gothein, and Felix Waldstein.[76] As much as the Democrats were concerned with pursuing that political will-of-the-wisp, the *Volksgemeinschaft*, they were, after all, bourgeois. Yet, the irony of all of this was that, in the eyes of the bourgeoisie, the German Democratic party, associated as it was with the Weimar Constitution and, at least to some degree with such things as the "Factory Council Law," really did not represent their interests. In the end, the ideology of this party, tailor-made to represent everybody, would represent almost nobody at all. Again, what was of ultimate importance in dictating decline for the DDP was its identification with the increasingly despised Weimar Constitution, and, in a broader sense, with parliamentary government. As we shall see, the Democrats themselves would become increasingly embarrassed by their own, at least in part, "creation." As it was, DDP support of the law was responsible for a considerable number of resignations from the party.

As early as February 14, 1920, Gertrud Bäumer published an article in *Die Hilfe* with the engaging title of "Parteifreie Politik." She pointed out that German youth was both disturbed by and distrustful of political parties. They were put off, she maintained, by the lack of willingness to sacrifice class and individual interests to the national interest which they saw as

---

[70] Wilhelm Ziegler, *Die deutsche Nationalversammlung 1919/1920 und ihr Verfassungswerk* (Berlin, 1932), p. 211.
[71] *Ibid.*, p. 209.
[72] *Verhandlungen der verfassunggebenden Deutschen Nationalversammlung. Band 332 Stenographische Berichte* (Berlin, 1920). Hereafter cited as VVDN, 4494B.
[73] *Ibid.*, 4494D–4495B.

[74] *Ibid.*, 4496B.
[75] *Ibid.*, 4496C.
[76] Ziegler, *op. cit.*, pp. 207, 211.

characteristic of political life.[77] The parties, she thought, would abandon their dogmatic positions once they found it necessary to take part in government and share responsibilities. However, she made it fairly obvious that her own sympathies lay with the younger generation which was "seeking, in truth, nothing other than the old national-social thought."[78] As we shall see in other contexts, Frau Bäumer was characterized by a sort of post-menopausal fascination for young people, at times even going so far as to share their tendency towards political romanticism. However, she was hardly alone in espousing that the German Democratic party in particular, and German political life in general assume a "party-free" tone.

The Kapp *Putsch* of March, 1920, did force the German Democratic party to join the Social Democrats and Centrists in assuming a "no compromise" stand, regarding the sanctity of parliamentary governments, albeit while in temporary exile in Dresden and Stuttgart. However, the party's most important representative in Berlin, the vice-chancellor and minister of justice, Eugen Schiffer, helped to put its position under somewhat of a cloud. In a series of conferences involving, among others, Martin Schiele of the conservative German National People's party (DNVP), Gustav Stresemann of the German People's party, Major Waldemar Pabst of the putschists, and General Walther von Lüttwitz, who was the commanding general of the putschist military forces and as the unsuccessful nature of the revolt became apparent, acting leader of the *Putsch* itself, Schiffer made his offices available for the conferences and also indicated that he would support amnesty for the rebels, thus undercutting the position of the Bauer government to which he was supposedly loyal.[79] Erich Koch, who was then minister of the interior and who would later play a leading role in the German Democratic party, did telephone Schiffer from Stuttgart, declaring that the Bauer government would disavow any agreements that he and those of Stresemann's ilk might make with the rebels.[80] Schiffer, protesting bitterly that the government had no idea of just how serious the situation in Berlin actually was, never made Koch's telephone call known to the negotiators.[81] Moreover, he put tremendous pressure on George Gothein, the other DDP representative in Berlin, to take part in the negotiations.[82] After March 17, i.e., the day that the *Putsch* came to an end, Schiffer disavowed his previous agreement for amnesty and, in the March 18 entry in his "Notes on the Kapp *Putsch*" (*Aufzeichnungen Kapp Putsch*), Koch recorded, with some irony, that Schiffer had finally found himself and was no longer quite as soft on the rebels as he had previously been.[83] Schiffer's double-dealings, while condemned by his own party in general and by Koch in particular, did reveal some of the weaknesses that were contained within the ranks of the DDP. His own commitment to republicanism was not terribly strong— nor to the party, for that matter (he would leave it in 1924)—and this made it impossible for him to maintain a strong position against those who threatened it. In this, he was at one with the admittedly anti-republican Stresemann; both displayed a remarkable ability to treat with the rebels when their success seemed imminent.

The same day that Koch recorded his somewhat ironical remark concerning Schiffer, the National Assembly met in temporary quarters at the art museum (Kunstgebäude) in Stuttgart. The president of the Assembly, the Centrist Konstantin Fehrenbach (soon to be chancellor), pointed out that the Kapp rebels had struck just when Germany was entering a period of order and hope.

But, the peaceful development was not congruent with the spirit of men who spoke much of a Fatherland, yet did not understand how to subordinate their personal and party interests to the general well-being.[84]

Fehrenbach, with some passion, declared that events in Berlin constituted a "monstrous crime" against the German people. Friedrich von Payer spoke for the Democrats. It was a bitter speech, reflecting the spiritual exhaustion of a man soon to retire from politics. In part, he reiterated much of what Fehrenbach had said. The German people had been cheated out of their hard-won internal peace. The interests of the whole had been threatened.[85] It would be years, von Payer went on, before distrust against Berlin would be extirpated from South Germany, particularly after this latest outrage.[86] However, he continued, the German Democratic party would not be panicked. "Under no conditions will the policies of our fraction be oriented to the right."[87] Von Payer thanked all those who remained loyal to the republic and then, with some circumspection, considering the delicacy of the issue, he suggested that the army and bureaucracy needed to be investigated and those "elements inimical to the *Volk*" rooted out.[88] At any rate, that *Einheitsstaat* which would end disorders of this nature would soon arrive.

Von Payer's speech was a strong condemnation of the Kapp freebooters, a collection of reason-enfeebled

---

[77] Gertrud Bäumer, "Parteifreie Politik," in: *Die Hilfe*, Nr. 8, 14 February, 1920: p. 116.
[78] *Ibid.*, p. 117.
[79] Hartenstein, *op. cit.*, pp. 165–178.
[80] Henry Ashby Turner, *Stresemann and the Politics of the Weimar Republic* (Princeton, 1963), pp. 57–61.
[81] Bundesarchiv Koblenz, Nachlass Koch-Weser, Nr. 24, Aufzeichnungen 'Kapp Putsch' von 15/3 bis 6/4, 1920, 89; Turner, *op. cit.*
[82] Turner, *ibid.*

[83] Nachlass Koch-Weser, *op. cit.*, p. 93.
[84] VVDN, 4899D.
[85] *Ibid.*, 4911B.
[86] *Ibid.*
[87] *Ibid.*, 4911C.
[88] *Ibid.*, 4911D–4912A.

mental dwarfs whose activities in Berlin were pretty well confined to such actions as canceling examinations at the University and confiscating matzo flour.[89] Yet, von Payer's speech was primarily concerned with order and unity of the German state. Under the circumstances, this is quite understandable. However, it is of significance that he devoted little time to a defense of the parliamentary government that had been so gravely threatened by events in Berlin. Von Payer's primary concern was with that threat to German unity posed by the *Putschists*. It was in search of unity that the Democrats rallied to the thinking of Friedrich Nauman before the First World War. This same fated search had led them to Weimar. It would continue throughout the Weimar period until that time when unity indeed would be attained by a movement which the Democrats could only regard as divisive.

To be sure, the Democratic party as a whole, as represented by Koch, was from the beginning, bitterly opposed to Kapp, and in this it differed substantially from its neighbor on the right, the DVP. However, as Hartenstein points out, the events of March, 1920, seemed to push both the DDP and the DVP into embarrassing proximity insofar as the tone and contents of their respective *Aufrufe* for the elections of June 6, 1920, were concerned. Both parties declared themselves opposed to any form of dictatorship; both were opposed to corruption in government; both were in favor of the unified Reich; both called for a forceful foreign policy and for revision of the Versailles Treaty; both called for class reconciliation and for the defense of private enterprise.[90] Indeed, the only ways in which they differed were these: who was responsible for restoring order to Germany and was or was not Germany in good shape politically and economically? Since the DDP was identified by the voters as being part of that bumbling system that had come within a whit of being toppled by a handful of ludicrous political misanthropes, and since bourgeois fears of the left were ebbing, it lost heavily in the elections of June 6, receiving only 2,333,700 votes (8.3 per cent of those voting) and returning but 39 delegates to the Reichstag (as we have seen before, in the elections of January 19, 1919, the DDP had polled 5,641,800 votes (18.6 per cent of those voting) and had sent 75 delegates to the National Assembly). The similarities between the campaign platforms of DDP and DVP and the collapse of the former in the 1920 elections pointed to several interesting phenomena: (*a*) While the DDP was formerly committed to republicanism, it was able to coat this over with a triple-thick layer of patriotic veneer. In a word, statism was really the guiding principle of the party; a statism which, at times, made it difficult to discern any appreciable difference between it and the more conservative DVP. (*b*) Despite this willingness to compromise—at least during election campaigns—the party was nevertheless identified with the republic and all of its weaknesses. Whether or not members of the party were aware of this unhappy paradox, their willingness to indulge in statist fantasy was to continue unabated until the fall of the republic itself. Such was the powerful legacy of statism in German political life.

In the June 3, 1920, issue of *Die Hilfe*, just three days before the election, Karl Würzburger printed an article with the same name as that of Bäumer's one of February 4. In this article, Würzburger extolled the national and social orientation of the party. The Democratic party, he said, was not in favor of state socialism; not at all. Rather, it considered itself to be representative "of the entire individual life of society and *Volk*."[91] It was a party which was willing to take up the political tasks of the state.[92] The greatest of these tasks, Würzburger maintained, was that of work. In an extremely interesting statement, he remarked that only through democracy could the German people go from parliamentarianism to a "system of experts" which, without regard to party, could lead to the development of a national-social work program.[93] Here, we can note two rather interesting themes: (1) the tendency, common to many democrats, of seeing the party as a sort of non-political party of the whole; and (2) to see parliamentarianism as something provisional and scarcely necessary for democracy. Certainly such a point of view was not common only in Germany. However, in a nation in which parliamentarianism was so underdeveloped and in which a sort of *völkisch* democracy was often espoused, such an attitude must be seen as being particularly dangerous.

It is of some interest that the German Democratic party considered itself to be a party of work without necessarily being a proletarian class-party. It was such an opinion which allowed Bäumer on March 4, 1920, in an article, "Bürgerliche Ideale," to maintain that love of work was at the basis of bourgeois culture much as it was in socialism. Thus, she reasoned, the bourgeois class, or rather, that portion of it represented by the German Democratic party, had nothing to fear from socialism.[94] Whether or not she was consciously representing the thinking of Max Weber is difficult to say. However, emphasis upon "work" as distinct from "proletarian class-interest" was characteristic not only of the German Democratic party but of the radical right

---

[89] Erich Eyck, *A History of the Weimar Republic*, translated by Harlan P. Hanson and Robert G. L. Waite (2 v., New York, 1970) 1: p. 151.

[90] Hartenstein, *op. cit.*, pp. 210–211.

[91] Karl Wurzburger, "Parteifreie "Politik," in: *Die Hilfe*, Nr. 23, 3 Juni, 1920: p. 341.

[92] *Ibid.*

[93] *Ibid.*

[94] Gertrud Bäumer, "Bürgerliche Ideale," in: *Die Hilfe*, Nr. 19, 4 Marz, 1920: p. 149.

as well.[95] This once again underscores the point that, no matter what their differences in regard to racist ideology, both the Democrats and the radical right, e.g., Moeller van den Bruck, were heir to that same tradition which saw the state (or *Volksstaat*) as being somehow greater than the sum of its parts. Thus, unity of state-life was *ipso facto* the important concern for Germany's democrats. Parliamentarianism and party-life had to take a back seat to broader concerns of state. As early as 1919, Meinecke had called for a strong presidency, one which could act as a counter-balance to the Reichstag and to party majorities. These views were echoed in a 1920 article by H. G. Erdmannsdorffer, who also chose to view the president as a counter-balance to the Reichstag and exulted in his dependency only on "the peoples' will."[96] It was this sense of *Staatsnotwendigkeit* and *völkisch* unity which caused Bäumer to cry out that the party spirit and infighting which prevailed in the Reichstag made her ashamed to be a member of parliament. In this article which, astonishingly enough, when we consider that it appeared in 1920, was entitled "The German Parliament in the Fateful Hour" ("Das deutsche Parliament in der Schicksalstunde") she put special blame on the Social Democrats and on the German National People's party (DNVP) for emphasizing party interest above *Volk*-unity.[97]

At the same time, though, the electoral disaster of June 6, 1920, caused some members of the party to question whether or not the DDP could continue to declare itself to be the party of no class or interest group. In a meeting of the *Vorstand* on June 10, 1920, Hermann Fischer declared that many bourgeois were convinced that the DDP had not done enough to represent their interests *vis-à-vis* the Social Democrats.[98] Bernhard Grund lent support to Fischer. The fears of Koch, Bäumer, and others of entering a coalition with the DVP, one seemingly dictated by the results of the election, had to be overcome, even if the SPD itself did not participate in the coalition. At this meeting, a clash between two groups within the DDP had become apparent. On the one hand, there stood Koch and Bäumer, still reaching for the ideal of class reconciliation, for the *Einheitsstaat* that had eluded Germany in 1848, 1871, and now apparently in 1918 as well. On the other hand, there stood people like Hermann Fischer who, republican though he was (at least in his own mind), nevertheless seemingly had grasped the ironic fact that, if the DDP were to survive as a republican party, it might well have to align itself with bourgeois interests which were clearly anti-republican, e.g., with the DVP.

This point of view had become a quite powerful one, at least within the *Vorstand*, by the end of 1919, and was clearly represented in the meeting of this committee on December 3, 1920. Here, Petersen suggested that if the DDP were unable to work with the SPD in the government, it had to be willing to work with the DVP. Friedrich Wachhorst de Wente, who was active in agrarian Democratic politics, agreed. Furthermore, he added, he agreed with party comrades in Schleswig-Holstein, who had all but suggested that, at least in their conservative area, DDP and DVP merge into a new bourgeois party of the middle.[99] If the DVP were to refuse such a suggestion, he thought, the DDP could only benefit from the refusal. However, Otto Nuschke and Anton Erkelenz were against fusion at any level. There was no guarantee, the latter said, that such a fusion party would hold together anyway. Besides, the DVP had identified itself with the "yellow" trade unions. If there was a fusion now, Erkelenz warned, "you would have a unified workers' party from Legien to Stegerwald."[100] Despite Erkelenz's warning, the *Vorstand* eventually agreed—against the votes of Bäumer and Nuschke—that at least the Schleswig-Holstein Democrats could make overtures to the DVP that a unified Schleswig-Holstein *Landespartei* be formed. This, of course, would in no way commit the national DDP to move in the same direction.[101] The overtures had no practical results, to be sure. However, as early as 1920, events within Germany had forced many in the DDP to seek out that unity with the anti-republican DVP that had escaped them in 1918. For republican parliamentary government to function, alliances with anti-republican factions seemed to be necessary, particularly inasmuch as the most powerful of the "republican" parties, the SPD, had been estranged from the government. It is not surprising that, as time went on, Germany's liberal Democrats became ever more suspicious of the parliamentary system itself.

In 1920, Theodor Heuss who, in his memoirs pointed out quite correctly that he never was in favor of such quasi-totalitarian devices as the plebiscite, exhibited a

---

[95] On the German right-wing's differentiation between "worker" and class-conscious proletarian see George L. Mosse, *The Crisis of German Ideology* (New York, 1964), particularly pp. 20–22, 100–102, and 262–264. Also Fritz Stern, *The Politics of Cultural Despair* (New York, 1965), particularly his discussion of the ideology of Moeller van den Bruck. David Schoenbaum's *Hitler's Social Revolution* (New York, 1967) is also most revealing on this subject, while George L. Mosse's *Nazi Culture* (New York, 1966) contains some interesting Nazi writings on the subject of workers and the *Volk*.

[96] Preussisches Geheimes Staatsarchiv, Hauptabteilung XII-III, H. G. Erdmannsdörffer, "Die Wahl des Reichspräsidenten," in: *Das demokratische Deutschland*, 2 Jahrg, Nr. 8, 22 Feb., 1920: p. 133.

[97] This article first appeared in the April 1, 1920 (Nr. 14) issue of *Die Hilfe*. The source which is being utilized here is *Das demokratische Deutschland*, 2 Juli, Nr. 20, 19 Mai, 1920: pp. 393–394.

[98] Bundesarchiv, Koblenz, R45III/16, Sitzungen des Vorstandes des DDP (Protokolle), 1920: p. 45.

[99] *Ibid.*, p. 87.
[100] *Ibid.*, p. 93.
[101] *Ibid.*, p. 96.

somewhat ambivalent attitude towards parliamentary democracy. In an article entitled "Towards the Turn of the Year" ("Um die Jahreswende"), which appeared in a Democratic party newspaper *Der Beobachter* on December 31, 1920, Heuss made the following observations:

We affirm parliamentary democracy as the only form in which the self-supporting state could create a new organism . . . which will make justice and stability possible; but, it is only a form, and is not an object of party power struggle but an instrument with which the parties should be of useful service to the state. Where we suffer is in lack of feeling for this total state responsibility.[102]

Here again, we can see several rather prominent notions: (1) that parliamentary democracy was only a form, and (2) that this form must provide the means by which parties could be "useful" to the state. Again, although perhaps not as clearly as in the case of Meinecke and others, we can see that Heuss was adhering to that traditional dualism that had developed in German political life and thought during the nineteenth century. The state stood above and beyond the various forms through which it functioned.

As we have noted before, several prominent Democrats attempted to justify the emergence of parliamentary democracy from a purely *Real*-political point of view; this particular phenomenon was the one form of government that divided Germany the least and in essence Germany could be held together only through such a state-form. Some Democrats, however, carried this attitude a bit further, into the realm of foreign policy. Such a point of view was expressed in a pamphlet written by Professor Walter Schücking, in 1920 entitled "Auf dem Wege zur deutschen Demokratie." Schücking took a strong position against the pre-World War social order. The tragedy of German history, he proclaimed, was the failure of the 1848 revolution.[103] The basic failure of pre-1914 Germany, one which in fact had led Germany to defeat, had been a "lack of democracy." Germany had been unready for war inasmuch as it had lacked a "unified will."[104] Here, Schücking was emphasizing something that Meinecke had previously examined in his *Nach der Revolution* of 1919; the necessity of having a unified state in order to secure this state in an age of mass warfare and mass armies. However, Schücking carried this analysis into the postwar period, attacking the Kapp putschists of 1920 as individuals who had really threatened the entire German people. Now, in order to gain that trust among foreign nations which would be necessary if Germany were to be able to overturn the unjust treaties of Versailles and St. Germain, democratic rule must be preserved.[105] Those who threatened the democratic order thereby also threatened Germany's position in the world. Professor Schücking called upon the great Ranke himself, in pointing out that external and internal affairs were inextricably intertwined. Thus, a threat to the internal order was an implicit threat to external goals. In an article in *Das Demokratische Deutschland*, September 26, 1920, Professor Ludwig Bergstrasser was a bit more positive along these lines. He accused the German Democratic party of not being interested enough in foreign policy, emphasizing that the most important fact of national life was the Treaty of Versailles.[106]

The attitude towards the party's role which had emerged by 1920 was a rather interesting one indeed. First of all, the Democratic party established itself as a republican party with its roots in the Weimar Constitution. However, many of its members were unable to break free from an historically sanctified view of the state, which saw it as being somehow above the mundane course of day-to-day life. The party role and even the role of such things as elections were thus somewhat limited. Here again, a critique by Walther Rathenau is of some interest.

In this moment June, 1920, we are emerging into formal democracy in its most grandiose form; as a final novelty in the mode of 1848. No breath of a new thought has arisen in Weimar; the old liberalism celebrates its golden wedding anniversary in patricide and crinoline. In no land is Biedermeier democracy more dangerous than with us and at no time was it more dangerous than today.[107]

Again, much of what Rathenau has said reveals fine insights into the weaknesses of the Weimar Republic. Certainly, the choice of Weimar itself pointed to a certain pompous, pseudo-Goethean self-satisfaction. However, as in earlier criticisms, Rathenau's 1920 essay serves also to reveal his own somewhat dualistic view of the state:

Since when should someone seriously believe that he rules the state with his portion of sovereign will because he, in accordance with the proposition of the lesser evil, had carried out an act of voting?[108]

It was a "Schwindel," Rathenau proclaimed, that the "perplexed government which emerges from it [the elections] can be seen as 'embodying state power.'"[109] Perhaps, Rathenau suggested in another essay of 1920, some sort of *Direktorium* consisting of "the three most capable men of the cabinet" ought to be set up. At any rate, "That would be a far better solution than the

---

[102] Heussarchiv, Stuttgart, *Politische Schriften, Der Beobachter, Blatt der DDP Württemburg*, Freitag 31, Dezember, 1920.
[103] Preussisches Geheimes Staatsarchiv, Hauptabteilung XII-III, Walter Schücking, *Auf dem Wege zum deutschen Demokratie* (Berlin, 1920), p. 6.
[104] *Ibid.*, p. 7.
[105] *Ibid.*, p. 11.
[106] Preussisches Geheimes Staatsarchiv, *Das demokratische Deutschland*, 2 Jahrg., Nr. 20, 26 September, 1920: p. 615.
[107] Rathenau, *op. cit.* (*Reden Wir Deutsch*, Juni, 1920), p. 317.
[108] *Ibid.*
[109] *Ibid.*, p. 318.

rule of factions according to the model of the Polish Reichstag."[110]

The period 1918–1920 was a time of troubles for the Weimar Republic. Certainly, one can explain the criticism of parliamentary and party life then extant on this basis. However, one cannot avoid noting that criticism of parliamentarianism and of those party activities which are seen as constituting the politics of pluralism was not something which developed only late in the history of the Weimar Republic; but that it was, in fact, something which was prominent among many democrats almost from the beginning, albeit it tended to become more prominent as the Weimar period waxed on.

From 1920 until 1925 the republic existed as an institution fairly secure against enemies on the left but threatened from time to time by enemies on the right. There were revolts, assassinations, and *Putsches*, of course, 1923 being an exceptionally active year. Although the government itself did reign, at times it appeared not to rule, even though threats of magnitude of that faced in 1920 seemed to be things of the past. Germany's bourgeois Democrats, facing the problem of a nation divided against itself, continued to reveal uncertainties and inconsistencies in regard to parliamentary rule and the role of political parties.

As we have seen, there did exist, in the German Democratic party, that element which sought to identify the party with specifically middle-class interests, especially since the electoral defeat in June, 1920. Another example of this was an editorial which appeared in the January 27, 1921, issue of *Der Demokrat,* which was graced with the somewhat apocalyptic title of "The Middle-Stand in Danger!" ("Der Mittelstand in Gefahr!"). Here the case was made that the German Democratic party was really the only true party of the middle class. The parties of the right represented the great capitalist interest of Germany, while the Social Democrats of course constituted a threat inasmuch as they stood for proletarian class interests and socialism.[111] Only the German Democrats stood for the middle. Yet, even here we are confronted with a somewhat equivocal attitude. This concerns the use of the word *Stand*—a virtually untranslatable word, which implies a sort of stratum within an organic *Volk*-community rather than a formally economic class. Again, the use of this word underscored the attitude which many members of the Democratic party held in regard to the state: it was, or should be, an organically unified commonweal.

It is true that by 1921 several Democrats were able to put a finger upon a basic, vitiating weakness of German political life. This consciousness was perhaps best expressed by Leo A. Freund in an article, "Unpolitische Politik," that appeared in the April 17, 1921, issue of *Das Demokratische Deutschland*. Half regretfully, Freund remarked that "Party politics compels the *tribunas plebs* to sacrifice one's 'unshakable' principles or political convictions to the masses."[112] The trouble with the German political community was not political, but rather, a tendency towards a sort of fuzzy-minded idealism which ran counter to the basic tenets of political life.[113] With the exceptions of Erkelenz and, as we shall see, of Heuss, Freund's somewhat practical view of what politics is all about was not widely held.

The problem which many Democrats seemed to face whenever they attempted to confront the issues of Democracy and parliamentarianism is perhaps best revealed in an article which appeared on July 14, 1921, in *Der Demokrat*. Here, the editorial staff of the journal heaped praise upon Dr. v. Campe of the German People's party for noting that, although parliamentarianism and democracy were supposed to have been the cure-alls for everything that ailed Germany, the German people "does not know how to use them."[114] The two institutions had been vitiated through the belief that majority rule was the law of the day. "Inner values" had been forgotten in a ruthless sacrificing "of the few to the many."[115]

Der Demokrat responded as follows:

These are excellent, valuable and unfortunately all too true words which the entire citizenry ought to take to heart. For many Germans, democracy is still a strange garment; one must become accustomed to new clothes. The suit can be altered a bit, but we must never think of laying it aside.[116]

The journal went on to applaud von Campe's brave statement that:

Democracy will be the basis of our state—or we will cease to exist. And, our entire political life will develop within the framework of parliamentarianism, or we will be reduced to total impotence.[117]

The journal applauded von Campe's recognition that *Real*-political factors dictated that Germany had to be ruled by parliamentarianism. The German Democratic party itself would be a lot stronger, the journal maintained, if it had not chosen to put *Staatsnotwendigkeit* ahead of party advantage (*Parteivorteil*). "Away from all party politics!" the journal enthused. What was needed was the "cooperation of all positive, creative strengths which hold firm to the idea of the state."[118]

---

[110] *Ibid.,* "Was wird werden?" 4-12-1920, p. 320.
[111] Institut für Zeitgeschichte, München, "Der Mittelstand in Gefahr," in: *Der Demokrat,* 2 Jahrg. Nr. 27, January, 1921: p. 83.
[112] Preussisches Geheimes Staatsarchiv, *op. cit.,* Leo A. Freund, "Unpolitische Politik," in: *Das demokratische Deutschland,* 3 Jahrg, Nr. 15, 17 April, 1921: p. 346.
[113] *Ibid.,* p. 347.
[114] Preussisches Geheimes Staatsarchiv, "Ein Frontwechsel?" in: *Der Demokrat,* 2 Jahrg., Nr. 28, July 14, 1921: p. 541.
[115] *Ibid.,* p. 542.
[116] *Ibid.*
[117] *Ibid.,* p. 543.
[118] *Ibid.,* p. 544.

To be sure, stands taken on the basis of *Staatsnotwendigkeit* often necessitated backing extremely unpopular measures. In 1921, for example, the party came out in favor of accepting the reparations figure arrived at by the Allied governments at the Spa. In defending this course of action before the Reichstag, Ludwig Haas declared that, if his fraction were to vote its feelings, the Allied Reparations Ultimatum would be rejected. However, one had to bear in mind the future of the German people and thus make a "responsible decision."[119] Germany, he declared, was in no position to resist and, if any part of Upper Silesia (a plebiscite regarding its fate was soon to take place) were to be saved and the Rhineland occupation ended, the ultimatum had to be accepted.[120] Everything possible had to be done to protect the *Volk* and the state, even as all Germans would work together to end the shame and injustice of Versailles.[121] Most Democrats joined the Social Democrats, Centrists, and Independent Socialists in the majority vote to accept the ultimatum. Such an act implied a considerable degree of political courage. However, acts of this nature also accentuated the party's tendency to identify interest of state with itself, thus placing it in an extremely contradictory role insofar as its belief in republicanism was concerned.[122] Naturally, as mentioned previously, the old statism had a role to play in this. Its influence upon even a determined defender of the republic such as Theodor Heuss can be seen in his 1921 essay "Democracy and Self-Government" (Demokratie und Selbstverwaltung"), in which he attempted to find roots for principles of self-government in such historical phenomena as the old German legal concept of *Genossenschaft* and in the Prussian reform movement. The essence of democracy, Heuss maintained, was this: "State power comes from the people." However, what people were involved here? "The sum total of individuals to whom the state has assented to give a say in public matters."[123] Such a point of view would naturally lead to the conclusion, which Heuss drew in a later speech, that it behooved the German Democratic party—indeed, any party—to view itself as "an instrument of the state."[124]

Quite early, prominent German Democrats displayed a tendency to view the German Democratic party as being a sort of mediator between left and right and also, in this capacity, an educative organization. In his "Easter Observations" (*Osterbetrachtungen*) of March 26, 1921, Meinecke had suggested that the German Democratic party need not be discouraged by its miserable performance at the polls. Rather, its real importance was derived from its very existence as a middle party, one whose ideas could perhaps influence the German People's party on the right, and the Social Democratic party on the left.[125] The old Naumann ideal of an enlightened bourgeoisie serving to construct "bridges" between right and left was coming through again and, considering the rather pathetic falling-off of the party since 1919, it was coming at a rather appropriate moment. Even Anton Erkelenz, who, as we shall see, would remain devoted to the democratic republic till the very end—in fact, deserting the party for the Social Democrats when he thought that it had abandoned the principles of parliamentary democracy by joining the *Jungdeutsche Orden* to form the *Staatspartei* in 1930—assigned a somewhat nonpolitical, or perhaps, super-political role to the Democrats. In an essay of December 21, 1921, Erkelenz pointed to what he called the great "community of need" (*Not*) of the German people. There were the needs:

to overthrow the class struggle
to reconstruct the German people inwardly and outwardly
to educate the subject to become a state citizen
to overthrow materialism through an Idealism which is practical and which rejoices in struggle
to preserve Reich and republic
for understanding between city and country
for self-responsibility in freedom
for true liberalism, i.e., the free, self-responsible man is the goal of society
for protection of man against the spirit-killing effects of the machine, the state, the bureaucracy[126]

Here, we can see those goals with which, Erkelenz supposed, the state ought to be concerned, or rather, goals with which the German Democratic party as it embodied the state ought to be concerned. We can observe that, for Erkelenz, the state or the party which represented it had the role of being both a mediator between classes and an educator. He had fused the national-socialist state of Naumann with the Fichtean state-as-educator. At the same time, one can discern a concern with overthrowing that depersonalization which Erkelenz, among others, associated with the industrial age. Erkelenz never turned consciously against parties and parliamentarianism. However, he also placed the party in the position of being a sort of didactic *Staatspartei*, which would educate the German people

---

[119] *Verhandlungen des Reichstages* (hereafter cited as VR) 1. *Wahlperiode 1920. Band 347. Stenographische Berichte* (Berlin, 1921), 3640C.

[120] *Ibid.*, 3641A-D.

[121] *Ibid.*, 3642A-D.

[122] On the self-sacrificing attitude of the party on the question of reparations see the June 16, 1921, issue of *Der Demokrat*. Also, the November 17, 1921, issue of *Der Demokrat*, which was concerned primarily with the Bremen *Parteitag* of 12-14, November, 1921. Rathenau's speech, in which he attacked the Silesian Seccession to Poland while defending the retention of *Erfüllungspolitik* ("policy of fulfillment") is of some interest.

[123] Preussisches Geheimes Staatsarchiv, *op. cit.*, Theodor Heuss, *Demokratie und Selbstverwaltung* (Berlin, 1921), p. 5.

[124] Institut für Zeitgeschichte, *Der Demokrat*, 2 Jahrg., Nr. 46, 17 November, 1921: p. 899.

[125] Meinecke, *Politische Schriften und Reden*, p. 316.

[126] *Op. cit.*, Anton Erkelenz, "Die Ewige Aufgabe der Demokrat," in: *Der Demokrat,* 2 Jahrg, No. 51, 22 Dezember, 1921: p. 1001.

toward political democracy. At the same time a strong state role in the economy was precluded. For virtually all prominent Democrats, however, the party had a certain pedagogical or didactic role, which was of particular importance in a nation with so weak a tradition of self-government.

The assassination of Walter Rathenau on June 24, 1922, and Chancellor Wirth's dramatic pronouncement that "The enemy lies on the right!" seemed to rouse many Democrats to undertake a dramatic defense of parliamentary democracy and the Weimar Constitution.

On June 25, 1922, Dr. Carl Petersen made an emotional speech before the Reichstag, declared that Rathenau's services to Germany had been continuous and invaluable. The republic that he had represented had saved the country from Bolshevism and, if Germany were to be able to rebuild itself completely, the republic had to remain.[127] Yet, even during this speech, Petersen fell back upon a common democratic position; viz., that national duty compelled all Germans to back the republican state form. In this context, he accused the German right of lacking that important "feeling for national duty."[128] However, Petersen did go on to say that it was the duty of all who supported the republic to "emphasize the republican constitution of our state form" and to stand four-square behind this constitution.[129] To this, the extreme left responded with the cry "Like Gessler!" apparently indicating that the anti-republican sentiments of the Democratic *Reichswehrminister* were fairly well known. This forced Petersen into stating a gentlemanly sort of falsehood.

Whoever knows our friend Gessler, knows that he has stood and will stand, without any reservation or half-heartedness, upon the ground of the republican constitution.[130]

If Petersen had survived to read "friend Gessler's" postwar memoirs, his faith in the latter's republicanism might well have suffered something of a shock. However, Petersen's defense of parliamentary government was about as strong a one as was made by a member of the Democratic party upon the floor of the Reichstag. In the June 30, 1922, issue of *Der Demokrat*, Erkelenz angrily declared that Rathenau had been murdered because enemies on the right feared that the republic was finally consolidating itself,[131] and, in a dramatic essay, "Am Grabe Rathenau," the journal declared:

Germany and the existence of the republic are today one and the same. It alone can safeguard and defend internal peace. Even the so-called 'peaceful and constitutional fight' against the republic leads us into civil war.[132]

The collective citizenry had to make the decision to strengthen the republic and parliament. All parties had to agree "to protect the constitution." There was no talk now of republican democracy being one of the "forms" of a transcendental state. The lines were drawn. Even Meinecke, who, on June 11, 1922, in an article, "Signs of Political Progress in Germany," rather grumpily emphasized that "we have arrived at democracy not out of enthusiasm, but out of necessity, out of reason of state,"[133] felt compelled to condemn strongly the youthful excesses of Germany's right, sickened by a surfeit of idealism. In an article, on August 6, 1922, "The Spirit of Academic Youth in Germany" ("Der Geist der akademischen Jugend in Deutschland") he attacked its lack of "psychic balance" and its obvious tendency towards reaction.[134] To be sure, he and others of his ilk found right-wing youth "easier to work with" than left-wing youth; however, the immediate danger to the state was definitely from the right.[135]

The Rathenau assassination, and the unity of left and center which it seemed to bring about aroused a determined pro-republic, pro-parliamentarianism feeling which was slow to die. In a speech on May 15, 1923, Erkelenz took a strong stand against any possible German Democratic party unification with the DVP, a possibility that had been considered by individuals of both parties since 1918. Now, Erkelenz stated without equivocation that such a unity could only be achieved if agreement were reached on the basic questions of constitution and state-form. A great coalition could be achieved only when both parties agreed on the essential issues, and Erkelenz gave the DVP little cause to think that the Democratic party would back away from its formal commitment to parliamentary democracy. Theodor Heuss who, as we have seen earlier, had exhibited a certain dualistic attitude towards the relationship between party life and the state, now came out more strongly than ever before for parliamentary democracy. In an article in the *Leipziger Tageblatt*, December 25, 1923, he deprecated the notion of a "best state" which is able to provide for human happiness. Such a state, he maintained, existed only in the realm of philosophers.[136] True democracy, he said, is no guarantee for happiness; indeed, there would always be an element of unrest in it because, in a pluralistic society, new elements were constantly being introduced and advanced.[137] This article was one of the most important defenses of pluralism that arose from Democratic ranks during the Weimar period, and it served to set Heuss apart from others in the

---

[127] VR, *op. cit.*, Band 356, 8062B.
[128] *Ibid.*, 8062C.
[129] *Ibid.*, 8063C.
[130] *Ibid.*
[131] Anton Erkelenz, "Walther Rathenau," in: *Der Demokrat*, 3 Jahrg., No. 25/26, 30 Juni, 1922: p. 393.
[132] *Ibid.*, p. 395.

[133] Meinecke, *op. cit.*, p. 336.
[134] *Ibid.*, p. 341.
[135] *Ibid.*, p. 342.
[136] Heussarchiv, *Politische Schriften*, 1924, Theodor Heuss "Entfaltung der Kräfte," in: *Leipziger Tageblatt*, 25 Dezember, 1923.
[137] *Ibid.*

party, who persisted in endowing the state with certain powers and functions beyond those melioristic ones assigned it by traditional Western liberalism.

There was, however, another reaction to the Rathenau assassination and the underlying spirit of murderous anarchy to which it testified, and this reaction can be seen in an article in *Der Demokrat,* August 9, 1922. In part, this bore a resemblance to some of the more common demands of the German Democratic party. The democratic state, it claimed, rose and fell with its citizenry. For the state to have any meaning, all must participate in it and the new state had to be "deeply anchored in the heart of its citizenry more than any earlier state form." [138] However, the reader could detect something of a shift in mood. Previously, many Democrats accepted parliamentary democracy as Germany's fate. Now, for the first time, the Democratic party exhorted the German people to be "stronger than our fate!" [139] An effort was being made to view the republic as something heroic accomplished in the face of a cruel fate; a fate that had externalized itself in the form of German political impotence abroad and anarchy at home. Yet, the obverse of such a belief was a sense of hopelessness and resignation as great as that which characterized those democrats who saw Germany's fate as republicanism.

Events between 1922 and 1924, years which saw the Rathenau murder, the invasion of the Ruhr by French and Belgian troops, the attempted Nazi coup in Bavaria, the forceful stamping out of Communism in Saxony, and also the rule of Germany by decree under Article 48 of the Weimar Constitution, seemed to bring out the full range of democratic attitudes towards the republic and towards pluralism.

The question of passive resistance in the Ruhr, inflation, and troubles in Bavaria were very much on Koch's mind when, on October 8, 1923, he spoke up in favor of that "rule by decree" (i.e., under Article 48) demanded by Chancellor Gustav Stresemann to facilitate his government's dealing with the problems of inflation and upheaval. "We are not of the opinion," Koch said, "that this crisis is so inextricably intertwined with the essence of parliamentarianism that one can make parliamentarianism itself responsible for it." [140] At the same time Koch took a position which demonstrated the impossibility of the DDP and the SPD ever really coming together. He questioned whether or not his party could support Socialist demands for an eight-hour day.[141] Government failure to support this measure, plus the lack of severity in dealing with the right in Bavaria were the reasons why the SPD bolted Stresemann's second cabinet on November 2, 1923. Koch also strongly condemned the Communists of Saxony and Thuringia for going against the Berlin government and the army. Turning to the left portion of the Reichstag, he declared, "For us, democracy is freedom bound to order, and a capable democracy will always defend itself against destroyers of order such as you." [142] Koch then made the rather curious statement that the radical left of Saxony and Thuringia was not very Marxist. It was, rather, one-sided, standing as it did only for the interests of the workers![143]

Koch was careful, it must be pointed out, not to condemn disorders in Bavaria too severely, at least not to the same degree that he did those Communist ones in northeastern Germany. He only made the somewhat ironical observation that the Bavarian government, which had not banned the Nazi *Völkischer Beobachter,* had banned the Democratic newspaper in Nürnberg as being leftist.[144] Of course in pursuing this course, Koch was trying to give support to Stresemann's own policies of the bourgeois center and slightly right of center. The former did acknowledge the fact that the old nineteenth-century liberal Eugen Richter had a point when he referred to the dangers inherent in an unlimited statism. Yet, Koch declared, an enabling act was necessary to allow the government to take meaningful action against the economic and political problems which plagued Germany.[145]

Koch's speech points to the impossible position of the German Democratic party. Declaring itself to be above class and interest group, it was nonetheless bourgeois in composition and mentality. Democracy was freedom bound to order, and it is obvious that most Democrats could have had little real empathy for the chauffeur who, in February, 1919, remarked to Troeltsch, "'The people don't want order; but socialization; they expect a bettering of their condition, and see only a worsening.'" [146] Just how representative the opinion of this chauffeur actually was is, of course, open to question. However, while Troeltsch had some sympathy for it, it is obvious that the bourgeois nature of the German Democratic party had to cause it to elevate order over change, to say nothing of socialization. Yet, as seen before, this same party was one of the three "constitutional" parties and, in the eyes of a bourgeoisie moving ever more to the right, this made the Democrats partners in the sorry tale of disaster and humiliation that had constituted German national life since 1918.

The withdrawal of the Social Democrats from Stresemann's cabinet and the refusal of the DNVP to

---

[138] Institut für Zeitgeschichte, *Der Demokrat,* 3 Jahrg., Nr. 29/30, 9 August, 1922: p. 449.
[139] *Ibid.,* p. 450.
[140] VR, *Band 361,* Berlin, 1924, 11990D.
[141] *Ibid.,* 11993D.
[142] *Ibid.,* 11992B.
[143] *Ibid.,* 11992C.
[144] *Ibid.*
[145] *Ibid.,* 11995D–11996A.
[146] Ernst Troeltsch, *Spektator Briefe: Aufsätze über die deutsche Revolution und die Weltpolitik 1918/1922* (reprint, Tübingen, 1924, Darmstadt, 1966), p. 38.

support it, led to Stresemann's downfall on November 22, 1923, when a coalition-sponsored, i.e., Center, DVP, and DDP, vote of confidence failed by a vote of 156 to 231. A new government was then formed under the chancellorship of the Centrist Wilhelm Marx, with the Democrats again participating in it. A new enabling act, this one with the support of the Social Democrats, was introduced and, during the debates over it, which took place between December 5 and December 8, 1923, Haas of the Democratic party defended parliamentary government as Koch had done so earlier. The Reichstag had not been responsible for the economic and political crises that had engulfed Germany, he declared. Rather, the government of Stresemann must be blamed. Parliamentary problems simply pointed to the confused state of mind of the German people.[147] At this time, the DNVP and its supporters were making noises to the effect that they too, opposed as they were to parliamentary government, nevertheless wanted to enter it. Haas attacked this notion. The DNVP had attacked the republic throughout Germany. It could only be disruptive. Also, Haas continued, DNVP participation in the government would only widen the gap between the bourgeoisie and the workers at a time in which reconciliation was the order of the day.[148] As the Social Democrats had done in August, 1914, all should support the Reich no matter what its particular form might be. This had to be done, not for superficial reasons, but for reason of state. Somewhat wistfully, Haas added that he wished that the government would emphasize the word "republic" when it spoke of itself and the German nation.[149]

Again, in Haas's defense of parliamentary government, order and reconciliation stand out as most prominent. Also prominent is a sense of desperation. The emphasis upon reason of state points to this as does the 313 to 18 vote in favor of the enabling act, which took place on December 8, 1923.

This same sense of desperation, tinged with a bit of fatalism was displayed by the then party head, Erich Koch (later, he would add the name of his constituency to get Koch-Weser) when, in a meeting of the party committee (*Parteiaussuss*) on January 27, 1924, he persuaded it to accept the temporary dictatorship that had been imposed under Article 48. Now, he said, Germany finally had that dictatorship for which so many had longed, which was necessary if Germany were to save herself from "the eternal crisis-foolishness" that had characterized the nation for so long.[150] The year 1923 had proven that the Democratic party could not count on the Social Democrats or the German National People's party to behave in a responsible manner (as we have seen, the Social Democrats had walked out of Stresemann's government because it considered it unfair in its treatment of Communists in Saxony and weak in dealing with the right in Bavaria, while the latter party opposed Stresemann's ending of passive resistance in the Ruhr). Stresemann himself had been forced to fall back upon the powerful right wing of his own party. The Democratic party, Koch maintained, was now on its own, having to content itself with opposing an "excess of power" from the right or from the left. The despair which would eventually drive Koch to seek an alliance with a collection of statist/romantic bundists was clearly evident.

In the March 15, 1924, issue of *Die Hilfe,* Erkelenz emphasized that any sort of anti-parliamentary agitation could eventually lead to a dictatorship.[151] He defended the foreign policy of the republic by pointing out that there were no foreign troops in Berlin despite the tensions of the Ruhr occupation and that there had occurred no Bolshevik revolution.[152] Democracy's development, Erkelenz maintained, was not something that would occur magically; it had to be created by all democratically minded men. Only then would Germany have that state which approximated the democratic ideal, viz., "strong, expert leaders, at the head of free, self-conscious people, joyful in responsibility.[153] Erkelenz's defense of parliamentary democracy was echoed by that of Heuss who, in an article appearing in *Der neue Albbote* on April 29, 1924, defended the role of political parties. It was certainly true, Heuss maintained, that the state could do with fewer parties and that parties often represented groups whose interests clashed with those of the state. However, the parties constituted "the steps which lead to the state."[154] Political life would be unthinkable without them.

Others within the Democratic ranks, though, displayed a somewhat more traditional view of the role of parties and party life. Here, Meinecke's article of April 20, 1924,[155] "Before the Reichstag elections" ("Vor den Reichstagwahlen"), can be cited. The parties of the middle of 1924, Meinecke claimed, were serving that same interest of *Volksgemeinschaft* that had surfaced so heroically in 1813. *Volksgemeinschaft* was their creed, one which they were using in combat against the "*Volk*-dividing radicalism of the right and the left." Again, Meinecke reiterated his thought that the German Democratic party's value subsisted not in its role as a party with special interests, but rather as a bridge between the two halves of the nation: the

---

[147] VR., *op. cit.,* 12308C-D.
[148] *Ibid.,* 12310B-12310D.
[149] *Ibid.,* 12312C-12313B.
[150] Bundesarchiv, Sitzungen des Parteisasschuss der. DDP, R45 111/12, 50.

[151] Anton Erkelenz, "Die Krisis den Demokratie in Deutschland," in: *Die Hilfe,* Nr. 6, 15 Marz, 1924: p. 91.
[152] *Ibid.*
[153] *Ibid.,* p. 92.
[154] Heussarchiv, *Politische Schriften,* 1922–1924, Theodor Heuss, "Sammlung oder Zersplitterung," in: *Der Neue Albotte,* 24 April, 1924.
[155] Meinecke, *op. cit.,* p. 365.

working class and the bourgeoisie.[156] In the May 4, 1924, elections, in which the DNVP, the Nazis, and the Communists registered strong gains at the expense of the Weimar coalition parties and the DVP, the Democratic party fared very badly, dropping to an, until then, all-time low of 1,655,100 votes (5.7 per cent of votes cast) and 28 delegates. The still-critical economic situation as well as some opposition against the Dawes Plan were responsible for the debacle. However, the DNVP failed to gain cabinet posts because of the opposition of the Centrists and the DDP, and thus the Centrist Marx held on to the chancellorship.

At an "extraordinary *Parteitag*," held on November 2, 1924, in Berlin, Koch vigorously defended the actions both of the DDP Reichstag fraction and of those DDP members of the government who had refused to work with the DNVP. Through its attempting to utilize the issue of the Dawes Plan as a means of gaining cabinet posts, the German Nationalists were a threat to the state, Koch declared.[157] There was a necessity for the German people to get accustomed to living under the "democratic-republican state form" and to recognize that Germany was better off now than she had been during the previous five years.[158] However, Koch went on, Stresemann's willingness to call in the DNVP to take part in the government went against virtually everything positive that had occurred in Germany and certainly was opposed to the former's own attempts to work for a responsible foreign policy. Koch then made the trenchant—although, from a purely parliamentary point of view, somewhat questionable—observation that so long as there existed a struggle between republican and monarchical principles, the DNVP simply could not be trusted in the government.[159] After emphasizing that the DDP was a true party of the middle, Koch went on to acknowledge that there were some Democrats, most prominent among them, Eugen Schiffer, who did not agree that the DNVP had to be excluded. After all, though, Koch remarked, the DDP was a "party of heads" in which each member was entitled to his own opinion. This rather comforting observation was an attempt to cover over two important facts. First of all, there had arisen that old clash between those in the party, like Koch, who continuously emphasized the necessity of the party's acting to unify the nation, to bring together proletarian and bourgeois, left and right, and those who were more willing to work with bourgeois circles, even those of the far right if necessary; people who, perhaps with some political realism, viewed the DDP's efforts to build bridges towards the proletariat as being rather futile anyway. Secondly, the issue over the DNVP's role in the government was causing some of the DDP's right wing to break away from the party. The most important of these people was, of course, Eugen Schiffer.

Bernstorff followed with a significant address in which he voiced an opinion shared by many Democrats, *viz.*, that only through a good foreign policy could the republican government be strengthened. Moreover, a democratic-republican government was absolutely necessary in that "World history is nothing else but a development of democracy."[160]

Reichminister for Economics Eduard Hamm als spoke against the admission of the DNVP to the government. He then made a remark which did arouse some protest (*Widerspruch*) among the assembled delegates. "Most of us became republican at first only through the pressure of events."[161] Any other stateform after the World War would have meant only further war and annihilation. Hamm's remarks, as controversial as they seemed to have been to some of his colleagues, pointed to that attitude of "fated republicanism" which, as we have seen, was extremely common in Democratic ranks. Parliamentary crises such as that of 1924, a crisis that had been in large measure due to the unwillingness of the DDP to accept DNVP participation in the government, made it far easier for many Democrats who had been suspicious of or hostile to parliamentary government from the beginning to feel themselves justified in these beliefs. At the same time, of course, they were responsible for a gradual disillusionment on the part of those Democrats who had had at least a guarded faith in the possibilities of parliamentary rule.

In view of the substantial opposition of the extreme right, meaningful government action was impossible, and new elections had been called for, these to take place on December 7, 1924. The DDP viewed these elections with some trepidation and this was revealed in the rather defensive attitude betrayed by Dr. Külz who in an article of December 4, 1924, bitterly attacked the parties for pressing "interest politics against state politics" and he called for a sense of political responsibility on the part of the voter.[162]

Külz's fears were not entirely realized. Because of the improving economic situation, the Weimar Coalition parties registered gains (so unfortunately had the DNVP). However, Marx was forced to resign in favor of Hans Luther.

In the parliamentary debates, as we have seen, the German Democratic party did attempt to defend parliamentary government while, at the same time,

---

[156] *Ibid.*, p. 367.
[157] Bundesarchiv, Koblenz, R 45III4, Deutsche Demokratische partei Parteitag. *Ausserordentlicher Parteitag der DDP an 2. Nov. 1924, Berlin*, p. 2.
[158] *Ibid.*, p. 4.
[159] *Ibid.*, p. 5.

[160] *Ibid.*, p. 14.
[161] *Ibid.*, p. 24.
[162] Bundesarchiv, Nachlass Külz, 1924/1925, 34, Wilhelm Külz, "Der Tag der Selbstbestimmung des Volkes," 4 Dezember, 1924 (no journal or newspaper entry given).

putting itself forward as a super-class party of order and conciliation. Yet, as seen particularly in Haas's speech of December 5, 1923, parliamentary government was defended more and more on the basis of reason of state. At the same time, the bourgeois DDP's attempt to present itself as a non-class, non-interest group party (really, a non-party, one would assume) was patently absurd. Almost nobody bought that particular argument. The constituents of the Social Democratic party could not vote for a group which, cries of class conciliation and national unity to the contrary, was obviously bourgeois. The bourgeoisie, suspicious, if not contemptuous of the DDP's participation in a governmental system which seemed not to be working (and, as we shall see later, of the participation of large numbers of Jews in the Democratic party), increasingly tended, as Bernhard Vogel and Rainer-Olaf Schultze have pointed out, to vote Nazi in times of crisis, and DNVP in times of calm.[163] Moreover, from late 1924 on, the rise of so-called "interest parties," e.g., the *Wirtschaftspartei*, which quite frankly came out in the defense of bourgeois class interests, posed an increasing threat to the German Democrats.[164]

Political clashing, electoral disappointments, and the growing strength of the DNVP, Nazis, and the "interest parties" caused some in the Democratic party to demand that it make up its mind what it was: whether it was a part of mass democracy or of a traditional, bourgeois liberalism. In other words, the differing brands of "liberalism" represented in the party clashed head on. Of interest here are two articles which appeared in *Die Hilfe* in 1924. The first article appeared in the April 1 issue of the journal, and was written by Kurt Wolf, an individual who was associated with the youth organizations connected with the party. Wolf claimed that the parliamentary turmoil and internal disorder that had characterized Germany up to that time was due to liberalism and not to democracy. Interest politics, Wolf suggested, was a phenomenon of traditional liberalism and the party would do well to work towards the creation of a true freedom, one which could arise only with democracy and not with liberalism.[165] On November 1, 1924, Robert Corwegh published an article entitled "Democratic Party at the Crossroads" ("Demokratische Partei am Scheideweg"). This article took precisely the opposite view from that of Wolf. The Democratic party, Corwegh maintained, had driven itself into a corner with the Social Democrats, and thus to defeat because of its overemphasis upon democratic ideas. A meaningful alliance with the Social Democrats was out of the question anyway, so the Democratic party would have to return to the old liberalism if it were to be able to hold onto its constituents.[166] The Germans, Corwegh said, lacked a true national consciousness anyway. Thanks to the Hegelian tradition, they tended to view the state as something far off and remote. Liberalism represented the way to bind state and *Volk* together inasmuch as it was in itself an attempt to mediate between the general, as embodied in the state, and the individual. Thus, Corwegh maintained, if the German people were to gain a true state-consciousness, liberalism was a necessity.[167] These essays were of immense significance for two reasons: (1) they pointed to that division within the party between left and right, i.e., between those who thought that the German bourgeoisie had to display more of an interest in and sympathy towards the great mass of the German people, and those who adhered to that point of view which saw the state as being in effect emboided within an enlightened stratum of the bourgeoisie; and (2) they underscored the existence of points of view opposed to the pluralistic society. First of all, Wolf's essay represented an attack on what he considered to be the clumsy impedimenta of liberal constitutionalism: parliaments, clashing of interest groups, etc. He was opting for a sort of "direct democracy." Corwegh was falling back upon a variety of statist thinking—interestingly enough, an anti-Hegelian variety—which had characterized Naumann, Weber and, in the 1920's, Meinecke. For Corwegh, the state found concrete embodiment in an enlightened bourgeoisie, steeped in the tradition of *Realpolitik*. Both points of view held but scant brief for parliamentary republicanism. Approaching the problem from two different angles both Wolf and Corwegh pointed out those anti-republican biases which had developed within German political speculation and which made it impossible for parliamentary democracy ever to have a certain hold even within the ranks of democrats.

In January of 1925, the newly appointed Luther government found itself in an extremely precarious position. On the urging of the DVP, Chancellor Hans Luther, an "independent" (i.e., in fact, a conservative), the reactionary German National People's party (DNVP) had been drawn into the government. The Democrats turned against this government, Gessler avoiding the moment of truth by declaring himself to be now "independent" from the party, although not formally resigning from it. However, the leader of the Democratic party, Koch, was quick to assure the German people that the party had no intention of urging a no-confidence vote against the government.[168] To

---

[163] *Die Wahl der Parlamente und anderer Staatsorgane: Ein Handbuch.* Herausgegeben von Dolf Sternberger und Bernhard Vogel (Redaktion von Dieter Nohlen. *Band I: Europa. Erster Halbband,* Berlin, 1969), p. 267.
[164] *Ibid.*, pp. 267–268.
[165] Kurt Wolf, "Krisis der Demokratie," in: *Die Hilfe,* Nr. 7, 1 April, 1924: p. 117.
[166] Robert Corwegh, "Demokratische Partei Am Scheideweg," in: *Die Hilfe,* Nr. 21, 1 November, 1924: p. 385.
[167] *Ibid.*
[168] Bundesarchiv, Nachlass Koch-Weser, Nr. 94, Das Inner politische Geschehen, 1925, 5, Erich Koch-Weser, "Die Opposition der Demokraten" (Reichstag address).

be sure, the party was disappointed that the Center had been unwilling to take a step to the left in repudiating Luther's policies and that the DVP had persisted in supporting Luther. The Democratic party would always have this problem, though, because, of the bourgeois parties, only it was really in favor of the parliamentary system.[169] Again, we can observe the curious role in which the German Democratic party found itself cast: only the Democrats were truly pluralistic in a situation in which pluralism was a necessity of state. As Dr. Ludwig Haas put it in a Reichstag speech on January 22, 1925: "There is no state authority without the republic, and whoever fights against the republic, deals a blow to the principle of state authority."[170]

On January 16, 1925, Meinecke made a most interesting and revealing speech before the *Demokratische Studentbund* in Berlin. In this address, he emphasized that the principle that allowed him to go over from a conservative position to the German Democratic party was his belief that the "state must be free and powerful and the nation must be unified and, within itself, brotherly minded."[171] Class interests had to be assiduously avoided and all interests had to be examined "not from the standpoint of class interest, but from the standpoint of central state interest."[172] Again, the role which many democrats assigned to the party was clear: the party represented interests of state. Seen from this angle, Meinecke was being perfectly consistent when he maintained that a government which extended from the Social Democrats to the anti-republican German National People's party was most desirable and that it was imperative that the republic not alienate the right, as the old monarchy had done with the left. "Enthusiasm for the republic should not be demanded as a prerequisite for governmental ability."[173] A new republican-conservative party would really be the best possible thing and, insofar as the constitution itself was concerned, the excess of parliamentarianism that Meinecke saw in it should be abolished. Here, Meinecke was adamant in stating: "I view the parliamentary system as an unavoilable transitional form."[174] There can be little doubt that Meinecke stood to the right of many of his party-comrades. However, as we have seen in the essays of such people as Wolf and Corwegh, Meinecke's position was not an isolated one, although he admittedly stated it with more eloquence. Within both right and left groups within the Democratic ranks there were many who tended to view parliamentary democracy either as an "unavoidable transitional form" or as a colossal bore.

The year 1925 was important in the history of the Weimar Republic. Friedrich Ebert, its first president had died and a new president was to be elected by popular vote. The Democratic party was quick to leap into the breach by offering the name of Otto Gessler as the candidate of the middle, because he stood above party interest.[175] Gessler's candidacy was torpedoed by Stresemann, ostensibly because the latter suspected that Gessler's role as *Reichswehrminister* might embarrass Germany abroad.[176] However, since Stresemann later voted for Hindenburg with little mental anguish, Koch was undoubtedly correct when he questioned Stresemann's motives in refusing to accept Gessler; in fact, Koch somewhat dramatically accused Stresemann of stabbing Gessler in the back, ostensibly for personal reasons.[177] There can be little doubt that Gessler was in fact betrayed by Stresemann. However, his own republican pedigree was a bit questionable, to say the least. As Heuss put it, "The simple truth is: Gessler was and remained, in his heart a monarchist. This had made . . . cooperation with the army officers easier."[178] Just how far Gessler was willing to go in cooperating with the officers of the *Reichswehr* would not become clear until a year or so later. However, even after World War II, Gessler made no secret of the fact that he was never enthusiastic about the republic and that he had made little effort to hide his lack of enthusiasm from others.

My political passion did not belong to the Weimar Republic. The past, the Bismarck-Reich possessed my heart. The democratic republic in its gray mantle, with its superpolitical pressures and . . . party fighting was, for me, only a . . . necessary, fated form.[179]

Of course, he served the republic. "But to serve it and to represent it are two different things."[180] In fact, throughout his memoirs, one can see that Gessler was apparently made far more uncomfortable by "doctrinaire" Democratic friends and colleagues, than by the forces of reaction which threatened the republic. A particularly irritating individual in Gessler's eyes was Anton Erkelenz, another one of those "doctrinaire" Democrats who believed that the army could be made democratic "through the simple command 'left face, march!'"[181] Fortunately, Gessler had been able to preserve the apolitical nature of the *Reichswehr* by recognizing, along with such stalwart constitutionalists as von Seeckt, *Chef des Truppenamtas Oberst* Hasse and von Schleicher, the fallacy of the position that "this

---

[169] *Ibid.*
[170] *Ibid.*, 43 Ludwig Haas, *Reichstag* Speech of 22 January, 1925, "Die deutsche Demokratie und des Kabinett Luther."
[171] Meinecke, *op. cit.*, p. 377.
[172] *Ibid.*, p. 369.
[173] *Ibid.*, p. 377.
[174] *Ibid.*, p. 378.
[175] Bundesarchiv, Sitzungen des Parteiausschuss der DDP. R45 111/12, *168* (1 May, 1925).
[176] Turner, *op. cit.*, pp. 194–195. Also see Gessler, *op. cit.*, pp. 334–335.
[177] *Op. cit.*, Nachlass Koch-Weser, Nr. 32, Tagebuchartige Vermerke von 3.1–18.12, 1925, 59, 13 Marz, 1925.
[178] Gessler, *op. cit.*, p. 70.
[179] *Ibid.*, p. 336.
[180] *Ibid.*
[181] *Ibid.*, p. 409.

republic, with its non-functioning democracy, was the eternal and last word in German state history; in the conviction that a change would and must take place sometime, I was at one with both chiefs, even if differences in degree certainly played a role."[182] Finally, Willy Hellpach, the president of Baden, was chosen as the standard-bearer of bourgeois German democracy. The Centrist Wilhelm Marx was eventually chosen as the candidate of his party, while the parties of the right chose Karl Jarres as theirs. The SPD put forth Otto Braun and the Communists, Ernst Thälmann, while Ludendorff ran in an "independent" slot, receiving the tacit support of the Nazis. In the first election on March 28, 1925, no one candidate received a majority, with Hellpach a poor fifth, behind Jarres, Braun, Marx, and Thälmann, in that order. For the second election, all republican parties, including the SPD, agreed to support Marx, while the anti-republicans hastened to exhume General Paul von Hindenburg and thrust him into the political ring as their own. The lines were drawn. On the one hand, the German electorate was confronted by Marx, a man "who seriously wants to uphold and advance the present state form and the Weimar Reich constitution."[183] On the other hand, one could see troglodyte-Hindenburg who, as the journal *Der Demokrat* pointed out in an article on April 23, 1925, would be a serious embarrassment in foreign affairs and besides, was a person who represented everything that despised democracy and the republic.[184]

Naturally, Hindenburg was elected. Immediate Democratic response to this was despair. This was reflected in a May 7, 1925, article in *Der Demokrat*. "We believed," the journal said, "that the German people, to an overwhelming extent, would let themselves be directed by thought and not by feeling; we are now confronted by the fact that this is not so."[185] The journal expressed dismay that the two things which seemed most to influence voters was the Hindenburg name and the fear of a Catholic president. The journal also expressed regret "that some of our own members voted for him."[186] Now, of course, all Germans had to rally behind Hindenburg. At any rate, when he took the oath to the republic, it would constitute a moral victory of sorts, inasmuch as he would no doubt feel bound by his oath. Indeed, some Democrats attempted to draw something positive out of the carnage. An example of this was an essay by Külz that appeared in the November 8, 1925, issue of the *Plauener Sonntags Anzeiger*. Here, in seeking support for his claim that the German democratic republic was "stronger today than ever!" Külz apotheosized Hindenburg's taking of the oath to the republic as constituting a triumphant moment in the history of parliamentary democracy.[187]

As far as Reichstag activity was concerned, the Democratic party distinguished itself in the debates over acceptance of the Treaty of Locarno and the League of Nations, which took place between November 24 and November 27, 1925. Koch, masterfully playing upon German feelings against Versailles, declared in his speech of November 24, that Locarno was a step on the way towards understanding and freedom for Germany. It was thus the first step in the overthrow of the Versailles Treaty.[188] Moreover, Germany had to enter the League because "the isolation in which she finds herself is, in the long run, unbearable."[189] Recognizing that German signing of the Locarno Treaty and her entry into the League of Nations implicitly would involve a renunciation of colonial ambitions, Koch went on to attack colonialism, declaring that the crushing of primitive peoples who simply did not have "quite as good weapons as the European peoples" was evil in itself.[190]

On November 26, the German Democrat Dernburg spoke on behalf of Locarno and entering the League of Nations. Among other things, he tried to link Locarno to the Bismarckian spirit of *Realpolitik*. He also suggested that America probably would not give money to Germany as long as the latter were not in the League.[191] The last, somewhat unwise, remark was quite logically answered from the right with the cry "America also is not in the League of Nations!"[192] Apparently not too embarrassed by this, Dernburg went on to declare that the will of the German people was for peace, and that, implicitly, Locarno and the League of Nations were steps in that direction. The German Democratic party joined the majorities which, on November 27, 1925, voted for German approval of the signing of the Locarno Treaty (299 to 173) and Germany's entrance into the League of Nations (279–183). The radical right, the *Wirtschaftspartei,* and the Communists joined in voting against both measures. Once more, the German Democratic party had been able to justify its stand for interests which were at least controversial, by cloaking itself in the mantle of national interest.

The duel between Corwegh and Wolf over what the course of the party ought to be continued into 1925. In the August 1, 1925, issue of *Die Hilfe,* Corwegh launched an attack on parliamentarianism, among other

---

[182] *Ibid.*, p. 292.
[183] Institut für Zeitgeschichte, *Der Demokrat* 6 Jahrg, Nr. 7, 9 April, 1925, p. 177.
[184] Institut für Zeitgeschichte, "Vor der Entscheidung," in: *Der Demokrat* 6 Jahrg., Nr. 8, 23 April, 1925: pp. 209–210.
[185] Institut für Zeitgeschichte, "Hindenburg Reichspräsident," in: *Der Demokrat*, 6 Jahrg, Nr. 9, 7 May, 1925: p. 225.
[186] *Ibid.*, pp. 225–226.

[187] Bundesarchiv, Nachlass Külz, Nr. 74 "Innere Politik," 88, Wilhelm Külz, "Wie stehts um uns" in: *Plauener Sonntags Anzeiger,* 8, November, 1925.
[188] *VR. op. cit., III. Wahlperiode 1924. Band 388. Stenographische Berichte* (Berlin, 1926), 4524B–4524C.
[189] *Ibid.*, 4526D.
[190] *Ibid.*, 4527B.
[191] *Ibid.*, 4591B–4592B.
[192] *Ibid.*, 4592B.

things, suggesting that parliamentarians ought not to be paid. "A professional parliamentarian is no longer in the position to represent the interests of his people," Corwegh remarked.[193] Such people were pretty much against parliamentarianism anyway, inasmuch as they were loyal only to their respective parties, upon which they depended for their daily bread. German youth was rapidly being alienated. Corwegh went on to attack all political parties, except the German Democratic party, for being interest parties. The German Democratic party, he reiterated, must become a true liberal party and independent. With complete lack of humor, he suggested that the party approach all political problems on the basis of the categorical imperative.[194] Corwegh also attacked the list-system of balloting and proposed instead that candidates be elected on the basis of powerful personalities. In the December 15, 1925, issue of *Die Hilfe*, Wolf, in an article entitled "Pure Democracy" ("Reine Demokratie") waxed mystical over German youth and its political role. German youth, Wolf suggested, wanted to elevate *Gemeinschaft* over "limitless individualism." German youth stood in hidden opposition to liberalism, and its opposition stemmed from youth's longing for a "super-individualistic (not contra-individualistic) *Gemeinschaft*."[195] Youth wanted a "spiritual streaming-together" which might—but must not—find its embodiment in Führer personalities, "political or unpolitical."[196] Wolf was well aware of the mileage that Germany's radical right was obtaining from its anti-political stance. He seemed to be saying that somehow, the healthy mysticism and ingenuous patriotism of youth ought to be captured by a truly democratic state which, if not anti-liberal, went beyond liberalism and all the mumdane impedimenta that characterized it. "We want democracy, not merely liberalism. We need to show a hard hand against the misuse of freedom. We need hard hands in order to create true freedom."[197] Again, Corwegh had demanded that the party move back to being a liberal party which, through application of the categorical imperative to the major problems of national life, would serve as a sort of national/state conscience. Wolf was opting for a wholesome, collective *Volk*-community. Both Corwegh and Wolf were, as ever, beyond the bounds of the parliamentary system.

The period 1919 to 1925 saw the German Democratic party playing an extraordinarily active role in the various Weimar governments of the time. However, such a role must have appeared to have been ever more anomalous as support of the party itself continued to fall off, the slight rise in voting totals in December, 1924, to the contrary. During this time, the German Democratic party, for reasons both ideological and agitational, was forced ever more into the position of claiming to represent everybody, of justifying its actions on the basis of a super-interest "national interest," even though some in the party had questioned this course of action. To be sure, particularly in the Reichstag debates, the German Democrats continued to defend republicanism and, implicitly, political pluralism. However, even in the debates, republicanism was defended on the basis of "necessity of state" and, in the essays and journal articles of many Democrats, parliamentarian republicanism was coming more and more into question. Again, it is well to underscore the irony of all of this. In the eyes of the Democrats, they were the state, moreover the state in its republican form. However, their claim to represent everybody, a natural legacy of left-wing bourgeois republican thought which had its roots in the pre-World War I period, was baldly anti-republican (or most certainly, anti-pluralistic). A tendency endemic to German political theory and political life understandably was reflected in the German Democratic party, *viz.*, the desire to avoid political clashing and disorder through sublimation in pursuit of the *Volksgemeinschaft*.

Yet, caught between the rising strength of so-called "interest parties," e.g., the *Wirtschaftspartei*, which frankly claimed to represent no one but those of a particular class or interest group, and the radical right, which also claimed to represent everybody but rejected republicanism in general and the Weimar Republic in particular, the Democrats had to, and did, look more and more pathetic. Bourgeois though they were, they were forced into the position of not officially representing bourgeois interests, although as we have seen, many in the party were opposed to this position. At the same time, their statism—itself a bourgeois political philosophy—was tied, by condition and circumstance, to a form of government increasingly despised by the class from whose ranks they had come. Increasingly isolated from the bourgeoisie, the Democrats could not claim to represent proletarian interests either, at least not with the time-honored consistency of the Social Democrats. As we have seen, particularly with Robert Corwegh, some Democrats were aware of this problem. In the period 1925–1930 the Democratic party was increasingly on the defensive and, eventually was forced to all but abandon republicanism. The next two chapters will be devoted to describing this process.

IV. STATE AND REPUBLIC, 1925 TO 1930: THE LAST ATTEMPTS TO DEFEND PARLIAMENTARY REPUBLICANISM

Between December 4 and December 6, 1925, the German Democratic party held a *Parteitag* in Breslau.

---

[193] Robert Corwegh "Kein Parlamentarismus?" in: *Die Hilfe*, Nr. 17, 1 August, 1925: p. 370.
[194] *Ibid.*
[195] Kurt Wolf, "Reine Demokratie," in: *Die Hilfe*, Nr. 24, 15 December, 1925: p. 493.
[196] *Ibid.*
[197] *Ibid.*

During this congress, the tensions that had been so evident within Democratic ranks previously came out into the open. Willy Hellpach, the unsuccessful Democratic candidate for president, made a vigorous defense of democracy. Implicitly criticizing some of his colleagues, Hellpach attacked those who would defend democracy purely on the basis of "usefulness." Such defenses were weak, Hellpach suggested. Rather, what was needed was a defense on the basis of democracy's ethical worth.[1] Then, Hellpach went on to make one of those blunt remarks that, so often, have led people to conclude that Germans seem to lack any sensitivity towards sectarian differences. Christianity and democracy went together, Hellpach remarked; rather, Protestantism and democracy went together. About Catholicism, he was not so certain. Judaism was unmentioned. This theme, which Hellpach would pick up later in several published works, aroused the anger of Theodor Heuss who, as a Protestant, took issue with Hellpach's somewhat sweeping remarks.[2]

Despite Hellpach's ingenuously packaged bombshell, the most significant speech at the 1925 party congress was undoubtedly that of Koch. After making general remarks about the current political situation, the necessity of stronger policies against economic cartels, the question of European unity and so on, he went on to admit that the parliament was certainly not the only form of expression for democracy. Yet, the balance between a strong executive and a responsible legislature achieved in the United States was not really possible in Germany. Moreover, what problems there were with the functioning of Germany's parliament were due not to the constitution nor to the institution of parliamentary government itself; but, rather, to the suddenness of the transition between monarchical and parliamentary government forms.[3] The political parties, particularly, had to become aware of their responsibilities and take their actions seriously. As for the DDP, it had to continue its policy of attempting to build bridges between the working class and the bourgeoisie. It had to continue to guard against the dangers of socialization on the one hand and large-scale capitalism on the other.[4] The greatest threat to democracy, Koch concluded, was "interest politics" of the sort that Germany had seen since the establishment of the republic. The important questions of the day were not those of political parties, but those which concerned the state.[5]

In this address, we can see Koch very much on the defensive, as much against his own growing doubts as to the efficacy of parliamentary government in Germany as against those inside his party and out who were opposed to parliamentary government. On the one hand, he declared that parliamentary government had to be given the opportunity to work. On the other, his attacks upon interest politics and his call for an increasing emphasis on matters of state were really hardly consistent with an adherence to republican pluralism. Yet, the unhappy political realities of 1925 Germany seemed to have forced him into this sort of position, while his continued emphasis upon the "bridge-building" role of the DDP was beginning to sound more and more absurd. Moreover, Koch's "statism" ran counter to the views of some in his party, most prominently (at least at this party congress) that of Anton Erkelenz who, in an address of his own, declared that state intervention in the economy could not take the place of true economic democracy.[6] By the end of 1925, the DDP leadership was more than ever on the defensive, particularly regarding the role of parliamentary government. It was a defensiveness which, in the end, would turn upon itself as the attitude of this leadership became indifferent, if not hostile, to parliamentary republicanism. At the same time, differences within party ranks, e.g., between Koch's non-socialistic statism and Erkelenz's non-statist economic democracy (the didactic role of the state remained unquestioned) would continue to grow apace.

On December 5, 1925, Chancellor Hans Luther handed in his and his cabinet's resignation. The Social Democrats, although they might well support him in questions of foreign policy, would not participate in a government headed by him, and the DNVP, which had been invited to participate in the government on the assumption that they would cooperate in crucial issues of state, had voted against the government's foreign policy. The only way out now was to form a new coalition government, one which would exclude the DNVP and, in some way, include the Social Democrats. At first, President Hindenburg approached the Centrist Fehrenbach and then, after he declined the offer, the Democrat Koch-Weser (he had added the constituency name). The DVP announced that it was willing to participate in a cabinet headed by a Democratic chancellor and consisting in part of Social Democrats. However, the latter party refused to go along. They were bitterly opposed to the DVP over the issue of the eight-hour day and, as we have seen, the Democrats themselves had offered small comfort in this regard.[7] After further fruitless negotiations, Luther was again *Reichskanzler*, heading a bourgeois cabinet, *viz.*, Centre, German People's party, German Democratic party, and Bavarian People's party. This cabinet was formed by January 19, 1926, and, on January 27, 1926,

---

[1] Bundesarchiv, Koblenz, R 45III/5. Sechster ordentlicher Parteitag der DDP am 4/6 Dezember, 1925 in Breslau, pp. 11–12.

[2] *Ibid.*, pp. 14, 39.

[3] *Ibid.*, pp. 65–66.

[4] *Ibid.*, pp. 70–72.

[5] *Ibid.*, p. 76.

[6] *Ibid.*, p. 150.

[7] Erich Eyck, *A History of the Weimar Republic*, translated by Harlan P. Hanson and Robert G. L. Waite (2 v., New York, 1970), pp. 49–50.

the new government appeared before the Reichstag to receive a vote of confidence. Dr. Theodor Heuss arose to make his maiden Reichstag speech. First of all, he defended the foreign policy of Luther and Stresemann, especially the entrance of Germany into the League of Nations. He also made a strong defense of parliamentary government. Governmental crises, he declared, contributed to a better, stronger government. To say that parliamentary democracy was incapable of rule was absurd. English parliamentary democracy had faced many crises as well. Talk of a dictatorship as a solution to Germany's woes was nonsense.[8] In spite of everything Heuss declared, "the republican state stands." [9]

With the obviously somewhat less than enthusiastic support of the Democratic party, Luther got his vote of confidence, 160 to 150, with all 130 Social Democrats abstaining. Again, the logic of Weimar Republican politics had placed the Democrats in the position of participating in a bourgeois coalition, divorced from the strongest single source of support for the republic, the Social Democrats. The embarrassment of having to work with the DNVP was gone; but still, of their three coalition partners, only one party was formally committed to parliamentary republicanism. The isolated position of the German Democratic party brought out the demand that it become the cornerstone (or at least a cornerstone) of a new, bourgeois liberal party. In a February 15, 1926, essay in *Die Hilfe*, Anton Erkelenz remarked that one great party of the center would represent the proper solution to parliamentary confusion.[10] However, in the same breath he scotched this notion by pointing out that the DVP and the Democratic party could not unify immediately, because of the former's adherence to monarchical principles. Unlike such individuals as Meinecke, Erkelenz never saw the possibility of creating a greater *Staatspartei* stretching from the Social Democrats all the way over to the left wing of the DNVP. In an April 15, 1926, essay in *Die Hilfe*, he suggested that there was not enough real contact between the Reichstag and the government. To allow for this, Erkelenz suggested that attention be focused on the English system, with its parliamentary state secretary and its speaker of the house.[11] If the government and the Reichstag could somehow be brought closer together, the former might be more sensitive to public needs and anxieties while the Reichstag would gain a sense of responsibility that it hitherto lacked.

In the spring of 1926, the Democrats (and probably, most prominent among them, Koch-Weser) received a most instructive lesson as to how the phenomena of initiative and referendum, devices which, as we recall, Koch-Weser had been most eager to sew into the constitution as a counter-balance to parliamentarianization, could be used in an embarrassing way. The Communists, soon joined by the Social Democrats, circulated a petition calling for the expropriation, without compensation, of the wealth of Germany's departed princes. Having obtained far more than the signatures of one-tenth of the electorate (as required by the Weimar Constitution), they were able to place the proposed confiscation measure before the Reichstag. The radical right, i.e., the National Socialists and some members of the DNVP, were overjoyed, because this allowed them to offer up a delightful measure of their own calling for the "expropriation of bankers, princes of speculation and other national parasites," one obviously designed both to embarrass the left and to voice the anti-Semitic feelings of the right.[12] This "supplementary measure" was not accepted, and the Reichstag then voted 236 to 141 against the original petition-grounded motion of the Communists and Social Democrats, the German Democratic fraction voting with the majority. According to the constitution, the measure now had to go before the public in the form of a referendum. On June 20, 1926, it did, and the referendum was defeated, obtaining only 15,500,000 out of an eligible electorate of forty million. As we shall see, however, this referendum issue produced one rather serious side issue. Before looking at this, though, there is yet another issue to be considered.

As we will recall, the Weimar Constitution had provided that the colors of the new German flag be black, red, and gold, while those of the merchant flag were to be black, white, and red (i.e., the old imperial colors) with a black, red, and gold jack in the corner. In May, 1926, President Hindenburg issued an order, dutifully countersigned by Chancellor Luther, declaring that both flags were to be flown outside of German legations and consulates outside of Europe, and outside of legations and consulates located in European seaports. Hindenburg was delighted with Chancellor Luther's willing cooperation, but, while visions of Tannenberg danced in his head, a parliamentary explosion erupted. The matter was not at all ameliorated by a letter sent by Hindenburg to Luther declaring that the former had had no intention of tampering with the national colors. However, Hindenburg added ominously, the furor over his decree showed "'how threatening and dangerous to our people the unresolved question of the colors has become.'"[13] All that this indicated was that Hindenburg seemed to be still un-

---

[8] *Verhandlungen des Reichtages III. Wahlperiode 1924. Band 388. Stenographische Berichte* (Berlin, 1926) (hereafter cited as VR).
[9] *Ibid.*, 5185A.
[10] Anton Erkelenz, "Parlamentarismus und Parteiwesen," in: *Die Hilfe* Nr. 4, 15 February, 1926: pp. 60–61.
[11] Anton Erkelenz, "Kritik an Regierung und Parlament," in: *Die Hilfe*, Nr. 8, 15 April, 1926: pp. 135–136.

[12] *VR III. Wahlperiode 1924 Band 389. Stenographische Berichte* (Berlin, 1926), 7190.
[13] Quoted in Eyck, *op. cit.*, p. 67.

certain as to what the colors, constitution or no consitution, ought to be, and that Luther shared this uncertainty.

Luther appeared before the Reichstag on May 11, 1926, and he was violently attacked by the Social Democrats. On May 12, 1926, Koch-Weser who, as we recall, had been in favor of retaining the old colors in 1919, made a bitter speech in which he attacked the Social Democrats for refusing to participate in the government in the first place and Chancellor Luther. The chancellor himself, Koch-Weser declared, was responsible for the crisis that had broken over Germany resulting from the flag issue. His lack of judgment and responsibility had convinced the Democratic fraction that "cooperation with the chancellor is not possible any more, and that we would remain in the cabinet only to assume the responsibility for a policy dependent upon the DNVP and overwhelmingly influenced by them."[14] The Democrats were leaving the government not because they were unwilling to work on the flag issue. However, there had to be a positive solution to the problem, one which "concurs completely with the new Reich and with republican Germany, and acknowledges the deep and abiding significance of the colors of the republic."[15] Walther Rathenau had fallen "for and under the flag," he continued and, for the first time, millions of Germans had gained a sense of "state conviction" (*Staatsgesinnung*) under it. Efforts had to be undertaken to "keep these millions" bound to the state, and further crises of this nature had to be avoided.[16] Declaring his complete recognition of everything that Luther had accomplished, particularly in the realm of foreign policy, Koch-Weser declared that he could no longer go along with him now. A German Democratic motion of "disapproval" (a degree above "no confidence") was passed 177 to 146, with the DNVP abstaining and the DVP voting against it.

Koch-Weser's speech was a powerful one. To be sure, the theme of the *Einheitstaat* could be discerned—the millions of Germans who had gained a sense of "state conviction" under the republican colors. However, it took a great deal of moral courage for Koch-Weser to speak out against a man in whose cabinet he had served, if not with enthusiasm, then at least faithfully. There can be little doubt that, as Eyck put it, Koch-Weser's eloquent speech and the disapproval motion that came out of it, "finished Luther off" in a rather decisive manner.[17] Nevertheless, Koch-Weser's stand reveals all the more the incredibly awkward position of a bourgeois republican party during the Weimar period. First of all, the speech ended a period in which the Democratic party had participated in a bourgeois coalition, one in which the Social Democrats had refused to participate. Only six days earlier, Koch-Weser and the German Democrats had joined in defeating a Communist and Social Democratic-sponsored motion calling for the confiscation of royal wealth. Now, the Democrats were voting with the Socialists, while the DVP, the bourgeois party with which coalition had been, in the eyes of some Democrats, possible, was on the opposite side of the fence and the DNVP, in its abstention, stood in opposition to both the Democrats and the DVP. Voting for the national interest, especially if one belonged to a bourgeois, republican party, was a thankless task in Weimar Germany.

Less than a month after his denunciation of the Luther government, Koch-Weser was again speaking out on a prominent and divisive issue of the day. We must recall the referendum on confiscation of royal wealth, which was made necessary by the defeat of the Socialist and Communist-sponsored measure of May 6, 1926, on the floor of the Reichstag. Between May 6 and June 20, 1926, there was initiated a bitter campaign against the confiscation proposal. The campaign was directed by Friedrich von Loebell, who had served in the government of Wilhelm II. In this capacity, he had been able to persuade President Hindenburg to write a letter—for national publication—in which the aging patriarch denounced the proposal of the left as being illegal and immoral. This obviously ran afoul of the Weimar Constitution, Article 50 of which stated that the chancellor had to countersign all presidential orders and decrees. It was obviously against the spirit of the constitution, which had intended that the president be above politics and partisan issues (as usual, of course, siding with the right, as opposed to the left, was, by definition, above politics). On June 10, 1926, Koch-Weser, decrying the fact that some people had not desisted from dragging the president "into the forefront of the political struggle," made the further point that Bismarck himself had declared that representatives of the government ought to appear before the public only in "ministerial dress" and that failure to do so raised serious constitutional issues.[18] Koch-Weser insisted that democratic, parliamentary, or liberal considerations were beside the point here. The issue was a "constitutional" one, and had been even during Bismarck's time. Again, Koch-Weser was doing his bit in defense of the Weimar Constitution. However, he felt constrained to obviate the possibility of attack from the right, by somehow tying his criticism of von Loebell and, implicitly of Hindenburg, to the imperial, Bismarckian past. Moreover, as we shall see later on, in intra-party circles and meetings, Koch-Weser's frustration at the events of spring, 1926, will be reflected in an increasing skepticism as to the efficacy, at least in Germany, of parliamentary government.

---

[14] VR, *op. cit.*, 7192.
[15] *Ibid.*
[16] *Ibid.*, 7196B–C.
[17] Eyck, *op. cit.*, p. 68.
[18] VR, *op. cit.*, 7433C.

Wilhelm Mommsen, in an article of August 1, 1926, attempted to construct a more positive defense of the Weimar Constitution. It, he claimed, had not created chaos, but, rather, had overthrown a previous chaotic condition.[19] The real danger, Mommsen suggested, was not that the democratic form itself could be overthrown, "but that basic political, ethical, and national thoughts, which are supposed to find expression in this form appear to be heavily endangered."[20] The most formidable threat to the Weimar government and the constitution for which it stood did not come from anti-republican or anti-democratic elements, but rather from the avowed supporters of parliamentary democracy. It was up to them to give "contents" to the new state form and to demonstrate a sense of responsibility for the whole.[21] The German people had to be educated to be political and to realize that "Democracy and republic rest not upon rights but upon duties of each member towards the state."[22] In Mommsen, we can still observe a basic dualistic attitude towards the state and political life. However, unlike such commentators as Gessler and Meinecke, he did not seem to view parliamentary life as transient nor political parties as being inimical to the state interest. He avoided, at least for the moment, falling into the trap of seeking to defend the pluralistic society by demanding that everyone vote for the only party which represented fate-dictated pluralism, the German Democratic party. Indeed, Mommsen made the interesting and somewhat perceptive observation that the greatest danger to the republic would come when opponents of democracy learned to use and to act through democratic forms.[23]

The greatest single effort on behalf of the republic also appeared in 1926. This was Heuss's thoughtful work, *Staat und Volk*. In this book, Heuss did not suggest that Germany ape any other nation in establishing a parliamentary government, particularly that of England. However, he did point out that, at least in practice, "parliamentarianism" really antedated democracy and thus had a fairly well-established historical pedigree of its own.[24] At any rate, he suggested, one could hardly blame parliamentarianism for Germany's woes inasmuch as parliamentary government had had virtually no power to speak of.[25] Heuss supported a basic precept of the German Democratic party in claiming that centralization of the state was hardly "un-German" inasmuch as the princes themselves had pursued such a policy during the eighteenth and nineteenth centuries.[26] In this context, Heuss broke with many democratic adherents to organic state concepts by questioning whether any state could be thought of as being organic.[27] Heuss could not dispose of the notion that the state needed some kind of "aristocratic element" which, being above demagoguery or party-conflict, could provide for those things useful to the state. However, Heuss, as earlier, refused to condemn political parties. "Parties are the companions of democracy, even those parties which combat and reject democracy."[28] Parties were natural functions of "social currents and structures, at the same time, however, also of state life elements, in the narrow sense."[29] By qualifying his recognition of the role of parties in state life with the phrase, "in the narrow sense," Heuss did indicate that he felt that there were elements of state life which were beyond politics. However, such a point of view did represent a modification of the old dualist position to which many in the DDP clung with great assiduousness. Furthermore, Heuss echoed earlier statements by pointing out that the parties were concerned with fighting for power and position within the state; indeed, the ultimate goal of all parties was state life.[30] Such a statement was indicative of the fact that Heuss, while still assuming that a certain gap existed between state and mundane politics, did not assume that there existed a qualitative difference between the two realms; one was in fact the object of the other. Heuss went on to attack the German political parties, particularly to the extent that all of them—significantly, Heuss did not exempt the Democratic party from this—were ideological parties and that each of them claimed to represent the "interests of the whole."[31] With extreme perceptivity, Heuss attacked the German approach to constitutionalism and democracy; this approach was childish and it was embodied in both the parties themselves and in the system of proportional representation, both of which were designed to capture the entire "will of the *Volk*," an absurd impossibility according to Heuss.[32] Those people who criticized dirty politics and "party intrigues" did so from the point of view of "*literati*-vanity."[33] Parties and interest groups were the lifeblood of political life.

Heuss's work was hardly a blanket endorsement of every aspect of Weimar-period politics. However, unlike other writers that we have considered, Heuss did not attack parliamentarianism as such, and he evidenced a genuinely positive attitude towards parties, while concurrently deprecating the notion that a party

---

[19] Wilhelm Mommsen, "Zum Verfassungstag: Sicherung der Demokratie," in: *Die Hilfe*, Nr. 15, 1 August, 1926: p. 301.
[20] *Ibid.*
[21] *Ibid.*, p. 302.
[22] *Ibid.*, pp. 302–303.
[23] *Ibid.*, pp. 301–302.
[24] Theodor Heuss, *Staat und Volk: Betrachtungen über Wirtschaft, Politik und Kultur* (Berlin, 1926), p. 62.
[25] *Ibid.*, p. 63.
[26] *Ibid.*, pp. 53–54.
[27] *Ibid.*
[28] *Ibid.*, p. 147.
[29] *Ibid.*
[30] *Ibid.*, pp. 147–158.
[31] *Ibid.*, p. 152.
[32] *Ibid.*, p. 156.
[33] *Ibid.*, p. 167.

could claim, with any validity, to represent the interests of the whole. In a word Heuss, while maintaining a somewhat guarded attitude towards much of Weimar-period political life, did not seek out anti-parliamentarian or anti-party solutions. As we have seen, Heuss himself was not entirely free from certain attitudes that were inimical to the pluralistic society. However, insofar as constitutional speculation was concerned, he, more than any other Democrat excepting Erkelenz, generally remained within the matrix of parliamentary democracy.

Thus, we can see that by the mid-1920's the German Democratic camp, as well as the party which supposedly embodied it, contained several prominent strands of opinion in regard to pluralism, parliamentary democracy, and interest politics. The basic attitude, though, one which influenced most Democrats to one degree or another, was a very obvious statism, a view which quite consciously refrained from identifying the German state (Reich) with any of those forms dictated by historical necessity, and which was also responsible for the superclass, "above interest" position of many in Democratic circles. German democrats, even, at times, those sharing the position of a Heuss, seemed to see themselves in the role of adjusting to a new series of circumstances. The republican form might indeed be valid, but in no case could the German state be viewed as being coextensive with a particular, time-conditioned form. The citizen was seen, more often than not, as having a duty towards the state itself, rather than the republican form.

This attitude carried over into campaign literature itself. As an example of this, we can study a 1928 fly-leaf addressed to "Democratic Workers and Employees" ("Demokratische Arbeiter and Angestellte"). The victory of social democracy would take place during the May 20 elections, the fly-leaf proclaimed. This would be the social democracy of the German Democratic party if, "on election day, all democratic workers and employees fulfill their duties as state citizens." [34] The German Democratic party came out in favor of lower taxes and reduced tariffs. However, what is important for our purposes was the party's attempt to utilize the traditional "national idea" of Naumann's day, to rally proletarian support. "The national idea attains its highest fulfillment in social thought," the party proclaimed, while it declared that proletarians ought to be "not labor-slaves, but colleagues and economic citizens." [35] Again, most prominent here, were two Naumann-like principles: (1) that duty to the state transcended class, and (2) that class-reconciliation was the highest order of the day.

The attitude of much of the party to the state was also revealed in its attitude towards the army. On December 3, 1926, the *Manchester Guardian* published an article in which it was revealed that the *Reichswehr* and the Soviet army had had a working relationship for some time and that Russian and German war industries had been exchanging advice and materials. The German Social Democratic newspaper, *Vorwärts!* broke the news in Germany on December 9. These revelations embarrassed just about everybody except the Social Democrats. On December 6, 1926, Philip Scheidemann of the Social Democratic party made a Reichstag speech deploring the fact that the German *Reichswehr* had a working arrangement with the Red army and that German industry had exchanged materials with its Russian counterparts. Gessler's attitude (as expressed in his autobiography and, it would seem, before the *Reichswehr* committee of the Reichstag) while, in view of his position as defense minister, in part understandable, was nevertheless threaded through with casuistry; the 300,000 Russian mortar shells mentioned by Scheidemann—shells which were of "excellent quality" (Gessler quoted a critic with just a hint of professional pride)—were to be used only in the case of a Polish attack.[36] Supposedly this was understood both by the Russians who provided the *Reichswehr* with factories in which to manufacture them, and by the *Reichswehr* itself. As for mutual experiments with poison gas—well, as pointed out in an article in the *New York Commercial,* poison gas was "the most humane of all death devices," and besides, little if anything came of them.[37] With this apparent effort to convince posterity of the ultimate humanitarianism of the *Reichswehr,* Gessler indignantly rejected Scheidemann's revelations as hysterical and insignificant, except, of course, to the degree that they were treasonous and contrary to the national interest.

In an SPD-sponsored no-confidence vote on December 19, 1926, the Democratic party joined the minority in defending the government, which fell due to SPD fury at the rearmament revelations and DNVP hostility to a government that had excluded them. In attacking the *Reichswehr,* Scheidemann seemed to have trodden upon a raw nerve. Theodor Heuss, who had always held that state life was the legitimate object of the parties had declared, in an article of August 16, 1926, that because this was so it was "no wonder that the parties often mix in where they don't belong, i.e., in the army." [38] This seemed to represent the attitude of most Democrats, for, outside of Ludwig Quidde, the rather isolated Bavarian pacifist, only Erkelenz seems to have been seriously exercised by the thought that the *Reichswehr* was engaged in some sort of expansion policies. In 1927 he published an article in *Die Hilfe*

---

[34] Preussisches Geheimes Staatsarchiv, Hauptabteilung, XII, IV, Nr. 142.
[35] *Ibid.*
[36] Gessler, *op. cit.,* p. 199.
[37] *Ibid.*
[38] Heussarchiv, *Politische Schriften,* 1926, Theodor Heuss, "Zur Stellung der Reichswehr," in: *Wille und Weg,* Nr. 16, 16 August, 1962: pp. 233–234.

accusing the *Reichswehr* of working hand-in-glove with the right-wing veterans organization *Stahlhelm* in order to provide for a large trained reserve and for greater political influence. Koch-Weser received an angry letter from Gessler accusing Erkelenz of utilizing falsified documents in his attack on the *Reichswehr* and demanding that he be disciplined in one manner or the other.[39] The upshot of it all was a somewhat cool letter exchange between Koch-Weser and Erkelenz, the former demanding that Erkelenz investigate his sources and use greater discretion in the future, the latter maintaining that the documents used were not falsified and questioning Gessler's reliability. Perhaps Erkelenz felt freer to do this, inasmuch as Gessler had resigned from the party on January 28, 1927, because of possible clashes of interests and also because the new Marx government of January 29, 1927, contained four members of the DNVP and was, for this reason, unacceptable to the DDP who took no part in it. As a matter of fact, the DDP joined the SPD in voting "no confidence." The measure lost 235–174. At any rate, the view that the army was above politics had its supporters within the Democratic ranks, even while the DDP, for political reasons, was unable to participate in a government dominated by people who had approximately the same attitude.

To be sure, the Democrats were not alone in attacking those who would infringe upon the alleged super-political character of the army. As Eyck points out, both the Centrists and the DVP were upset at Scheideman for "interfering" in an area which concerned the national interest and national security and hence was "above politics."[40] However, considering the impressive intellectual pedigrees of so many of the leaders and spokesmen of the German Democratic party, it is surprising that so few of them seemed to recognize the fact that, at least in Germany, and probably elsewhere as well, an army "above politics" had been and was an impossibility, and at least the recent history of Weimar Germany should have told them that a "non-political" army was *ipso facto* a right-wing army. Koch-Weser seemed, at least in part, to recognize this. In a speech of February 4, 1927, one in which DDP lack of confidence in the new Marx government was expressed, he remarked that, for the far right, the army was depoliticized, of course, when the far right was in charge.[41] However, he failed to develop this theme any further and, as we shall see, Koch-Weser would adhere with almost painful assiduousness to the notion of a "depoliticized" army until his enforced exile.

As we have seen above, many Democrats and the German Democratic party in particular assigned a moralizing role to the state. Just how far some of them were willing to go in support of this definition was evidenced in another great controversy of 1926, that surrounding a clerical-supported law, proposed by the Democratic minister of interior, Wilhelm Külz, to protect youth from "trashy and dirty literature" (*Schund und Schmutzgesetz*). This proposed law, which derived constitutional support from Article 118, split the Democratic party. Koch-Weser himself was opposed to the law, seeing in it a threat to freedom of expression.[42] Theodor Wolff, Ernst Lemmer, Anton Erkelenz, and Ludwig Haas, among others, also opposed it. However, strong support for the measure came from, among others, Theodor Heuss, who declared, in an article of June 16, 1926, that dirt had little to do with art anyway. Moreover, trashy and dirty literature was produced on a "wage-contract basis" the result being, "capitalistic, mass wares."[43] In an article of one week later, Heuss candidly stated that the "democratic and social state, in keeping with its own essence, has the right, perhaps the duty, to act in an educational manner."[44] Whether or not such a point of view stemmed from a neo-Fichtean idea of the state as educator or from the Biedermeier side of Heuss is difficult to say. He was, of course, joined in his support of the law by such friends of youth as Bäumer who, as we shall see, saw democratic opposition to it as in large measure stemming from a Jewish plot.

During the actual debates over the law, which took place between November 27 and December 3, 1926, both Heuss and Bäumer spoke vociferously in its defense. Heuss declared that he agreed that "freedom of art" creativity had nothing whatsoever to do with the state. However, the type of literary trash affected by the law was a sort of "wage-contract" art which had little to do with creativity (this portion of Heuss's speech was really a repetition of his article of June 16, 1926).[45] Furthermore, the law was concerned with a sort of "underworld" type of literature, one which propounded a "false heroism" and was responsible for "a confusion of ethical values, as well as those of taste."[46] Heuss went on to say that the establishment of "examining offices" (*Prüfstellen*) would assure that the government would not be able to impose an exces-

---

[39] *Op. cit.*, Nachlass Koch-Weser. Nr. 96, Erkelenz' Artikel gegen die Reichewehr in Die Hilfe, 1927, 1.

[40] Eyck, *op. cit.*, pp. 98–100.

[41] *VR III Wahlperiode. 1924. Band 391* (Berlin 1927), 8836B–C.

[42] Nachlass Koch-Weser, *op. cit.*, Nr. 36, Tagebuchartige Vermerke 11.1–21.9. 1927, 58, 17 February, 1927.

[43] Heussarchiv, *Politische Schriften*, 1926, Theodor Heuss, "Von 'Schund und Schmutz,'" in: *Weser Zeitung*, 16 Juni, 1926.

[44] Heussarchiv, Theodor Heuss, "Für und wieder das Schundgesetz," in: *Stuttgarter neues Tageblatt*, 23 Juni, 1926. Such a position would seem to contradict that taken by Heuss in *Staat und Volk*, where he declared that state interference in art could lead only to mediocrity. See *Staat und Volk*, pp. 255–259.

[45] *VR, op. cit.*, 8233D–8234A.

[46] *Ibid.*, 8234D.

sively one-sided or unfair form of censorship.[47] In a speech of December 3, 1926, Gertrud Bäumer made a passionate address on behalf of the law. This law, she said, was concerned with the conditions under which youth must live. The literature with which it was concerned served to ruin youth's world outlook, to reduce its senses to a state of "imbecility" and further, to "weaken its capabilities of resistance."[48] Youth had to be protected against cheapness and trash, against the "fateful consequences of capitalism."[49] Spiritual freedom was a good concept, Bäumer said, but it applied only to those worthy of it.[50] With a final, shrill blast against the Social Democrats for not cooperating with the Democrats in working on the law, Bäumer concluded her address. The law was passed on December 3, 1926, by a vote of 248 to 158. The Democratic Reichstag fraction split almost right down the middle. Twelve voted for the law, fifteen were against it, and there was one abstention.

Theodor Wolff, disgusted over his party's split position on a law which he saw as palpably inimical to freedom of expression, had expressed his opposition in a series of somewhat snide articles in the *Berliner Tageblatt*. In the *Tagebuch* of Ernst Feder, editorial colleague of Wolff, the following was recorded: " 'The debate over the *Schundgesetz*. What a cultureless debate over culture!' " Also mentioned in the *Tagebuch* was the somewhat shocked attitude of many Democrats regarding Wolff's attacks. " 'Heuss is thinking: "The tone!" With laughing eyes [and with] fury in her heart, his wife stands beside [him]. The [*sic*] Bäumer is indignant.' "[51] The indignation of Heuss and Bäumer was amply repaid by Wolff's scorn and the *Schund und Schmutzgesetz* was responsible for driving the newspaper editor out of the German Democratic party.

At the same time, there were those in the party who were perpetually and frantically concerned with somehow expanding its base. As things developed, this effort was more and more in a right-wing direction, in the direction of the DVP. Again, there is little reason that this should be surprising. The fact that Germany's "left-wing" Democrats were, despite "bridge-building" claims to the contrary, bourgeois in origin and in economic and political outlook, was responsible for fundamentally separating it from its Weimar coalition partner, the SPD. By the same token, the bourgeois nature of the party allowed at least some of its members to seek union with another party, many of whose members were actually opposed to the principles for which the so-called "Weimar Coalition" supposedly stood. At a November 6, 1926, meeting of the party *Vorstand*, Peter Stubmann attacked those efforts that were being made by some Democrats, e.g. Koch-Weser and Fischer, to come to some sort of understanding with the DVP through the rather amorphous (but rather conservative) *Liberale Vereinigung*.[52] In his attack, he was supported by Erkelenz and Frankfurter, the latter of whom made a most telling point. No one in the left wing of the party, he declared, sought out union with the SPD. However, the right wing of the party (here, he was referring to Fischer, who was interested in union for economic and social reasons, not Koch-Weser, who was interested in union simply to expand the base of the DDP) was definitely interested in union with the anti-republican DVP.[53] To all of this, Fischer, who, like many others in the DDP, had been at least interested in a possible merger with the DVP for some time, replied that one ought not to judge the *Liberale Vereinigung* too harshly. He also thought that any efforts to come to terms with the DVP could only serve to strengthen their own party.[54]

The concerns of Fischer and others to try to tie the German Democrats down to one basic source of support, i.e., the bourgeoisie, were as myopic as those that were being made to create a mass party based upon no particular interest whatsoever. After all, the bourgeoisie already had parties and interests groups, e.g., the DVP, DNVP, and the *Wirtschaftspartei*, which, unhindered by continuous efforts in the direction of social and economic ecumenism, could be far more consistent in representing the interests of one class. Thus, it is not at all surprising that the party leadership continued on the same search for the *Volksstaat* that had characterized it from the beginning. Again, it is well to point out that the search for the *Volksstaat* (or *Volksgemeinschaft*) had been a prominent part of German bourgeois political speculation for some time. Within Democratic circles there were, one could say, two bourgeois political tendencies: (1) the drive for the *Volksstaat*, hallowed by German political theory, and (2) the concern to represent the interests of the bourgeois class in particular. Of course, these tendencies could, and often did, go together. However, particularly as the German Democratic party slid from disaster to disaster, the number of those prominent in Democratic circles who were concerned with the party's defining its position would grow.

Nevertheless, the official stance of German Democracy remained, by and large, that of a superclass (and at times, superpolitical) party. This can be clearly seen if one considers the party congress of 1927. Here, the party again made the brave attempt to represent itself as the choice for just about everybody. To be sure, there were warnings. In his address of April

---

[47] *Ibid.*, 8236B.
[48] *Ibid.*, 8368C.
[49] *Ibid.*, 8368D.
[50] *Ibid.*, 8369B.
[51] Gotthart Schwarz, *Theodor Wolff und das Berliner Tageblatt* (Tübingen, 1968), p. 216.
[52] Bundesarchiv, Koblenz, R 45 III/20. Sitzung des Vorstandes der DDP 6 November, 1926: p. 38.
[53] *Ibid.*, p. 40.
[54] *Ibid.*, pp. 42–43.

21, 1927, Dr. Mommsen warned that German youth was feeling estranged from Democratic politics and that this could pose a grave threat for the future. However, his answer to this was that German youth had to be made to feel that the Democratic party was the party of national unity. Only through this, he said, could youth feel itself to be a part of history.[55] Thus, according to Mommsen, the DDP had to strengthen its position as being a superclass party rather than weaken it. The party certainly did make an effort in this direction. On the one hand, it came out in favor of reduced income taxes for the middle class as well as for reduced interest rates in general. Former finance minister Peter Reinhold, who introduced the above suggestions, also called for an economy based on "social and ethical sensitivity," not on materialism, one in which the entire people would be elevated.[56] Anton Erkelenz declared that, if the German economy were to prosper, the working class needed a higher wage so that it too could participate more effectively in a market economy. Greater technical training was also necessary. Greater purchasing power and greater efficiency were needed, not complex and self-defeating state programs.[57] On the other hand, Dr. Heno Bollinger called for government support in establishing a strong, self-supporting middle class. Small firms and hand-workers had to be protected against large capitalism on the one hand and the well-organized industrial proletariat on the other.[58] Very much in the spirit of the "above class" ethos was the *Yearly Report of the Reich Party Leadership* for 1926, in which the leadership pointed with alarm to the growth of class consciousness on the part of the bourgeoisie. Here, it called attention to the *Wirtschaftspartei,* a group which, in its class self-centeredness and materialistic rapacity, was even worse than the SPD.[59]

Speaking on April 24, 1927, Heinrich Mann declared that "social conscience is the beginning of republic," and that the republic had not been an historical accident for those who had attempted those reforms necessary to prepare for it.[60] In a most interesting definition of "republic" he went on to declare that it was "the state which is open to thought." [61] Democracy, he said, could have no dogma; each citizen had to be responsible for the other. In a further attempt to represent the interests of all citizens, the party came out in favor of a strong farm policy. Taxes were to be reduced and a tariff policy, which would encourage German farmers to produce inexpensive goods, was also suggested. At the same time, technical training for the small farmer was to be encouraged and a vigorous settlement policy to increase the number of farmers *vis-à-vis* the large estate owners was proposed. Of course, the party maintained that such a program would pose no threat to the large estate owners, whose property would be left pretty much intact.[62] In brief, the party had come out for reform for everybody with social or economic displacement for none.

It was in partial response to the extremely catholic nature of the program hammered out at the 1927 *Parteitag* that, at the June 21, 1927, meeting of the *Vorstand,* Richard Frankfurter declared that the reason the DDP was dying was its effort to represent everybody. Such a course, he said, was absolutely impossible. The party had to come out more strongly against the SPD and against large-scale capitalism.[63] In other words, Frankfurter was calling upon the party to strengthen its appeal to the middle class. He was vigorously attacked by Frau Uth and Hermann Hummel, both of whom declared that it was the strength of the DDP that it represented no special class or interest and that it had to continue on this course, having, in the words of the latter, "too much of a mission to fufill." [64] In the end, it was the superclass (i.e., formal "statist") position that won out in the leading ranks of German bourgeois Democracy. The challenge of the "special interest" group was more or less brushed aside.

Democratic efforts to push Germany towards that magic "state of conciliation" continued of course. This can be most clearly seen in two speeches by Democrats during the Reich budget debates of February, 1928. On February 11, Gustav Schneider spoke on behalf of improved laws on behalf of labor. He decried the "spiritual alienation" from work and from each other which characterized both employer and employee, and he declared that all working people, whether blue or white collar, needed greater protection.[65] In a machine age, with an accelerated "work tempo," new and improved working laws were needed.[66] In all of this, the state had to play a more important role than ever before. On February 15, 1928, Ernst Lemmer spoke on behalf of farmers, land workers, and the middle class. With some bitterness, he attacked those tradition-bound *Junkers,* who hired Polish land workers while 60,000 jobless Germans searched the countryside in vain. For many, Lemmer said, love of the Fatherland stopped when it came to hiring foreign workers.[67] At the same time, he admitted, there was occurring a general flight from the land, which the state could not stop.

---

[55] Bundesarchiv, Koblenz, R 45III/6. Siebenter ordentlicher Parteitag der DDP am 21/24 April, 1927 in Hamburg, p. 78.
[56] *Ibid.,* p. 197.
[57] *Ibid.,* pp. 203–215.
[58] *Ibid.,* pp. 219–231.
[59] *Ibid.,* p. 309.
[60] *Ibid.,* p. 327.
[61] *Ibid.,* p. 332.

[62] *Ibid.,* pp. 104–115, 116, 127–135, 154–155, 360–361.
[63] R45 III/20 *op. cit.,* pp. 92–93.
[64] *Ibid.,* p. 98.
[65] *VR III. Wahlperiode. 1924 Band 394* (Berlin, 1928), 12749B.
[66] *Ibid.,* 12749C–D.
[67] *Ibid.,* 12863B.

Nevertheless, the state could hinder it, to some degree, by improving the social and cultural life of the *Landvolk*. Also of importance, Lemmer said, was the protection of the German *Mittelstand;* "a healthier *Mittelstand,* capable of life, assures social peace and creates German culture." [68]

Again, what the speeches of Schneider and Lemmer reveal is the well-established German Democratic tendency of attempting to please everybody, and thus to form that long sought-after "bridge" between bourgeoisie and proletariat, one which would bind the whole nation together in *Volksgemeinschaft*. Of course, as is well known, the Nazi party had and would do the same thing, and would enjoy considerable success in the process. Equally well established is the fact that the Nazis' claim to represent the working class (as well as everyone else) met with just about as little success as that of the Democrats. However, bourgeois support was something they could rely upon, at least in times of crisis. The Democrats, being in the unfortunate position of attempting to hold up the edifice of republic in cooperation with a confessional party and an avowed working-class party with which it could cooperate only occasionally, were increasingly despised by the bourgeoisie. This class, in either its "new" form (white collar employees, bureaucrats, and so forth) or its "old" (craftsmen, small traders, etc.) could hardly have been receptive to the Democratic call for *Volksgemeinschaft*. Such a call came from that party in large measure responsible for parliamentary republicanism, an institution but grudgingly accepted in times of tranquility and despised in times of trouble. Furthermore, as we shall see, it was viewed by many as that "Jew party." The Democrats, of course, would attempt to deal with some of these objections; but, in the end, the Nazi call for *Volksgemeinschaft* would be the successful one.

In the meantime, however, the German Democratic party had been forced to face an issue every bit as complex and divisive as the one presented by the *Schunde und Schmutzgesetz*. In January, 1928, defense minister Otto Gessler who, until 1927 had been a member of the German Democratic party, resigned because of bad health and the scandal which resulted from the disclosure that his ministry had been presenting the Reichstag with false budget figures (the true ones, however, were presented to the budget committee) and that this same ministry was also investing government funds in various projects. Among such projects was the Phoebus Film Corporation, a firm that, after absorbing some millions of taxpayer contributed marks, quietly went bankrupt. Gessler was replaced by General Wilhelm Gröner, who had once served as quartermaster general of the German army after Ludendorff's dismissal in October 1918. One of Gröner's pet projects was the strengthening of the German navy. According to the Versailles Treaty, Germany could build armored ships, "pocket battleships" as they were somewhat derisively called, to replace the six old battleships she had been allowed to keep. Already in the 1920's, it had been discovered that, by making certain adjustments in armor and armament, a rather efficient warship only slightly slower than a conventional cruiser and possessed of far more imposing fire power, could be produced (the *Graf Spee,* of course, was such a warship). Gröner, over Social Democratic, Democratic, and Communist opposition, succeeded in persuading the budget committee of the Reichstag that a first installment on such a cruiser (known, for the time being, as *Panzerschiff A*) ought to be made. On March 14, 1928, Gröner brought the matter before the Reichstag. He declared that, in view of Germany's greatly reduced army and also, considering the fact that her eastern frontier, i.e., the border with Poland, was constantly threatened, the construction of such a ship was of utmost importance. Gröner further stated that he was supporting this project as a believer "in a sound and intelligent pacifism—though not in one which leads to servile submission." [69]

Haas of the Democratic party declared his support of the new defense minister. He also stated that, in his opinion, "no army in the world is of use if the entire people does not stand behind it." Gessler had not recognized this, Haas admitted, and now it was the task of the new defense minister to make certain that all classes stood behind the new *Reichswehr,* as they had behind the army during the war.[70] Haas did state, however, that he, like Gröner, was in favor of a "healthy pacifism," one that, presumably, was able to reconcile the desire for peace with the maintenance of national strength. He disavowed what he called "pathological pacifism" as being just as dangerous as "pathological nationalism."[71] After declaring that the army had, somehow, to be made loyal to the republic just as it had been loyal to the old monarchy, and after attacking the propagators of the "stab in the back myth" (*Dolchstosslegende*), Haas went on to the issue of *Panzerschiff A*.[72]

---

[68] *Ibid.*, 12865B. It would appear that Lemmer is talking about the "traditional" German middle class of craftsmen, small traders, and small landowners. The German Democratic party had the tendency—widely shared at that time—to group white-collar "employees" with the working class. Larry Eugene Jones points out that the *Wirtschaftspartei* tended to represent the "old" *Mittelstand*, while the "new" *Mittelstand* attempted to work through such parties as the DVP and the DNVP. Both groups, of course, came to represent a strong source of Nazi voting strength. See Larry Eugene Jones, "The Dying Middle: Weimar Germany and the Fragmentation of Bourgeois Politics," in: *Central European History* 5, (March, 1972): p. 54.

[69] Quoted in Eyck, 2; *op. cit.,* p. 153.
[70] *VR, op. cit.,* 13401B–13402C.
[71] *Ibid.,* 13403A.
[72] *Ibid.,* 13404A–13405A.

No doubt with complete honesty, Haas said that he really did want to be convinced that the "cruiser" was necessary. However, the *Reichswehrminister* had not succeeded in convincing him that a cruiser somehow would be valuable in defending East Prussia and Silesia, especially if these territories already had been lost to a Polish ground attack.[73] Disarmament was really what was needed if Germany were to be secure. After all, particularly with regard to navies, Germany never could compete with the large powers anyway and small powers (implicitly Poland) could build up their navies just as rapidly and well as could Germany.[74] After thus tying "a healthy pacifism" to *Realpolitik*, Haas stepped down to somewhat unenthusiastic applause. After further debate, during the course of which sharp Social Democratic and Communist opposition to the building of the cruiser was evidenced, the majority of the Reichstag, against the opposition of Democrats, Social Democrats, and Communists, voted not to strike *Panzerschiff A* from the budget. However, when the budget was presented to the *Reichsrat*, Prussian Social Democratic opposition was able to hamstring matters to such a degree that it was decided that work on the cruiser ought best to be postponed until September 1, 1928. The Reichstag concurred in this decision.

In the meantime, of course, the disastrous elections of May 20, 1928, took place. which, as we shall see in due course, reduced the German Democratic party Reichstag delegation to the status of being a half-hearted cheering section for parliamentary republicanism. Despite Democratic losses, two of them, Herman Dietrich and Erich Koch-Weser, were given portfolios in Chancellor Hermann Müller's new cabinet, the former that of minister of food, the latter that of minister of justice. Democratic participation in the government was to prove embarrassing insofar as the "cruiser" issue was concerned.

On August 10, 1928, under pressure from Gröner, who inisted that an initial outlay of approximately 9.3 million marks for the ship would not be extravagant and that the cabinet would have full approval powers over the construction of further vessels, the new cabinet, Social Democrats included, approved the decision to commence construction of *Panzerschiff A* on September 1, 1928. During their very successful electoral campaign, the Social Democratic party had made much of the "cruiser" issue. Their slogan *Keine Panzerkreuzer, sondern Kinderspeisung* ("Not armored cruisers, but food for children") had been an effective one, and the fact that Social Democratic ministers had now joined their bourgeois colleagues in approving construction of precisely such a *Panzerkreuzer*, produced a crisis in SPD ranks. As for the reaction of the Democratic party, it would seem that, by and large, they approved of the decision to commence construction of the ship. At their annual convention, Koch-Weser, without indicating how he actually voted, outlined the reasons against construction of the warship. His remarks were received with phlegmatic calm. However, Dietrich had only to declare, "'I voted for the armed cruiser,'" to be greeted with thunderous applause.[75]

The reasons for Democratic approval of construction of the ship were not only militaristic ones, and, as we shall see, these came out in November, 1928, when the Reichstag reconvened. On November 15, Otto Wels spoke for the Social Democratic party. Cruiser production had to be halted, he declared. The will of the German people had dictated this in the elections of May 20.[76] The Social Democratic party was not interested in fighting against the *Reichswehr*, Wels maintained. Rather, it was concerned "with making it into a reliable instrument of the republic."[77] Furthermore, it was not just a question of one armored cruiser. Even Gessler, before his resignation, had suggested that there would be more. Picking up on a theme introduced by the Democrat Haas during the March debates, Wels questioned the military value of such a ship, and he concluded his address by declaring that there were social needs to be met, needs far more worthy of the eighty million marks projected as necessary to complete construction of *Panzerschiff A*.[78]

Gröner had threatened to resign if the Reichstag voted to halt construction of the ship, and Wels's speech seemed to be an effective one which could have helped in bringing about just such a situation. However, on the day following Wels's address, November 16, Ernst Lemmer, of the then greatly reduced Democratic fraction, made a rather effective speech of his own. At first, he took the customary Democratic "above party" stance. It would be "from the party-political standpoint, more comfortable and easier" to support the Social Democrats, he maintained.[79] In view of the, according to Eyck, favorable response of the DDP as a whole to cruiser construction, there was considerable casuistry involved in such a remark. However, Lemmer went on, he and his delegation could not go along with the SPD demand that construction be halted. The past Reichstag had been for it, even though the Democrats had voted against it. The *Reichsrat*, in setting up September 1 as a target date, had indicated that they would go along with any decision made between March and September 1, 1928, and, of course, the new cabinet itself, on August 10, 1928, had been for construction. Quite accurately, Lemmer maintained that Wels's speech seemed to be going against a cabinet

---

[73] *Ibid.*, 13406B–C.
[74] *Ibid.*, 13406B.
[75] Quoted in Eyck, 2, *op. cit.*, p. 162.
[76] *VR, op. cit., IV. Wahlperiode. 1928. Band 423 Stenographische Berichte* (Berlin, 1929), 324A.
[77] *Ibid.*, 325B.
[78] *Ibid.*, 327C–331B.
[79] *Ibid.*, 388B.

that had been appointed by Hermann Müller of his own party.[80] Lemmer did not mention this specifically, but the situation of the Social Democratic ministers was especially poignant. The left-wing of the Social Democratic delegation had forced through a resolution which required Social Democratic ministers to support the SPD motion to discontinue construction of the cruiser, and thus to vote against themselves. What was at stake here, Lemmer continued, was the whole system of parliamentary government. "The failing is not in the system, but in men who don't know how to use it."[81] Lemmer did raise some objections to the construction of the cruiser, and he agreed with Wels that certain social, economic and cultural needs were very great indeed. However, the constitutional issue was the one of greatest concern and thus, in defense of parliamentary procedure, the German Democratic party had to spurn the Social Democratic demand that construction of *Panzerschiff A* be halted. When the vote was taken, the Democrats joined the majority which was against the Social Democratic motion. The vote was 257 to 202, with 8 abstentions. A no confidence motion presented by the Communists was then handily defeated, 393 to 62 with 5 abstentions.

Lemmer's defense of parliamentary government—in reality, a defense of the Weimar Constitution—was a fine one and there can be little doubt that, from a constitutional stand-point, he was correct. No matter how great the SPD success had been in May, 1928, a decision made by the cabinet which resulted from this success could not be retroactively overturned, even if the now greatly expanded SPD delegation, which, of course, also resulted from the May election. wished to honor a commitment made to its constituents. If such a precedent were to have been set, Lemmer was suggesting, parliamentary government would soon become an impossibility. All in all, Lemmer's speech was one of the most stridently pro-parliamentarianism ones ever to come from the mouth of a Democrat, either on the floor of the Reichstag or elsewhere. There are two little bits of irony, however, which need to be examined. First of all, it is curious (to say the least) that Lemmer's defense of parliamentary government was directed against a motion made by one of the Democratic party's "Weimar Coalition" partners. As mentioned above, the Social Democratic party—at least before the First World War—had been in the position of being a class party which nevertheless bore the burden for constitutional reform. The German Democrats had been statists before the war, and they were statists after it. The fact that the "cruiser issue"— no matter how real the constitutional problems flowing from it actually were—was the one that could summon forth parliamentarian principle from Democratic ranks, served to push Democrats and Social Democrats farther apart than ever. However, the Democrats were turning towards the right anyway, as we have seen already and will see again, and this brings up the second bit of irony. The German Democratic party, from time to time, had rallied to parliamentary republicanism on the floor of the Reichstag (although, as seen above, this was usually done in the name of reason of state) and, in a 1927 publication *Die Krisis des deutschen Parlamentarismus,* two Democrats, Willy Hellpach and Graf zu Dohna, had expressed a sort of guarded optimism in regard to the role of parliamentary life in Germany. Despite the general decline in the role of parliaments throughout Europe, parliamentary life could survive in Germany if certain reforms were undertaken, *viz.,* the limiting of interest politics, speaking time on the floor of parliament, and the limiting of the use of no-confidence votes.[82]

However, in Democratic publications and committee meetings, questioning of parliamentary government and cries for the super-political *Volksgemeinschaft* had been numerous from 1919 to 1928. Moreover, as the party went from electoral disaster to greater electoral disaster, such phenomena became more and more common. The *dénouement* of all of this will be the virtual formal abandonment of parliamentarianism, pluralism, and, some will say, tolerance as principles of the German Democratic party. Of course, this would be done under the pressures of a public for which the party, in its republican guise, had decreasing relevance. Naturally, a significant indication of this loss of relevance was the national elections of May 20, 1928. Although these elections gave Germany a Social Democratic chancellor for the first time since 1920, the voting totals for the Democratic party sank to an all-time low of 1,505,700, only 4.9 per cent of the total vote. The obvious fact that Germany's electorate was turning its collective back upon the party, and seemingly upon that parliamentary democracy which it represented, served to increase that sense of despair that we have observed within Democratic ranks. It did not create anti-republicanism or anti-parliamentarianism within Democratic ranks in general and the party in particular. As we have seen, statism was present from the beginning. Rather, the decline of parliamentary democracy within the ranks of its bourgeois exponents made the compromisers more willing to seek extra-parliamentary solutions while, at the same time, it allowed those who had always been suspicious of parliamentary democracy and had always clung to a statism which they had used to rationalize their enforced acceptance of such a state form, to retain their old attitudes.

In 1928 Gertrud Bäumer published a most interesting work which amply reflected the spiritual confusion

---

[80] *Ibid.,* 388C–388D.
[81] *Ibid.,* 359A.
[82] Professor Dr. Willy Hellpach and Professor Dr. Graf zu Dohna, *Die Krisis des deutschen Parlamentarismus* (Karlsruhe, 1927); see especially pp. 3–4, 6, 12–15, 35.

of many Democrats. In many ways it was an extremely perspicacious analysis of such issues as democracy in Weimar Germany, the role of liberalism and so on. On the other hand, this work, *Grundlagen demokratische Politik* ("Foundations of Democratic Politics") was also indicative of Bäumer's own turning away (at least in part) from such things as pluralistic republicanism and liberalism. A large degree of political romanticism, something that would become ever stronger in Democratic circles, could also be detected.

Perhaps as a partial criticism of her own party, Bäumer began the work by pointing out that every party, every special interest, claimed to represent the welfare of the whole people.[83] The issue of importance, often obfuscated by these claims, was that of the relationship of the state power to the people. State power, she declared, had to be "rooted in *Volkstum*," in the "corpus mysticum of national community."[84] *Volkstum*, in its turn, had to grow in political consciousness, but it could not if classes or groups stood against it. Here, we see a most interesting notion of national community, one that presupposed the existence of some form of unified *Volk* spirit, one that was often hidden, if not threatened, by class or special interest groups. This rather anti-pluralistic, or at least extremely romantic, view of the relation(s) between classes and a presumed unity of *Volk* spirit was explicitly anti-political in tone, and can be compared to some of the Neo-Conservative notions that were being bandied about in Germany at that time. In Germany, Bäumer claimed, the class problem, i.e., the continued confrontation between proletarian and bourgeois, did exist. However, she said, the issue was really one of a sort of "proletarian complex," that stemmed "much more from an ailing [sense of] self-respect and a wounded freedom instinct, than from materialistic avidity."[85] Like many German bourgeois political philosophers and politicians, Bäumer chose to view proletarian problems as being those "of the spirit," rather than as outgrowths of the material conditions of society. Nonetheless, Bäumer remarked that this "complex" represented "the Achilles heel" of German power, and had to be dealt with in the near future.[86] What had to be done, Bäumer suggested, was to treat all people like the *Volk* and not a mass. The term "masses" was, for Bäumer, a disturbing one. The term *Volk*, on the other hand, hallowed as it was by more than a century of German political mysticism, had all sorts of ingenuous, if not downright cuddly, overtones about it.

Bäumer differentiated rather sharply between democracy and liberalism. The former represented an "active" position towards freedom, the latter (and here Bäumer was obviously considering that "classical" liberalism of the nineteenth century), a "passive" position towards freedom.[87] This liberalism, she said, tended to function as the "watcher" or "governor" of power, and not live in power itself. For this reason, she said, liberalism had "no productive strengths" and, because of its emphases upon individualism and passive freedoms, "liberalism is very often misused by special interests."[88] Liberalism could serve as a criterion of positive criticism *vis-à-vis* the state. "As criterion it is necessary, as political principle [it is] too thin, and thus dangerous.[89] As for the state itself, it had very positive roles to perform, the most important of which was to allow for the full cultural and political development of the people.[90] At the same time, though, in economic areas, the state ought to leave things be. "Private Enterprise," being full of struggle and thus "of life," was preferable to state interference, much less control.[91]

Bäumer viewed the relationship of leader to people as being a dialectical one, in which the leader embodied the mature (or at least maturing) strengths of his people. In this regard, Bäumer admitted, Mussolini looked good on paper; in fact, he seemed to come across as a democratic leader. However, she continued, power could not be confined to one group, otherwise the development of the people would be stilted or one-sided.[92] Returning, as she often did, to her opening theme of the relationship between state and *Volk*, Bäumer made the interesting observation that state power had to be rooted in a self-conscious nation, this latter being a people which "develops as a collective personality, whose members know and feel themselves as parts of it."[93] Throughout most of Bäumer's writings on politics, one can see the important roles of such notions as that of unconsciously held ideas of unity, the state as a sort of organizer and/or concretization of unconsciously held ideas, and so forth. These vestiges of political romanticism remained strong in Bäumer, and would become increasingly important in her own thinking as Weimar parliamentary republicanism slid to its doom.

As for the role of parliamentary government itself, Bäumer made the interesting observation that the "parliamentary system" had been designed to embody, "in a healthful way," the dynamism of the political strengths in Germany, and, most of all, "to bring people together and to the state."[94] Parliament was not to

---

[83] Gertrud Bäumer, *Grundlagen demokratische Politik* (Karlsruhe, 1928), p. 1.
[84] *Ibid.*, p. 5.
[85] *Ibid.*, p. 12.
[86] *Ibid.*

[87] *Ibid.*, p. 18.
[88] *Ibid.*, p. 21.
[89] *Ibid.*, p. 21.
[90] *Ibid.*, p. 23. Parenthetically, such an attitude towards the role of the state helps to explain Bäumer's attitude towards the *Schund und Schmutz* law of 1926.
[91] *Ibid.*, p. 22.
[92] *Ibid.*, pp. 30–31.
[93] *Ibid.*, p. 35.
[94] *Ibid.*, p. 41.

have served or to serve as a mediator between interests or even, really, as a vehicle for compromise. Parliament was to be the means towards state unity, if not necessarily the apotheosis of this unity. Once again in Democratic literature, we can see the extremely important role that state unity had to play. It was in this context that Bäumer once again exalted the national socialist ideal of Friedrich Naumann.[95] This ideal was to become more and more of a poignant rallying cry for German Democrats as the state order was increasingly threatened.

One cannot gainsay the fact that Bäumer put her finger upon several problems that were damaging German parliamentarianism, viz., the instability of governments based upon continuously changing parliamentary majorities, and the loss of faith in parliamentary government on the part of the German people (how much faith they in general or many Democrats in particular had from the start is, of course, open to question) as the role of interest politics became ever more apparent.[96] At the same time, however, Bäumer made a most interesting observation, one that seems to point toward an increasingly skeptical attitude towards that *Volk*, which was otherwise the normative grounding for all political life. Despite everything that one could say against it, Bäumer said, the parliamentary system was a necessary means of keeping the life of the *Volk* (*Volksleben*) moving along.[97] However, the functioning of the system was a "natural functioning of the political maturity of the people." A government could not be any better than the people from which it stemmed.[98] This interesting balance between a romantic attitude towards the *Volk* and a certain cynicism regarding its political maturity would be more thoroughly developed in her 1930 work, *Sinn und Former Geistiger Führung* ("Meaning and Forms of Spiritual Leadership"), where the role of dynamic leadership becomes of utmost importance.

Again, the underlying theme of the 1928 work was that of national unity. The old, Naumannesque theme of winning the workers to the state remained central to Bäumer's concerns (and in an increasingly pathetic manner to the concerns of most other Democrats as well). In her expressions of interest in the problems of industrial society, Bäumer even went so far as to condemn (using in part the language of Naumann) those who sought to adhere to romantic anti-industrial and anti-Semitic doctrines.[99] Of course, to anyone familiar with Bäumer's own bucolic, romantic tendencies, such expressions must have seemed a bit casuistic.

In the final analysis, unity was the overriding necessity of the day: unity of classes, unity of cultural training (education) and, of course, the unity of state (*Einheitsstaat*). As time passed and disorder increased, Bäumer would become even more strident and romantic in her demands, and even less concerned with parliamentary government.

Grundlagen demokratische Politik can be seen as being representative of Democratic attitudes during the late Weimar period, although admittedly, Bäumer was a bit more romantic than many of her colleagues. She was for parliamentary government, but only to the degree that it functioned to ensure state unity. She was sensitive to the needs of the working class (or rather what she thought its needs were), but any substantive altering of the capitalist system of production was out of the question. She was, in some ways, close to being *völkisch* in her attitude towards the German people; yet, she really was beginning to question whether they were mature enough to conduct their own political affairs, especially as German bourgeois democracy and the party that represented it seemed more and more to be stymied by parliamentary disorder and electoral disaster. Bäumer was becoming increasingly desperate. Perhaps parliamentary government, even that kind accepted by Bäumer as the *sine qua non* of mature political life, would not and could not work. What then?

It is interesting to note that, by 1928, Theodor Heuss had come to share Bäumer's criticism of liberalism. In an article entitled "Demokratie und Parlamentarismus: ihre Geschichte, ihre Gegner und ihre Zukunft" ("Democracy and Parliamentarianism: Their History, Their Opponents and Their Future"), Heuss was skeptical of liberalism's efficacy in the modern world because it lacked "the state idea" and because of its ahistorical assumptions about the human race.[100] While attacking various authoritarian and irrational ideologies, Bolshevism-Fascism, racism, etc., Heuss came out as rather uncertain as to the role of parliamentary government in German life. Parliamentary government had no deeply rooted tradition in German life, and German suspicions of it from the very beginning had served almost to cripple it from the start.[101] At the same time, Heuss remained positively committed to democracy which, being more concerned with the collective well-being of the nation rather than the individual, was still of value in the modern mass society.[102]

Individuals such as Erkelenz had made repeated and desperate attempts to rally Germans to that cause which he saw as embodied within his own party. In an April 15, 1928, article, "Subjects or Citizens" ("Untertanen

---

[95] *Ibid.*, p. 48.
[96] *Ibid.*, pp. 49–53.
[97] *Ibid.*, p. 51. One assumes here that what Bäumer meant, particularly in view of her earlier statements about the role of parliament, was "moving" the people in the direction of the state.
[98] *Ibid.*
[99] *Ibid.*, p. 75.

[100] Theodor Huess, "Demokratie und Parlamentarismus: ihre Geschichte, ihre Gegner und ihre Zukunft," in: *Zehn Jahre Deutsche Republik: ein Hanbuch für Republikanische Politik*, herausgegeben von Anton Erkelenz (Berlin, 1928).
[101] *Ibid.*, pp. 107, 110–111. As we will see, in a 1928 newspaper article, Heuss referred to the Reichstag as "dying."
[102] *Ibid.*, p. 116.

oder Bürger"), Erkelenz declared that the republic and the constitution had allowed the German people to become citizens rather than simple subjects of an all-powerful state.[103] The subject had had everything decided for him by an all-powerful monarch. Now, "We all wear the crown of citizen of the German Republic."[104] It was, in some ways, far harder to be a good citizen than a good subject. However, it was well worth the effort. In the same issue, there appeared an editorial attack upon the notion of "direct democracy," claiming that such notions would lead, in the end, to an emphasis upon the Führer personality, and thus to a destruction of the democratic order. However, such defenses of parliamentary democracy had the tone of desperation about them. By 1928 even Theodor Heuss had characterized the Reichstag as dying.[105] The election disaster of May 20, 1928, was the last straw. In an article in *Die Hilfe,* June 1, 1928, Erkelenz put much of the blame for this unhappy occurrence upon the "effects of parliamentarianism": the parliamentary system was forcing the electorate either to the left (SPD) or to the right (DNVP), or towards those pure interest splinter parties such as the *Wirtschaftspartei*.[106] This mildly anti-parliamentary statement was exceptional for Erkelenz and, in its official capacity, for the party as a whole. It was the rule, however, for such individuals as Gessler, Meinecke, Wolf, Corwegh, and of course, Bäumer, who used the election disaster of 1928 as an excuse to cast furtive glances in the direction of *Jungdeutsche Orden*. However, she was not alone.

The despair of German Democrats was amply reflected in the *Vorstand* meeting of June 14, 1928, in which the mood was characterized by a sort of breast-beating "where did we go wrong?" attitude. Peter Stubmann declared that the party had not been sensitive enough to the needs of several groups, the lower and middle *Beamte,* tradesmen and employees (precisely those classes or groups, of course, which would stream to Nazism after 1930). He also charged that Koch-Weser's participation in discussions with the *Liberale Vereinigung,* as well as his mutterings about a possible union with the DVP had caused many to distrust DDP leadership.[107] Both he and Erkelenz agreed that the party was too much centered in urban areas, e.g., Berlin and not enough in smaller communities and the countryside.[108] Erkelenz was also quite bitter about recent efforts, in this case those of former party member Theodor Wolff, to form a new, broader republican party. The Centre was not interested, nor was the DVP and, at any rate, the latter was farther right than ever before.[109] Koch-Weser declared that the primary reasons for the defeat were two: viz., that the German people really were not interested in what he called the "great issues," such as that of a unified state, and that the party was in need of a new economic program.[110] Koch-Weser suggested also that the party ought to focus more attention upon those groups which, he assumed, were not as interested in "class politics" as the others—artisans, employees, and civil servants.[111] Again, it is of interest to note that these groups, presumably not interested in "class politics," would be excellent recruiting grounds for the Nazis. An interesting attitude emerges here, namely Koch-Weser's perennial search for the "non-class," "non-interest" wave of voting strength. Now, he had focused somewhat myopic eyes upon sorts of "non-class classes."

Frankfurter and George Bernhard attacked Koch-Weser for his flirtations with the *Liberale Vereinigung* (and implicitly the DVP), while others, with some degree of political realism, one would fear, declared that the identification of the DDP as a "Jew party" had hurt it a great deal. In this regard, the rather liberal agrarian Friedrich Wachhorst de Wente remarked: "It would be of great value for us if our Jewish party friends would stay more in the background."[112] Hartmann Freiherr von Richtofen attempted to explain the electoral disaster of May 20 in the following manner: working-class people would naturally stick with their own party, the SPD, while the fight against the DVP was proving to be unfruitful. Furthermore, the Berlin press had been of no use at all; in fact, it had done the party much harm. "We cannot gainsay the fact," said von Richtofen, "that the Democratic party is considered to be the party of Jewish capitalism."[113] Koch-Weser noted that the only reason that the Jewish question had become important within the party was the behavior of such people as Theodor Wolff and Ernst Feder.[114] As we have seen, Wolff, the general editor of the *Berliner Tageblatt,* had left the party over the *Schund and Schmutz* controversy, while Feder, who was a well-known jurist and a political editor on the *Berliner Tageblatt,* had taken periodic shots at what he thought to be weaknesses in the party leadership.[115] For Georg Schreiber, too, the

---

[103] Anton Erkelenz, "Untertanen oder Bürger," in: *Die Hilfe,* Nr. 8, 15 April, 1928: p. 172.
[104] *Ibid.*
[105] Heussarchiv, Politische Schriften, 1928, Theodor Heuss, "Der Sterbende Reichstag," in: *Nürnberg–Fürth Morganpresse,* Nr. 33, 22 February, 1928.
[106] Anton Erkelenz, "Die Auswirkungen des Parlamentarismus auf den Volkswillen," in: *Die Hilfe,* Nr. 11, 1 Juni, 1928.
[107] R 45III/20 *op. cit.,* pp. 173–174.
[108] *Ibid.,* pp. 174–175.

[109] *Ibid.,* p. 176.
[110] *Ibid.* pp. 178–180.
[111] *Ibid.,* p. 179.
[112] *Ibid.,* p. 189.
[113] *Ibid.,* pp. 191–192.
[114] *Ibid.,* p. 192.
[115] For an interesting view of Democratic political life during the Weimar period, see Yearbook XIII (1968) of the Leo Baeck Institute, where Ernst Feder's diaries (1930–1932) have been reproduced.

Jewish issue was an important one. The party, he thought, was unpopular because people identified it with institutions "dominated" (*sic*) by the Jews, e.g., the warehouses and the banks.[116] Erkelenz and Hermann Dietrich spoke out against the elevation of the Jewish question into a position of prominence, the former declaring that such an attitude eventually would drive everybody out of the party, while Dietrich stated that the role of the Jewish question had not been so important as previously.[117] What all of this points to, of course, is the importance of the Jewish question in Weimar politics and the mixed attitudes, in Democratic circles, to a strong source of support for Weimar republicanism—the Jews. We will examine this problem in more detail in a later chapter.

Throughout the meeting, the question of the party's claim to represent everybody came up again, stronger than ever. As we have seen, Stubmann and even Koch-Weser had agreed that civil servants, employees, artisans, and tradesmen needed more attention. Theodor Tantzen joined them in this, declaring that much middle-class support had to be available, and that the party had to be more economically liberal.[118] Hellpach, with some perspicacity, declared that the DDP could never become a party of employees and civil servants. Rather, it had to become a party of the "self-employed," jurists, teachers, doctors, etc.[119] At the same time, however, several members of the *Vorstand* took pot shots at Fischer and his *Hansa-Bund* for being too narrowly middle class and for being against "economic democracy."[120] Frau Bäumer maintained that the party was far too much identified with the cities, and that German youth had to be won over to its cause.[121] Liberalism was finished, she said. The future of German democracy rested with youth. This position would become an extremely important one within German Democratic ranks and, as we shall see, would have interesting consequences.

The June 14, 1928, meeting of the *Vorstand* of the German Democratic party was an important one. Out of it, there came the general feeling that the DDP had failed to win over substantial elements in all strata of the population and that, indeed, it had to become more of a middle-class party (even though there was some quarreling over which part of the middle class it should endeavor to represent). At the same time, though, with the possible exception of Hermann Fischer, the Democratic leadership was most reluctant to abandon the official party position of being above class and special interests. This point of view came through most clearly in the case of the party chairman, Koch-Weser. Yet, there really was no particular contradiction in this attitude, *viz.*, that the DDP could not really draw much from the working-class supporters of the SPD and hence had to become more of a middle-class party, but that the super-class, super-interest position must not be abandoned. Implicit in this was the recognition that the traditional call for "non-class" and/or "non-partisan" politics always had come from bourgeois circles that had been and were eager to mask their own interest politics behind the baroque façade of the national interest. By 1928, however (and far more so later, of course), there were other parties on the political horizon who, not being identified with the Weimar Republic and all of its problems, were able to utilize the "non-partisan" approach far more effectively than the beleaguered Weimar Democrats. For the present, though, it was Bäumer's call for youthful revivification that would have the greatest effect upon the future of Democratic politics.

For some in the German Democratic party, gestures towards such groups as the *Jungdeutsche Orden* did not stem from romantic or statist points of view, but were merely efforts to expand the base of the party and thus to strengthen it. Cynicism as to the limited appeal of the party had become rife by the late 1920's and it was reflected in a rather bitter letter from Friedrich Mück to Theodor Heuss on June 16, 1927. The party, Mück declared, was finished. It had become "a kind of bowling club for several fellows with an abundance of grey matter; but not for a greater portion of the people."[122] Moreover, suggesting that young blood was necessary if the party was to be able to draw upon a greater portion of the electorate merely reflected good political sense. It was in keeping with this notion that the party began entertaining ideas of approaching the *Jungdeutsche Orden* as early as the autumn of 1928.[123] By 1929 even Erkelenz began talking of the positive aspects of this youth movement of the right, although he was careful to point out that it seemed to lack a concrete political program.[124] The same *Biedermeier* aspect in Heuss which caused him to support the *Schund und Schmutz* law made it impossible for him ever to feel very comfortable about the medievalism and romanticism which he saw with the *Jungdos*. However, it is important to note that, for many Democrats, fascination with the *Jungdos* accompanied a gradual loss of faith in parliamentary democracy.

This loss of faith in parliamentary democracy was helped along by a bitter parliamentary crisis, which broke out in January and February, 1929. After the

---

[116] *Op. cit.*, p. 195.
[117] *Ibid.*, pp. 192, 193.
[118] *Ibid.*, pp. 194–195.
[119] *Ibid.*, p. 190.
[120] *Ibid.*, pp. 184, 235.
[121] *Ibid.*, p. 185.

[122] Heussarchiv, Friedrich Mück/Theodor Heuss Briefwechsel. Letter: Mück to Heuss, 16 June, 1927.
[123] As an example of this see: Bundesarchiv, Stizungen des Vorstandes der DDP. R45 III/20, 232 (*Vorstand* meeting of 20 October, 1928).
[124] Anton Erkelenz, "Jung und Alte," in: *Die Hilfe*, Nr. 8, 15 April, 1929: pp. 181–182.

1928 elections, Hermann Müller was confronted with the problem of setting up a "Great Coalition" cabinet, i.e., one that would reach from the Social Democrats over to the right-wing DVP. The fate of this coalition hinged upon the role of the Centrist party. At first, there was only one representative of the Centre party in the cabinet, Theodor von Guérard, who was minister of transport. However, in January and February, 1929, the Centrists demanded three seats in the cabinet. The DVP declared that it would agree to this only if it were allowed to have two seats in the Prussian government. The Centrists refused to countenance this and, in protest, yanked von Guérard out of the "Great Coalition." Particularly in view of increasing budgetary problems, the "cruiser issue" and the necessity of maintaining a united government front *vis-à-vis* the allies (discussions on reparations payments were just beginning in Paris), the parliamentary crisis of February, 1929, was particularly embarrassing. To be sure, the Centrists eventually did get the two extra seats (in April, 1929); Adam Stegerwald became minister of transport and Josef Wirth, minister of occupied territories. However, to preserve the so-called "Great Coalition," Erich Koch-Weser had to resign as minister of justice, inasmuch as Guérard was now given this post, and also, of course, because of the weak electoral position of the DDP. The Democrat Hermann Dietrich did remain as minister of food. However, Koch-Weser's enforced resignation in the name of governmental unity was a bitter blow for the party and for Koch-Weser personally.

Koch-Weser's bitterness towards parliamentary government was expressed in the remark that the party had to emphasize "that parliamentarianism is not democracy's only form of expression," and that "parliamentarianism, in the form in which it is presently practiced, a form which allows the state to disappear behind the parties, does not correspond to the basic thoughts of the current system [i.e., the Weimar Constitution]."[125] As part of an increasing party demand for reform of the electoral system, Koch-Weser attacked the proportional system of election, a system that had allowed interest groups to come before the state.[126] In an interesting reversal of an old political bromide Koch–Weser remarked that a state rested "on men, not on laws," and that strong personalities were needed to help bring youth to the state.[127] Emphasis upon strong personalities was to characterize the program of the German Democratic party from 1929 to its demise in 1930. For many, such as Koch-Weser, these personalities were not to be *völkisch*/romantic supermen, but rather, individuals who were able to rise above parliamentarianism and the parties in support of the state. Individuals such as Heuss questioned the possibility of one party representing the state. However, these were in the minority, and most prominent democrats agreed with Meinecke, who called for a great, center party. "The goal must be: a great *Staatspartei* of the middle, reaching from Koch-Weser to Lindeiner-Wildau. But it must be striven for along organic, not mechanical, paths."[128] Meinecke, who never ceased urging that parties had to overcome the "partialities" within themselves, was perhaps a more articulate representative of that point of view shared by Gessler, Corwegh, and since the late 1920's by Koch-Weser also: that parties and parliamentarianism were only transient impedimenta; that the state alone—one which could not be identified with any particular constitutional form—survived. It was in part this point of view which was responsible for the abortive alliance with the *Jungdos* and elements of the *Volksnationelen* in the summer of 1930, an alliance which effectively destroyed the German Democratic party as a self-contradictory experiment in pluralism.

At the same time, an effort to qualify the ecumenical statism of the party was reflected in the new economic program that was unveiled at the Mannheim *Parteitag* on October 5, 1929. This document was largely the work of Gustav Stolper who, since 1928, had been working on it at the behest of Koch-Weser. In the program, the true economic position of the Weimar Democrat came through more than ever. First of all, Stolper maintained, the German nation suffered two burdens, lack of capital and payment of reparations.[129] Stolper then went on to say that, since the war, the "power positions" of the classes had changed. Once, the proletariat had been dominated by the bourgeoisie. Now it had become "the politically ruling class."[130] In view of the course of German political and social history during the republic, it is difficult to see what Stolper meant by this. Most probably, he was simply referring to the important role of the SPD as a "Weimar Coalition" partner, either in or out of the government, as well as to the chancellorship of Müller. Now, Stolper said, other classes had to become the objects of social measures—the small farmers, the *Mittelstand*, threatened by large-scale capitalism on the one hand and the proletariat on the other, merchants, and technical employees. The war had ended the ability of these "classes" to support themselves.[131] The state had to step in and assist them. Charges of "statism" were beside the point. Whether one was for it or against it, the state was now in a paramount

---

[125] Institut für Zeitgeschichte, "Zukunftsaufgaben der DDP," in: *Der Demokrat*, 10 Jahrg., Nr. 11/12, 15 Juni, 1929, p. 320.
[126] *Ibid.*
[127] *Ibid.*
[128] Meinecke, "Mindestmandatzahl für die Parteien," in: *Kölnische Zeitung*, 2 Dezember, 1929, *Politische Schriften und Reden*, ed. Georg Kotowski (Darmstadt, 1958), p. 433.
[129] Gustav Stolper, *Die wirtschaftliche-soziale Weltanschauung der Demokratie*, Mannheim Parteitag. 5 Oktober, 1929, Berlin, pp. 5–6.
[130] *Ibid.*, pp. 6–7.
[131] *Ibid.*

position *vis-à-vis* the economy and would remain so for the foreseeable future. Manchester liberalism was finished.[132]

Stolper himself continuously emphasized the role of the state in German economic development. Stolper called for a revision of the Reich finances, with clearer divisions between the uses of those taxes collected at the national, state, or community level.[133] Tax-free income had to be raised from 2400 RM to 2600 RM and, so long as the German economy in both public and private sectors suffered from a lack of capital, income-building and saving had to be encouraged.[134] Stolper called for higher alcohol and tobacco taxes and for the eventual elimination of the tax on trade (*Gewerbsteuer*). This tax had been particularly galling to the trading elements of the *Mittelstand*.[135] To encourage economy in government, all expenditures (*Ausgaben*) ought to be fixed, or at least planned out, for the next ten years, with ample provision made in case of overexpenditure.[136] Over a period of time, the income tax, especially for the lower and lower middle classes, had to be reduced and, at any rate, tax relief provided for those hurt by inflation.[137]

Stolper then went on to consider the "public," i.e., state-owned, area of the economy. This area, always an important one in German life owing, among other things, to the Prussian tradition, had grown for four reasons: (1) political—local and state governments responding to public demands, (2) social—in response to social problems created by the war, (3) financial—lack of capital, loss of credit, etc., and (4) technical—the Reich having to take a hand in such areas as energy exploitation and use.[138] Now, Stolper said, it was necessary for the public sector to be limited to those areas in which it did not compete with the private. Moreover, a sharp line had to be drawn between purely economical spheres of activity and those of a more political nature.[139] Monopolies, which Stolper blamed on a lack of equitable capital distribution throughout the economy, had to be accepted when necessary and combatted when not necessary.[140] As to be expected, Stolper came out against socialism. Capitalism was needed, more than ever before. However, the dehumanization of labor through mechanization had to be ended. Working people needed shorter working days and more variety in their work. Sounding a bit like Bäumer, Stolper declared that labor's problems were "psychic" not material.[141] The workers now had power in the state (!), and still nothing seemed to be going right. The workers had to be made to feel themselves part of something, not simply own the means of production.[142] The SPD, Stolper said, wanted "to proletarianize the owners; we want to make owners of the proletariat." Stolper declared that this was "the cardinal difference which separates us from socialism or Bolshevism."[143] In this context, Stolper, like Erkelenz, came out in favor of schemes of profit-sharing. As for wage hikes, Stolper, contrary to Erkelenz, thought that a bit of working-class self-discipline was necessary. Should one cash in now or, allowing a firm to have more money at its disposal for capital investment, invest in the future?[144]

The "class-struggle" ideology of the SPD had to be combatted at all levels and a general reform of arbitration proceedings had to be undertaken.[145] At the same time, certain industries, e.g., the construction industry, had to receive massive state aid. Housing, after all, was not "an interest problem."[146]

Finally, Stolper listed twelve points which, for him at least (and presumably most of those in the DDP), constituted "Democracy." Emphasized here were such things as the possibility of social and economic equality of interest in a free state, rejection of class struggle or dictatorship, freedom of the individual and of property, the combatting of mass poverty, and faith in the individual rather than the mass. "Democracy believes in free human beings, not in the state machine." However, the state had to guarantee that no single interest group or class "can put its private fate before that of the general community."[147]

What Stolper was calling for was, in reality, more or less the semi-welfare state with which the Western World has become quite familiar especially since World War II. The notion of deficit spending was absent, of course, and, in some strange way, Stolper, in calling for working-class self-discipline regarding wages and a pro-*Mittelstand* policy on the part of the government, did seem to be more openly asserting that what was good for the middle class was good for the country. However, as a bourgeois economist, the author of the Mannheim Program of the DDP only was being honest as to where the interests both of his party and the class it represented truly lay (or where he thought they did, at any rate). Yet, the "above-class" call of the party, the desire to "build bridges" remained unabated. Again, this should not be surprising, in view of the traditional liberal-bourgeois search for that

---

[132] *Ibid.*, p. 8. Whether or not Manchester liberalism ever had played much of a role in the German economy was a moot point, of course. In his *The German Economy: 1870 to the Present*, trans. by Toni Stolper (New York, 1967), Gustav Stolper comes to the conclusion that it did not.
[133] *Ibid.*, pp. 11, 14, 16.
[134] *Ibid.*, pp. 11–12.
[135] *Ibid.*, pp. 13–14.
[136] *Ibid.*, p. 17.
[137] *Ibid.*
[138] *Ibid.*, p. 20.
[139] *Ibid.*, pp. 2, 21.
[140] *Ibid.*, p. 22.
[141] *Ibid.*, p. 28.
[142] *Ibid.*, p. 28.
[143] *Ibid.*, p. 30.
[144] *Ibid.*, p. 32.
[145] *Ibid.*, p. 34.
[146] *Ibid.*
[147] *Ibid.*, pp. 34–42.

"above class" posture which would yet allow this class to keep property and profits intact.

At the party congress, however, Stolper's program did not go unchallenged. Gustav Schneider feared that Stolper's weak stance on wages could be interpreted as being favorable to "yellow" trade unionism. At the same time, he questioned whether profit-sharing schemes had been or ever would be effective. He also viewed Stolper's stand on monopolies as being weak.[148] The Young Democrats also found Stolper's approach to be too conservative. They declared that they did not share the latter's confidence in the system and that the state had to play a far stronger role than that allotted to it by Stolper. More government, rather than private, monopolies were needed.[149] However, the voice of big business, in the form of *Generaldirektor* Andreas Colsmann, declared that Stolper's approach was far too one sided in the other direction; that economic realities were being sacrificed for social goals. The notion that workers ought to share in corporate profits was not really a just one. Did they share in the risks of business, and would they want to share in the risks? Furthermore, Stolper seemed to be accepting public ownership as given. Colsmann saw the need for a more positive statement demanding that the public sector of the economy be greatly limited.[150] At any rate, the attitude of German Democrats towards Stolper's program was mixed. On the one hand, there stood the Young Democrats, Schneider and, for that matter, Erkelenz, who felt that Stolper's program was a concession to the entrepreneurial interests of the party. On the other hand, there stood the business interests themselves, as embodied in Colsmann, the *Hansa Bund,* and Hermann Fischer, who took issue with Stolper's willingness to accept a large public sector of the economy and who questioned the entire profit-sharing scheme. In the end, as we shall see in a later chapter, the Democratic economic program will be a sort of watered-down version of the one offered by Stolper in October, 1929.

Yet, the Stolper program was of immense significance, and, perhaps more clearly than any other action or statement of Germany's Weimar Democrats, reveals why its efforts to "build bridges" between bourgeoisie and proletariat, as serious as such efforts were on the parts of many, had to fail. The bourgeois nature of these German Democrats, amply revealed in a strong statism combined with a functional approach to the economy, made such efforts at national ecumenism futile. At the same time, even in the eyes of members of the German Democratic party, the party was hardly bourgeois enough. The quest for the "party-above-parties" and "above classes" would continue, but in the direction of the right.

At the end of March, 1930, Hermann Müller, harassed by opposition from left and right as he attempted to deal with the massive problems of economic depression, resigned. The Centrist, Heinrich Brüning, who succeeded him, would have the dubious distinction of dissolving the last Reichstag in which the Nazis and the Communists, taken together, constituted a minority of the total number of delegates. He would also have one other dubious distinction, *viz.*, he, in conjunction, of course, with President Hindenburg, would implement Article 48 for the last time. The reason that Article 48 was promulgated concerns the Democrat Hermann Dietrich, who had been minister of food under Müller, at first minister of economics under Brüning and, in July, 1930, had been switched over to the unenviable position of minister of finance (as we have seen Koch-Weser had left the Müller government in April, 1929, because of cabinet reshuffling; and hence Dietrich was the only Democrat left in the cabinet). On July 7, 1930, Dietrich presented his financial proposals to the Reichstag. Dietrich's plan envisioned a drastic cutting of government expenditures, increased direct and indirect taxes and a $2\frac{1}{2}$ per cent tax on the salaries of government officials. All of this was designed, of course, to provide the Reich treasury with an increased cash reserve necessary to meet the exigencies of economic and fiscal crisis, *viz.*, the paying back of short-term loans, bond premiums and the funding of relief projects. Debate on the bill began on July 15, 1930, and almost immediately, it was in trouble. On July 16, 1930, article two of Dietrich's bill, which concerned the tax on the salaries of government officials, was defeated 256 to 193, Social Democrats, Communists, Nazis, and most members of the DNVP joining together to accomplish this. That evening, the cabinet issued two emergency decrees, under powers vested in it by Article 48.

On July 18, 1930, Hermann Dietrich spoke out in defense of the emergency decrees against a Social Democratic motion that they be lifted. His financial measures, i.e., his proposed taxes, were "a necessity of state." He added that the government would "fight for this state with the means that the constitution places at its disposal."[151] Bitterly, he struck out against "interest politics," declaring that the time had come for the German people to decide whether they were "a heap of interests or a state people."[152] Oscar Meyer, a Democratic delegate spoke up, declaring that he had been opposed to the imposition of Article 48. Tragically, he thought, the government had been compelled "to fulfill the duties of the Reichstag."[153] He then went on to recite a rather dreary litany of all the sacrifices made by his party in the name of *Staats-*

---

[148] Bundesarchiv, Koblenz, R 45III/7. Achter ordentlicher Parteitag der DDP am 4/6 Oktober, 1929 in Mannheim, 200–202.

[149] *Ibid.*, pp. 213–214.

[150] *Ibid.*, pp. 208–210.

[151] VR, *op. cit.*, *Wahlperiode 1928. Band 428. Stenographische Berichte.* 6516C.

[152] *Ibid.*, 6517A.

[153] *Ibid.*, 6519A.

politik: his party had been willing to participate in virtually any cabinet, it had worked with the SPD (or tried to), it had always appreciated that state stood above party. All measures, either of the party or of the government to which at least one of its members belonged, had failed. Hence, the emergency decrees were necessary and the Social Democratic motion to annul the decrees had to be defeated.[154] In the voting that followed, the SPD, the Nazis, the Communists, and most members of the DNVP joined together in passing the Social Democratic motion 236 to 222. Displaying a marvelous capacity for political strategy, Brüning then read a presidential decree dissolving the Reichstag. This most unhappy of parliaments would not convene again until after the September 14, 1930, elections, which greatly reduced the strength of the new *Staatspartei,* successor to the German Democratic party. The last role of any appreciable significance had been played out by this party in July, 1930.

Between 1925 and 1930, the German Democratic party was more than ever before on the defensive in regard to republicanism in general and the Weimar Republic in particular. As we have seen, some Democrats, e.g., Theodor Heuss, did rally to the defense of the Weimar Republic, and defense of it continued on the floor of the Reichstag. However, the continued growth of "interest parties" such as the *Wirtschaftspartei,* as well as the DVP and the DNVP, and issues such as the expropriation of princes' wealth, the *Schunde und Schmutzgesezt* and *Panzerschiff A,* which served to separate the German Democratic party from its Weimar Coalition partner, the Social Democratic party, put the Democrats in a very awkward position indeed, this being reflected in the 1928 elections. The problem seemed to be that, because of its superparty position, the DDP could not satisfactorily represent anybody. This was the result of attempting to reconcile a pre-World War I statism with a form of parliamentary democracy which had to be interest-oriented. The Social Democratic party was a class, and hence implicitly interest, party. Such "interest parties" as the *Wirtschaftspartei* quite openly declared that they represented only one group or the other, while the DVP and DNVP, also "class parties" of sorts, could link their particular *Überparteilichkeit* to openly anti-republican sentiments, something which the DDP, also a "class party," although many in it sought not to be too obvious about it, certainly could not do. From 1929 on, of course, anti-republican sentiment grew apace as social and economic disaster beckoned. Such a situation had to doom the DDP.

Yet, even before the crises attendant upon international depression reared their several heads, members of the Democratic party were questioning the very tenets of parliamentary republicanism. Koch-Weser was an example of this, and it is perhaps the best commentary upon Democratic frustrations regarding their increasingly unwanted position as representatives of parliamentary government that Koch-Weser, until 1930 the head of the German Democratic party, wrote a book, *Dennoch aufwarts!* which, appearing in the somewhat fateful year of 1933, contained biting attacks on parliamentarianism as well as upon the avarice of political parties.[155] Assuming, however, that most Weimar-period Democrats did accept parliamentary democracy, either out of *Real*-political motives or, as in the case of Erkelenz, because they genuinely believed in the pluralistic society, the Democrat in particular and his party in general were faced with a rather unhappy paradox: his was the only non-class, non-confessional party which stood for pluralism. Hence, alternately impelled by a desire to provide those traditional bridges between bourgeoisie and proletariat and by a desire to infuse Germany's moribund bourgeoisie with pluralistic vigor, the Democrat and his party had to assume a most non-pluralistic stance. If one were a supporter of Weimar republicanism, one had to vote for the Democrats. As Theodor Heuss somewhat perceptively observed, the party was already in power in the form of the republic.[156] Whatever weaknesses vitiated the latter's effectiveness or aroused the scorn of left- and right-wing opposition, brought also scorn and ridicule upon the members of Germany's most precocious "bowling club," which could respond, of course, only by demanding, in a most unpluralistic manner, that people either vote for or seek unification with the only party which, by virtue of its acceptance of parliamentary democracy in the name of *Staatsnotwendigkeit,* was Germany's true *Staatspartei.* The assuming of the title *Staatspartei* in 1930 was simply the translation of a long, at times desperately, cherished belief into reality.

The survival of a traditional statism had done much to vitiate the somewhat gossamer republicanism of Germany's Democrats. However, particularly in the forming of the *Staatspartei* in 1930, elements of political romanticism, of the new, *völkisch* politics of the twentieth century, could be found.

V. THE WEIMAR DEMOCRATS TURN TOWARD POLITICAL ROMANTICISM. THE FORMATION OF THE *STAATSPARTEI* AND THE BACKGROUND OF THIS ACTION

In the history of German political philosophy, formal statism has always existed in somewhat un-

---

[154] *Ibid.,* 6519A–6519C.

[155] This will be discussed in a later chapter.
[156] Heussarchiv, *Politische Schriften,* 1920, "Zur Problematik der deutschen Parteienpolitik," in: *Die Hilfe,* Nr. 19, 1 Oktober, 1926: p. 408. Also see Sigmund Neumann's discussion of this in his *Die Parteien der Weimarer Republik* (rev. ed., Stuttgart, 1965), p. 49.

comfortable proximity to political romanticism, the linch-pin being an organic approach to political thought and history. Statists tended to view the state as the organic entity worthy of perusal and support; political romantics, on the other hand, tended to be more *völkisch* in their approach. Transition from one point of view to the other was not very difficult inasmuch as it often implied no more than semantic changes. The history of German political liberalism was hardly free from statist elements. Political romanticism was also present in no small degree, and this tended to take two forms: (1) an exalting of youth, not merely in a practical sense, i.e., to draw them into democratic politics, but in a spiritual sense as well; (2) a reaction against modernization, especially the big city, and an anti-Semitic bent that tended to accompany it. Political romanticism was not something that was confined to one group of people but rather was a mood which, from time to time, was shared by virtually all Democrats. However, there can be little doubt that certain Democrats were more prone to this sort of thinking than others, probably the best known of them being Gertrud Bäumer.

The tendency to glorify youth as somehow representing an ingenuous, superpolitical purity was well established in German history before the First World War. More often than not, such a phenomenon was characteristic of the radical right but, by the end of the First World War, rightists, the intellectual left, such as that grouped around the journal *Weltbühne,* and many Democrats all shared a somewhat worshipful attitude towards the younger generation.[1] Among Democrats this phenomenon evidenced itself rather early. From the beginning, some Democrats were concerned with bringing youth into the Democratic orbit and into politics. However, they realized that the amalgam of often inchoate emotions which made youth so attractive could be negative when placed within the realm of political life. An article in *Das demokratische Deutschland,* February 15, 1919, proclaimed that youth had to be trained for politics. Indeed, the article suggested, the German Democratic party had the important task of teaching youth "to think politically" and "to act politically."[2] Youth had to be politicized, even if this meant removing the aura of ingenuous romanticism with which it had been traditionally shrouded. Youthful support of the state was a necessity, but this support had to come from a youth educated to the political realities of republican life.

However, this point of view clashed with another, perhaps more deeply seated one, eloquently expressed by Adele Friedländer. In *Das demokratische Deutschland,* Frau Friedländer made the remark that a youthful political movement could succeed only if it had "a soul."[3] She felt that complete agreement on all important questions could be attained if such an organization of political youth stretched over the entire Reich. What she called for was a "community of conscience," *Gesinnungsgemeinschaft.* Youth could be a source for this, inasmuch as it was characterized by "the belief in the power of the idea. The belief in the power of personality."[4] It was in these areas, she thought, that youth and the old liberalism came together in a fashion propitious for the new republic. Frau Friedländer viewed youth as an eternal source of new ideas and she was enthralled by its ingenuous idealism. Such an attitude was not confined to essayists who wrote in the journals of the German Democratic party. In his 1919 work, *Nach der Revolution,* Friedrich Meinecke himself took occasion to step away from the powder-stained world of *Realpolitik* and to focus upon one of the, to him, primary solutions to Germany's woes. This was to be found in the souls of "happy wandering youth," those merry and seemingly thoughtless vagabonds through whom Germany, around the turn of the century, had gained a new appreciation for its lanscape and *Kultur.*[5] What Meinecke was referring to, of course, was the *Wandervogel,* many of whose members found it disarmingly simple to fuse the study of landforms with *volk*-racism. Meinecke's tendency to overlook such problems was reflected in his previously mentioned 1922 address on the Rathenau murder. As discussed above, while he attacked the youth of the radical right for its lack of balance and for its reactionary activities, he was careful to concede that rightwing youth was "easier to work with" than the youth of the left.[6]

Ernst Lemmer, who was closely associated with the Young Democrats, in an article appearing in the *Berliner Tageblatt* on August 20, 1921, reported on a week-long meeting of Democratic Youth. "The week's work was dominated not by considerations of appearances, nor tactics, but by will, without dogmatic adherence to clarity, and to the setting-up of spiritual/political goals."[7] Lemmer went on to claim that youth was not romantic, but that it still shrank away from party discipline and routine. Lemmer's enthusiasm

---

[1] On the leftist worship of youth see Istvan Deak, *Weimar Germany. Left-wing Intellectuals: Die Weltbühne, A Political History of the Weltbühne and Its Circle* (Berkeley, California, 1968).

[2] Preussisches Geheimes Staatsarchiv, Berlin, Hauptabteilung XII-III. "Die Demokratische Jugendbewegung," in: *Das demokratische Deutschland,* 1 Jahrg., Nr. 10, 15 Feb., 1919, pp. 230–231.

[3] *Ibid.* Adele Friedländer, "Von der Seele der Jungdemokraten," in: *Das demokratische Deutschland,* 1 Jahrg., Nr. 30, 6 July, 1919: p. 711.

[4] *Ibid.,* p. 712.

[5] Friedrich Meinecke, *Nach der Revolution* (München, 1919) pp. 69–70.

[6] Friedrich Meinecke, *Politische Schriften und Reden,* ed. George Kotowski (Darmstadt, 1958), p. 339.

[7] Preussisches Geheimes Staatsarchiv, Hauptabteilung XII-III, Ernst Lemmer "Jugend und Partei," in: Berliner Tageblatt, Nr. 393, 20 August, 1921, quoted in *Der Demokrat: Mitteilungen aus der Deutschen demokratischen Partei,* 2 Jahrg., Nr. 30, 22 September, 1921: p. 744.

over German youth, though, would seem to indicate that his attitude towards it was hardly negative, despite his strictures against its lack of discipline. However, there could be little doubt that the German Democratic party was whistling in the dark insofar as its ability to obtain or retain a hold on German youth was concerned. Ernst Lemmer, Kurt Wolf, and others might well have been making strenuous efforts to exalt youth and to maintain the Democratic Youth organizations as viable elements within the party life; but, by 1922, it had become obvious to many that youth was abandoning both the Democratic party in particular and the republic in general. At a meeting of the party *Vorstand* on June 26, 1922, Heinrich Landahl warned: "The danger is at hand that this youth will desert the party and all other coalition parties and seek out new forms." [8]

The party's answer to this threat was to attempt to keep the allegiance of youth by becoming more radical, in a spiritual sense at any rate. The January 5, 1923, issue of *Der Demokrat* was introduced by appropriate quotations from the racist-nationalists Paul de Lagarde and Treitschke, the gist of them being that youth always will be ready to fight for a concrete ideal.[9] Perhaps the youth-oriented egalitarianism of these individuals blinded the party to the vicious racism espoused in other, perhaps better-known, writings. However, this incident pointed to a characteristic response of many German Democrats to the threat posed by youth's streaming to the right: the attempt to head off such desertions by stealing some of the *völkisch*-idealistic thunder that had always been characteristic of German right-wing radicalism. Many Democrats viewed youth as somehow representing a unity that transcended the realm of parliamentary disorder and party bickering. We have already seen the attitudes of both Corwegh and Wolf on this; Corwegh criticizing parliamentary disorders in part because they alienated youth, while Wolf exalted the youthful ideal of a unified state above parliamentary bickering and dissention which he said characterized liberalism. As democratic critics of parliamentarians became ever more vociferous, demands for a spiritual rejuvenation of the party as well as for fusions with non-party bundist groups grew apace.

As might be expected, one of the most vociferous supporters of this new direction was Gertrud Bäumer, the party's leading exponent of political romanticism. Bäumer, whose somewhat mystical views of state leadership and the *Volk* would lead her to write one of the most mystical political diatribes ever produced by a Democrat (*Sinn und Formen Geistiger Führung*, 1930) was quick to seize upon a Democratic party/bundist union as representing a way out of parliamentary stagnation. In an article that appeared in *Die Hilfe* after the election disaster of May 20, 1928, Bäumer claimed that the loss of the German Democratic party was due to people voting along interest lines. The democratic spirit, she said, was not something which drew sustenance only from material and social interests. It was in this context that she turned towards a new phenomenon, the *Jungdeutsche Orden*. This group might well have presented a rather inchoate picture, however Bäumer spoke approvingly of its opposition to the "party essence." [10] Significantly enough, she tied this somewhat positive attitude towards the *Jungdos* with a virulent attack upon big-city cynicism and moral relativism:

This democracy, which is rooted, not in the pompous relativism of liberal big-city dwellers, but in many *völkisch* and soil-bound strengths . . . is conservative-bourgeois in all questions of conscience.[11]

The average supporter of democracy, she maintained, was a believer in firm religious and moral principles and, like her, he was angered by the cosmopolitan cynicism evidenced in the *Berliner Tageblatt*.[12] The old Weimar coalition, she remarked, was *kaputt* and a new alliance between the DDP and the DVP, while possible, was not likely. What was really needed, was a new weaving-together of liberal, social, and Fascist elements.[13] She saw youth as a necessary ingredient in bringing this new party into being.

Gertrud Bäumer's opinions as expressed in this article were of immense significance in that they pointed to several elements which were present in the *Weltanschauungen* of many Democrats. Most important of these was a tendency towards flirtation with romantic ideas and a concurrent tendency to deprecate the cosmopolitan cynicism that they associated with big cities and, as we shall see later, when we focus upon the problem of anti-Semitism, with the Jews. Suspicious of parties and parliament, and seeing their suspicions confirmed in the chaos of Weimar political life, many Democrats turned towards a fusion with avowed superpolitical bundists as a way out of the spiritual impasse in which they found themselves. As we have seen, even Erkelenz had expressed some interest in the *Jungdos,* although it was an interest that was rather quickly dissipated.

There was, of course, yet another reason why the German Democrats gradually drew closer (or attempted to) to the youthful idealists of the 1920's. As we have seen earlier, the Democrats were well aware of the fact that German youth was tending more and more to eschew republican politics. Consequently,

---

[8] Bundesarchiv, Koblenz, *Sitzungen des Vorstandes der DDP,* R 45/III/18, *57–58.*

[9] Institut für Zeitgeschichte, *Der Demokrat,* 4 Jahrg., Nr. 1, 5, January, 1923: p. 1.

[10] Gertrud Bäumer, "Konsequenzen des Wahlausfalles," in: *Die Hilfe,* Nr. 12, 15, Juni, 1928: p. 270.

[11] *Ibid.*

[12] *Ibid.*, p. 271.

[13] *Ibid.*

the flirtations with such groups as the *Jungdeutsche Orden* must be viewed as being, in part, dictated by tactical considerations. This was certainly the case for Koch-Weser, who can hardly be described as having been a wild-eyed romantic. However, for such people as Bäumer, and others whom we have considered earlier, a strong streak of political romanticism had been part of their political *Anschauungen* from the beginning. Moreover, the feeling on the part of many Democrats, from Koch-Weser to Bäumer, that it was necessary for German democracy to turn towards youthful, *völkisch* and, to a large extent, antipolitical support, is a rather poignant commentary upon state of German bourgeois political life during the Weimar period. The image of the German Democratic party, i.e., that of a predominately bourgeois party rooted in the city and deriving considerable support from Jews, "plutocrats," and liberal cosmopolites, had to be radically altered, if not expunged altogether. At the same time, of course, efforts to achieve some sort of alliance with the *Orden* were part of the continuous Democratic drive (at least on the part of its leadership) to broaden its shrinking electoral base. Talk of fusion with the DVP remained constant throughout, although most Democrats seemed to be aware of the increasingly conservative course of the party, especially since the death of Stresemann.[14]

By 1929 Democratic interest in party rejuvenation and in youthful spiritualizing of political life had achieved an apogee. One of the most interesting articles to appear on the subject was published in the January 1, 1929, issue of *Die Hilfe* by a Dr. Kneisel. In this article, entitled "Demokratie und Jugend," Kneisel reminded the party—as if it needed any reminding—that youth had been totally alienated from democracy. The problem, he said, was not merely that of youth, but of the German people as a whole who, he maintained, were by and large unpolitical in nature. Rather, they tended to be moved by feelings, fantasy, and atmosphere.[15] The democratic *Volksstaat* would be far more effective, he thought, if it could be viewed as something deeply rooted in German history, if it could draw upon those irrational strengths as captured in art and in poetry.[16] The forces of reaction, he warned, were already making use of historical myth in rallying support to their cause. If youth in particular and the German people in general were to be won for the democratic republic, its defenders would have to endeavor to do the same.[17] Dr. Kneisel was not alone in urging the party to make better use of the impedimenta of mass political life, movies, visual and oral propaganda, etc. What is of particular interest for us, though, is his assertion that youth itself was irrational, and that this irrationality had to be accommodated.

In the April 15, 1929, issue of *Die Hilfe,* Anton Erkelenz also made a point of reflecting upon the irrationalities that seemed to motivate and to drive German youth. Here, he focused primarily upon that calling card to right-wing irrationalism, the "front experience"; something which, Erkelenz suggested, had become of inordinate importance to the young. To be sure, he noted, many of the "older" generation had also been exposed to this experience, but such an occurrence was psychologically more important for the young, inasmuch as it had occurred at the beginning of life. The older generation, on the other hand, had had many of its views formed before the war.[18] Youth today, Erkelenz dilated, was neither politically educated nor politically active. Those who had matured before the war had had the invaluable experience of acting politically, of attempting to reform the state of the Hohenzollerns.[19] While attacking the immaturity and presumptuousness of German youth, Erkelenz did display his usual somewhat guarded interest in the *Jungdos*. It was, he thought, somewhat difficult to grasp what this group really had in mind and to discern what was merely propaganda for them and what was "factual reality" as they conceived it.[20] Yet he expressed admiration for their attempts to rise above factionalism, while hoping that they would be a bit more concrete in regard to a political program.[21] While Erkelenz was somewhat uncertain as to what position the German Democratic party ought to take in regard to the *Jungdos,* the party *Ausschuss* itself was not quite so hesitant and, at a meeting in Leipzig on April 28, 1929, Helmut Jaeger mentioned that feelers had already been sent out to the *Jungdos* and that he hoped that something useful would come of them.[22]

If Erkelenz was undecided and the party committee as yet uncommitted as to what position the Democratic party ought to take in regard to the *Jungdos,* Bäumer approached the issue with that romantic attitude with which she is so often identified. On June 1, 1929, in an article in *Die Hilfe,* she pointed with satisfaction to a radio discussion that Koch-Weser had had with Artur Mahraun, *Hochmeister* of the *Jungdeutsche Orden,* on May 26 of that year. The *Jungdos,* she said, were not critical of the techniques of parliamentarianism, but of its accomplishments. The *Jungdos*

---

[14] As an example of this, see the report on the May 5, 1930, meeting of the party *Vorstand*. Bundesarchiv, Koblenz, p. 45 III/22 Sitzungen des Vorstandes der DDP (Protokolle), 1930. Especially, pp. 28–30.

[15] R. Kneisel (no first name given), "Demokratie und Jugend," in: *Die Hilfe,* Nr. 1, 1 January, 1929: p. 14.

[16] *Ibid.,* p. 15.

[17] *Ibid.*

[18] Anton Erkelenz, "Jung und Alte," in: *Die Hilfe,* Nr. 8, 15 April, 1929, p. 180.

[19] *Ibid.,* p. 181.

[20] *Ibid.,* pp. 181–182.

[21] *Ibid.*

[22] Bundesarchiv, Sitzungen des Parteiausschuss der DDP, R 45/III/15, 18.

were, after all, idealistic young men who felt themselves to be bound to the state and to a system of super-partyism.[23] They sensed "idealism as a *Real*-political force" and were opposed to interest politics and to that enervating cynicism that had become associated with German political life.[24] Referring with some approval to one of the *Jungdos*' heroes, she remarked that the source of Mussolini's strength was "that he dared, as a politician, to appeal to the peoples' thoughts of and readiness for sacrifice."[25] Bäumer, like Erkelenz, noted that the *Jungdeutsche Orden*, for all of its idealism, seemed to lack a true political program, and she attacked Mahraun's somewhat medieval notion of basing political life upon an organic "neighborhood principle." Such a thing would fragment political life even further.[26] However, on the whole, Bäumer's view of the *Jungdos* was a positive one indeed. Erich Koch-Weser, who had been in contact with the *Jungdos* for some time, took the occasion on July 15, 1929, to call upon the DDP to reach out for youth more than ever. In all of this, the organizations of Democratic Youth were far from silent and the July 15, 1929, issue of *Der Demokrat* reported that the Young Democrats of East Prussia had sharply criticized the German Democratic party for its lack of youthfulness.[27] A later issue, that of August 15, 1929, contained a plea of the German Young Democrats for an all-Europe youth war against Fascism and Bolshevism, indicating that, to some extent at least these Young Democrats were somewhat to the left of such lovers of youth as Bäumer who, as we have seen, saw things to admire in Fascism and in Mussolini.

Despite occasionally professed loyalties to parliamentary democracy, the impetus for some sort of alliance with idealistic youth was too great to be overcome, and in the summer of 1930 the new *Staatspartei* was proclaimed, a party which initially drew much of its support from Mahraun's *Jungdeutsche Orden*. As we shall see, not all Democrats welcomed this fusion with enthusiasm, some actually resigning from the party. For the time being, though, we must consider what the *Jungdeutsche Orden* and its party Führer, Artur Mahraun, actually represented.

The *Jungdeutsche Orden* was established in 1920. The manifesto was in large part written by Mahraun himself and, although some splintering within the *Orden* did occur between 1929 and 1930, most of the points were adhered to with considerable assiduousness. In some ways, the manifesto utilized much of the rhetoric of the formal political parties. It called for a *Volksstaat* with *Staat* and *Volk* becoming one.[28] However, it also reflected that spiritual impact which the First World War had upon the younger generation. In this regard, "the community of front-comradeship" was emphasized.[29] To those who had participated in the war (the *Feldgrauen*), "war is the highest moral aspect of the citizen's fulfillment of duty."[30] The real enemy to Germany was viewed as being plutocracy and "the monied interests." They, plus the continued domination of Roman Law, represented divisive and spiritually enslaving powers that were fast sapping Germany's strength, and, as such, they had to be suppressed. Naturally, the temptation to refine a general attack on plutocracy into a doctrine of consistent anti-Semitism was great indeed, and many of the *Jungdos* displayed extreme forms of anti-Semitism, while the order itself was closed to Jews. However, at least in the manifesto, anti-Semitism was not terribly strong, Mahraun in fact indicating that anti-Semitic doctrines had been vitiating to previous national movements.[31] Nevertheless, there could be little doubt that the movement as a whole took a decidedly unfriendly attitude towards Jews. Such an approach was dictated by the negative attitude displayed by the movement in regard to the cities. Strong attacks upon the "rootless, city elements" were also to be found in the manifesto, as well as constant emphases upon the virtues of rootedness.[32] In discussing religion, Mahraun was careful to point out that in his view every Christian was entitled to his own church. Germany was, in his eyes, a Christian state, and it is interesting to note that this was one of the few actual *Jungdo* points that was carried over into the manifesto of the *Staatspartei*.[33]

As regards parliamentarianism and political parties, the attitude of the *Jungdos* was indeed negative. Mahraun viewed parties as inimical to the unity of *Volk*, and he made the petulant observation that other *völkisch* movements (one presumes the Nazi were included) were losing their strengths because they were rooted in the party system.[34] As Mosse points out, the *Jungdos* were too elitist to participate in vulgar mass politics, and this estrangement from the masses naturally led them to take a dim view of all political parties while at the same time working to limit their own strength.[35] Naturally, the *Orden* was anti-republican, being opposed to any political order "which contradicts the predetermined essence of the Ger-

---

[23] Gertrud Bäumer, "Das Ethos der Politik," in: *Die Hilfe*, Nr. 11, 1 June, 1929, p. 268.
[24] *Ibid.*
[25] *Ibid.*, p. 269.
[26] *Ibid.*
[27] Institut für Zeitgeschichte, München, "Jungdemokratische Arbeit in Ostpreussen," in: *Der Demokrat*, 10 Jahrg., Nr. 13/14, 15 Juli, 1929: p. 373.

[28] Artur Mahraun, *Das Jungdeutsche Manifest* (2nd ed., Berlin, 1928), p. 4.
[29] *Ibid.*, p. 8.
[30] *Ibid.*, p. 9.
[31] *Ibid.*, p. 22.
[32] *Ibid.*, p. 174.
[33] *Ibid.*, p. 180.
[34] *Ibid.*, p. 22.
[35] George L. Mosse, *The Crisis of German Ideology* (New York, 1964), p. 228.

man."[36] Instead, it took a firm stand upon the grounds of a pure German idealism—"the moral foundation of the *Volksstaat*"— which consisted of cheerful fulfillment of the citizen's duty and subordination of the individual to the interests of the whole.[37] "This German idealism," Mahraun went on to say, "is the mystique of the front race, from which it draws its entire strength."[38] With such an outlook, it was not surprising that Mahraun placed emphasis upon the role of the hero: "The fanatic schemes; the heroic man affirms."[39] Great emphasis was placed upon political responsibility for the individual citizen. However, almost in the same breath, Mahraun went on to proclaim that the *Volksstaat* of the future would be based not upon freedom, but duty.[40] He called not for a mass state, but for a true *Volksgemeinschaft*, and like so many who have played around with that mystical but explosive term, he saw parliaments as being divisive of the *Volk*.[41] The basic unit of the *Volksgemeinschaft* was to be the neighborhood (*Nachbarschaft*). The leader (*Führer*) of the organic *Volksstaat* was to be a man bound by heart to his followers (*Gefolgschaft*).[42]

Naturally, Mahraun was in favor of plebiscites as opposed to formal elections, and he called for a free economy with responsibility to the whole. To handle those problems regarding women and culture, Mahraun proposed the establishing of a *Frauenkammer* and a *Kulturkammer*. Calls for the return of colonies, internal settlement, and the return of the Polish Corridor rounded out the manifesto of the *Jungdeutsche Orden*. This was the group that had been so lauded by Bäumer and patronized by individuals like Koch-Weser. All in the German Democratic party must have known that, insofar as the party was at least formally committed to republicanism, alliance with this collection of medieval bundists would be tantamount to intellectual suicide. Certainly, it was such for the party as a whole, at least to the degree that it remained committed to the program of December, 1919. However, for many so-called Democrats, commitment to the republic and commitment to Germany had become two different things. We have already seen how statism had remained snugly ensconced within Democratic ranks during the Weimar period. Romanticism, e.g., that of Bäumer, was the primary impetus, besides that one provided by tactical considerations, which drove Germany's Democrats—or at least those in the party—to ally themselves with *völkisch* youth.

It is only fair to point out that, despite his admiration for the idealistic strengths that Mussolini had been able to arouse among Italians, Mahraun remained somewhat suspicious of Italy and of Italians. He tended to view Italy as being weak in human and material resources, dependent to a great extent upon England and, because of the vexing question of the Tyrol, more of an enemy than a friend to Germany.[43] By 1929 the *Orden* seemed to be eager to find expression for its curious *völkisch* notions within established political forms, e.g., the German Democratic party.[44] Nevertheless, Mahraun's group, despite official disavowals of anti-Semitism, anti-republican sentiments, and so on, was to a large extent irrational and *völkisch* in its approach to political life. It was hardly a group devoted to parliamentary democracy and the pluralistic society.

Certainly, German Democrats, particularly those in the party, had some notion as to what the *Jungdeutsche Orden* was all about, even if they had not read the complete manifesto. Mahraun himself had been in contact with Koch-Weser for some time. In a revealing letter of April 23, 1930, which should have been an eye-opener for Koch-Weser as well, Mahraun spoke of his plans to talk with members of the *Volksnationelen* as well as with Koch-Weser himself over the formation of the new *Staatspartei*. As particularly important goals, Mahraun emphasized, "human beings rooted in and bound to the soil of the homeland," the fight against mechanization and class division and the advancement of the true "Christian/conservative spirit."[45] How the latter point might have struck Koch-Weser, who, as we have seen, was in part of Jewish ancestry, is an interesting question. However, in Mahraun's further call for "renewal of the party essence itself," he was in full agreement with Koch-Weser who had despaired of party life earlier, and with such unregenerated political conservatives as Friedrich Meinecke. Certainly, many Democrats hardly viewed their flirtation with political obscurantism as representing a sacrifice of principle, and the German Democratic party pressed ever closer towards the goal of unification with the *Jungdeutsche Orden* and the political party tied to the *Orden*, the *Volksnationelen*.

At the same time, Koch-Weser was also concerned with that hoary task of somehow bringing in the DVP to add to a broadly based coalition of the middle. However, negotiations between the DDP and DVP came under fire from the left wing of the former, and he was gradually forced to eschew such efforts. Negotiations between the two parties came to an end in May, 1930. Those with the *Volksnationelen* and the *Jungdeutsche Orden* continued, however, and on July 27, 1930, the formation of the new *Staatspartei* was announced.[46]

---

[36] *Ibid.*, p. 37.
[37] *Ibid.*, pp. 40–41.
[38] *Ibid.*, p. 41.
[39] *Ibid.*, p. 45.
[40] *Ibid.*, p. 49.
[41] *Ibid.*, pp. 61–63.
[42] *Ibid.*, p. 121.

[43] Mahraun, *Gegen getarnte Gewalten* (Berlin, 1928), pp. 89 ff. Cited in Klaus Hornung's *Der Jungdeutsche Orden* (Düsseldorf, 1958), p. 48.
[44] See Hornung, especially pp. 87–90.
[45] Bundesarchiv, Nachlass Koch-Weser, Nr. 101, 105.
[46] *Ibid.*

Not all Democrats were thrilled by the efforts of the German Democratic party to add a sort of *völkisch* zest to its platform. Most prominent among them was Anton Erkelenz who, on July 29, 1930, sent a telegram indicating his resignation from the party to Koch-Weser. The party, Erkelenz indicated, had done great things on behalf of parliamentarianism and democracy, and it had striven to ameliorate the problems that had developed between left and right in Germany. However, the ruling clique had little real understanding of internal and foreign policies, and more important, it had become victimized by "nationalistic and anti-socialistic" slogans. The party had abandoned the workers, one of the best defenses of the republic, and Erkelenz felt that he could do more fighting on their side. Hence, he was leaving the German Democratic party for the Social Democrats.[47] Koch-Weser, it seems, took little notice of this. Indeed, in response to DVP criticism of the new *Staatspartei* he sent a letter to Ernst Scholz asking whether his party now would be ready to participate in the great adventure of the new *Staatspartei*.[48] The offer was spurned. Ludwig Quidde also departed to form the little-known *Radikaldemokratische Partei*.

On the right, the *Hansa Bund* representation in the DDP hardly greeted the formation of the new party with enthusiasm. Supporting the statist economic policies of the Brüning government, in which Hermann Dietrich, as finance minister, was playing an important role, had been difficult enough for these more-or-less traditional capitalists.[49] Now, this union with a collection of seemingly radical romantics, who denounced "plutocrats" with great vehemence, was just one more difficult thing to swallow for those representatives of big business who had chosen to place their faith in republicanism.[50] Hermann Fischer and company remained with the party, or rather, became part of the new *Staatspartei,* but with somewhat muted enthusiasm.

Gertrud Bäumer tried to cast oil upon politically troubled waters. In an article, "Generationspolitik," she admitted that youth was a bit fuzzy as to actual state forms. However, state thought was strong among them, and their emphasis upon positive "national goals" represented a definite improvement upon party politics.[51] She then mentioned letters from Josef Winschuh and others, all praising the efforts to form a new, unified *Staatspartei*. The August 20, 1930, issue of *Der Demokrat* contained articles by Lemmer and Hermann Dietrich calling, in the first case, for youth to wage war upon divisiveness by joining the new *Staatspartei,* and, in the second, for radical reforms of party structures and an overthrow of interest-politics.[52] The DDP, Dietrich declared, was ready for a new party of the middle. Now, it was up to such parties as the DVP to recapture state thought and develop a progressive outlook, "the preconditions," Dietrich thought, "for the maintenance of the parliamentary system in Germany."[53] Such a statement must have struck many as a bit ironic in view of the attitudes held by that group with whom the befuddled Democrats were seeking an alliance. However, consistency, at least in regard to the defense of parliamentarian principles, had never been a strong point of Weimar Democrats.

Fusion with the *Jungdos* and elements of the *Volksnationalen* was unavoidable and, on August 22, 1930, a manifesto of the new *Deutsche Staatspartei* appeared. The points of this manifesto were the following.[54]

1. "State/political renewal." Here, the *Staatspartei* called for the "development of the German Republic into a true social and national German *Volksstaat*. This *Volksstaat* should be built upon the living unity of *Volk* and *Staat*. Power stems from the *Volk*." The *Staatspartei* called for a new voting law, a parliament free from the politics and machinations of the various classes and groups, a parliament whose policies would "serve the well-being of the collective *Volk,* the economy and the state."

2. The German *Staatspartei* proclaimed that it stood on "communal *Volk* foundations" and it declared that special allegiances to confessional, economic, and class interest groups were contrary to the interests of the whole.

3. It stood for a voting reform and against the evils of the "present party system." It came out in favor of smaller electoral districts (*Wahlkreise*) so as to "elevate personal qualities" and thus make personality important in elections.

4. The *Staatspartei* called for reform of the *Länder* and the *Länder* parliaments and for a strong, centralized Reich power. Like Koch-Weser and others, it called for the end of particularism and for the binding together of Prussian and Reich governments.

5. It called for governmental reform insofar as office-holding was concerned. State servants and public officials ought to be selected on a non-party basis, with talent as the only criterion.

6. The new party boldly announced that it would approach issues only from a "state-political point of view," and that it was against the SPD if it threatened to harm the state. The party also declared itself against "any attempt to erect a dictatorship of the minority."

7. The party called for unity in foreign policy and for revision of the 1919 treaties. It also called for revision of the Young Plan.

---

[47] *Ibid.,* Nr. 105, 61.
[48] *Ibid.,* 159.
[49] See Hermann Fischer's later comments on this to Dietrich at the September 11, 1932 meeting of the *Gesamtvorstand,* as quoted in footnote number 10, page 56 of Erich Matthias and Rudolf Morsey, *Das Ende der Parteien 1933* (Düsseldorf, 1960).
[50] Hornung, *op. cit.,* pp. 100–101.
[51] Gertrud Bäumer, "Generationspolitik," in: *Die Hilfe,* Nr. 32, 9 August, 1930: p. 796.

[52] Institut für Zeitgeschichte, Ernst Lemmer, "An die junge Generation," and Hermann Dietrich. "Die Staatspartei Kampft für Deutschlands Zukunft," in: *Der Demokrat,* 11 Jahrg., Nr. 16, 20 August, 1930: pp. 359–362.
[53] *Ibid.,* p. 363.
[54] The following is a precis of the *Staatspartei* Manifesto of August 22, 1930, as presented in Wolfgang Treue's *Deutsche Parteiprogramme, 1861–1954* (Göttingen, 1954), pp. 148–151.

8. The party demanded "a settlement policy which will create a healthy balance between the over-populated west and the under-populated east." The party also picked up an earlier notion of the old Democratic party by declaring that it was in favor of establishing a ring of German farm settlements in the east in order to establish "a peaceful fortification line of German culture and of German soil."

9. The party called for the overthrow of caste and class prejudices. "The citizen of a *Staatsvolk* should not be evaluated according to his ancestry and possessions, but according to the value of the individual for the duration and the future of *Volk* and *Staat*."

The briefest section of the manifesto was that devoted to "cultural-political clarification." However, it was in many ways the most interesting, inasmuch as it evidenced many of the emotional longings of Germany's Weimar Democrats. The following points constituted the *Staatspartei's* program on cultural policy:

1. First of all, the party declared that the basis of cultural policy was "the national unity of the German *Volk*." It called for "respect for the traditional values of the German past" combined with "proud beliefs in the future of the nation." In a broader sense "German cultural policy should substitute the soulish values of German humanity for the presently overvalued material interests and economic advantages."

2. The party proclaimed that German culture was a Christian one and that the state should preserve it as such.

3. Religious differences ought to be respected, the party declared, but attempts should be made to bridge them over and to allow each religion to contribute to and to serve the *Volk* community.

4. The party placed great emphasis on youth and upon education for all, particularly insofar as it created a sense of *völkisch* unity and consciousness of duty to youth. The schools had to become centers of religious and moral strengths. Education for all, regardless of social class, was demanded. Basically, the *Staatspartei* was calling for that same unified school system that had been so strongly espoused by the Democratic party.

5. The party declared that all influences that were destructive or divisive of the *Volk* were to be fought, while healthy strengths and influences were to be encouraged. Such a notion fit in rather well with the thinking of such people as Heuss and Bäumer, who took, as we have seen, stands against what they considered to be forces of degeneration.

On questions of economic and social policy, the *Staatspartei* was a bit more detailed than the old Democratic party had been.

1. First of all, the party called for reform of the state and "reconstruction of its governmental and taxation system." The state controlled over half of the income of the *Volk* anyway; therefore, the party felt, it had responsibility for equal distribution, the building of capital and accumulation of capital.

2. The party came out in favor of private enterprise and against "all socialistic experimentation." Here, it bore a marked resemblance to the early demands of the Democrats in 1919. It resembled the old Democrats to the extent that it demanded that all have access to gaining property and that economic leaders had to show a social conscience.

3. A new tax policy was called for, one which would be responsive to economic pressures within the various classes and would "encourage elevation of income and property development in all levels of the *Volk*." The middle class was too heavily taxed, the party declared.

4. The party called for a renewal of financial responsibility on the part of communities.

5. The party called for state support of the various self-help agencies in society.

6. The party demanded a stock law "which protects the stock owner against governmental arbitrariness and the misuse of capital power."

7. The party demanded that the public be protected against cartels and monopolies and such things as price fixing.

8. The party demanded a trade policy which recognized the "involvement of the German economy in the world economy" and secured the economic interests of Germany *vis-à-vis* the world.

9. The party demanded that public involvement in the economy be limited to those areas in which public ownership was more efficient and cheaper than private ownership.

10. The party demanded sharp control over public-controlled industries and their tax equalization with private industries.

11. The party called for the support of German agriculture through the lowering of taxes and interest rates and through technological and organizational measures which would allow it successfully to hold its place in relation to foreign competition.

12. The party called for the securing of the social security system of Germany, particularly its protection against reaction. "Social policy should be borne by the social conscience of the entire *Volk*."

13. It demanded active and "responsibility-conscious labor unions," and the protection of workers' rights, "above all, strongest protection of older employees."

14. The party called for the reform of arbitration or settlement laws in the interests of social peace, reforms which would "prohibit a one-sided misuse of them to the detriment of the economy or of social well-being."

What the *Staatspartei* in fact represented was a step in the direction of the functional state. Classes were to remain classes, yet all were to serve the state. The state was to abstain from direct economic influence except when such an influence would be beneficial to the public order. In a way, such an attitude, at least in economics, bore a marked resemblance to American New Deal policy in the 1930's, or, more generally, to the sort of welfare-statism that has become a mode of life in the West since World War II. However, there was a difference here, a difference which concerned the definitions of state and political life. These definitions can be discerned in the very first point of the *Staatspartei* manifesto. We shall recall that the *Staatspartei* called for a parliament that would "serve the well-being of the collective *Volk*, the economy and the state." In essense, the party was calling for the subordination of class and group interests to a state which it itself, by virtue of its title, was claiming to represent. The party, point two declared, "stood on communal *Volk* foundations." In other words, the party stood above class or special interests and was declaring itself to be a party of all the people. In a very real sense, those views which were implicitly represented in the formation of the Democratic party in 1918/1919, which had become ever more explicit during the 1920's, now were expressed in the *Staatspartei* platform. One could, however, also observe a certain *völkisch* slant that had been absent from the earlier platform of the Democratic party. The emphases upon the *Volksgemeinschaft,* moreover, one that was "Christian," pointed in this direction.

As for republicanism, this approach which had been, at least formally, the *raison d'être* of the original Democratic party, was virtually abandoned. Point one emphasized that the republic was to constitute merely a step in the direction of a higher form of *Volksstaat.* The traditional role of parliament, that of representing various interest groups whose attitudes and demands would be subjected to mediation and compromise, had been abandoned and, as seen above, it was now seen as a tool of the unified *Volksstaat.*

As a whole, Germany's Democrats expressed satisfaction with this, as events would prove, very temporary alliance with state and *Volk*-conscious youth, and they hastened to voice exuberant hosannas over the new party. Hermann Dietrich, the somewhat harassed Democratic finance minister, in a speech made at Karlsruhe on August 4, 1930—eighteen days before the appearance of the manifesto—called for a rebirth of idealism and for a new *Staatsvolk.* "Young men to the front," he proclaimed. "Away with senile parties. Away with dictatorship games." [55] Friedrich Meinecke, in the *Kölnische Zeitung,* August 3, 1930, talked of the need for "large, healthy state parties" and for a concurrent limitation upon the powers of parliamentarianism.[56] He hoped that the secession of Treviranus and Westarp from the DNVP could lead to the formation of a "large, conservative *Staatspartei,* which would augment that *Staatspartei* that was being formed in the center.[57] The new journal of the *Staatspartei, Mitteillungen des deutsche Staatspartei,* in its issue of September 18, 1930, proclaimed that the major purpose of the party was the following:

The German *Staatspartei* does not have the intention, as did earlier parties, of being merely an organization whose purpose is votes. It wants to be a living, *Volk*-movement which will not be ruled by a party apparatus, but whose spirit is itself governed by the *Volksstaat* idea.[58]

With some pride, the journal announced that Artur Mahraun had been made "extraparliamentary Reichsführer" of the *Staatspartei.*[59] The sight of Democrats calling for "large *Staatsparteien* throughout the political spectrum" and exulting in the supplanting of political parties by a "living, *Volk*-movement"—to say nothing of their satisfaction in establishing the post of "extraparliamentary *Reichsfuhrer*"—is perhaps one of the most singular commentaries upon the weakness of parliamentary democracy in Weimar Germany.

The coalition that constituted the *Staatspartei* did not last very long. As Theodor Heuss points out in his *Erinnerungen,* the *Jungdos*' medieval romanticism did not provide the basis for much interest in day-to-day political life.[60] Furthermore, in the Reichstag elections of September 14, 1930, which saw the Nazis obtain 107 seats while the *Staatspartei* obtained only 20 (down 5 from the DDP Mandates in the May 20, 1928, elections), more than half of the *Jungdos,* according to Heuss in a letter of October 13, 1930, voted Nazi.[61] A considerable amount of distrust began to be evidenced against that portion of idealistic youth with which German's half-hearted Democrats had hoped to ally themselves. On their part, the *Jungdos* felt uncomfortable in a party which many Democrats saw as simply being a continuation of the old German Democratic party. On October 3, 1930, Mahraun wrote a letter to Koch-Weser expressing the above sentiments, which marked the formal withdrawal of his quaint organization from the coalition.[62] Six of the twenty *Staatspartei* delegates elected to the Reichstag, *Jungdo* delegates, left immediately. Because of his role in the ill-conceived and, more important, unsuccessful attempt at amalgamation of *Biedermeier* and youthful radicalism, Koch-Weser was forced to resign not merely his chairmanship, but even his mandate.

Despite the considerable disappointment of having a sizable portion of the *Staatspartei* coalition pack up and leave, the Democratic wing persisted in its goal of forming a superparty *Staatspartei.* The manifesto of August 22, 1930, was never rejected or even revised and, at an "extraordinary *Reichsparteitag*" of November 8–November 9, 1930, at Hannover, the old German Democratic party officially became the *Staatspartei,* Hermann Dietrich assuming formal leadership. In a speech on the first day, honorary chairman Petersen, who had headed the party after the death of Naumann in 1919, spoke a brief eulogy over the corpse of the old Democratic party. This party, he said, was the only one besides the Centre, that had "unconditionally and without reservation, given credence to the *Volksstaat.*"[63] In pursuit of this goal, the party had had to perform many unpleasant tasks. Many of its members had been against accepting the terms of Versailles and changing the flag. However, the party had had to go

---

[55] Bundesarchiv, Nachlass Dietrich, Nr. 222, Die Reichstagwahlen, Juli-Dez., 1930, 41.
[56] Meinecke, *Politische Schriften und Reden, op. cit.,* p. 437.
[57] *Ibid.*
[58] Bundesarchiv, Nachlass Külz, Nr. 17, Grundung des Deutschen Staatspartei, o.D. Juli-Nov., 1930: 59.
[59] *Ibid.*
[60] Theodor Heuss, *Erinnerungen,* 1905–1933, Tübingen, 1963: p. 393.
[61] Heussarchiv, Stuttgart, Hopf/Heuss Briefwechsel, Heuss letter to Hopf, October 12, 1930.
[62] Bundesarchiv, Nachlass Koch-Weser, Nr. 106, Zussammenbruch der Staatspartei, Bd. I, Schriftwechsel, o.d., 1930, 48.
[63] Bundesarchiv, R. 45/III/83, aussenordentlicher Reichsparteitag, DDP, 11.

along "because we always placed interest of the *Volk*-community above interests of the party."[64] This had been no mere class party, Petersen proclaimed, but a party for all people. With some bitterness he contrasted the noble performance of the DDP with that of the SPD, whom he accused of practicing interest politics at the expense of the whole.[65] Basically, the *Staatspartei* that was founded on November 9, 1930, was the old Democratic party, minus such people as Erkelenz and Hellpach, the latter resigning on November 9, the very day that the Democratic party became the *Staatspartei*.[66] However, in its new guise, many of its members felt just as free as before, if not more so, to indulge in that neo-romantic fantasying and sniping at liberalism that had characterized so many Weimar Democrats. One week before the transformation of the German Democratic party into the *Staatspartei*, Bäumer published another one of her lead-footed assaults on the modern, skeptical age. Entitled "Dennoch Staatspartei!" the article attacked what she called "relativistic liberalism" as well as "formal democratic rationalism." What was really needed she thought, was some sort of *völkisch* idea. After all, democracy lived only to the extent that it was *volkstümlich*.[67] The tone of Bäumer's writings would remain constant until the demise of the party in 1933. However, Kurt Goepel went even further in the exposition of romantic palaver. In an essay of December 5, 1930, entitled "Jugend und Staatspartei," he seemed to be calling forth the spirit of the old *Wandervogel* movement that had so enthralled Meinecke in 1919. "The idea of German youth," he proclaimed, "is simply Germany, Fatherland, homeland." In a mechanized age, city folk longed for the countryside, for healthy sport, and for clean fresh air. The state had somehow to provide this ideal picture and, for the younger generation, become "the expression-form of the *völkisch* will to national community."[68] Sounding somewhat like Rathenau during his more romantic moments, Goepel called for an end to the proletarianization of man. *Lebensraum* had to be provided for youth, and youth's strong demands for leadership had to be answered.[69] In the January 5, 1931, *Blätter der Staatspartei* an editorial stated that the German people had to be made aware that the state was the very "embodiment of the Reich idea." The *Volk* that had to fight to preserve this state was not a "mechanical" type, but rather, an "organic unity of the community of living, future, and past races."[70]

In these words, which could well have been set down by Edmund Burke, the journal gave articulate expression to one of the most profound longings of the Democratic German: to escape the pettiness and meanness of political life, as he saw it, and finally to achieve that unity of *Volk* for which Naumann had striven unsuccessfully. Only for many Democrats, such as Meinecke and Bäumer, individuals who had never been able to accept the industrial age and urban iconoclasm, Naumann's dream now stood divested of all *Real*-political coverings. What remained was a super-political emotionalism that was expressed in admiration for youthful idealism, contempt for formal political parties, and dislike of urban centers, from which, ironically enough, the democratic tradition in general and the Democratic party in particular drew most of its strength.

Again, particularly in light of the massive turning away from parliamentarianism in particular and democratic politics in general, it is obvious why the German Democrats felt constrained to take the radical course they did, i.e., that attempted alliance with youthful anti-pluralistic enthusiasm that resulted in the formal establishment of the *Staatspartei*. Yet, this merely underscores an irony of Weimar political life; viz., that in order to save the Weimar Constitution, one had to reach for solutions that were hardly applicable within constitutional parameters, even those of the particular constitution in question. Moreover, the enthusiastic fervor with which many Democrats (with obvious exceptions, such as Fischer on the right and Erkelenz on the left) reached for outright statist and/or romantic solutions to the woes of Weimar-period Germany, can be seen as being an obvious testimonial to the power of such ideas in the circles of bourgeois Democracy.

VI. THE GERMAN DEMOCRATS AND THE JEWS

Democratic attitudes toward the big city and toward the cosmopolitan cynicism associated with city life raises the question of Democratic attitudes toward the Jews. One must say "attitudes" instead of "attitude" in that there was no general Democratic position toward the Jews. The Democratic party itself, deriving in fact a good deal of its support from Jews, took official stands against anti-Semitism. Even the *Staatspartei* never espoused overt anti-Semitism. However, the official party position hardly represented Democratic views as a whole. It is often difficult to see a consistent right-wing attitude on the parts of individual Democrats.

---

[64] *Ibid.*
[65] *Ibid.*, 12, 14.
[66] See Hellpach's statement in the Nov. 9, 1930 *Hannoverischen Kurier*, in Bundesarchiv, Nachlass Külz, Grundung der Deutschen Staatspartei, Nr. 116, o.D. Juli-Nov., 1930.
[67] Gertrud Bäumer, "Dennoch Staatspartei!" in: *Die Hilfe*, Nr. 44, 3 November, 1930: p. 1083.
[68] Institut für Zeitgeschichte, Kurt Goepel, "Jugend und Staatspartei," in: *Blatter der Staatspartei*, 11 Jahrg., Nr. 23, 5 Dec., 1930: p. 543.
[69] *Ibid.*, p. 544. *Lebensraum* is not being used in a militaristic sense. The author is merely calling for a de-emphasis of urban life.
[70] Preussisches Geheimes Staatsarchiv, Rep. 92 Nachlass Meinecke, Nr. 98, Blätter der Staatspartei, 1 Jahrg., Nr. 1, 5 Jan., 1931: p. 1.

Some Democrats, such as Meinecke, remained quite cool—if not somewhat hostile—to Jews, while maintaining a basically anti-republican stance as well. Others, such as Heuss and Koch-Weser, attempted, at least for a while, to defend republicanism, but, at the same time, did display a certain anti-Semitic bias. What the 1920's revealed was merely that anti-Semitism was an attitude endemic to German bourgeois life.

Naturally, anti-Semitism was not something that developed in the ranks of the democratic bourgeoisie during the 1920's. Anti-Semitism in the ranks of the *Bildungsbürgertum* was a phenomenon that had deep roots. In his *Erinnerungen,* Meinecke admitted to having been a "rugged anti-Semite" during his younger years,[1] and, as we have seen, on September 27, 1918, when defeat was all but a foregone conclusion, he had expressed his doubts about the future of Germany in the following manner: "No state could rule for long on the basis provided by the protaganists of the left, with their Jewish, sentimental-soft ideas."[2] Meinecke's attitudes remained essentially unchanged during the Weimar period. Another example of anti-Semitism within Democratic ranks was to be found in the enigmatic figure of Walther Rathenau, an individual who served as a living example of Jewish self-doubt, if not actually self-hate. Indeed, Rathenau went much farther than Meinecke in his own peculiar, quasi-racist variety of anti-Semitism. This phenomenon has been rather well covered in other contexts, and in fairness to him it must be noted that he did not survive long enough into the Weimar period for us to obtain a complete picture.[3] However, Rathenau's spiritual anti-Semitism, when combined with his state worship and cultural romanticism, put him in a very dubious position insofar as support of republican democracy was concerned.

One cannot gainsay the fact that, compared with its monarchically inclined neighbor, the DVP, the DDP was extremely liberal on the "Jewish Question." While the former party was not officially anti-Semitic, point 11 of its program, entitled "Religion und Kirche" declared that the party "sees in Christianity a keystone of German culture and German folk-life."[4] Ironically enough, as we have seen, the *Staatspartei* of 1930 had been forced to take somewhat the same position in its own program. However, in the beginning, the DDP took no such position, at least officially. Compared to the DNVP, of course, the DDP certainly must have appeared to have been a bastion of religious tolerance. In an almost complete adherence to the famous Tivoli program of the old Conservative party—at least on the "Jewish Question"—the DNVP, in point 11 of section one ("Volks und Staatsleben"), declared that it sought to preserve the German people from any type of "foreign influence" and that, therefore, "we fight against any disintegrating, un-German spirit, whether it stems from Jewish or other circles."[5] While individual members of the German Democratic party did express reservations about the Jews and their role in German life, such statements as that contained within the official program of the DNVP were rare.

At first, the DDP itself did take a positive stand against anti-Semitism. George Urdang, in an article of August 10, 1919, entitled "More Honesty" ("Mehr Ehrlichkeit"), maintained that the greatest problem that concerned democracy was the "Jewish Question" and that the party would have to display a great deal more forthrightness in taking a stand against anti-Semitism.[6] The party would have to try to prevent that situation in which "a certain, disgraceful complex of attitudes which is tied up only with a substandard morality—not, however with any variety of ancestry—will be blamed on a particular race."[7] The "haggling spirit" and concern for profit were to be found amidst all elements of the population and not only among the Jews. Other articles appearing in organs of the Democratic party emphasized that anti-Semitism was especially unjust in view of the sacrifices that German Jews had made in defense of the land.[8] A far stronger attack on anti-Semitism was that made by the philosopher Constantin Brunner (who was a converted Jew, né Leo Wertheimer) in an article addressed "An die deutschvölkische Jugend." "Does one have to hate the Jews in order to be German?" Brunner asked. All *völkisch* arguments, however sophisticated they might be, were really only arguments to "kill all the Jews."[9] With some passion, Brunner went on to exalt the Jewish community for its war effort. "The worst of the fallen Jews is to be more greatly praised than the best of the fallen non-Jews; for he has sacrificed his life for monsters and enemies like you instead of for his

---

[1] Friedrich Meinecke, *Strassburg, Freiburg, Berlin* (Stuttgart, 1949), p. 27.

[2] *Ibid.,* p. 266. See above, p. 36.

[3] On Rathenau's "Anti-Semitism," see Solomon Liptzin's *Germany's Stepchildren* (New York and Philadelphia, 1961), pp. 139–151. Also Robert A. Pois, "Walther Rathenau's Jewish Quandary," in: *Yearbook* 13 (1968) of the Leo Baeck Institute.

[4] Wolfgang Treue, *Deutsche Parteiprogramme 1861–1954* (Göttingen, 1954), p. 117.

[5] *Ibid.,* p. 109.

[6] Preussisches Geheimes Staatsarchiv, Berlin, Hauptabteilung XII-III, George Urdang "Mehr Ehrlichkeit," in: *Das demokratische Deutschland,* 1 Jahrg., Nr. 35, 10 August, 1919: p. 820.

[7] *Ibid.,* p. 821.

[8] *Ibid.,* Hauptabteilung XII-III, a very early example of this is to be found in Heinrich Gerland's "Deutsche Demokratische Partei und Deutschnationale Volkspartei," in the December 28, 1918 issue of *Das demokratische Deutschland* (Jahrg. 1, Nr. 3).

[9] *Ibid.,* Constantin Brunner *An die deutsche völkische Jugend* (pamphlet, *circa* 1924?), p. 11.

land."[10] Attacks on the radically anti-Semitic *Deutschvölkische Schutz und Trutz Bund* were also made, and, in a somewhat amusing article in the August 4, 1921, issue of *Der Demokrat,* the party attempted to point out the dangers of racism by showing how Rhenish separatists were using racist arguments to declare their independence from Prussia! (in their view, Prussians were "in the majority Slavs, who have accepted the German language," while the *Urdeutschen* were to be found ensconsed in the Rhineland).[11] With few exceptions, anti-Semitism was absent from official party literature. Nevertheless, in private party meetings, particularly of the party committees and in the writings of individual Weimar Democrats, anti-Semitic attitudes or observations were disturbingly common.

At least one of these observations came from a rather unexpected source: Max Weber. In the *Journal of Modern History* (June, 1967), Professor Bruce B. Frye has reprinted "a most interesting letter from Max Weber to Carl Petersen, the then leader of the DDP, explaining why he was resigning from the *Parteiausschuss.*" Besides indicating a rather commonly held antipathy towards the activities of the Reichstag, and declaring that his position as academician precluded political involvement, Weber—in this letter of April 14, 1920—pointed out that he did not agree with the DDP's selection of members for the investigating Committee, i.e., that committee set up by the Weimar government to investigate the causes for the defeat of 1918. Somewhat petulantly, Weber observed that "Jews should not have been seated" on this committee.[12] He went on to declare that he was not an anti-Semite himself; but, as Frye points out, he seemed to resent Jews sitting in judgment upon German statesmen and soldiers. This attitude, held by one of the most liberal members of the DDP, at least on the Jewish question, was indicative of a commonly held resentment in regard to the party's dependence upon Jewish membership and support.

One of the most prominent sources of this support was a republican press in which Jewish-owned, and in part edited, newspapers played a major role. The *Frankfurter Zeitung* (Kurt Simon), the *Berliner Tageblatt* (Rudolf Mosse and Hans Lachmann) and the *Vossische Zeitung* (Hermann Ullstein; brought up as a Christian, but of Jewish ancestry) were the three main sources of editorial support for the so-called "left-wing" German bourgeoisie. These newspapers might well have "led the German press in news service and prestige."[13] However, their bitter attacks, particularly those of the *Berliner Tageblatt,* on German annexation and self-alienating policies during the war, and their bitter opposition to militarism and monarchical tendencies during the Weimar years, caused many supporters of the DDP to view them as sensationalist at best and, in the case of Gessler, as corrupting influences at worst. Attacks on the major sources of editorial support for the party in particular and the republic in general were frequently expressed by many members of the party. The bitter attacks upon the *Berliner Tageblatt* by the admittedly annexationist Stresemann in November, 1918, in which he, among other things, accused the newspaper of contributing to "the disintegration of the homeland,"[14] were increasingly to find echoes in Democratic ranks as the Weimar period waxed on. The fact that the "Jewish press" bulked large in the support of the DDP and of the republic was, for many members of the party, unfortunate, and it is at times difficult to ascertain whether or not attacks on these papers were merely attacks upon editoral policies, or whether the fact that these papers were owned and edited by Jews added substantial spice to the sauce. As we shall see, the tendency to identify the Jews with a certain cosmopolitan cynicism and sacrilege in regard to the German past put such attacks under something of a cloud.

As early as 1922, the German Democratic party itself was being attacked as the "Jew party" and the term "Asphalt Democrat" had become a common one in German political parlance. In a meeting on June 22, 1922, of the party *Vorstand,* committee member Karl Böhme complained that anti-Semitism was very damaging to the party. He himself used the term "Asphalt Democrats" to describe that variety, an often obnoxious one, of city-bred people upon whom the party had become dependent for support.[15] Many members of the Democratic party were already finding that urban support of the party was not to their taste and in a letter of April 23, 1922, one Herr Deines told Dietrich that one of the primary reasons he was leaving the party was that it would never win over the bourgeoisie, especially since it was backed by the *"Frankfurter Zeitung* and the *Berliner Tageblatt."*[16] Certainly many Democrats, perhaps justifiably so, from a tactical point of view, were beginning to feel that the involvement of Jews and the "Jewish press" in the party was unfortunate. In a letter from Friedrich Mück to Theodor Heuss on December 3, 1922, this Heilbronn Democrat, who had previously indicated that he was, if anything, a philo-Semite, remarked that the Democratic party in his region had decided to combine voting lists with the

---

[10] *Ibid.*, p. 13.

[11] Institut für Zeitgeschichte, München, "Die Rassentheorie als Gefährdung der National Einheit," in: *Der Demokrat,* 2 Jahrg., Nr. 31, 4 August, 1921: pp. 604–605.

[12] Bruce B. Frye, "A Letter from Max Weber," in: *Journal of Modern History* 34, 2 (June, 1967), p. 122.

[13] Paul Kosok, *Modern Germany. A Study of Conflicting Loyalties* (Chicago, 1933), p. 279.

[14] Wolfgang Hartenstein, *Die Anfänge der deutschen Volkspartei, 1918–1920* (Düsseldorf, 1962), p. 45.

[15] Bundesarchiv, Koblenz, Sitzungen des Vorstandes der DDP, R 45/III/16, 23.

[16] *Ibid.*, Nachlass Dietrich, Nr. 67, Allgemeine Korrespondenz, April–Oct., 1922, Bd. I, Buchstab, A–F.

bourgeois parties rather than with the Social Democrats. In conservative Württemberg this was the only way. Should the party, he asked, be forced into an alliance with the Social Democrats "only because of the *Frankfurter Zeitung*, the Jews and the doctrinaires?"[17]

Although overt anti-Semitism did not appear in official DDP publications, various Democrats were not so squeamish about expressing their views in private and even, in Meinecke's case, publicly. In his diary, Koch-Weser records that, on January 11, 1925, he and a Jewish friend, Wassermann, attended a Zionist meeting. With some relief, Koch-Weser recorded that virtually all the Jews he met there were tolerable. "The more Zionist [they are]," he observed, the less they have of those usual unlikeable qualities associated with Jews, "the unfortunate half-obsequious, half-pretentious appearance which is indeed part of their insecurity in *Deutschtum*."[18] During the mid-1920's, relatively few Democrats attacked the Jews as a religion or group. Most bitterness was focused upon Jewish influence, particularly in the press, and towards that variety of cosmopolitan cynicism with which Jews were associated. In a letter to Philip Wieland, dated January 2, 1925, Heuss told of his concern that the DDP was considered, by the *Frankfurter Zeitung* and the "even worse" *Berliner Tageblatt* to be a party of the left.[19] Friedrich Meinecke was always annoyed that anti-Semitism had been used in attacks upon the republic and upon his own party. In his previously considered 1922 essay written after the Rathenau murder, he pointed out that many Jews in Communist, Democratic, and Social Democratic ranks were being driven even farther to the left by anti-Semitism,[20] and, in a 1925 essay, "Republik, Bürgertum und Jugend," he proclaimed that "a good political cause will certainly not be made worse by the fact that it is also represented by Jews."[21] However, in an address on April, 1926, "Die deutschen Universitäten und der heutige Staat," ("The German Universities and the Contemporary State"), he attacked the "left press" for showing a certain "impiety" towards the German past. From time to time, he suggested, this press had shown (besides its usual good sense in protecting the public interest) a "somewhat Jewish resentment."[22]

In this regard, it is both interesting and important to note that Meinecke's reaction against the Jewish press was shared by another Democrat of some prominence, defense minister Gessler, who had succeeded Gustav Noske at that post after the Kapp *Putsch* of March, 1920. In his memoirs, *Reichswehrpolitik in der Weimarer Zeit,* Gessler mentions, with apparent resentment, the bitter attacks launched upon the government by a portion of the Berlin press after the Kapp *Putsch* was defeated. While acknowledging the fact that such an attack was probably in part a "reaction to the anti-Semitism which had found open expression in the *Freicorps*," Gessler still voiced his opinion that Mosse (of the *Berliner Tageblatt*) and Ullstein (of the *Vossiche Zeitung*) had been unwarrantedly severe in their criticisms of the government.[23] Gessler's attitude towards the Jews was one which was fairly typical of the more prominent members of the party. Throughout his autobiography, he generally managed to maintain a tone of outward "neutrality" in regard to the Jews. However, his own inclinations were rather clearly revealed inasmuch as he tended to identify the—to him—most degenerate elements of Weimar life with big-city Jewry. In this regard, Gessler launched a detailed and quite vitriolic attack upon literary cynicism, cosmopolitanism, and pacifism. Concerning the last subject, Gessler remarked: "I considered it and still consider it today to be one of the most serious weaknesses of the Weimar system that it, out of its liberal ideology, did not tear out this big city degeneracy root and branch."[24] Gessler, in this work, broadened his approach to one concerned with explaining what he considered to be the roots of Weimar-period anti-Semitism. Here, his argument can be seen as representing an elaboration upon Meinecke's own previously mentioned malaise in regard to the left-wing Jewish press. "With cold cynicism," Gessler remarked

they [the Jewish big city literary circles and press] tore down everything upon which healthy German national feeling depended and treasured each phenomenon of decadence as a sign of the progress of civilization. It was an oversight of their racial comrades that they did not consider it important to draw a sharp line of demarcation here, before the public.[25]

In statements of this nature, Gessler bore a striking resemblance to some of the individuals who were striving perhaps more systematically to overthrow the system of which he was ostensibly a part, and to whose defense his *Reichswehr* was supposedly dedicated.

The tendency to see the Jews as, in some way, being at the heart of all that was decadent and cynical was reflected in the attitudes of some of the more idealistic members of the party. On February 17, 1927, Koch-Weser recorded in his diary that Gertrud Bäumer, who was in favor of the *Schund und Schmutz* law, saw the generally negative attitude of the Reichstag

---

[17] Heussarchiv, Stuttgart, Friedrich Mück-Theodor Heuss Briefwechsel.
[18] Bundesarchiv, Nachlass Koch-Weser, Nr. 32, Tagebuchartige Vermerke, 31.
[19] Heussarchiv, Philip Wieland-Theodor Heuss Briefwechsel.
[20] Friedrich Meinecke, *Politische Schriften und Reden*, ed. George Kotowski (Darmstadt, 1958), p. 339.
[21] *Ibid.*, p. 374.
[22] *Ibid.*, p. 412.

[23] Otto Gessler, *Reichswehrpolitik in der Weimarer Zeit* (Stuttgart, 1958), p. 127.
[24] *Ibid.*, p. 173.
[25] *Ibid.*, pp. 173–174.

delegation as an indication that it "had fallen under the influence of the Jewish-liberal circles of Berlin."[26] Somewhat huffily, she had informed Koch-Weser that she was leaving the delegation. Koch-Weser noted, with some amusement, that he finally had succeeded in quieting her down.

By the mid and late 1920's, opinions questioning the advisability of depending upon Jewish support for the party had become more prevalent. In a meeting of the Party *Vorstand* on March 26, 1927, one Herr Brunner (not Constantin Brunner) spoke enthusiastically of the Austrian equivalent of the DDP, the *Bürgerliche Demokratie* group. However, financial help from the DDP would be unwelcome, he thought, because those who received any money from it would also receive the taint of being a "Jewish-preserved party." With some understatement, he noted that the Austrian Democrats probably would not desire that.[27] In a letter of May 29, 1928, from George Freck to Hermann Dietrich, the former mentioned that one of the reasons for the party's defeat was that the trading middle class and farmers espoused this belief: "Yes, the Jews, who are with the Democrats, rule and have us by the throat."[28] For many, Freck maintained, "Democracy is the party of the Jews."

As we have seen, the same sort of attitude towards Jewish support of the party could be seen in the June 14, 1928, meeting of the party *Vorstand* where many members of this committee saw Jewish influence in support of the Democratic party as having decidedly detrimental effects.

A source of at least mixed support for the Jews came from Willy Hellpach. In 1928 he published his *Politische Prognose für Deutschland*, in which he attacked the whole myth of the pure race. (He did not deny that there were such things as races, however.) He criticized the Germans for a culturally conditioned love of fantasy and "feeling" (*Gefühl*), one that made an understanding of the day-to-day machinations of politics rather difficult, to say the least. In part, this tendency towards fantasy had made parliamentarianism impossible in Germany, he thought.[29] Besides the German inability to live by parliamentary rules, Hellpach also blamed the decline of parliamentarianism upon a general world-wide tendency in that direction (much as he had in his earlier work *Die Krisis des deutschen Parlamentarismus*); parliament, he said was "too humane" and "too wordy" to function well in a mass age, and particularly in Germany). Jews, he thought, were characterized by what he called the "unstraying rational coolness of their Mosaic doctrine."[30] This, Hellpach seemed to prefer to the Germans' tendency towards romanticism. The stereotyping of Jews was ugly, Hellpach said, and the tendency of Jews to settle in cities and to concentrate in the middle class did not help matters any.[31] Moreover, the "earthiness" of the Jews and their rejection of the irrational and fantasy made them anomalies in a nation of apolitical romantics. This, and the entrance of many Eastern Jews into Germany, was causing them to "stand out," something that they should assiduously avoid.[32] Yet, Hellpach said, the Jews were needed for the state, and it was the task of democracy to make certain that positions were open to them. Earlier in the book, however, Hellpach had made the remark that Jews ought not to concentrate in the Democratic camp, but rather spread around among the other parties.[33]

Nevertheless, despite Hellpach's "mixed" attitude towards Jews—anti-Semitism was bad, but the burden of dealing with it rested to a large extent on the Jews themselves—his attitude towards democracy itself was a strangely provincial one. The source for democracy had to be found among the German peasantry, which despised liberalism and was indifferent to "tolerance," which, Hellpach declared, was a big-city phenomenon.[34] He repeated his idea, expressed at the 1925 party congress, that the DDP had to seek out the spiritual roots for democracy in evangelical Christianity.[35] Again, Hellpach emphasized that Catholicism, because of its emphasis upon hierarchy, was poor soil for democratic growth.

Hellpach's 1928 book presents the reader with a somewhat confused picture. He was opposed to anti-Semitism and did not take the notion of pure races very seriously. He saw an active role for Jews in the state. Yet, he more or less accepted anti-Semitism as "given," and the Jews as being inherently different from their Christian German countrymen. His tying democracy to freedom-loving but most certainly intolerant peasants, as well as his attack (for such it was) upon Catholicism for being inherently undemocratic, pointed to a stance which was not merely illiberal. In the context of 1928 Germany, it was almost unthinking. In many ways, Hellpach's mixed position towards Jews in particular and tolerance in general, and towards the roles of race, city, and countryside, can be viewed as representing a sort of *précis* of that of many Democrats, who, harassed by parliamentary crises and electoral disasters, also either hoped that the Jews would not stand out so much in Democratic ranks, or began to feel a genuine resentment towards them (assuming that they had not before). Tolerance, either

---

[26] Bundesarchiv, Nachlass Koch-Weser, *op. cit.*, 58–59.
[27] Bundesarchiv, Sitzungen des Vorstandes der DDP, R 45/III/20, 72–73.
[28] Bundesarchiv, Nachlass Dietrich, Nr. 221, Bd. III, Die Reichstag Wahlen, 20.5, 1928, 55.
[29] Willy Hellpach, *Politische Prognose für Deutschland* (Berlin, 1928), pp. 50–56, 145–147.

[30] *Ibid.*, pp. 125–126.
[31] *Ibid.*, pp. 366–369.
[32] *Ibid.*, pp. 370–375.
[33] *Ibid.*, p. 260.
[34] *Ibid.*, pp. 209–210.
[35] *Ibid.*, p. 255.

towards Jews or Catholics, for that matter, was being strained, as was parliamentary democracy itself.

Of course, opinions such as these are commentaries not merely upon the party and attitudes of its members, but upon the general state of the German electorate as well. To be a Jew party was to assure defeat. However, there could be little doubt that many members did not consider the Jews to be unexpendable and, as we have seen in the cases of Bäumer and Gessler, anti-Semitic attitudes were hardly absent from the party itself. As always, much criticism was directed against the liberal Jewish press, whose support of the party was seen in ever more negative terms. In discussing the impending concordat crisis, Koch-Weser, in his diary entry of July 5, 1929, could not resist taking a swing at those clergymen "who make themselves beloved by the Jewish clique à la Berliner Tageblatt, by their caressing of Jews and Catholics. Generals, countesses, and pastors who assume a friendly posture towards the Jews are the only ones who impress the Berliner Tageblatt." [36] With some approval, Koch-Weser included in his diary an article in the June 19, 1929, issue of the Leipziger Volkszeitung, a Social Democrat newspaper, which contained bitter attacks on the Democratic press. "Ullstein and Mosse," the article said, "are trampling their party down with elephant feet. . . . The anti-Semites in Berlin are being gorged by the 'Jewish press.'" [37]

With so apparent a tendency to view the Jews as being a rather discrediting element in the German Democratic party, it is small wonder that possible Jewish objections to the alliance with the Jungdos were overridden in a most cavalier fashion. One day after the secret alliance with the Jungdos had been consummated on July 28, 1930, the party Ausschuss held a stormy meeting over it. In an eloquent statement, one which soon was to be made public in the journals of the German Democratic party, Koch-Weser declared that Mahraun had personally denied to him that the Jungdeutsche Orden was anti-Semitic. Indeed, Koch-Weser seemed to be indicating, the real burden of proof for commitment to principle rested upon the Jews:

Do you wish to prevent young people from going over to the National Socialists and extremists? Come into our organization; work together with the former Volksnationalen; show them what good Germans you are; then you will, in view of the direction in the new party, also fulfill a task ["mitzvos?"] in the Jewish sense.[38]

Ernst Mosisch expressed some reservations about the Jungdos, particularly inasmuch as they had refused to do away with their "Aryan paragraphs," those which forbade entrance to Jews. In this, he was joined by the well-known Democratic pacifist Professor Ludwig Quidde.[39] Bruno Weil, a member of the party committee and also a leading member of the Centralverein deutscher Staatsbürger Jüdischen Glaubens, joined in questioning the role that anti-Semitism had played in the Jungdos. However, he was satisfied by joining Hans Muhle in stating "Anti-Semitic instincts cannot be allowed to find a place in the construction of the new party."[40] Gertrud Bäumer added her pious denunciation of anti-Semitism to the others, and the party Ausschuss finally agreed on the new program. The forthright statements of the party Ausschuss against anti-Semitism have caused some, P. B. Wiener among them, to place a great deal of emphasis upon the adherence of the Staatspartei to hallowed democratic and egalitarian principles. However, those "completely different, private views" mentioned by Wiener as being suppressed in the committee room were most important for people such as Bäumer and Koch-Weser who, Koch-Weser privately and Bäumer more publicly, did indeed feel that Jewish influence—if not Jewish members—had become "an unacceptable burden for the party." [41]

A truly incredible example of Democratic insensitivity to Jewish, or for that matter, Freemason feelings is described in Theodor Heuss's Erinnerungen. Heinrich Himmler wrote, or had written, a booklet entitled Der Reichstag 1930. In this salacious treatment of the Reichstag delegates, Heuss found himself described as being Jewish. Nazis all over Germany seemed to pick this up and in Schwenningen, in Heuss's native Württemberg, a local Nazi newspaper referred to him as "the noted Jew and Freemason" Heuss.[42] Heuss's Democratic colleagues there attempted to pursuade him to institute libel proceedings against the newspaper! Heuss said that he had to explain to these people that he had friends "of Jewish ancestry" as well as some who belonged to Masonic lodges, and that they might well feel offended by such a course of action.[43]

Although Staatspartei campaign literature did come out against race hatred, anti-Semitism as a campaign issue was not totally precluded. W. S. Allen, in his The Nazi Seizure of Power, quotes a Staatspartei member who, campaigning in the Hannoverian town of "Thalburg," called for laws in which Jews would be

---

[36] Bundesarchiv, Nachlass Koch-Weser, Nr. 36, Tagebuchartige Vermerke, 5–61.

[37] Ibid., Nr. 37, 75.

[38] Institut für Zeitgeschichte, "Deutsche demokratische Partei für deutsche Staatspartei," in: Der Demokrat, 11 Jahrg., Nr. 14, 15, 5 August, 1930: p. 333. See also Entscheidungsjahr 1932, ed. by Werner E. Mosse and Arnold Paucker (Tübingen, 1968), p. 294.

[39] Quidde later quit the Staatspartei to form the unimportant Radikaldemokratische Partei.

[40] Mosse and Paucker, op. cit., p. 295.

[41] Ibid.

[42] Theodor Heuss, Erinnerungen (Tübingen, 1933), p. 407.

[43] Ibid.

allowed citizenship "only according to their character and accomplishments."[44]

A few Jews, such as Theodor Wolff who had been considerably impressed by the non-anti-Semitic Fascism of Mussolini, were so influenced by the youthful virility of the *Jungdos,* that they found it relatively easy to accept the new *Staatspartei.* However, many Jews were not so easily impressed; among them was Ernst Feder, as mentioned above, noted author and, until June, 1932, an editor on the *Berliner Tageblatt.* As early as April 8, 1930, he made mention in his diary of the right-wing course of the party, singing a lugubrious swan-song to it in the entry of April 24, 1930.[45] On July 7, 1930, he recorded his dismay over the fact that the "Reich committee" (*Parteiausschuss*) of the party offered "no resistance" to the "stab-in-the-back" (*Dolchstoss*) that Koch-Weser (in his diary, Feder refers to him as "Koch") and Meyer had accomplished by joining the DDP with the *Jungdos.*[46] Indeed, the general Jewish reaction against the new party caused Koch-Weser to state, in a somewhat bitter letter to one Herr Graff, that he could not understand why the Jews were so annoyed because the *Jungdos* refused to accept them into their ranks. After all, he did not feel angry because Jewish organizations denied entrance to him.[47] As we have seen, the eventual electoral disaster of September 14, 1930, one which saw the *Staatspartei's* mandates fall to an all-time low of fourteen, (after the departure from the *Staatspartei* Reichstag delegation of six of the *Jungdos* who could not reconcile their quaint medieval principles with modern politics) plus various internal difficulties with the *Jungdos,* led to a rupture of the party and to Koch-Weser's enforced resignation (he was even compelled to surrender his own mandate). Koch-Weser, dejected and alone, withdrew to the sidelines of political life and ensconced himself in a position of extreme bitterness.

In a letter to a Dr. I. S. Schmerz on April 23, 1931, he expressed agreement with the latter's view that no one of their generation could support the sort of liberalism that was embodied in the *Berliner Tageblatt.*[48] In a diary entry of December 7, 1931, Koch-Weser mentioned that he had been talking politics with one Frau Gutmann, of whom he wrote that "nothing is as unsympathetic as this type of Jewess ... who creeps about in a hunchbacked posture." She was the sort who would make it, though, even if the Nazis came to power.[49] In this context, it is interesting to note that Koch-Weser was forced to leave his law firm in 1933 because of a Jewish grandmother and that he died in 1944, an exile in Brazil.

The falling away of Jews from the *Staatspartei* brought out a great deal of bitterness on the part of many of its members, who had decided to stick it out for the duration. At a meeting of the *Vorstand* of the *Staatspartei* on April 28, 1932, Heinrich Rönneburg bitterly attacked the Jews for "betraying" the *Staatspartei.*

The Jews, in a shabby fashion, have left us in the lurch. Through agitation from house to house, from mouth to mouth, through letters and handbills they have spoken out against us.[50]

One of Herr Rönneburg's colleagues, Herr Zeitlin, rather pointedly remarked that:

It is noteworthy that when people search for a scapegoat, they always seek out the Jews. For a Jewish voter, the course to the *Staatspartei* was already a heavy burden. Afterwards, this has been underscored recently by a racially pure [*rassereinen*] *Landesliste.*[51]

A certain touchiness was also revealed in a letter (undated, but probably one of March, 1933) from Külz to the *Centralverein deutscher Staatsbürger Jüdischen Glaubens.* For some time, this organization had been attacked by the Nazis and other right-wing groups as being a Communist-oriented if not a Communist-directed, organization. Now with Hitler in power, the organization had called upon leading members of the *Staatspartei,* e.g., Dietrich and Külz, to come out in defense of Jews in general and itself in particular. In this reply, Külz noted that it was unworthy of a Christian people to be anti-Semitic, and that he himself would continue to fight anti-Semitism whenever and wherever it appeared. However, he added, "I must say, if I wish to be completely open, that for me this struggle over German citizens of Jewish belief is often very difficult." He went on to observe rather petulantly that often, after having defended a person attacked by anti-Semites, the same individual whom he had just defended attacked him (Külz) over a "rather doubtful issue."[52] It was also his sad experience, Külz went on to say, that Jews had not supported him in elections as much as would have been possible for them to do. Apparently feeling that a tit-for-tat attitude in regard to prejudice was somehow justified, Külz closed his remarks by stating that in the battle against anti-Semitism the Jews themselves had to play a more positive role.

---

[44] W. S. Allen, *The Nazi Seizure of Power* (New York, 1965), p. 34.

[45] "Searchlight on the Decline of the Weimar Republic: The Diaries of Ernst Feder," by Arnold Paucker, in *Yearbook* 13 (1968) of the Leo Baeck Institute, pp. 161–234.

[46] *Ibid.,* p. 189.

[47] Bundesarchiv, Nachlass Koch-Weser, Nr. 105, Gründung der Staatspartei, Schriftwechsel, 1930, 249.

[48] Bundesarchiv, Nachlass Dietrich, Nr. 129, Allgemeine Korrespondenz Bd. III, Buchstaben G-J, Jan. 1931–July 1932, 40–42.

[49] Bundesarchiv, Nachlass Koch-Weser, Nr. 40, Tagebuchartige Vermerke, 3.

[50] Eric Matthias and Rudolf Morsey, ed., *Das Ende der Parteien* (Düsseldorf, 1690), p. 79.

[51] *Ibid.*

[52] Bundesarchiv, Nachlass Dietrich, Nr. 265, Reichstag und Preussenwahlen 1933, Nov. 1932–Marz, 1933, 82.

Perhaps a somewhat more revealing remark was made by Theodor Heuss on May 7, 1933, in a letter to Friedrich Mück. First of all, he noted that his son had been most upset to find his father's name on a Nazi-drawn-up "Pillory (*Schandpfahle*) of the German nation." It was sad, Heuss mused, that his son seemed to be experiencing only the negative aspects of the time. After all, nobody could prevent students from taking various forms of action. Heuss expressed satisfaction with some of the individuals with whom he had been grouped. However, he was most distressed to find himself in the company of individuals who were part of that "deeply rooted Jewish *Literatentum* against whom I have fought all these years; and it is less pretty to perish in history with these."[53] Perhaps, one could argue that Heuss was afraid of the censor, and, as we will see later, he himself had written an extremely perceptive critique of the Nazi party (indeed, this was one of the reasons that his name appeared on the "Pillory"). However, there was no reason for him to express a positively anti-Semitic attitude unless he genuinely felt it.

Many of Germany's more prominent Weimar-period Democrats—admittedly not the Democratic party itself—were, in ways both subtle and unsubtle, anti-Semitic. Theirs was not a systematic racial anti-Semitism, but rather a somewhat gentlemanly *Biedermeier* variety which saw the Jews as being an occasionally obnoxious, often loud, group of people, who somehow did not really fit into German life. In considering the sources for this feeling, we would do well to examine Armin Mohler's *Die Konservative Revolution in Deutschland: 1918–1933*.

In this work, the author maintains that German anti-Semitism can be divided into two mainstreams: first of all, there was the "aristocratic" variety of anti-Semitism, utilized by individuals like Max Liebermann von Sonnenberg in order to draw people to the Conservative party; second, there was the more "democratic" variety, stemming from the small town and rural bourgeoisie, a group which felt threatened by the proletarians and by the industrial bourgeoisie of the large cities and which concurrently saw the Jew, in both his radical and capitalistic stereotypes, as the cause of its misery. Mohler suggests that Otto Boeckel of Hesse was an early example of this more democratic variety.[54]

The author does not go into this much further, but there can be little doubt that both Nazism and the "New Conservatism" of the 1920's with which Mohler is concerned derived much of their motional impetus from a strong reaction against what they considered to be the metropolitan cynicism and un-*völkisch* cosmopolitanism of the industrial big cities. The Jew stood out both as representative of the soulless rationalism which had spawned the industrial age and, observed through the prism of archetyping, as the rootless cosmopolite who drew his very substance from the un-German metropolis. The degree to which this complex of ideas penetrated into all aspects of German life is certainly open to question. But there can be little doubt that many Germans conceived of there being deep-seated and palpable differences between German Jews and their Christian fellow countrymen. Unhappily, it would appear that many good German liberals—members of the republican German Democratic party—shared this point of view.

The identification of the Jew with big-city life was natural, perhaps even logical. After all, most Jews in Germany and elsewhere lived and still live in metropolitan areas. However, some of the statements of various Weimar-period Democrats indicate that the Jew was identified with big-city life in a very particular way. Naturally, German Jewry itself contributed to the construction of the stereotype, much as any minority group tends to do. Jews were largely engaged in financial activities and in publishing, and the Jewish influence bulked large in the republican press. Such scandals as that involving the brothers Sklarek who, in 1929, were correctly accused of corrupt practices in the city government of Berlin, did not help matters. Moreover, an un-*völkisch* and critical, if not cynical, attitude, was not unusual among Jewish publicists and *litterateurs* and this, in view of the influence of various forms of idealism in Germany, could hardly have summoned forth positive feelings for that group whose influence seemed inordinate when one bore in mind that it constituted only one-twentieth of the population.

The guilt of the Weimar Democrat was simply that, despite his own generally impressive *Bildung,* he was unable to go past the raw data and observations with which he was confronted. Where he was often critical philosophically or politically, he was almost näively uncritical in accepting the existence of a particular "Jewish problem." Certainly, this was not *the* "Jewish problem" of the German radical right, nor did he see the Jews as necessarily representing a destructive form in German life. However, the Weimar-period Democrat was generally unable to see the Jew as contributing a vital and important aspect of the German system. The German Democrat fitted well the situation described by the Jewish drama critic Alfred Kerr:

Even people of sensitive nature could put up with such things as when, on the Day of Atonement, a boor would call a gentleman with a prayer book "damned Jewish dung!" Or when a major of the "Eleventh" (regiment) would publicly declare on the streetcar: "There are so many pregnant Jewish women—makes you want to vomit!" These things did not hurt. But when enlightened, well-meaning, and considerate friends said "The Jewish gentlemen"—that hurt.[55]

---

[53] Heussarchiv, Friedrich Mück/Theodor Heuss, Briefwechsel.
[54] Armin Mohler, *Die Konservative Revolution in Deutschland 1918–1932* (Stuttgart, 1950), p. 41.

[55] Istvan Deak, *Weimar Germany's Left-Wing Intellectuals, Die Weltbühne. A Political History of the Weltbühne and its Circle* (Berkeley and Los Angeles, 1968), p. 25.

Those who, between 1933 and 1945, attempted to destroy the Jewish community throughout Europe were those who would hurl the epithet "damned Jewish dung" or would make the crude remark attributed to the major of the Eleventh Regiment. However, it was the attitudes of "enlightened" individuals, such as those who make up the German Democratic party, that made it possible for the Nazis to carry on a program of mass extermination with little resistance or even protest on the part of the most liberal and sensitive portion of the German community. Nevertheless, it is certainly true that the German Democratic party and many of its more prominent members, e.g., Heuss, battled long and hard first to put down the Nazi party and later to prevent its coming to power. We must now take a closer look at the Weimar Democrats and their struggle against Nazism.

VII. THE DEMOCRATIC REACTION TO NAZISM

As we have seen, Democratic reaction to anti-Semitism was somewhat mixed. On the one hand, the German Democratic party itself, even in its *Staatspartei* form, as well as many of its members remained adamant in maintaining an official position against anti-Semitism. However, many individual Democrats espoused anti-Semitic views, either privately or, in some cases, publicly. Furthermore, political romanticism and elements of statism were not absent from Democratic ranks, even from the Democratic party itself. As Democrats, then, the Weimar variety left a considerable amount to be desired.

However, at least during the Weimar period, the party was one in its fight against Nazism. Some of this we have already touched upon in considering its attitude towards anti-Semitism. However, the reaction of the party towards the Nazi movement as a whole requires a more searching examination. Again, we shall be able to perceive certain problems and inconsistencies, particularly when we examine the views of individual democrats. However, the Democratic party as a whole exhibited adamant opposition to Nazism, at least up until the *Ermächtigungsgesetz* of March, 1933.

The attitude of the Democratic party towards Nazism was in large measure determined by two primary elements in its own ideology: (1) its concern for national unification, and (2) its support of industrial growth based upon private enterprise. Nazi anti-Semitism played a role in eliciting a negative response on the parts of most Democrats. However, this was not as important a factor as one might imagine. This will become particularly clear when we examine the writings of some non-Jewish Democrats, e.g., Heuss and Meinecke. One of the first significant commentaries upon the Nazi movement emerged from the November 11, 1923, meeting of the party *Vorstand*, which took place two days after Hitler's ill-fated attempt to seize power in Munich. After a prolonged debate, the party *Vorstand* came out in support of "national unity of the Reich against particularistic and reactionary enemies."[1]

Any governmental policy which did not provide for the necessary security against such groups had to be "unconditionally rejected by the DDP on grounds of domestic and foreign policy."[2] Such a stand was, in a way, indicative of a certain degree of spiritual confusion on the part of the Democratic party, inasmuch as Hitler's revolt, to which the *Vorstand* was referring, was not "particularistic." To the historian, the obvious difference between the "los von Berlin" of von Kahr and the "nach Berlin" of Hitler had been overlooked. However, it is clear that the Democratic party viewed Nazism as something that was intrinsically inimical to national unity and, at a meeting of the *Parteiausschuss* on January 27, 1924, Koch declared that the government certainly should have acted more decisively in the Bavarian case, particularly in view of the strong action that it had taken against the government in Saxony.[3] The view of the Nazis which saw them as disruptive to national unity and thus as inimical to the national interest was a common one among Democrats.

Theodor Heuss's *Staat und Volk* of 1926 contained a rather vigorous attack on Nazism, comparing the "up-rooted" type who flocked to Hitler's standard—jobless proletarians, handworkers, and intellectuals—to those who flocked to the standard of Kurt Eisner in Munich.[4] However, Heuss was primarily concerned with discerning the roots of Fascism, of which he apparently felt Nazism to be a part. Fascism, he claimed, stemmed from a desire for "daring action," a result of the "heroic romanticism" that had come out of the war. In its most prominent Italian form, he said, it was sort of an overcompensation for the obvious lack of military success that Italy had had in the war.[5] Quite perceptively, Heuss pointed out the prominent role of the Führer in a Fascist movement, and that "Fascism has become an international problem, like Bolshevism, albeit in different tones."[6] Heuss saw the German call for a Führer or a "strong man"[7] as a sign of weakness, due to unbridgeable social division. Much of what Heuss said, particularly his emphasis upon the *Führerprinzip*, would be repeated in his *Hitlers Weg* of 1932.

One of the most comprehensive attacks upon Nazism, at least insofar as campaign literature was concerned, appeared in 1926 in a series entitled *Zur demokra-*

---

[1] Bundesarchiv, Koblenz, Sitzungen der Vorstandes der DDP, R 45 III/19, 52.
[2] *Ibid.*
[3] Bundesarchiv, Sitzungen des Parteiausschusses der DDP, R 45 III/12, 51–53.
[4] Theodor Heuss, *Staat und Volk* (Berlin, 1926), p. 95.
[5] *Ibid.*, p. 96.
[6] *Ibid.*, pp. 97-98.
[7] *Ibid.*, p. 100.

tischen Politik. In pamphlet No. 140, entitled *Die Nationalsozialisten,* the Democratic party mounted a several-pronged attack upon the Nazis, one which would later be in part embodied in Theodor Heuss's anti-Nazi *Hitlers Weg* of 1932. First of all, the pamphlet condemned Hitlerian anti-Semitism. The Nazi party, it was stated, was just another anti-Semitic party, relying upon shopworn and prejudice-tainted arguments.[8] Such vitriolic anti-Semitism made it impossible for any respectable German political party —at least the German Democratic party—to work with the Nazis in any way. As strong as was the DDP attack on Nazi anti-Semitism, the party came down a lot harder upon Nazi economic policy and upon Nazi flirtation with some of the ideas of Italian Fascism. No doubt with its eye upon winning further bourgeois support, the Democratic party attacked the Nazi economic program as being strongly Marxist in nature.[9] Here, it is obvious that the party was taking the term "national-socialism" quite seriously, without really considering the Nazi twenty-five-point program. As Heuss would later point out, Nazi economics, such as it was, drew most of its content more from the romantic socialism of Weitling or Dühring than from Marx, and again, the Democratic party, while it would always remain critical of Nazi economics, did not make too much of the Marxist charge until 1930. However, the somewhat curious accusation that the Nazis were anti-national was one which remained fairly constant, and this was particularly emphasized in the 1926 pamphlet. Here, the Democratic party charged that Hitler, because of his interest in Mussolini and in Italian Fascism, had sacrificed the South Tyrolean Germans to their Italian oppressors.[10] Hitler's unscrupulous abandonment of this persecuted German minority in the name of political expediency disguised as ideology was condemned as a *deutsche Kulturschande* of the first magnitude.[11] Certainly, the pamphlet intimated, a party which was willing to sacrifice the interests of Germans abroad would not hesitate to do the same to Germans at home if and when it should ever be able to come to power.

As strong as the 1926 pamphlet was in attacking Hitler and the Nazis, it is fairly obvious that, at this point at least, the Democratic party did not take the Nazi threat very seriously. There was some reason for this, of course. While the Nazis had obtained 32 seats in the Reichstag election of May 4, 1924, they had fallen off to 14 seats in the election of December 7, 1924. In the 1925 elections, the Nazi-supported candidate, Ludendorff, had received only 250,000 votes in the first one, and the party had been forced to join with the DNVP and the DVP in backing Hindenburg.

However, by 1927, the German Democratic party was being forced to take the Nazis a bit more seriously. In the November 24, 1927, issue of *Der Demokrat,* Werner Stephan called the party's attention to an otherwise somewhat insignificant election in Braunschweig. The Democrats had retained their two mandates in the Braunschweig *Landtag,* but had lost 1,832 votes—from 14,775 votes obtained in the 1924 elections, to 12,943 votes. The National Socialists had kept their one mandate while gaining 846 votes; they had obtained 9,474 votes in 1924 and 10,320 votes in 1927.[12] This National Socialist success, while not of national significance was, in Stephan's eyes, somewhat ominous because the party seemed to be fairly well financed, while the Democratic party seemed to be running into some problems along this line.[13] Although Stephan, in this essay, was more concerned with the threat to national stability which he saw as posed by large Social Democratic gains in Braunschweig, his concern over growing Nazi strength is of particular interest.

In the May 20, 1928, Reichstag elections, which, as we have seen, were a disaster for the Democratic party, the Nazis gained only 12 seats. However, growing Nazi strength in the various *Länder* had become an issue of serious concern for the Democratic party by 1929. The November 5, 1929, issue of *Der Demokrat* contained an article entitled "National Socialism: A Growing Danger" ("Der Nationalsozialismus—eine wachsende Gefahr"), and it correctly pointed to the successes which the National Socialist party was enjoying in various portions of Germany. In the *Landtag* elections in Saxony, the journal said, the Nazi vote had risen from 74,333 to 133,792, while those of Lippe had shown a rise of 1,037 to 1,671.[14] What were the reasons for this success? The journal pointed to what it called "one-sided agitation" and to the support of Hugenberg of the DNVP.[15] There were emotional reasons as well. Nazi terror in the cities certainly had a coercive effect, while the party's characteristic emphases upon uniforms and stirring martial music had played a more positive role in drawing various groups of people to the movement.[16] Of importance also was the traditional Jewish scapegoat. Ominously, *Der Demokrat* emphasized the success that the Nazis were enjoying by appealing to an "atavistic anti-Semitic instinct."[17]

---

[8] Preussisches Geheimes Staatsarchiv, Berlin, Hauptabteilung XII-III, *Zur Demokratischen Politik* (1926), Nr. 140, *Die Nationalsozialisten.*
[9] *Ibid.*
[10] *Ibid.,* pp. 5–6.
[11] *Ibid.,* p. 6.

[12] Preussisches Geheimes Staatsarchiv, Hauptabteilung XII-III, Werner Stephan, "Verärgerungswahlen," in: *Der Demokrat,* 8 Jahrg., Nr. 22, 24, November, 1927: p. 493.
[13] *Ibid.,* p. 494.
[14] Institut für Zeitgeschichte, München, "Der Nationalsozialismus—eine wachsende Gefahr," in: *Der Demokrat,* 10 Jahrg., Nr. 21, 5, November, 1929: p. 537.
[15] *Ibid.*
[16] *Ibid.*
[17] *Ibid.*

While the German Democratic party had always taken strong stands against reaction in general and against the role of anti-Semitism in German social and political life, truly serious concern with the Nazi party in particular was something that began with the waxing economic crisis which eventually helped to doom the republic. The party's response to the economic crisis was embodied in some proposals—watered down elements of Dr. Gustav Stolper's October Program—which were put forth by the "Reich Employee Committee of the DDP" (*Reichsarbeitnehmerausschuss der DDP*) in December, 1929. Essentially, the committee saw Germany's primary weakness as stemming from a lack of capital. Such a weakness could be compensated for through new "economic leadership," one that could protect the national economy against lack of capital.[18] Committees ought to be set up to protect not merely the private sector of the economy but the public sector (*Volkswirtschaftliche*) as well. Both transaction gains and the extension of credits ought to be rationalized in order to prevent overproduction, which would lead to yet further unemployment.[19] The most inimical forces in the German economy, those that had led to lack of capital and overproduction, were those of plutocracy and monopoly. Only a true economic democracy, the committee suggested, could really provide for Germany's economic needs. However, the Nazi solution was no answer either; and the committee launched an attack upon the somewhat bucolic Nazi economic program. This attack was somewhat different from that of 1926. Now, there was no longer the question of a hidden or non-hidden Marxism in the Nazi program. Rather, the committee took issue with the romanticism inherent in the National Socialist approach. An economy could not be built upon a collection of small farmers and a somewhat rustic middle class.[20] Capital accumulation was the goal, but it could hardly be attained on the basis of that rustic, economic primitivism espoused by the National Socialist party.

From the winter of 1929 until the Nazi take-over in 1933, the German Democratic party and individual Democrats waged a bitter war against the Nazi party. Again, the interesting argument that the Nazis were anti-German-national came to the fore. An example of this could be found in the March 5, 1930, issue of *Der Demokrat*, in which a Koch-Weser address of February 17, 1930, was reprinted. In the address, Koch-Weser chastised Hitler for an unseemly interest in an alliance with Fascist Italy. Germany, Koch-Weser suggested, had had enough of the Italians as "allies" in the last war. Furthermore, the way in which the Italian government was handling the South Tyrol question was scandalous.[21] The danger that National Socialism posed to German youth was obvious and on June 4, 1930, in an article entitled "The Danger of National Socialism" ("Die Gefahr des Nationalsozialismus"), Josef Hutter pointed out that the Nazi movement was deriving considerable strength from youth.[22] Like earlier articles, his seemed to recognize that the Democratic party in particular and democracy in general were losing whatever influence they might have had over German youth. The same sentiments were expressed by Dr. Külz in an address given in the fall of 1930. He blamed the rise of Nazism on a general radicalization of political life that was taking place in Germany at that time. It was difficult to deny, Külz stated, that the Nazi movement, with its admittedly strong national energies, found considerable support among the German people, "above all, among the youth."[23] However, Külz opined, a party which utilized the methods of the Nazis "could never lead a state or satisfy a people."[24] With some accuracy, Külz referred to National Socialism as a movement which embodied mass feelings and instincts. He pointed to its use of romanticism and the organic idea of state. Somewhat inaccurately, Külz proclaimed that state leadership could not be built upon dictatorship and mass psychosis.

In 1930 the *Staatspartei* did attempt to revive that old, somewhat forced identification of the Nazis with the Communists. This was done in regard to the Nazi farm program. A *Staatspartei* hand-bill of 1930 entitled, "Farmer in Need!" ("Bauer in Not!"), called upon the farming population to turn to that one party that had displayed serious interest in farming problems, the *Staatspartei*. The DNVP represented only the interests of large-scale farmers, while both the SPD and the Nazis had effectively sabotaged any effective program of farm aid (the *Osthilfe*). The Nazis were actually "wolves in sheep's clothing." They were, in fact, "Marxists, who want to scrap private property and even expropriate land and soil without indemnity."[25] Naturally, so forced a comparison between the Nazis and the Communists was designed to appeal to the well-recognized conservative side of the German farmer.

One of the strangest and, to the reader, most ambivalent attacks upon Nazism was that made by Friedrich Meinecke in the *Kölnische Zeitung*, dated Decem-

---

[18] Bundesarchiv, Sitzungen des Vorstandes der DDP, Vorschläge des Reichsarbeitnehmerausschuss derr DDP. Zur Abänderung des Wirtschafts programmes entwurfes von Dr. Stolper, p. 10.
[19] *Ibid.*, p. 11.
[20] *Ibid.*, p. 12.
[21] Institut für Zeitgeschichte, Erich Koch-Weser, "Demokratische Reichspolitik," in: *Der Demokrat*, 11 Jahrg., Nr. 5, 5 March, 1930: p. 99.
[22] Josef Hutter, "Die Gefahr des Nationalsozialismus," in: *Die Hilfe*, Nr. 25, 21, Juni, 1930: p. 620.
[23] Bundesarchiv, Nachlass Külz, Nr. 16. Gründung der Deutsche Staatspartei, o.d., Juli–Nov., 1930: 126.
[24] *Ibid.*, 127.
[25] Preussisches Geheimes Staatsarchiv, Hauptabteilung, XII-III, Nr. 145.

ber 21, 1930. First of all, Meinecke, exhibiting that preoccupation with foreign policy characteristic of the Historicism to which he was committed, declared that the Versailles peace is the "final and strongest source of national socialism." [26] As we have seen, Meinecke was never very comfortable insofar as parliamentarianism was concerned and, in the 1930 article, he declared that the democratic principle was more secure with the will of a *Volk*-elected president. However, the article was concerned primarily with the Nazi threat. In attacking Nazism, Meinecke strove to be as fair as possible. Indeed, he discerned some valuable elements in the Nazi movement, *viz.*, "strong national will, the passionate feeling of our political dependency and the ethical revolt against big city dirt." [27] However, these valuable characteristics were weakened, Meinecke thought, by the movement's tendencies towards exaggeration and demagoguery; tendencies which seriously flawed what idealism it may have had and also made it useless and perhaps dangerous in terms of *Realpolitik*.[28] To save itself from the threats posed by such groups as the Nazis, the German bourgeoisie would have to take that single most useful idea from right- and left-wing radicalism, the idea of "strong and concentrated government power," and utilize it to overthrow political divisiveness. Meinecke's attitude towards Nazism was definitely negative but, as was the case with other Democrats, it was not the racism and super-nationalism of the movement that turned him away, although such elements obviously did not appeal to him. Rather, his sense of political and historical propriety was offended by the raucous nature of those who followed Hitler.

In the March, 1931, issue of the *Zeitschrift für Politik*, Werner Stephan published an article entitled "Zur Soziologie der National-Sozialistischen Deutschen Arbeiterpartei." First of all, Stephan claimed that the Nazis were contradictory insofar as ideology was concerned (the same point will be made by Theodor Heuss in his 1932 work). They claimed to be "socialists," yet the Führer was himself a student of Mussolini and, in turn, of Pareto and Sorel, and none of these people were socialistic. The seizure of power was the only true goal of the National Socialist party.[29] Stephan, like many Democrats, tended to underplay the role of Nazi ideology. However, what made his article significant was his attempt to determine the sources of Nazi voting strength. Analyzing various *Länder* elections, Stephan came to several interesting conclusions. The Nazis, he said, did extremely well in highly agricultural areas such as Oldenburg, East Friesland, and Schleswig-Holstein.[30] Moreover, Stephan pointed out, the Nazis were strongest in highly Protestant areas of Germany.[31]

Stephan then went on to make an interesting analysis of election results in Berlin. The Nazis did extremely poorly in the labor district of Wedding and in the upper middle-class ("Villa") district of Zehlendorf. However, they did extremely well (25.8 per cent of the vote) in the middle-class district of Steglitz.[32] The same phenomenon held true in Bremen, where the Nazis obtained only 11.1 per cent of the vote in the working-class districts, 27.7 per cent of the vote in the upper middle-class districts and a most impressive 47 per cent of the vote in middle-class districts.[33] The results of Stephan's analysis ought to have been sobering for German Democrats. The Nazis were scoring heavily in those areas of the population in which the DDP was attempting to establish a strong anchorage for itself, *viz.*, the farming population, and the middle class. To be sure, the so-called "bourgeois middle," i.e., the DDP, also did fairly well, at least in Berlin, in those districts which bulked large in the Nazi voting columns, *viz.*, 23.5 per cent. However, the ability of the Nazis to appeal to the middle and lower middle classes was alarming.

What did it all mean, Stephan asked rhetorically. It meant that the middle class was no longer interested in preserving the social order. Many of those who voted Nazi were uprooted members of the middle class, as were many of the Nazi delegates in the Reichstag.[34] Also, Stephan noted, youth was strongly represented in the Nazi party. Two-thirds of the Nazi Reichstag delegates were less than forty years old.[35] Again, the author emphasized the fact that the Nazis were gaining a great deal of support from those members of the middle class threatened by the depression, people who felt that they had nothing to lose and thus could not be blamed for voting Nazi. The DNVP and DVP seemed to be attracting people in more secure positions. These parties (and, one thinks, Stephan was referring to the DDP as well) seemed to have no understanding for the miserable conditions that prevailed in middle-class ranks. The Nazi party was the party of all those bourgeois who felt threatened with imminent proletarianization.[36] Throughout Stephan's quite perspicacious article, there was the tone of desperation.

By 1932, though, there were some in the still-born *Staatspartei* who were urging that Germany's tattered Democratic forces fight fire with fire. At a March 19, 1932, meeting of the *Parteiausschuss*, committee mem-

---

[26] Meinecke, "Nationalsozialismus und Bürgertum," in: *Politische Schriften und Reden*, ed. George Katowski (Darmstadt, 1958), p. 443.
[27] *Ibid.*
[28] *Ibid.*
[29] Werner Stephan, "Zur Soziologie der Nationalsozialistischen Deutschen Arbeiterpartei," in: *Zeitschrift für Politik*, Band XX, II. März, 1931: p. 793.

[30] *Ibid.*, pp. 794–795.
[31] *Ibid.*, p. 796.
[32] *Ibid.*, p. 797.
[33] *Ibid.*
[34] *Ibid.*, p. 799.
[35] *Ibid.*, p. 800.
[36] *Ibid.*

ber Nuschke suggested that the *Staatspartei* would do far better if it learned to play dirty as the Nazis had done. Among other things, Nuschke thought that it would be useful if the party were to spread it about that the Nazi party was having financial problems and that Hitler was a Catholic.[37] Nuschke's admittedly admirable attempt to emulate the Nazis in basing political campaigns upon sheer dirt was an act of desperation. Such desperation was certainly well justified. The year 1932 was to be excellent for Nazi hopes. Some of this desperation was reflected in frantic letters which the head of the *Staatspartei* in Württemburg, Albert Hopf, sent to various groups and individuals, among them, Theodor Heuss. One of the most disturbing letters was sent to the Wirtherd *Ortsverein* of the *Staatspartei* on May 13, 1932. Here, Hopf pointed out that, in the *Länder* elections of April 24, 1932, the Nazis, the DNVP, and the farmer's organization of the DNVP, the *Bauernbund,* had joined forces, and that the social-evangelical *Christlicher Volksdienst* might well be joining them before too long. Ominously, Hopf reported, the *Süddeutsche Zeitung* was talking of an evangelical government coalition. However, in a letter of May 27, 1932, Hopf announced with some pride that the Württemburg *Staatspartei,* without much assistance from the national leadership, had prevented the Nazis from entering the government, as well as providing that the government enjoyed the confidence of the *Landtag*.[38] Of course, the Democrats were swamped in the July 31, 1932, elections, gaining but 371,800 votes which sent four delegates to the Reichstag.

Despite such occasionally encouraging missives, most German Democrats seemed to realize that the Nazi threat was extremely serious and a measure of fatalism began to evidence itself among them. A good example of this is to be found in a *Hilfe* article of June 11, 1932, entitled "The Future of National Socalism" ("Die Zukunft des Nationalsozialismus"). The author of the article, Professor Carl C. Thalheim, exhibited a great degree of perceptiveness when, like Werner Stephan, he stated that one of the primary sources of strength for Nazism stemmed from lower middle-class fears of proletarianization.[39] Furthermore, the Nazi party, through its emphasis upon organic thinking, indicated that it was aware of the needs and ideals of youth. For these reasons, Professor Thalheim strongly maintained that National Socialism would be around for a long time, especially as such groups as the Social Democrats seemed to lack any sort of understanding of it.[40] He suggested that, at some point in the future, people might well lack the strength to offer effective resistance to so tantalizing a program.

Many Democrats seemed to be well aware of the Nazis' successful use of romanticism. Professor Thalheim's article evidences such an awareness and, on August 15, 1932, in a letter to party chairman Dietrich, Dr. Max Clauss also called attention to the fact that the younger generation, being largely under the influence of a bundist romanticism, was very much taken with Nazism.[41] Dr. Clauss's answer to this problem was similar to ones that we have considered previously: the republic in general and the *Staatspartei* in particular must root themselves in the countryside of Germany. The cities, e.g., Berlin, were either chauvinistic or radical in attitude. Democracy and republicanism both had their natural roots in the countryside.[42] Dr. Clauss's identification of chauvinism as a big-city phenomenon must have raised Dietrich's eyebrows. However, his attempts, dictated either by idealism or expediency, to provide a bucolic, *völkisch* tone for the republic, which would presumably help to immunize it against the more extreme *völkisch* tendencies of Nazism, was not an isolated phenomenon.

At least one member of the *Staatspartei*, Heuss's Württemberg friend Reinhold Maier, thought that the party's attitude towards the Nazis was most unrealistic. In a letter to Dietrich on May 9, 1932, he suggested that it was wrong for the leadership of the *Staatspartei* to state that it would never work with the Nazis. Such a statement, Maier said, would merely strengthen Nazism. Maier thought that the *Staatspartei* ought at least to maintain contacts with the Nazis, even though he appreciated the fact that working with them would present considerable difficulties.[43] The party did maintain an officially hostile attitude towards the Nazis until the end although, as we have seen, individuals like Meinecke displayed a certain degree of ambivalence. However, Meinecke's ambivalence was not the closest that some Democrats drew to the Nazis. As is well known, one of the founders of the German Democratic party, Hjalmar Schlacht (who left the party in 1925 over the issue of confiscation of princes' property) found it rather easy to provide substantial economic advice and assistance to the Nazis once they came to power. The prominent Democratic politician and one-time head of the Badenese government, Willy Hellpach, who left the newly formed *Staatspartei* in 1930, lent a degree of ideological support to Hitler after the latter came to power.[44] Perhaps the most remarkable case

---

[37] Bundesarchiv, Sitzungen des Parteiausschuss der DDP, R 45 III/58, 56.

[38] Heussarchiv, *Briefwechsel*, Albert Hopf/Theodor Heuss, letters of 13 Mai, 1932, & 27, Mai, 1932.

[39] Carl C. Thalheim, "Die Zukunft des Nationalsozialismus," in: *Die Hilfe,* 11 Juni, 1932: p. 573.

[40] *Ibid.,* p. 574.

[41] Bundesarchiv, Nachlass Dietrich, Nr. 224, Die Reichstagwahlen, Bd. VI, Die Wahl 5.11.1932, Juni–November, 1932: p. 49.

[42] *Ibid.,* p. 50.

[43] Heussarchiv, *Briefwechsel* Reinhold Maier/Theodor Heuss.

[44] Among other things, Hellpach, who was a medical doctor and who had training in psychology, wrote two works in which he expressed his satisfaction with the National Socialist regime. These two works were both of a racist nature, *viz.,*

of all, however, is that of Rudolf Diels, a prominent member of first the German Democratic party and then the *Staatspartei*. As a prominent civil servant he had at one time fought Nazism, going so far as to provide legal assistance to Jews who had been slandered. Diels was also a member of the Democratic Club, a group of prominent Democrats, many of them Jewish, who represented a sort of social and ideological auxiliary to democratic political life. His performance in the Prussian government was somewhat mixed.[45] However, he certainly seemed to have been a committed Democrat; indeed, Ernst Feder remarks at one point in his diaries, that Diels would have preferred to have been a Social Democrat.[46] However, by late 1932 Diels had altered his attitude somewhat and the November 7, 1932, entry in Feder's diaries records that Diels had informed a colleague that he was leaving the Democratic Club because he "had become anti-Semitic."[47] Diels was also formally expelled from the club, although several of its non-Jewish members sought to keep him. It is extremely interesting to note that former Democrat—and member of the Democratic party and Democratic Club—Rudolf Diels was to be the first head of the Gestapo, a post which he retained until 1935.[48]

Naturally, most former members of the Democratic party, the *Staatspartei* and the Democratic Club did not go over to the Nazis. However, little resistance was to come from Democratic circles and that strange admixture of romanticism, statism and vestiges of *völkisch* thinking that found a home within at first the Democratic party and later the *Staatspartei* certainly did not serve to obstruct a member's movement in the direction of National Socialism.

Nevertheless, it must be pointed out that clear parliamentary opposition to the Nazis did take place. One of the most significant *Staatspartei* attacks upon the National Socialists—an attack made by delegate Dr. August Weber upon the floor of the Reichstag—found its way into pamphlet form, where it shared space with another parliamentary attack, made by Dr. Rudolf Breitscheid of SPD.[49] In his address, Weber declared that the Nazis were a source of divisiveness in national life and that they made a hideous impression abroad.[50] He also attacked them strongly for their brutality, at the same time protesting the leniency with which convicted Nazi thugs were treated by Germany's right-wing judiciary.[51] He condemned Nazi desires to work closely with Fascist Italy. Again and again, Weber, with great passion and in the face of cynical jeering from the Nazi delegates, condemned the Nazi party as an organization of murderers.[52] With disgust, he recited some of the words of a well-known Nazi marching-song, that all would go well "when Jewish blood spurted from the knife."[53] Weber's attack upon Nazi brutality was a strong one; in fact one of the strongest to emerge from Democratic circles during the last days of the Weimar Republic. Part of his anger may have been due to the fact that he had a Jewish wife. For this reason, he would go into exile in England in 1939. On May 11, 1932, Theodor Heuss, under the nose of Reichstag vice-president Göring, vigorously attacked the very principles of the Nazi ideology. The *völkisch* notions of the Nazis were not only absurd, he remarked, but dangerous as well. Foreign countries with large German minorities might well use these very same notions against the Germans.[54] (This rather interesting, albeit sophistic argument, will be used again in Heuss's *Hitlers Weg*, which also appeared in 1932.) The previous day, Reichstag vice-president Göring had declared that Bismarck's Germany ought to serve all Germans as a model for things to come. Very well, Heuss said, but one must also recognize all the mistakes the Iron Chancellor had made as well as all of his virtues. Here, Heuss picked up a theme common to Democratic thought. Had not Bismarck divided the German *Volk* through his campaigns against Catholics and Socialists? Furthermore, had not his suppression of parliamentary government left a terrible legacy for the future, and had not all of his negative activities served simply to deprive the German people of any sense of "state responsibility"?[55] Naturally, there was implicit in these remarks by Heuss the idea that the Nazis would make the same mistakes as Bismarck, if not worse ones. Of course, both Göring's and Heuss's referring to the legacy of Bismarck—each, naturally, for his own purposes—left something to be desired insofar as the usages of historical analagy were concerned. However, Heuss went further. The Nazis seemed to think, he said, that only the "totalitarian power state" they envisioned would

---

Einführung in die Volkerpsychologie (1938) and *Mensch und Volk der Grosstadt* (1939). In the latter work, Hellpach, while indicating that cities were an important part of any modern state and that it would be romantic nonsense to attempt to do away with them, still viewed them and their inhabitants as "unnatural," an attitude which is currently being voiced by present-day environmentalists, albeit without racial implications.

[45] See Arnold Paucker's "Searchlight on the Decline of the Weimar Republic: The Diaries of Ernst Feder," in: *Yearbook* 13 (1968) Leo Baeck Institute for a discussion of Diels & his somewhat incompetent and/or treacherous behavior in the so-called "Abegg Affair" of September, 1932. See p. 226 in particular.

[46] Paucker, "The Diaries of Ernst Feder," in *Yearbook* 13 (1968) of the Leo Baeck Institute, p. 173.

[47] *Ibid.*, p. 230.

[48] *Ibid.*, p. 165.

[49] *Republikanisches Bibliothek. Band II. Wider den Nationalsozialisten* (Berlin, 1932).

[50] *Ibid.*, p. 73.

[51] *Ibid.*, pp. 83–86.

[52] *Ibid.*, pp. 88, 90–93.

[53] *Ibid.*, p. 95.

[54] Theodor Heuss, *Erinnerungen 1905–1933* (Tübingen, 1963), pp. 417–418.

[55] *Ibid.*, pp. 422–423.

be a truly effective one. Such was not the case. All statesmen of any perspicacity whatsoever knew that "every state signifies power" and that, if threatened by anyone, the Nazis included, it could and would defend itself with all means possible.[56] Heuss concluded his address by launching a far-reaching attack against the character and style of that "Third Reich" which the Nazis were assuring people was on its way. "The outfitting of the Third Reich will be based on a gigantic clearance sale of freshly varnished and dressed up white elephants from the Wilhelmine epoch, and of this, gentlemen, I think that we have had quite enough." [57] With great bitterness, Heuss attacked the primitive Nazi ideas on economics and class relationships. There was nothing at all new about them, he said. Rather, they were simply the product of "a combination of German romanticism and utopian, early socialism in the manner of Weitling and Proudhon." [58] Furthermore, in claiming to be *völkisch,* the Nazis were not being entirely truthful, inasmuch as a good part of their ideology seemed to embody the elitism of the Frenchman Sorel and the Italian Pareto.[59] Of course, in declaring that the coming "Third Reich" was to consist of stale remnants of the Wilhelmine past, Heuss was making something of an error. However, his attack upon the National Socialists was both a strong and a courageous one and this, combined with his soon-to-be-discussed work *Hitlers Weg,* would give the Nazis ample reason to remember him once they came to power.

The most important document to emerge from the Democratic struggle against Nazism was the small book which Theodor Heuss published in 1932. As we have seen, August Weber, a fellow *Staatspartei* member, also produced a work attacking the Nazis, and attacks against the extreme right and upon anti-Semitism had always constituted a fair portion of Democratic and *Staatspartei* literature. However, Heuss's attack upon Nazism was perhaps the most substantive to emerge from Democratic pens during the pre-Hitler time and because of this it behooves us to examine it fairly closely.

First of all, Heuss focused upon Hitler himself. Unlike other Democrats, Heuss did not question the sincerity of some of Hitler's positions. Hitler truly believed, Heuss maintained, in the criminality of those he dubbed "November Criminals." [60] Moreover, Hitler's betrayal by von Kahr in 1923 added to his view of himself as being a political martyr, betrayed by friend and foe alike. Imprisonment had been one of the best things possible for Hitler, inasmuch as it had allowed him to put down his observations in the form of *Mein Kampf.* As for influences upon Hitler himself, Heuss pointed to those of Lueger and von Schönerer. The former had been strongly, if somewhat expediently, anti-Semitic and anti-Hapsburg.[61] While Heuss's treatment of these influences was rather brief, this represented one of the earliest efforts to discern ideological roots for Nazism, and it stands in welcome contrast to the views of individuals such as Meinecke, who preferred to view the Nazi phenomenon as representing one of those demonic and somewhat accidental outbursts of nature in history.[62] Since 1923, Heuss pointed out, Nazism had gained in influence and in impact and Hitler certainly had reason to be proud of what he had accomplished. His twenty-five-point program was a work of genius, particularly inasmuch as it corresponded to a cultural peculiarity of the Germans. "The passion for the program is a special talent of the Germans; it goes back to the pre-parliamentary period and had been but slightly modified during the decades of German constitutionalism." [63]

The National Socialist ideology *per se,* i.e., divorced from its racist underpinnings, was deeply rooted in German history, Friedrich Naumann being perhaps the most prominent exponent of it. However, Heuss remarked, Hitler's movement did not stem from this political phenomenon, "but out of an historical situation: the course of the war, revolution, and the results of Versailles." [64] With good reason, Heuss suggested that Hitler probably never read a book by Naumann. Hitler's main contributions to political life were hardly in the realm of political theory anyway. "What he lent it was temperament, complete agitational devotion and propaganda style." [65] To be sure, Heuss said, such people as Willy Hellpach (who, as we have seen, was to support Hitler ideologically once he had attained power) saw Hitler as being in the tradition of such "national socialists" as Fichte, Lassalle, and Naumann. However, the literature of the movement pointed to the influences of Houston Steward Chamberlain, Oswald Spengler, Othmar Spann, and Adam Müller, rather than to the influences of prominent national socialists of the past. Here, Heuss pointed to the "historical/philosophical system" which Chamberlain and Wagner had provided for Hitler and to Spengler's somewhat snobbish "Prussian socialism." [66] Spann's emphasis on the *Stand* basis of the state was also of considerable importance.[67]

---

[56] *Ibid.,* p. 435.
[57] *Ibid.,* p. 437.
[58] *Ibid.,* p. 428.
[59] *Ibid.,* p. 433.
[60] Theodor Heuss, *Hitlers Weg, Eine historisch-politische Studie über den Nationalsozialismus* (7th ed., Stuttgart, 1932), pp. 1–2.
[61] *Ibid.,* p. 16.
[62] See Meinecke's post-World War II, *Die deutsche Katastrophe* (4th ed., Wiesbaden, 1949), for examples of this, particularly chapter VIII. "Der Zufall und das Allgemeine."
[63] *Op. cit.,* p. 21.
[64] *Ibid.,* p. 25.
[65] *Ibid.,* p. 26.
[66] *Ibid.,* p. 28.
[67] *Ibid.,* p. 29.

Heuss spent considerable time in examining the role of racism in the National Socialist movement and, unlike some other Democratic thinkers of the time, he recognized that this role was a pivotal one. Racist concepts were absurd, Heuss thought. After all, Europe was a mixture of races anyway and there was little to be gained by such thinking. Should one end up investigating the roots of one's own family?[68] In this regard, Heuss made the somewhat questionable remark that many of the tacticians of the movement had found it unwise to take racist teachings too literally. Even Hitler had been forced to refrain from overemphasis upon race just as he had largely rejected the program of Nazism's economic expert, Gottfried Feder. For all of these reasons, Heuss maintained, the somewhat opaque writings of Alfred Rosenberg had never really been accepted as party literature.[69]

Heuss spent considerable time on the question of Hitler's anti-Semitism. The use of anti-Semitism by the Nazis was hardly new, the author pointed out, although the role of the *Untermenschen* theory had added a bit more intellectual spice to the sauce. With a certain aristocratic blandness, Heuss chided the Jews for lowering themselves to the level of the Nazis in replying to attacks made upon them. Furthermore, quarrels among the Jews, particularly over the Zionist question, "certainly do not make their situation any easier."[70] Naturally, extreme racist anti-Semitism created a problem for orthodox German Christians since Judaism had provided the basis for Christianity. However, Heuss pointed out, the Nazis were attempting to get around this spiritual impasse by claiming that Christianity was a sect tinctured by German influences and that Jesus had fought against orthodox Jewry.[71]

With some perceptiveness, Heuss maintained that the Jews, through their efforts to prove statistically their value to Germany, were actually reinforcing the notion of the "Jewish parasite" which, through power and influence, was eating away at the moral fiber of the nation.[72] However, Heuss himself attempted to defend German Jewry by pointing out its contributions to the war effort. With some vehemence, he attacked the desecration of Jewish cemeteries by Nazi hoodlums while also condemning as inaccurate the Nazi propaganda claim that the Jews controlled the press of Germany.[73] As of 1932, the author pointed out, the Nazi party had not yet decided to expel all Jews from Germany, but rather "to deprive them of their rights as citizens."[74] However, as Heuss had pointed out in his Reichstag speech, this would be an extremely dangerous policy for any German government to follow inasmuch as the governments of those nations in which there were large German minorities might well feel free to wreak havoc upon the large but isolated groups of Germans who lived within their own borders. This hypothesis led Heuss to the somewhat interesting conclusion that "'the blood-based' National-Socialist theory of state is more dangerous and destructive to the Germans, conceived of as people, than to the Jews."[75] This rather astounding observation made good agitational sense if we remember that concern for the Jews *per se* had never been a very strong point on the part of most German Democrats.

Heuss deprecated the Nazis' view of the state which, according to him, was unclear and muddled in the extreme. However, the notion of the functional, corporate state was not merely a brain child of Hitler or inspired by the movement which he headed but it went far back in European intellectual history, e.g., to Sismondi, the German Romantics and the Catholic Church (here no doubt, Heuss had in mind some of the ideas expressed by Leo XIII).[76] With some justification, Heuss questioned whether such a view of the state was really very important in Nazi thinking. What, then, was the basic source of strength for Nazism? "The Ethos of the National Socialist movement, and this is perhaps its strongest soulish achievement, lies in its being able to overthrow class and *Stand* differences and professional and educational differences in its great rhythm [which is] stronger than most of the other parties."[77] However, Heuss was himself doubtful as to whether the Nazi organic state would be any more harmonious than that of the liberals. Moreover, Hitler's own position regarding the *Volk* was uncertain. On the one hand he had an extremely positive and romantic view of the German people; on the other hand, his attitude was cynical and almost Nietzschean.

Heuss focused some attention upon the Nazis' attack upon parliamentarianism and their espousing of a more direct form of democracy *à la* plebiscite and referendum. Hitler had achieved much from such an attitude and here the author singled out a German "color-blindness" toward problems of the day and a tendency to blame them all upon the system of parliamentary democracy, which was not really responsible in the first place.[78] However, in keeping with the thinking of Sorel and Pareto, both of whom, Heuss pointed out, were influential in the formation of Fascist ideology, Hitler was really undemocratic, inasmuch as he placed primary emphasis upon a ruling minority, an elite.[79]

Heuss's considerations of the Nazi economic program were quite perceptive indeed. He admitted that the Nazis had a point when they spoke of some of the nega-

---

[68] *Ibid.*, p. 33.
[69] *Ibid.*, pp. 34–35.
[70] *Ibid.*, p. 39.
[71] *Ibid.*, p. 40.
[72] *Ibid.*, p. 41.
[73] *Ibid.*, pp. 41–42.
[74] *Ibid.*, p. 45.

[75] *Ibid.*, p. 46.
[76] *Ibid.*, p. 56.
[77] *Ibid.*, p. 58.
[78] *Ibid.*, p. 65.
[79] *Ibid.*, p. 68.

tive effects of industrialization, e.g., the uprooting of people, the loss of business independence, and so on. However, the author maintained, if there had been no industrial age in Germany, many national strengths would have been lost to those countries in which opportunities for employment would have awaited the arrival of substantial emigration.[80] Besides, those elements of agrarian reform that were to be found among Hitler's twenty-five-point program were there only for psychological effect. Those concepts of economic autarchy espoused by the Nazis were chimerical and Feder's war upon capitalistic rent and interest-slavery was ludicrous inasmuch as such phenomena were necessary in order to provide interest and capital for needed industrial growth.[81] The Nazis had, among other things, proposed that the state seize warehouses throughout Germany and then sell products at lower prices to small businesses in order to encourage the growth of that economic class, i.e., the lower bourgeoisie, from which they were deriving much of their strength.

The thought of transforming the great warehouses into oriental bazaars is, to say the least, original. That it is economically senseless in the modern, West-European metropolis does not have to be pointed out here.[82]

Throughout his discussion of Nazi economics, Heuss seemed to be taking the position that if the Nazis ever came to power, such schemes as proposed for agitational purposes would never be implemented. A close study of the German economy under Nazism would certainly substantiate this point of view.[83]

Heuss, as a self-conscious *Realpolitiker* in the Naumann tradition, was extremely critical of Hitler as a practitioner of foreign policy. In this context, he managed to take a pot shot at an old political foe, Eugen Richter. Heuss maintained that Hitler, like Richter, was opposed to a strong German colonial policy and to fleet-building. Whether or not Heuss was attempting to win the allegiance of the old imperialists for democracy is difficult to say. However, he was no doubt correct in maintaining that Hitler was more interested in Eastern Europe than in Africa.[84] As for Hitler's claim that, knowing war first-hand as he did, he would not be interested in embroiling Germany in a new conflict, this was ludicrous. Hitler was not only bellicose, but he also lacked the sort of political sophistication that had prevented the Allies from moving into Germany during the 1920's.[85]

Insofar as Nazi religious attitudes—other than those as regarded the Jews—were concerned, Heuss pointed out that in Germany there had been some precedence for the combining of political anti-Semitism with Christian piety. Here, he referred to Adolf Stöcker as a prominent example.[86] The tradition was not quite as strong insofar as Catholicism was concerned and Rosenberg, the party ideologue, was certainly anti-Catholic in the extreme. However, Heuss noted that there were some similarities between Hitler's social approach and those of the Catholic Church, particularly since the time of Leo XIII.[87] The author called upon the Church to reject "biological-naturalism," i.e., the Nazi emphasis upon race, with the same zeal with which it had condemned the materialism of the Marxists.[88] In one way, Hitler had really gone back to the Old Testament inasmuch as he too believed in a chosen people of sorts. This was merely Judaism turned about to place the Nordic race in such a position.[89]

Heuss placed considerable emphasis upon Hitler as a party leader and, in this context, compared him to Lassalle. The party had derived much support from its conception of itself as not really being a party at all, but a "movement."[90] However, this party, or movement, so irrational ideologically, was highly rational in terms of organization—party machinery, organization, offices, etc. An attempt to seize power would probably not work. However, Heuss pointed out, Hitler had placed tremendous emphasis upon propaganda and he had proved to be a master in grasping the feelings of a crown and of mob psychology in general.[91]

In the last portion of the book, Heuss took a shotgun approach to various topics regarding Hitler in particular and the German political problem in general. He called attention to Hitler's and the Nazis' anti-feminist attitudes and pointed out that this had found some support among conservative elements—women included—who did not wish to see women play prominent roles in public life.[92] Heuss also claimed that Hitler's post-1932 emphasis on legality had alienated him from many in his own party, who were beginning to view their Führer as becoming bourgeois.[93] Although Heuss said little more about this, one would assume that he was referring to the "left wing" of the Nazi movement, i.e., to the Strasser brothers, Ernst Röhm *et al.*

Heuss, continuing earlier efforts to defend parliamentary democracy, claimed that Weimar problems of parliamentary government were not due so much to the "system" which, Heuss maintained, was definitely elastic enough to handle them, but rather to the ways

---

[80] *Ibid.*, p. 81.
[81] *Ibid.*, pp. 85–87.
[82] *Ibid.*, p. 88.
[83] See David Schoenbaum, *Hitler's Social Revolution: Class and Status in Nazi Germany 1933–1939* (New York, 1966).
[84] Heuss, *op. cit.*, p. 97.
[85] *Ibid.*, pp. 100–101.
[86] *Ibid.*, p. 106.
[87] *Ibid.*, pp. 108–109.
[88] *Ibid.*, p. 113.
[89] *Ibid.*, p. 114.
[90] *Ibid.*, pp. 115–118.
[91] *Ibid.*, p. 131.
[92] *Ibid.*, pp. 134–135.
[93] *Ibid.*, p. 137.

in which the Germans handled the system. Rather pointedly, Heuss called attention to the fact that the very concept of "fairness" did not exist in the German mentality and that political life suffered from this lack. There was nothing "as nasty and as characteristic as this: that we must borrow the English word for this concept." [94]

As Heuss saw it, Hitler was in the process of toning down his propaganda in order to make his party and himself more respectable.[95] However, the organic nature of the Nazi movement, its emphases upon landscape and *Volkstum* remained, and Heuss took the occasion to take a pot shot at the organic approach of the Nazis. According to Hitler and his party, prewar Germany was characterized by courage, while postwar Germany was ruled by a gang of cowards, "traitor(s) to the German mission."[96] If this were indeed the case, Heuss maintained, there would have been a break in the "organic unity" of the German people and hence, by definition, no unity at all. However, much that was now occurring in German politics caused many to overlook this. Today, i.e., in 1932, the political parties were fighting each other with slogans of the nineteenth century and one could observe a general and systematic turning away from reason, "the methodization of the irrational, and through rational means." [97] Hitler was thus able to draw upon a very broad stratum of individuals, not only from the middle class, inasmuch as workers too often felt alienated, even from those parties which claimed to represent their interests. Thus, Heuss maintained, Hitler was in part correct when he said that his party transcended party lines and drew strength from all groups throughout Germany.[98] For now, Heuss thought, young farmers constituted the greatest single source of Nazi strength. Previously, farmers had been almost aggressively apolitical, but now they were not merely defending themselves and their interests but going over to the attack.[99] The farming interests of Germany, threatened by modernization and overproduction (and also, although Heuss did not go into this, by programs such as those of the Democratic party, which tended to encourage overproduction by calling for increasing numbers of farms), were sensitive to the promises of the Nazis, particularly to the concept of the autarchic state. The fact that the Nazis were also promising better rent to farmers on the one hand while promising cheaper goods for proletarians on the other was generally not noticed.[100]

The common ground for those adhering to Nazism, Heuss thought, was a general sort of "anticapitalistic feeling." This was drawn to both salient aspects of the Nazi approach: (1) the tendency toward a new order of some sort and (2) a definite revolt against the present, i.e., against parliamentarianism and the industrial society.[101] The German people, Heuss said, were in reality following Hitler and not the movement. When Hitler and the movement became routinized, as all political movements and their leaders had to do, much of this hysterical support would die down if not vanish altogether.[102] Briefly, Heuss was, consciously or unconsciously, applying a kind of Weberian critique to the Nazi party in general and to Hitler in particular. Much as Weber had predicted, rather accurately as things turned out, that the Social Democratic party would eventually be bureaucratized and routinized out of its ideological consistency, so Heuss saw Nazism and Hitler as being in rather the same position. Movement or no, Nazism and its present leader would go the way of all political parties and movements whether or not it succeeded in attaining power.

Hitlers Weg was the most significant anti-Hitler document to emerge from the ranks of Germany's Weimar-period Democrats. It was significant not only because it represented a consistent and well-written attack upon Hitler and the party he represented but also because it linked this attack with (1) an attempt to examine some of the sources of Nazism, i.e., an attempt to put the movement in some sort of historical context, and (2) an attempt to defend vigorously the Weimar Republic and its constitution. Both of these points were of great importance. First of all, Heuss's attempts to discern the roots of National Socialism and thus to put it in some sort of historical context stood in welcome contrast to the attitudes of many in Democratic circles who seemed to be unable to focus upon the movement as an historical phenomenon and were hence never able to understand it or to appreciate its hideous potentialities. Heuss's efforts are particularly impressive when we realize that, except for Theodor Geiger's work on National Socialism, by 1932 relatively little had been done on discerning the cultural and social roots of Nazism or of the anti-Semitism which comprised so much of its program. Heuss's little book was indeed a pioneering venture not only in political analysis but in cultural history as well. His efforts on behalf of the Weimar Republic were also quite impressive. As seen earlier, he was hardly uncritical of the republic or, for that matter, of political parties. However, his defense of parliamentary democracy remained a strong one right up until the fall of the republic itself. While virtually all Democrats, and the Democratic party as a whole, were highly critical of Nazism, very few of them, with the significant ex-

---

[94] *Ibid.,* p. 145.
[95] *Ibid.,* pp. 148–149.
[96] *Ibid.,* pp. 158–159.
[97] *Ibid.,* pp. 160–161.
[98] *Ibid.,* p. 164.
[99] *Ibid.*
[100] *Ibid.*
[101] *Ibid.,* p. 166.
[102] *Ibid.,* p. 168.

ception of Erkelenz whom Heuss did not like, were consistent in defending republicanism and/or political pluralism. In fact, as we have seen, the *Staatspartei* of 1930 in part represented a rejection of some of the salient characteristics of the pluralistic society. Heuss, though, remained adamantly republican until the end.

Naturally, *Hitlers Weg* did display a number of rather substantial weaknesses. First of all, Heuss's statement that the Nazi movement drew most of its intellectual and electoral support from the Treaty of Versailles is somewhat questionable, if not shortsighted. As a matter of fact, in his post-World War II *Erinnerungen*, he admitted that he probably overstated the importance of this phenomenon.[103] He also seriously underestimated the virulence of Nazi anti-Semitism, and his own highly critical attitude towards the cynicism and urban cosmopolitanism which he associated with Jewish *literati* came out in his statement that the Jews were responding badly to the Nazi attacks. Heuss did not seem to realize that the Nazi attitude towards the Jews could be externalized in a manner which would make vitriolic exchanges of billingsgate seem rather mild. However, few outside of the Nazi party really grasped this. Heuss was not—and perhaps could not have been—aware of the fact that Hitler and his movement could well avoid the dangers of routinization by placing great emphasis upon the extirpation of the internal enemy and by engaging Germany in a policy of continuous warfare. However, these criticisms must not obscure the fact that Heuss's work indicated that at least some of Weimar's beleaguered Democrats had a fairly good understanding of the Nazi movement and moreover understood what would probably happen if the Nazis came to power. Heuss, and such individuals as Professor Thalheim, displayed very profound insight into the significance and causes of the Nazi movement.

Hitler came to power as chancellor on January 30, 1933. Germany's Democrats certainly knew what this would mean. Heuss informed a Jewish friend that "this will be an evil time for you Jews,"[104] while Meinecke, in an essay entitled "Von Schleicher zu Hitler," attempted to point out what he considered to be the basic mistakes which had allowed Hitler to come to power. The most crucial of these he felt to be von Hindenburg's decision to dismiss Schleicher.[105] Meinecke, in his February 23 essay, "Von Schleicher zu Hitler," described the Nazi revolution as being a "revolution from above" which threatened to enslave half the German population through the other half which, through the Nazi movement, had come to power.[106] Exactly what Meinecke meant by this analysis is not clear; viz., did he mean a form of class dictatorship or merely that half of the electorate who had voted Nazi or DNVP were enslaving the half that did not? Meinecke professed not to hate the Nazis as men. Rather he hated "only the basically damaging ideas by which they allowed themselves to be intoxicated."[107] Furthermore, no doubt referring to Nazi opposition to "big-city dirt" and the like, Meinecke made the point of stating that several of the salient Nazi ideas were "common heritages of a better German past."[108] His main criticism of Nazism was the following: that the movement had attempted to develop these ideas "through splitting the *Volk* instead of through *Volksgemeinschaft*:"[109] Meinecke had had fought Nazism in the best ways that he knew how. Nevertheless, his understanding of the movement was never terribly acute; nor was his appreciation of and concern about what the movement's victory meant for German Jewry.

In the campaign for the March, 1933, elections, some Democrats attempted to grasp the bull by the horns. Külz, for example, attacked Goebbels for his statement that Prussia had been run, until July, 1932, by a Jewish conspiracy. Of the 12 *Oberpresidäntan*, 35 *Regierungspräsidenten*, and 400 *Landräter*, there had been not one single Jew. Of 35 *Polizeipräsidenten*, one had been a Jew. A party based upon "hatred and intolerance" could never succeed in becoming the spiritual base for the German people.[110] Naturally, in the atmosphere of Hitler's recent success, extensive campaigning took place under something of a cloud. In a somewhat pathetic letter of February 7, 1933, Külz pointed out the danger that phone conversations were being tapped.[111] The *Staatspartei*, in desperation, dared to combine lists with the SPD for the March 5, 1933, elections. However, this did the party little good. Although five mandates were sent to the Reichstag, the party's popular vote declined from one per cent of the electorate (336,500 votes) obtained in the November 30, 1932, elections (which sufficed to send two delegates to the Reichstag), to .8 per cent of the electorate (334,200 votes).

In an article in *Die Hilfe*, March 18, 1933, entitled "Unsere nationalsoziale Bewegung und der Nationalsozialismus," Gertrud Bäumer made an attempt to tie the thinking of Naumann, and the movement he presumably represented, to that of the Nazis. The rise of the Nazis to power, she thought, represented the "second explosion of long accumulated psychic explosives."[112] (What constituted the "first explosion"

---

[103] Theodor Heuss, *Erinnerungen, op. cit.*, p. 253.
[104] *Ibid.*, p. 168.
[105] Meinecke, *op. cit.*, 478.
[106] *Ibid.*, p. 481.
[107] *Ibid.*, p. 482.
[108] *Ibid.*
[109] *Ibid.*
[110] Bundesarchiv, Nachlass Külz, Nr. 19, Reichstagwahlen Bd. XI, o.D., Feb.–Marz, 1933 (undated speech), 5.
[111] *Ibid.*, 17.
[112] Gertrud Bäumer, "Unsere Nationalsoziale Bewegung und der Nationalsozialismus," in: *Die Hilfe*, Nr. 6, 10 Marz, 1933: p. 161.

is somewhat uncertain. Perhaps Bäumer was referring to the German "revolution" of 1918.) In the article, Bäumer emphasized Naumann's efforts to win the German working class away from Marxist internationalism, as well as his concern that the German nation remain militarily strong. Bäumer—and here she was being quite consistent with the position held by many Weimar Democrats, as well as that voiced by the now insignificant *Staatspartei*—maintained that it had always been of utmost importance for Germany that a superpolitical "national social policy" be implemented. "Now," she observed sagaciously, "this will be implemented [*vollziehen*] under different political forms [*Vorzeichen*] than those of democracy."[113] However, despite this change of forms, the basic issues and tasks confronting the German nation remained the same. These were "the binding of its [the nation's] possibilities of existence to certain economic and political presuppositions . . . [and] the task of, under these unprecedentedly difficult conditions, guiding the nation as a whole through its crisis."[114] Bäumer concluded by voicing her faith in the German people's ability to face up to the necessary tasks of the hour and, recognizing that the Nazis had done much to make German people aware of these tasks, she declared that Friedrich Naumann had anticipated, if not the rise of something like the Nazi party, then at least the dawn of a new age, i.e., that of "completed capitalism and perhaps the dawn of socialism."[115] As matters turned out, of course, it would seem that Bäumer, while quite sensitive to the powerful nationalism both embodied in and awakened by Hitler's party, took the socialism aspect of it far more seriously than did the latter. While it would be easy to suggest that Bäumer's article was written out of fear and with one eye on the censor, the tone of a sort of mystical *volkstümlich* socialism combined with an almost vulgar Machiavellism marks it as typical of that point of view characteristic of some Weimar Democrats.

On March 23, 1933, the Reichstag, with the notable exception of the Social Democrats, cut its own throat in voting for that "Enabling Act," and thus turning over all legislative activities of this somewhat moribund body to the Nazi/Nationalist dominated cabinet. The five-man *Staatspartei* delegation was split as to the stand it ought to take. Heuss and Dietrich thought that it should stand with the Social Democrats in voting "no" to the promulgation of the Enabling Act. However, the three other delegates, Heinrich Landahl, Ernst Lemmer, and Reinhold Maier, felt that, through accepting the act, "the possibility of legal development would be strengthened."[116] In other words, if Hitler were to have his actions legalized he would somehow be accountable for them. As Heuss points out, Dietrich did not want to go against the decision of his friend Heinrich Brüning of the Centre party, particularly as he and Brüning had been informed of the promises made by Hitler to Monsignor Kaas, promises which persuaded the leader of the Centre Reichstag delegation to vote in favor of the Enabling Act. Dietrich did not want to separate himself from Brüning, Heuss did not want to separate from Dietrich, and so things went.[117] The delegation thus unanimously voted approval for the Enabling Act. Reinhold Maier, speaking for the *Staatspartei* fraction, declared that the German people had voted for the present government on March 5, 1933. Moreover, the *Staatspartei* did feel that they could go along with the goal of national reconstruction as expressed by Chancellor Hitler in the Reichstag speech just delivered.[118] There were, to be sure, some remaining anxieties among the members of the *Staatspartei*. However, Maier said, he was sure that the government would welcome "an objective and loyal critique of its measures."[119] Maier did notice, however, that protection of civil liberties seemed not to have been covered in the new Enabling Act, and he went on to state that an independent judiciary and a professional bureaucracy had to be preserved. Nevertheless, Maier concluded with the following statement:

In the interest of *Volk* and fatherland, and in expectation of developments according to law, we subordinate our serious misgivings and vote for the Enabling Act.[120]

The party's reward for such cooperation was its forced dissolution on July 17, 1933, Heuss turning in the fraction's parliamentary papers "under protest." The period of internal emigration—and in a very few cases, active collaboration with the new regime—had begun.

Democratic attitudes towards the Nazis had been almost unanimously negative. Moreover, some Democrats, e.g., Heuss, had evidenced a quite sophisticated appreciation of what the Nazi movement meant in the context of German political life. However, one cannot gainsay the fact that, while the Democratic party (and later the *Staatspartei*) and individual Democrats stood opposed to Nazism, recognition of what the Nazi movement actually meant was sometimes rather muted. Heuss, while recognizing the role that racism played in the party, was not very concerned about the fate of German Jewry. Meinecke, Koch-Weser, and others saw the Nazi movement as evil because it disrupted

---

[113] *Ibid.*, p. 163.
[114] *Ibid.*
[115] *Ibid.*, pp. 163–164.
[116] Friedrich Naumann Stiftung, *Geschichte des deutsche Liberalismus, op. cit.*, p. 126.
[117] Theodor Heuss, *Der Mann, das Werk, die Zeit. Eine Ausstellung*, ed. Eberhard Pikart Pikart (Stuttgart, 1967), p. 178.
[118] *Verhandlungen des Reichstages. VIII. Wahlperiode. Stenographische Berichte. Anlagen zu den Stenographischen Berichten. Sache und Sprechregister. Band 457. Berichte Anlagen* (Berlin, 1934), 38B.
[119] *Ibid.*, 38C.
[120] *Ibid.*

the organic *Volk*-community, the latter being an ideal which of course existed at the base of Nazi political speculation as well. Party literature and individual statements of people such as Külz expressed a concern over Nazi anti-Semitism, but basically, this one aspect of the Nazi program which would be adhered to with scrupulous rigor was never subjected to the thorough scrutiny of the party or of the individuals who composed it. Even Koch-Weser, who was partly Jewish, who participated with a fair degree of vigor as a legal adviser to Jews (as did Hermann Dietrich), and who had been attacked or slandered by the Nazis, seemed in his public statements and his diaries to focus little attention on the Nazis as anti-Semites. The one former member of the German Democratic party, Otto Gessler, who would take part in the July 20, 1944, plot against Adolf Hitler—and who would suffer for this at the hands of the Gestapo [121]—evidenced little real concern over Nazism during the Weimar period, and certainly almost none at all in regard to its virulent anti-Semitism. In fact, as we have seen in an earlier chapter, he shared many of the right's bitter attitudes towards that cosmopolitanism and cynicism that was associated with republican Jewish circles. For most Democrats, at least in their public statements as Democrats, Nazism was evil because it was socialistic and/or utopian in its economic programs, because it was cynical and un-*real*-political in foreign policy, and because it was divisive of the German *Volk*. To be sure, some Democrats, e.g., Külz in his 1933 speech, did attack Nazi anti-Semitism. However, attacks on the Nazi party in general and Hitler in particular generally did not emphasize this aspect of the Nazi program. The reasons why this was so are not hard to discern.

As we have seen in the last chapter, the Democrats who took an active part in Weimar political life were most sensitive to the charge that "their party," i.e., the German Democratic party, was a "Jew party." To be labeled "Jew party" was tantamount to political death in Weimar-period Germany. The irony of it all of course was that the Jews constituted a fairly high percentage of the Democratic party's support. Loss of this support could prove to be somewhat irritating, if not embarrassing, as the *Staatspartei* discovered in the period 1930–1932. However, in its somewhat pathetic attempts to become a mass party or, as Bäumer would have preferred it, a mass *völkisch* party, the Democratic leadership found it necessary to play down much of the tolerance aspect of the party. To be sure, the German Democratic party was always officially against anti-Semitism. However, in party literature and in the statements of many Democrats, the Jewish connection had to be understated if the party were to be able to expand itself beyond the limits of being a "bowling club." Ironically enough, though, those uncommitted and/or conservative forces in the bourgeoisie which the party was attempting to tap were to swing over to the Nazi movement or, in the cases of Württemburg and Bavaria, over to anti-republican, right-wing groups such as the *Wirtschaftspartei*. However, the no doubt accurate assessment of the situation that one must avoid being labeled a "Jew party" if one wanted to enjoy even a modicum of success as a mass party was a fair commentary upon the state of mind of the German electorate, or at least of the German bourgeoisie. In this regard, it is valid testimony to the fact that anti-Semitism was a tremendous force in German Weimar-period political life, even for those politically somnambulent burghers who chose to cast their vote for the DVP, DNPV, or the *Wirtschaftspartei* rather than for the Nazis.

However, for some Democrats other factors were at work to determine their own responses to Nazism. Many in Democratic circles found themselves offended by several aspects of Weimar-period life. "Big city dirt," "cosmopolitan cynicism," the evil influence of "Jewish literary circles"—these phenomena proved offensive to those whom Fritz Ringer has aptly characterized as the "mandarins" of German social and cultural life. In other words, while the Nazi movement as a whole, particularly in its vulgar, somewhat irrational aspects, proved offensive to such people, some of its emotional underpinnings were shared by many who were ostensibly involved in defending the republic. As we have seen earlier, Gertrud Bäumer, who had little really to say about Nazism, could feel a certain attachment to the *Jungdeutsche Orden* and even to the Fascism which it in part represented. Even Theodor Wolff, offended by the seeming chaos of Weimar political life, could be somewhat receptive to the non-anti-Semitic Fascism of Mussolini's Italy. Koch-Weser, while defending individual Jews against Nazi attacks, could also be extremely active in attempting to form an alliance with a group, the *Jungdeutsche Orden*, which was avowedly racist, while he evidenced certain embarrassment over the Democratic party's needed reliance upon Jewish circles and the partly Jewish-dominated republican press. *Völkisch*, statist, and even anti-Semitic attitudes were not absent from Democratic circles in Weimar Germany or even from the Democratic party itself, and these no doubt had a vitiating influence on the Democratic struggle against an organization which, among other things, was much more systematic in its espousing of some of the same ideas. Even those who would suffer from Nazism, e.g., Koch-Weser, shared some of the emotional attitudes which contributed to its rise to power. Such attitudes serve to explain the general lack of resistance to the Nazis which characterized Germany's Weimar Democrats once the Nazis assumed power. To be sure, none of

---

[121] See Gessler, *Reichswehrpolitik in der Weimarer Zeit* for his reminiscences of this fearful period of his life. See also, *Theodor Heuss: Der Mann, Das Werk, die Zeit: Eine Ausstellung*, ed. Eberhard Pikart (Stuttgart, 1967), p. 234.

the individuals upon whom we have focused, with the possible exception of Diels, could ever have condoned much less have participated in the unspeakably brutal acts of the Nazis. However, their inability to offer any variety of substantive resistance to the regime must be viewed as unhappy testimony to the raw immaturity and moral weakness of German Weimar democracy and to the muddled spiritual postures of its most notable defenders.

VIII. TWO EXAMPLES OF DEMOCRATIC REJECTION OF REPUBLICANISM

As we have seen, German Democrats during the Weimar period were often somewhat nondemocratic, or at least nonrepublican, in their point of view. We have considered some of the nondemocratic, nonrepublican, or anti-Semitic ways in which that element upon which parliamentary democracy depended, the enlightened bourgeoisie, responded to the stresses and strains of Weimar life. Some of these attitudes were captured in two books which appeared during the last years of German democracy; one of these works was by Gertrud Bäumer, whose rather *völkisch*, at times anti-Semitic attitudes we have considered previously, while the other was written by the individual who, between 1924 and 1930, was chairman of the German Democratic party, Erich Koch-Weser. Bäumer's book, *Sinn und Formen geister Führung* ("Meaning and Forms of Spiritual Leadership") appeared in 1930, while Koch-Weser's work, *Dennoch aufwärts!* ("And Yet, Upwards!") appeared, ironically enough in 1933, the year in which Hitler came to power and also the year in which Koch-Weser was forced to go into exile, eventually settling in Brazil, where, in 1944, he died. Because these books do represent substantive critiques of Weimar political life as well as being important in their own rights as commentaries upon the confused spiritual states of at least two people who thought themselves to be democratic, this writer feels that they must be considered in an individual chapter.

Gertrud Bäumer, as we have seen, felt herself to be extremely close to Naumann and, in fact, she took over editorship of *Die Hilfe* from Naumann when he died in August, 1919. Bäumer was, among other things, an avowed feminist, a political idealist, and a romantic and we have seen evidence for at least the last two attitudes in those writings we have considered thus far. However, most of Bäumer's interests and avocations were non-political in nature (except to the extent that she was concerned with feminine emancipation; she co-edited *Die Frau* between 1893 and 1944 and also wrote several books concerned with the role of women in German cultural and political life). She wrote a number of books and essays on child psychology and various literary and philosophical topics, e.g., on tragedy, the poetry of Dante, and on Fichte, as well. By the time of her death, in 1954, she had established the reputation of being a sensitive, somewhat mystically inclined literary critic and poet.

Under Naumann's influence, a most powerful one, it would seem, Bäumer became seriously involved in politics. She basically accepted the Naumann national social(ist) ideal as well as his ostensibly *Real*-political analyses of German social problems and the role that Germany should assume among the family of nations. When Naumann participated in the formation of the new German Democratic party, Bäumer naturally joined him. While in the party, she served as a Reichstag delegate and, between 1919 and 1933, she served in the government as well, as a ministerial adviser to the Ministry of the Interior (it was in this capacity that she put pressure on Külz at first to support the *Schunde und Schmutz* law of 1926). However, Bäumer was far more of a romantic than Naumann and, unlike Naumann, she never really accepted that urbanization and, to some extent, depersonalization that characterized the industrial age. Moreover, she was never terribly happy with parliamentarianism (at least that form of it which prevailed in Germany) and, in many ways, she was a political romantic as well as a literary one.

Except for her studies of the woman's role in German history, Bäumer wrote very little on politics. However, as we have seen, her *Hilfe* essays, among other things, clearly pointed to a certain anti-urban, anti-rational and, in many ways, anti-political (in the narrow sense of the term) bias, while in private remarks she also evidenced a degree of cultural anti-Semitism. Her one major political work, *Sinn und Formen geistiger Führung*, appeared in 1930 and, at least in Clio's eyes, is not terribly well known. However, inasmuch as the book does bring together the opinions—at least on political leadership—of one who considered herself to be representative of German Democracy, it is important for the light it might cast in this realm.

Bäumer's book was concerned largely with the values which she saw as contributing to several varieties of spiritual leadership. The basic value, she felt, which allowed a particular individual to assume a leadership role in Germany—and presumably anywhere else as well—was the individual's reflection or embodiment of the common will of the nation. This will was most important and it transcended ephemeral constitutions and constitutional arrangements.

The German Reich does not subsist in the parchment of the constitution and not in the simple existence of a German parliament and in a German government; rather it sustains itself as a common will in all of its members.[1]

It was the leader's task to preserve this will and to win it for the state.[2] Here, we can see a remnant of

---
[1] Gertrud Bäumer, *Sinn und Formen geistiger Führung* (Berlin, 1930), p. 18.
[2] *Ibid.*

Naumann's old influence, i.e., in the notions that (1) the *Volk* possessed a will, or perhaps a tendency, which had to be *won* by the state, and (2) that the state was in the final analysis more important than the *Volk* and that the state in the form of the leader had to draw the people to it. To be able to utilize mass feelings for the benefit of the state, however, the leader must, from the first, be bound to the society he represented. In order for the leader to be able correctly to interpret mass tendencies or the mass will, society and the leader must have "a similar *Weltanschauung* or common ideas."[3] However, the leader must also be above mass pettiness and materialism, above the "merely biological effects of the great life-forces."[4]

Bäumer saw the leader as not merely being a manipulator or utilizer of mass feelings, but rather as one who also embodied elements of a higher, spiritual reality.

The leader does not create this world of value, the domain of the spirit. It leads to him. He sets it free. Indeed, this objective spiritual reality speaks from the leader, whose organ or instrument he is.[5]

This view of the leader went far beyond that held by political liberalism, or, for that matter, most aspects of political conservatism as well. Bäumer was viewing the leader as one who was providentially or at least spiritually (in the objective sense) ordained for his task. Bäumer viewed any form of leadership, in either a pedagogical or political form, as being comprised of three elements. "The essential core of leadership and its functioning is spiritual, but the serving means are magic and eros."[6] The primary task of the leader, the kernel of his leadership, was "the transmutation of the incorporeal kingdom of the spirit into living reality."[7] Here, Bäumer was clearly stepping away from such political theoreticians as Naumann or Max Weber, neither of whom saw the "word" as being in any manner transmuted into earthly reality. To be sure, Weber, in his emphasis upon charisma, seemed to be touching on something alluded to by Bäumer, the leader's utilization and control of mass passions. However, Weber meant this in a much more mechanical sense, and Bäumer's dualistic view of reality was something which he would have scorned. Obviously, for Bäumer, the leader had a great deal of power over those who followed him. However, she was adamant in emphasizing that the leader's control had to be exercised in a positive manner. He must not dominate people, but rather allow them to become themselves, to realize their own potential. Leadership which desired only to make others dependent upon it, "or works only in the sphere of personal and natural domination over others, is not only unfruitful but, in the literal sense, 'seduction'."[8] In this regard, Bäumer attacked the present-day interest in dictatorship. This form was a particularly bad permutation of the leadership principle. This longing for dictatorship pointed to a particular aspect of modern life.

In the increasing glorification of the dictator ... today, there is much of that impotent submissiveness to force and soulish/physical longing for pleasure [on the part of] the weak.[9]

Here, Bäumer seemed to be pointing to a sort of "flight from freedom" explanation *à la* Fromm in explaining why modern men seemed to be so susceptible to the "seduction" of dictators. Men were too easily coerced or too subject to spiritual laziness in order to be able to reject the lure of those who promised to assume responsibility for them. Her rejection of the dictatorial leader was of importance, but we must realize that every modern totalitarian dictator, with the possible exception of Stalin, has rationalized his rule on the basis of his serving as an instrument in the self-realization of his *Volk*. Bäumer's approach could explain, however, why she found it easy to admire individuals such as Mahraun; after all, he placed primary emphasis upon personality and personal leadership qualities. As we have seen, Bäumer was not terribly consistent in that she also found it easy to admire Mussolini as well.

The area which Bäumer thought should be most free from compulsion of any kind was that of education. Here, "magic," that element of leadership which was, for her, somewhat important in other realms, had no role to play at all. "Such magic in the relationship of the strong to the weak is a dangerous surrogate of educative effect."[10] Extrapolating further upon this, Bäumer stated the following: "There is no growth, no '*Bildung*' in the shadow of human 'power'."[11] Such a relatively "free" attitude towards education and cultural development rings strangely upon the ear when we recall that Bäumer was most concerned that the state prevent "obscene literature" and the like from being available to German youth. However, she was not the only Democrat whose romanticism was tempered by a *Biedermeier* posture towards morality. Bäumer went on to state that true education, i.e., self-development, was utterly lacking in the current (i.e., 1930) school system of Germany. Making a strong, albeit somewhat despairing, bid for the *Einheitsschule*, Bäumer pointed out that the present school system totally lacked any sort of spiritual unity. The teacher/student relationship, she thought, was also a bad one, since it had not provided for that "most intensive influence and union which, in the highest sense,

---

[3] *Ibid.*, p. 19.
[4] *Ibid.*
[5] *Ibid.*, p. 20.
[6] *Ibid.*, p. 24.
[7] *Ibid.*, p. 27.

[8] *Ibid.*
[9] *Ibid.*, p. 28.
[10] *Ibid.*, pp. 48–49.
[11] *Ibid.*, p. 49.

would be educational leadership."[12] Bäumer's implied attacks upon that *Kadavergehorsamkeit* which prevailed in the German classroom was part of a tradition which embraced Wedekind's expressionist play *Frühlungserwachen* and Heinrich Mann's *Professor Unrat*. It had overtones of a curious sort of spiritual radicalism about it. Yet, at the same time, it was linked to an equally curious sort of paternalism (or perhaps maternalism, in Bäumer's case), such as that reflected in Bäumer's efforts to somehow protect German youth from the corrupting influences of smutty literature and cosmopolitan cynicism. This dialectical fusion of *Biedermeier* morality with romanticism was a traditional one in German cultural history and was also strongly represented on the German Right, and in National Socialism. This movement was also concerned with capturing a following of youthful idealists while at the same time protecting them from "degenerate art" and the corrupt, Jew-dominated city.

In her 1930 work, though, Bäumer was concerned mainly with political leadership. In this realm, she thought, magic had an important role to play. "Political leadership," she maintained, "is perhaps the polar opposite of pedagogical."[13] She defined politics in the following way: "Politics is the struggle over legitimate power. Political leadership is exclusively leadership of will and leadership of action."[14] In this particular area, Bäumer adopted the somewhat *Real*-political language of her mentor Naumann or of Max Weber.

The measure of political action is neither the good, nor the true nor the beautiful. In which bloc of values does politics, above all, belong? Each political achievement represents a chain of deeds. Is the work of Bismarck, the unification of Germany, something 'good'?[15]

Apparently not uncomfortable in *Real*-political garments, Bäumer went on to point out that politics was in a different realm altogether than that of value.

The means of politics is "power." Its end is the "state." Insofar as the state is a power relationship, the object of politics is therefore "power" as well. The politician desires to influence the division of power.[16]

Politics was concerned with "what is", not with "what should be." It had to deal with facts and not with ideas, and it had to organize these facts into various power constellations. In this context, Bäumer seemed to break sharply from some of the attitudes displayed in her *Hilfe* essays. In these essays, as we recall, she seemed to view the *Volksstaat* as a sort of idealistic, supra-political goal of all political life. Now, in the 1930 work, she advanced the notion that idealism had a rather pragmatic role to play, *viz.*, it could be used as a sort of motor, a tool of political power, a means by which the leader could utilize mass desires for ego-fulfillment to attain political power.[17]

Bäumer placed particular emphasis upon Weber's differentiation between what he called the *Gessinungsethik*, or "ethic of conscience" and the *Verantwortungsethik* or "ethic of responsibility"; the latter was the ethic of politics and thus of success.[18] Again, we can detect an obvious *Real*-political tone in Bäumer's writings, one which, at least at first blush, contrasts strangely with her otherwise somewhat romantic *Weltanschauung*.

Magic Bäumer indicated, was of particular importance within the context of mass politics. The masses—somehow different from that *Volk* with which Bäumer felt so warm an empathy—were constantly being deceived by the newspapers and by the "illusion" in part created by the newspapers, that "the masses are pushing him [the leader] before them, instead of his pulling them."[19] However, Bäumer was quick to reestablish a symbiotic relationship between the leader and the people he led. Although the leader must lead a people rather than the other way around, his effectiveness could be judged only to the degree that he was able to summon forth innate spiritual powers within the breasts of his people. "In the final analysis, what is decisive for the politician is not what he himself creates, but that which he awakens."[20] Here, we can see a resolution of the seeming contradiction between Bäumer's view of politics as being rather coldly pragmatic, e.g., in its utilization of idealism for state-determined goals, and her more idealistic attitudes, as evidenced in the *Hilfe* articles, towards the *Volksstaat*. The leader had to act in a pragmatic manner in order to summon forth latent potentialities within his people. The people had to be guided, by whatever means possible, towards the realization of its highest capabilities. Here Bäumer's characterization of the highest form of leadership is of importance. For her, it was the blending together of the subjective desires of the leader and the objective needs of his *Volk* and his age.[21] This point of view, which in part reflected the Historicist tradition in which most members of the German *Bildungsbürgertum* were schooled, allowed her to retain a fair degree of idealism insofar as politics was concerned. There was, of course, a danger in this and Bäumer was quick to recognize it, *viz.*, that the subjective element might prove to be too strong and that its demonic character might prevail; in other words, that the leader might yield to naked egoism. This would have to be guarded against with great care. However, a certain degree of the demonic was essential,

---

[12] *Ibid.*, pp. 52–53.
[13] *Ibid.*, p. 61.
[14] *Ibid.*
[15] *Ibid.*, pp. 61–62.
[16] *Ibid.*, p. 62.

[17] *Ibid.*, pp. 64–67.
[18] *Ibid.*, pp. 66–67.
[19] *Ibid.*, p. 70.
[20] *Ibid.*, p. 75.
[21] *Ibid.*, p. 77.

Bäumer thought, because this constituted the "magical elemental strength of political leadership."[22]

Basic to political leadership, though, was the realization that the political leader had to approach his task from a "social-creative" point of view. He had to advance

the creative development of existing relationships toward a condition in which the strengths of *Volk* and *Staat* are fruitfully and effectively bound together; the life of the nation will be more richly revealed through the means of the state.[23]

The spiritual development of the collective *Volk* implied that any sort of "group interest" would have to be subordinated to goals which the leader himself had to determine. Such an attitude was not uncommon among Weimar Democrats, as we have seen, particularly inasmuch as they came to view the Weimar Republic as consisting of a "heap of interests" which had usurped or were attempting to usurp state power for their own respective uses.

Bäumer concluded the book on a somewhat metaphysical note, focusing upon the "Leadership of the Thinker" ("Die Führung des Denkers"). There were, she maintained, two types of ideas, those that illuminate and those that move. Galileo was an example of one who "illuminated" while Giordano Bruno was one who "moved."[24] The difference between the illuminating and the moving thinker was the following: "The one judges the cosmos; the other, widens the kingdom of life."[25] Thus, the illuminating thinker had more of a scientific bent. He judged the world, i.e., told us how it worked. In this regard, Bäumer thought, he was a very useful being. By definition, he was opposed to subjectivism and this could be very useful if not necessary. However, this approach could be misused (or overused) and a dangerous "intellectualism" could result.[26] The romantic side of Bäumer always rebelled against what she considered to be overemphases upon reason and science.

Bäumer expressed an implicit preference for the leader as a creator of "moving ideas" inasmuch as she saw leadership as having attained a special role when it entered this realm. The philosopher was one who "moved," i.e., widened the kingdom of life.[27] This particular variety of leader represented what he saw, not through symbols, i.e., mathematically, but through concepts and similar devices. The thinker of moving ideas could not, Bäumer thought, be a simple espouser of ideas. He himself had to be moved or disturbed by those thoughts with which he hoped to move others. He must be honest, and have a good soul or else his thinking would become meaningless in the long run.[28] The thinker—one feels here, that Bäumer is referring to all thinkers—cannot really create or be more than the simple material of the eternal. All that he could do was to provide a deepened understanding of that which was already there. "He has not been granted [the power] to create."[29] By implication, Bäumer was maintaining that only the aesthetician truly creates.

For Bäumer, the true leader had to realize that the subjective world of feeling and formal *Kultur* were not separate. For example, religion and *Kultur* were not unbridgeable opposites in the "essentially western form of the God experience."[30] The ultimate criterion of value was whether or not one's grasping of truth, "making the word flesh," as she put it, was time-bound to specific historical or national conditions, or whether it was eternal.[31] With the Old Testament prophets, she said, "this experience remained bound to contemporary political ideas."[32] Bäumer suggested also that the experience might be misused through the deceiving magic of false prophets. Her attitude toward the, in her eyes, somewhat mundane, Old Testament prophets is most interesting. A generally negative view of the Old Testament and, by implication, of those who worshiped by it, was characteristic of many German thinkers, e.g., Fichte and Wagner. While this would hardly point to any systematic variety of anti-Semitism, it would serve in part to explain, or to rationalize, some of the attitudes Bäumer displayed in other contexts, e.g., her tendency to view cities and those who inhabited them as being in some way more materialistic and less pure than those traditional and Christian souls who inhabited the countryside. Those whose attitude towards Judaism were negative, at least in the religious sense, were often critical of the Old Testament as being either mundane or not as transcendental in its message or value as the New Testament. The tragically confused Walther Rathenau was one who fell into this pattern.[33]

Bäumer's work is interesting from several points of view. First of all, in her desire to win the masses for the state she revealed an attitude that could well have been expected from a disciple of Friedrich Naumann. Her attitude towards political leadership bore, at times, a striking resemblance to that of Max Weber. However, at the same time, she evidenced a deep-seated political romanticism which neither of her two de-

---

[22] *Ibid.*
[23] *Ibid.*, p. 86.
[24] *Ibid.*, p. 112.
[25] *Ibid.*
[26] *Ibid.*, pp. 118–121.
[27] *Ibid.*, pp. 123–124.
[28] *Ibid.*, p. 130.
[29] *Ibid.*, p. 131.
[30] *Ibid.*, p. 142.
[31] *Ibid.*, p. 144.
[32] *Ibid.*
[33] For an example of Walther Rathenau's elevation of the New over the Old Testament and his emphasis upon the transcendental quality of the former, see his letter to Rabbi Daniel Fink of June 21, 1912. This is to be found in *Walther Rathenau Schriften*, edited by Arnold Hartung *et al.* (Berlin, 1965), p. 104.

ceased colleagues ever represented. She viewed the political leader as one who had some sort of mystical rapport with eternal truths, an individual who could summon forth the innate powers of a collective unconscious. In truth, the Weimar Republic, for Bäumer, was little more than writings on parchment, and her attitude towards the Reichstag had been a negative one almost from the beginning. While she was sincerely opposed to any formal dictatorship, her somewhat organic view of politics, one that presupposed the existence of a collective will of some sort or another, combined with her generally mystical view of the world of ideas (a literal phenomenon for her, it would seem) allowed her to evidence considerable sympathy for such anti-republican and quasi-racist groups as the *Jungdeutsche Orden,* while her defenses of the Weimar Republic, as a republic, were vitiated by a decidedly cool attitude towards day-to-day politics (as opposed to the metapolitics extolled in her 1930 book). In her romantically tinged prejudices, organic views of political life and worship of unfettered youth, Bäumer stood out as a living example of why political pluralism never achieved a firm anchorage in the *Bildungsbürgertum* of Germany.

Koch-Weser's book, *Und dennoch aufwärts!* was written under some duress. Even before the Nazis came to power, he had suffered a fair degree of humiliation as we have seen. After his efforts at forming an alliance with the *Jungdeutsche Orden* had miscarried, he had been deprived of his post not only of chairman of the now-bankrupt *Staatspartei,* but of Reichstag delegate as well. Moreover, some of the bitterness expressed in his diaries was reflected in this most interesting work. Unlike Bäumer's work, that of Koch-Weser's was devoted almost exclusively to the world of mundane political affairs, and intrusions of the metaphysical were rather few and far between.

Koch-Weser began the work by noting that the so-called "revolution" of 1918 had been a negative rather than a positive one. Turning his back upon previous notions, Koch-Weser maintained that "the feeling of the masses is primitive." [34] Instinct generally ruled. Moreover, the revolution was really meaningless in any truly political sense in that "the development of the idea of the liberal/democratic state form had been assured previously under Max von Baden." [35] Thus, the "revolution" was really one of the German people against itself and this in part explained the almost complete lack of unity among the participants. This criticism of the revolution of 1918 was a most cogent one, and it represented a complete reversal of the earlier position adhered to, at least formally, by many Democrats, viz., that 1918 represented a sort of watershed in German political history. Now, Koch-Weser was really stating that there had been no revolution at all, rather, a sort of uprising against homefront miseries, that was really directed against, not the monarchy, but the new liberal/democratic government.

Koch-Weser was not very critical of the Weimar Constitution as such, although he indicated that the old question of order and/or freedom had not really been resolved by it. The Germans had not lived under the Weimar system anyway, but rather under a degenerate form of it. Sounding somewhat like Theodor Heuss in the latter's *Hitlers Weg,* Koch-Weser noted that, "There is, even today, hardly a people that is so ready to turn against its *Volk*-comrades with such fanaticism as the Germans." [36] The middle parties (i.e., the Democratic party and, one would assume, the Centre party as well) had tried to keep abreast of the situation and to mediate bitter feelings, but little could have been done inasmuch as "The German believes that he shows character when he shows his teeth." [37] However, the parties were themselves to blame for the degenerating political situation in that they gradually eschewed their roles of being "servant(s) of the whole" and viewed themselves as serving their own interests. [38] Furthermore, the Weimar years saw a divergence between liberal and democratic interests, which was in part reflected in the Democratic party. "Liberalism," Koch-Weser maintained, "desires freedom from power; democracy, the possession of power." [39] While the divergence had been hidden before, in an era in which both elements were struggling against monarchical rule, they came into the open once the republic was established. Liberalism itself tended to disappear. It lacked, particularly in Germany, "party-building strengths" and it tended to degenerate into a system of assumed principles. [40] The German people had had enough freedom anyway, and the time had come for a more democratic emphasis to be made. However, the republic had never really made the transition between "so-called formal democracy to economic democracy and political liberalism had been mortally wounded by its lack of a positive program." [41] In a word, Koch-Weser was criticizing political liberalism for (1) not recognizing the need for a true democracy and (2) its lack of a concrete ideology. The latter point Koch-Weser himself had attempted to remedy through the abortive effort to fuse the old Democratic party with the *Jungdeutsche Orden.* Koch-Weser was extremely critical of parties which saw themselves and their own interests as representing the end-all and the be-all of political life. Hence, his explanation of the rise of anti-parliamentarianism, as

---

[34] Erich Koch-Weser, *Und dennoch aufwärts!* (Berlin, 1933), p. 3.
[35] *Ibid.,* p. 4.
[36] *Ibid.,* p. 79.
[37] *Ibid.,* p. 80.
[38] *Ibid.,* pp. 80–81.
[39] *Ibid.,* p. 82.
[40] *Ibid.,* pp. 82–83.
[41] *Ibid.,* p. 83.

exemplified in the Nazi and Communist parties, seems a bit strange. "In Germany, the parties have become nothing because they wanted to be everything."[42] What Koch-Weser of course meant was that the various parties attempted to elevate their respective interests to being representative of the whole. However, Theodor Heuss, as we have seen, had recognized that virtually every political party tended to see its interests and those of the collective whole or the state as being coterminous. Koch-Weser, particularly in view of his own attempts to form a *Staatspartei,* was driving himself into a logical corner: it was wrong for one political party to see itself as embodying state life while actually, it ought best to be willing to sacrifice itself to interests of state. However, it was wrong for the German people not to support that single group, as represented in the Democratic party and then the *Staatspartei,* which stood for reason of state. However, Koch-Weser seemed not to recognize this difficulty (at least he did not attempt to unravel it in this book) and his view of parties as being innately somewhat selfish if not rapacious enabled him to make the statement that parties calling for political dictatorship differed from ordinary political parties only in degree.[43] While this might have been true, Koch-Weser should have paid more attention to the Hegelian maxim that quantitative differences can become qualitative once a certain degree had been attained.

Koch-Weser, again seemingly unaware of the difficulties presented by such a position, declared that what the country now needed was a party of "reason and conciliation," which would bring the German people together in a "community of need" (*Notgemeinschaft*) while at the same time providing more leadership to serve the German people.[44] While calling for some form of new *Staatspartei,* Koch-Weser also attacked what he called the "party-state," i.e., that state of coalitions and party splinterings that had characterized the Weimar Republic up to that time. "The party-state is an entity which at no time had had the unified will of the *Volk* behind it. Without an independent and responsible head, the German state is not capable of existence."[45]

Koch-Weser's implied attacks on parliamentarianism soon came out into the open when he declared that this institution was a rather late form of democracy, "and not . . . the best" at that.[46] Here, he sounded strikingly like Meinecke and also Carl Schmitt, an early ideologist of Nazism, who was reaching somewhat the same conclusions.[47] Parliamentary government was proper only in England, Koch-Weser thought, and even there it was being threatened through the rise of a solidarity-conscious Labor party.[48] At any rate, parliamentarianism was finished if the parties who were absolutely opposed to the government were to constitute a majority in parliament. In Germany, Koch-Weser argued, the parliament had talked itself to death.[49] Government by discussion seemed to be an exercise in futility and, at any rate, fewer and fewer good people were being attracted to parliamentary careers. Like others of his own party, Koch-Weser was adamant in maintaining that the powers of the Reichstag were just too great for the good of the German people. The Reichstag should endeavor to become like the English parliament despite the fact that, as we have seen, Koch-Weser thought that true parliamentary democracy could take place only in England, and it should be concerned with major issues.[50] What Koch-Weser seemed to be implying here was that parliament had concerned itself with a manifold of issues, many of them minor, and had been in a way deflected from the truly great problems, e.g., economic democratization, which concerned the German people. Such a point of view could well be expected from one who had seen virtually everything for which he had fought, economic democratization, land reform, the *Einheitsstaat,* and the *Einheitsschule,* buried in parliamentary turmoil while other issues, e.g., the flag issue of 1926, were allowed to predominate. In view of this, Koch-Weser should have modified his earlier approach. Germany should have had a more mature parliamentarianism, with more actual power, rather than one that had allowed itself to be stagnated by trivia. However, what Koch-Weser gave with one hand, he took away with the other. He called for a strengthened presidency and for the upper house to work vigorously with the Reichstag to assist the president at arriving at decisions, particularly in the areas of finance and economics.[51] Thus the position of Koch-Weser's strengthened parliament was somewhat weakened by an implied subservient role to the president. What Koch-Weser might well have had in mind was the creation of such posts as parliamentary secretaries, such as those that existed in England, a course of action which, as we have seen, Erkelenz had suggested in 1927. However, he was not very clear on this point and, judging from earlier statements and from his emphasis on creating a party which would, in some

---

[42] *Ibid.,* p. 90.
[43] *Ibid.,* p. 95.
[44] *Ibid.,* p. 96.
[45] *Ibid.*
[46] *Ibid.,* p. 97.
[47] See Carl Schmitt's *Staat, Bewegung, Volk* (Hamburg, 1933) and his 1926 essay *Der Gegensatz von Parlamentarismus und moderner Massendemokratie.* Schmitt is discussed at length in Sigmund Neumann's *Behemoth* (New York, 1941), particularly on pp. 43–45, while selections from his writings have been reproduced in Harry Pross, *Die Zerstörung der deutschen Politik: Dokumente 1871–1933* (Hamburg and Frankfurt am Main, 1959) and in George L. Mosse, *Nazi Culture* (New York, 1966).

[48] *Op. cit.,* p. 98.
[49] *Ibid.,* pp. 105–106.
[50] *Ibid.,* p. 111.
[51] *Ibid.,* pp. 132–137.

way, be an embodiment of state spirit, his general view of the role of parliament, at least in the German context, must be seen as being more negative than positive. In the final analysis, Koch-Weser placed primary emphasis upon a kind of collective consciousness, much as Bäumer had done. The only possibility for Germany's salvation was "to fill the *Volk* with state spirit and the state with *Volk* spirit." [52]

Obviously critical of the old *Reichswehr*, Koch-Weser called for universal military training rather than for a professional army. A true people's army (*Volksheer*) was extremely important in that it was a sign of "order and love for the fatherland." [53] Koch-Weser emphasized, much as Gessler had claimed to do, that the army must be kept "far from party politics." [54] Even if Germany were to be threatened with civil war, Koch-Weser put his trust in a large people's army which would be completely divorced from politics. This attitude to a large extent explains why Koch-Weser had been so irritated with Erkelenz's 1927 attacks upon the *Reichswehr* and why he also tended to support Gessler, whose commitment to republicanism was somewhat less than ardent. He, like Gessler and, as we have seen, like Heuss also, viewed the army as being above politics, in effect, somewhat sacrosanct. One could be critical of it and offer suggestions for changes. However, active interference in military affairs by any political group was out of the question, while the army itself had to exist as a supra-political institution, consciously outside of political life. In a way, both the military and the politicians never quite seem to have recovered from the period of the Prussian Reform Movement, when Baron vom Stein declared that soldiers should never become citizens.

Koch-Weser spent some time on the question of Jews in German political life. Expressing both historical reality and his own prejudices, he remarked that most German parties did not want to work with the Jews inasmuch as they wanted to avoid being labeled as Jew parties.[55] Expressing some bitterness that Jews had turned away from the *Staatspartei*, he pointed out that many of them had gone over to the Centre party which, they thought, could offer them some protection against Nazi threats. The threats posed to the Jews by mass society, at least in Germany, caused Koch-Weser to make the somewhat perceptive remark that the Jews were perhaps better off under a monarchy than in a people's republic.[56] The implication, of course, was that most German Christians were, to one degree or another, anti-Semitic. Koch-Weser himself evidenced a certain degree of bitterness towards his semi-coreligionists. Because Jews had tended to support liberal and left-of-center causes, many had gained the notion that the Jews were, as a group, somewhat progressive. This was not true at all, Koch-Weser maintained. In fact, the Jews were more degenerate than any other people.[57] Whether Koch-Weser meant this in a religious sense, as had Rathenau, or whether he was using some other criterion to determine degeneracy is difficult to say. Judging from earlier remarks about Jewish defensiveness and/or obnoxious social behavior, one might assume that Koch-Weser shared some of the attitudes of Bäumer and others; namely, that the Jews represented a source of city-bred cynicism while Jewish religious practices had become outworn vestiges. There was, he thought, absolutely no danger of a united Jewish front threatening Germany. Inasmuch as the Jews were not unified on anything, such a threat was merely a "fairy tale." [58] "The solution of the Jewish question," he declared, "lies only in the assimilation of the Jews." [59]

Koch-Weser's *Und dennoch aufwärts!* was the work of an individual who had been embittered and demoralized by the course of republican life in Germany. His ideas and programs, the last of which involved an attempt to interject a certain youthful radicalism into the one bourgeois group which, on paper at least, remained committed to republicanism, had all failed. He was now a pariah, isolated from his former colleagues and harassed by a mass, revolutionary movement which threatened to destroy him. However, in his 1933 work, he was not breaking radically from past concepts and prejudices. Now, they had been merely brought together in a more organized form. His disgust with interest politics, with parliament and with the Jews, phenomena that had appeared in earlier private and occasionally in public writings, had been eloquently summed up in a work which called for the pursuit of that same mystical and elusive goal as had Naumann and the Democratic party of 1918: unity of *Volk* and sacrifice in the name of a greatly expanded state. Koch-Weser, while perhaps more positively inclined towards parliamentary government and political parties than such individuals as Bäumer or Meinecke, ended up seeing them as means to the end of *Volk*-unity, much as had other colleagues of his party. His attitude towards the Jews, while not racist—his call for Jewish assimilation certainly pointed this out—was tinged with the same vestiges of social and cultural anti-Semitism as those of Meinecke, Bäumer, and others. Koch-Weser, in political *extremis*, pointed to some of the basic problems which plagued Germany's Weimar-period Democrats: suspicion of parliamentary government, a tendency to view political norms and goals in terms of a suggested *Volk*-unity, and a rather non-systematic, but nonetheless real, anti-Semitic posture.

---

[52] *Ibid.*, p. 137.
[53] *Ibid.*, p. 222.
[54] *Ibid.*
[55] *Ibid.*, p. 263.
[56] *Ibid.*, p. 264.
[57] *Ibid.*
[58] *Ibid.*, pp. 266–267.
[59] *Ibid.*, p. 267.

Taken together, these two rather curious works, *Sinn und Formen geistiger Führung* by Bäumer and *Und dennoch aufwärts!* by Koch-Weser, can be seen as pointing to some of the significant problems that haunted Weimar republicanism. Naturally, political commentators have to recognize the not insignificant role of irrationality in politics and the fact that there are political decisions and influences which exist outside of any given formal political structure. However, for Bäumer, the various impedimenta of Western political life, parties, parliaments, the mediation of interests, were all seen as being somewhat tiresome, if not a little dirty. She, as well as Koch-Weser, assumed that there was a unified national will and that it was the task of the political leader somehow to tap or draw upon this will. She, as well as Koch-Weser, was a cultural anti-Semite. The fact that the authors of these works could consider themselves to be Democrats defending parliamentary government is a testimony to the political and intellectual bankruptcy of Weimar Germany's bourgeois Democrats. To be sure, in Koch-Weser's case, much of this despair did not appear until the mid-1920's. However, the traditions upon which he fell back once the despair had set in was that general admixture of romanticism, political dualism, and scattered *völkisch* elements that had constituted much of Germany's political tradition. The two works we have considered can be viewed as milestones on the road to political surrender to those demonic, yet understandable, forces which lurked below the surface of German life, and which were in part represented in the ranks of those committed to the defense of German democratic republicanism.

IX. CONCLUSIONS

Looking through the gigantic telescope of hindsight, we perhaps can say that what occurred within bourgeois Democratic ranks during the Weimar years—i.e., the subtle and, at times, not too subtle flirtation with various undemocratic or at least unpluralistic notions of political life—was both a result of German political history, at least since the beginning of the nineteenth century, and a result of the German Democratic party's peculiar position in Weimar politics. Let us now consider the first point.

Because of the relative lateness of German drives for unification, liberalism, as in part the offspring of the Revolutionary period and Napoleon, in part the legacy of German idealism, was closely wedded to nationalism from the beginning. A Fichte, for example, could remain sympathetic to the general goals of the French Revolution while, at the same time, espousing romantic political philosophy, e.g., the organic view of state expressed in his *Addresses to The German Nation* of 1808, and a virulent anti-Semitism. To be sure, the nationalist/liberal synthesis was one that was not confined to Germany. However, Germany's middle class lacked any sort of revolutionary or, for that matter, significant political experience. In this regard, the *Bildungsbürgertum* was no different from the majority of those who constituted the German middle class. A rising middle class may or may not have fought and won a civil war in England, and the French Revolution may or may not have been a purely middle-class phenomenon. However, what is important here is that many individuals of these respective national middle-class groups thought that such was indeed the case. The middle classes of the major nations of Western Europe saw their respective societies being molded in terms of their interests whether or not their own roles in these processes were as pronounced as they thought they had been. In Germany, particularly in Prussia, which was eventually to unify the nation, the middle classes had been kept in a position of political backwardness by regimes which depended upon the preservation of a noble class to supply officers for armies and staffs for growing bureaucracies. Even during the post-1815 period of "constitutionalism" in southern and western Germany, such constitutions as did appear were generally, with the notable exceptions of Württemberg and, in the 1830's, Baden, *oktroyiert*, i.e., granted from above. Certainly, in those areas that had been under strong French influence, i.e., Baden, Württemberg, Bavaria, and, after 1815, Rhenish Prussia, native bourgeois elements were sympathetic to constitutionalism. However, up until 1848 the German bourgeoisie, while concerned with questions of economic and political unification as well as with the extension and preservation of individual freedom, never staged a major revolt on behalf of its principles. In varying degrees, monarchism, if not absolutism, remained the prevailing and largely unchallenged principle throughout Germany.

The year 1848, of course, saw revolutions throughout Germany. However, the results were disastrous insofar as bourgeois political self-consciousness was concerned. Despite the overthrow of love-smitten Ludwig I of Bavaria and the granting of an extremely watered-down constitution in Prussia, 1848 market the demise, at least in the nineteenth century, of that noble synthesis between liberalism and nationalism. In Prussia, a bourgeoisie terrified of proletarian revolution welcomed Prussian troops back to Berlin while, at the same time, it raised little outcry over the extremely conservative constitution which was finally promulgated in January, 1850. The fugitives from the Frankfurt Assembly, observing reaction's progress throughout their respective fatherlands, could not help but to ponder the ineffectualness of the liberal pen when confronted with the absolutist sword. The history of German liberalism between 1848 and 1870 and, indeed, after unification as well, was one of continuous, if, in terms of Germany's unique history, necessary compromise with state authority or of retreat in the face of it. Moreover, the fragmentation of liberalism between 1878 and the turn of the century allowed first Bismarck and later Wilhelm II to embark upon various adventures and pseudo-crusades with little fear of interference from a united liberal front. Liberals such as Eduard Lasker might well have made an ethical point of sorts by seceding from their party once they saw it being too easily influenced or controlled by the state. An Eugen Richter might well have held forth for private initiative and personal freedoms in the face of autocracy. However, the ineffectiveness of the former and the, at times, ludicrous isolation of the latter, increasingly so even within his own somewhat beleaguered party, served simply to set the almost complete capitulation of German liberalism to the German state in a clearer perspective.

The lack of concrete political involvement that had characterized the German bourgeoisie during the eighteenth and nineteenth centuries, combined with a history in which political freedom had been defined as princely freedom *vis-à-vis* the empire had allowed for a most interesting view of politics and the state to develop. This was political dualism, and it permeated the writings of virtually every German liberal during the nineteenth and twentieth centuries. A dualistic view can be defined, in this context, as one which sees the state as being somehow divorced from or above the activities of formal political groups or parliamentary activities. Often Hegel is seen as being primarily responsible for the spread of such an attitude. However, he was not alone in this. With the possible exception of Wilhelm von Humboldt, virtually every German political thinker from Baron vom Stein to Friedrich Dahlmann viewed the state as being a more or less organic entity which was in some way more than the sum of its parts. These thinkers might well have differed radically among themselves on other issues. However, the tendency to see the state as being in some ways immutable was perhaps the most singularly pronounced phenomenon of German political thought. Political life was not seen as being unimportant or superfluous. However, it was, more often than not, viewed as being the activity which would bring more people to the state rather than one which was concerned with the mediation of interests.

The rise of Germany to the position of world power did necessitate a broadening of this attitude, and perceptive individuals, such as Friedrich Naumann, soon realized that the hallowed *Kaisertum* would have to be expanded to embrace that mass society which was developing in the wake of industrial growth. The Naumann "national-socialist" scheme was an effort in this direction, based upon one extremely important assumption: that there existed in Germany a cleavage between its two most important classes, the bourgeoisie, which was loyal to the state and supportive of all state efforts at imperialist expansion, and the proletariat, which lacked a consciousness of state citizenship and which was, more often than not, under the baleful influence of anti-state, revolutionary Marxism. In a way, Naumann took the Erfurt Synthesis of 1891, in which the German Social Democratic party swore allegiance to Marxist principles of dialectical materialism (if not, strictly, to those of revolution) more seriously than at least the leadership of this party. Max Weber was perhaps somewhat more realistic about the Social Democrats as a revolutionary force when he expressed the view that this party, in order to keep itself in being, would have to become as bureaucratized, routinized and as committed to the *status quo* as any other political party. However, in regard to policies of imperial expansion and the building of a fleet which such a policy necessitated, Naumann was no doubt correct in assuming that there was somewhat less enthusiasm on the part of the German proletariat than on the part of the bourgeoisie. Hence, his scheme of "winning the masses for the state" would seem to have had some valid point to it.

What Naumann's attitude actually represented was merely the application to political life of statist doctrines, such as had been expounded by many German liberals and glorified by the Historicist tradition of German historiography. As Naumann and his biographer, Theodor Heuss, never tired of pointing out, the question at hand was that of expanding state power, not that of political morality. A modern state, i.e., *circa* 1900, in order to achieve and retain a position of world power, had to have a strong basis of mass support. The traditional supremacy of an old, ossified economic and social class, the *Junker,* would have to be broken or at least diminished if Germany was to be able to engage in such heady programs of imperialistic expansion as were being suggested and/or in fact carried out. This necessitated the commitment of the proletariat to the state, as well as a more active voice for the Reichstag in the day-to-day affairs of state. In other words, the German state had to be expanded, if necessary, at the expense of the tradition-encrusted *Kaisertum*. Naumann's ideas were not confined to a limited, precocious circle of yea-sayers, but were in fact shared by some of the leading luminaries of pre-World War I German political life, e.g., Theodor Heuss, Friedrich Meinecke, Max Weber (who, however, tended to be less convinced of the importance of a politically conscious proletariat) and Walther Rathenau.

In schemes of this nature such things as political parties and parliamentary government, while not deprecated altogether, tended to assume roles of lesser importance than in the general liberal philosophies adhered to in the countries of Western Europe. Among German liberals, particularly among those who followed Naumann or adhered to an outlook similar to his, they were seen as means to an end, rather than as institutions possessing an intrinsic merit of their own. Germany's prewar liberals viewed reform mainly from the point of view of *raison d'état* and from this perspective, they often attacked traditional monarchists and *Junker* as being less interested in the state than they were. While reason of state is certainly not an illegitimate cause for reform, primary emphasis upon it would tend to vitiate or at least tone down moral commitment to such things as parliamentary government. What would happen if a parliament or a collection of political parties were to be viewed as being inimical to reason of state? What if they were to be seen as being destructive to national unity rather than as contributing to it?

What happened during the Weimar period was precisely this, *viz.*, that political pluralism became something that was seen by many Democrats as being inimical to *Volk*-unity and thus to the state. At the beginning, the Democratic party had been formed for two purposes: (1) to stand for republican principles, and (2) to unify the German nation. At first, republicanism and, presumably, the pluralistic society which it supposedly represented was seen as the one form of government that would divide the German people the least. Some Democrats, such as Erkelenz, welcomed the new republic with enthusiasm. Others, such as Meinecke, did not welcome but, rather, accepted it as being dictated by grim historical necessity. Between these two extreme reactions, there were those somewhat mixed ones of individuals like Heuss, Bäumer, Koch-Weser, and others. While some, such as Heuss and Koch-Weser, declared themselves for republicanism and the pluralistic society (Koch-Weser's views on this matter underwent a serious change over the years, as we have seen), others approached Meinecke's attitude, viewing the republic as something that had been dictated by brutal historical necessity. Individuals such as Bäumer saw the new state through prisms distended by political romanticism. Above and beyond the disparate individual reactions of Germany's Democrats, there was one, unifying reaction which tied all of them together: the determination at last to translate the unifying, statist schemes of Friedrich Naumann into reality. Naumann himself, of course, died in August, 1919, and the party in particular and German Democrats in general were thus deprived of his leadership and guidance quite early. However, his statist influence remained and individuals like Meinecke and Bäumer were forever in his debt.

Many German Democrats and, to some extent, the German Democratic party as a whole were influenced by a nexus of ideas which were not at all republican or democratic either in origin or content. Elements of political romanticism were also present, and these appeared from time to time in the thinking of virtually every important German Democrat, with the possible exception of Heuss, especially as German political life became ever more confused. Anti-Semitism, while never part of the programs of either the German Democratic party or the *Staatspartei* which took its place, was always present, to one degree or another, among those who belonged to either or both of the groups. Again, this was not the racist variety of anti-Semitism such as was apotheosized in the Nazi program. However, elements of social or cultural anti-Semitism were never absent from Democratic circles during the Weimar years and, even an individual such as Theodor Heuss who, according to his *Preludes to Life,* had been opposed to anti-Semitism of any kind when a youth, was not above making anti-Semitic remarks, albeit in private. The comments of such people as Heuss, and even more those of individuals like Bäumer, Meinecke, and Gessler, revealed the basic attitude that Jews were really not part of the German national scene. One ought best to be tolerant of them, but Jewish cosmopolitanism and/or cynicism—at least as they saw it—made the task not an easy one. This point of view was, of course, reinforced if not substantiated by the remarks of someone like Walther Rathenau, whose attitude towards his coreligionists was hardly clear.

For some Democrats, e.g., Koch-Weser, the rebellion against republicanism and the avowed rapaciousness of political parties occurred fairly late, i.e., in the mid-1920's. Others, however, such as Meinecke, took a distinctly negative attitude towards republicanism almost from the beginning and even Naumann, before the Democratic party really got off the ground, could criticize the vestiges of parliamentarianism that he saw creeping into Democratic circles. Thus from the beginning, i.e., even before German political life became torn by divisiveness and party conflict, there were those whose attitude toward parliamentarianism and party life was hardly republican in tone. One could perhaps argue that people such as Meinecke evidenced a great degree of perspicacity in arguing against parliamentarianism and political egotism from the beginning. However, there is another way of viewing such phenomena. The attitudes of such people as Meinecke, who thought in statist terms, who viewed political life as serving to strengthen a well-nigh immutable state, were precisely the attitudes which, if shared by enough individual citizens to say nothing of party leaders, made republican life impossible. As Theodor Heuss pointed out, every political party saw itself as embodying *Staatsgedanke* or the interests of state. It is one of the ironies of political life in Weimar Germany that probably only an avowedly confessional party, the Centre, and a supposedly class party, the Social Democrats, did not conceive of themselves as being *Staatsparteien.* The very concept of there being a *Staatspartei* was one that could easily have developed within the context of the German political tradition, i.e., a tradition which accepted the state as something that was both antecedent and superior to daily political life.

As bourgeois democracy was placed under stress, the situation worsened. Statist, romantic, and at times anti-Semitic elements became more and more prevalent within the party, the first two phenomena in fact being actually embodied within the platform of the *Staatspartei* founded in the summer of 1930. The somewhat *völkisch* orientation of the party pointed out two important problems of Weimar-period Germany: (1) that to become, or attempt to become, a mass political party, it was necessary to take on a more *völkisch* coloring, and (2) that liberalism under stress turned almost naturally in a more *völkisch* direction. Again, we are painfully reminded of the fact that any non-socialist party, if it desired to maintain itself in political life, could not be associated with Jewish support; nor could it stand for a sweet-reasoned republicanism. However, the attitudes of such people as Bäumer and even Koch-Weser did not evidence a deep-seated regret in being "driven" to ally democracy with radical, *völkisch* youth. *Völkisch* and statist elements, particularly the latter, always had been present in Democratic circles and the political crises of the Weimar period served simply to bring them to the surface. German liberalism under stress yielded to those elements that had always either constituted a significant portion of its own political *Anschauung,* i.e., statism, or had lurked below the surface, i.e., *völkisch* ideas and political romanticism. In the bitterly divisive Weimar period, those elements most prominent in German political thinking had to emerge.

As we have seen throughout this work, the German Democratic party, however uncertain the commitment of many of its members to parliamentary republican principles may have been, often did stand on such principles during the constitutional period and during the Reichstag debates. Yet, such stands merely underscore some of the rather unamusing ironies of bourgeois republicanism during the Weimar period. First of all, as seen above, defense of the republic in particular and parliamentary republicanism in general was often done on the basis of reason of state. In other words, Democratic defense of the state in its "republican form" was more often than not the primary tenet of the German Democratic party as it faced up to the monumental issues of the Weimar period. Perhaps of greater importance, however, were the positions which the party, in its at least partially sincere efforts to represent everybody (and thus be a *bona fide Staatspartei*) had to take. In the interests of the bourgeoisie it had to reject the Versailles Treaty in 1919. In the interests of the workers it had to come out, however grudgingly, in favor of the Factory Council Law of 1920. In the interests of the German nation *in toto* it had to advise acceptance of the Allied reparations demands in 1921. Broader questions (to it) of "interests of state" forced the party to support Stresemann's program of 1923, which crushed the left in Saxony and Thuringia while slapping right-wing wrists in Bavaria, a program which had to and did alienate the Social Democratic party, the most powerful member of the Weimar Coalition. Again, "interests of state" caused the German Democratic party in 1925 to come out in favor of the Locarno Treaty and entrance into the League of Nations, thus alienating it from those bourgeois circles represented by the *Wirtschaftspartei* and the radical right. Yet, as defender of bourgeois interests as well —above all of private property—the German Democratic party had to oppose the Social Democrats (and Communists too, of course) in coming out in 1926 against the expropriation of royal wealth. Again, in the interests of state unity, this party had to defend the colors of the Weimar flag.

The basically bourgeois nature of the party came out in its attitude towards Scheidemann's revelations regarding *Reichswehr*/Red Army cooperation, and this same attitude (or at least the *Biedermeier* aspect of it) was revealed in the support of some members of the DDP for the *Schunde und Schmutzgesetz* of 1926. In both instances, of course, the party was standing against the position of the SPD. And, irony of ironies, in 1928 the DDP, in part out of nationalistic motives but mainly on the basis of parliamentary principle had once more to alienate the Socialists by voting for the construction of *Panzerschiff A*. Throughout all of this, as indicated by the February, 1928, speeches of Gustav Schneider and Ernst Lemmer, the DDP continued to call for measures to alleviate the plights of small businessmen, employees, farmers, and the traditional "working class." "He who attempts to defend everything, defends nothing." The validity of this pithy maxim of Frederick the Great was amply proved by the career of the German Democratic party. It was attempting to defend the interests of the proletariat. But the non-bourgeois SPD could be far more consistent in this regard. Hence, the Democrats could count on little working-class support. It attempted to defend the interests of the bourgeoisie, particularly of the middle class, but, "interest parties" such as the *Wirtschaftspartei* and the more conservative DVP and DNVP could do this with greater consistency, while those farmers who did not vote DNVP had a host of interest parties of their own, e.g., the *Deutsche Bauernpartei* and the *Landbund*. Eventually, of course, large portions of the middle-class, and of the farming population as well, would be co-opted by the Nazis.

Yet, in terms of what the DDP was attempting to do, i.e., to build bridges left and right and thus to assist in the establishment of the hallowed *Volksgemeinschaft,* it had to have taken the stands it did, however disastrous these stands might have been for its voting strength. It had to make "sacrifices" in the national interest even though these sacrifices were to lead to the decline of the party. The bald fact which emerges here is that the German Democratic party really did not view itself as a "political party," but rather as a cornerstone of *Volksgemeinschaft*. Yet, the Democratic claim that they constituted a "party above parties" was vitiated by their identification with an at times hated *status quo*, i.e., the parliamentary government of Weimar. Thus, the bourgeoisie which would both see its interests represented in Nazism and be sensitive to the latter's claim that it was "a party of unity" (*Sammelpartei*), and hence "above special interests," could not respond to the Democrats' claim that they represented "a party of unity."[1] After all, the Democratic "unity," at least on paper, was tied to parliamentarianism and a vapid sort of liberalism seemingly incongruent with bourgeois middle-class interests and problems in the twentieth century.[2] Of course, the identification of the German Democratic party with "Jewish interests" did not help matters.

Naturally, the German Democrats were not unaware of these problems. Thus, throughout the Weimar period, particularly in articles, speeches, and committee meetings, the party membership, with the usual exceptions of such people as Heuss and Erkelenz, more and more displayed anti-parliamentarian and anti-pluralistic tendencies, as well as the desire to break free from "Jewish influence." The willingness of at least most Democrats virtually to abandon parliamentary republicanism in merging with the *Jungdeutsche Orden* in 1930 to form the *Staatspartei* was more than just an effort to build up a strong bourgeois "middle." It was also a concrete manifestation of the Democrats' belief that, in Weimar-period Germany, both super-parliamentary and *völkisch* demands had to be satiated. The existence of anti-parliamentary and *völkisch* attitudes within the ranks of the DDP testifies both to the prominence of such attitudes in Democratic circles and, perhaps more important, to their prominence among the bourgeoisie as a whole.

The attitudes displayed by German Democrats serve also to explain, at least in part, an extremely significant phenomenon of the Hitler period: the almost total lack of resistance on the part of those bourgeois circles that had constituted the Democratic group during the Weimar period.[3] To resist a terror machine such as that maintained by the Nazis one had to be committed with virtual fanaticism to one's own principles, be they embodied in Christianity, e.g., Sophie and Hans Scholl and Dietrich Bonhoeffer, Communism, e.g., the *Rote Kapelle* group in Berlin, or the conservative humanism of the *Kreissau Kreis*. The somewhat bemused Democrats of Weimar Germany were not unprincipled. However, the principles to which they owed allegiance were a rather mixed bag indeed. All of them were anti-Nazi and, as we have seen, Heuss wrote perhaps one of the most significant early analyses of the origins and meaning of the Nazi Party, *Hitlers Weg*. All of them were opposed to political violence and to militarism. However, their commitment to what could be called republican principles was somewhat unclear, to say the least. While the Nazi seizure of power was something against which the Democrats had fought ever since 1923, their own resolve to resist Nazism must needs have been weakened by two unfortunate problems: (1) a somewhat tenuous commitment to the republic that had just fallen, and (2) some sympathy, perhaps unconscious, with at least a few of the emotional underpinnings of Nazism. After all, as we have seen, many Democrats were alienated by the urban cynicism and "dirt" (to quote Meinecke) which they associated with some of the mundane aspects of pluralistic life. Many Democrats put their confidence in a youthful, at times almost unthinking, idealism. The *Staatspartei* as a whole, at least in its platform, evidenced an immense distaste for the tension-torn Reichstag. Naturally, the solutions offered and eventually put into effect by the Nazis were hardly compatible with Democratic attitudes. However, as opposed to dictatorship and to "final solutions" as the Democrats would have been, the emotional reaction of Democrats to the Nazis could not have been strong enough to sustain systematic resistance. A Heuss could well chide his son to look for the positive in the events of 1933, or a Meinecke could discover praiseworthy aspects of the Nazi program. These were not acts of cowardice, but rather, simple testimony to the deep-rooted nature of much of that for which the Nazis stood. They were also testimonies to the inability of German Democrats to perceive the destructive nature of some of their ideals when placed in the more systematic context of an ideology.

Yet, it is again necessary to point out that, paradoxically enough, the Democrats in general and the Democratic party in particular, while somewhat confused as to their attitudes towards republicanism, were,

---

[1] Larry Eugene Jones, "'The Dying Middle': Weimar Germany and the Fragmentation of Bourgeois Politics," in: *Central European History* 5, No. 1 (March, 1972): p. 54.

[2] Larry E. Jones, in his above-cited article, makes the assertion that none of the Weimar-period "parties of the middle," i.e., the DDP, the DVP, and the DNVP and its secessionists, the *Volkskonservativen*, were truly representative of middle-class interests, particularly those of the "new" middle class, i.e., white-collar workers, civil servants, etc. Outside of the fact that Mr. Jones's definition of "middle" seems to be a bit too catholic, his point that the National Socialist party was able to gather members of the bourgeois class disaffected because of this is a good one. However, at least in this article, consideration of the shared claim of the DDP and the Nazis—that they represented no one class and were hence "non-interest" parties—is not undertaken. See Jones's article pp. 24–25, 30–31, 33, 54.

[3] Weber, who was associated with the Conservative resistance group around the historian Gerhard Ritter, was an exception.

for the German electorate, symbolic of the republic and all the weaknesses and shortcomings they perceived in it. As Heuss pointed out in the 1920's (and Neumann in later writings) the Democratic party was the republic. To the extent that, on paper at least, it stood for parliamentarianism, the pluralistic society and religious toleration, the *magnum opus* of the Democrat Hugo Preuss, the Weimar Constitution, was the party incarnate. The German Democratic party and its supporters were thus placed in the impossible position of forever defending their own program to the degree that it was already embodied in the existing state structure. Furthermore, from this there flowed a most curious paradox. As we have seen, the Democratic party, as the only bourgeois political party that stood for the parliamentary republic, was forced to take a most unpluralistic view of things and demand that the electorate recognize that it alone stood for pluralism and republican democracy. The failure of many Germans to accept the republic and the weakness of the republican tradition in general drove the Democratic party and its supporters into an irresolvable logical impasse. The party, however much it attempted to accommodate itself to some of the objections and alternatives to republicanism, was forever doomed to be identified with that republic to which many Democrats were only formally dedicated.

As mentioned in the introduction to this work, there is another problem that can be observed in any study of the ideational content (or, perhaps, shift in such) of the German Democratic party. This problem is the increasing emphasis upon a sort of "functional statism" within party ranks as the republic slid from one crisis to another. As established in the text, this "statism" was a well-established part of German intellectual and political history long before the Weimar period and hence one should not overemphasize the role of post-World War I problems in bringing such a phenomenon to the surface. The statism of the German Democratic party in the 1920's was the statism of the prewar Naumann which was, in turn, a more concrete embodiment of the somewhat more reified statism of Leopold von Ranke. Yet, as the bourgeois, democratic Weimar republic faced crisis after crisis, the German Democratic party—again, partly in response to pressures from the class from which it had to derive most of its support—more and more tended to turn its back upon pluralism and parliamentary government. The solution for which, for reasons tactical and ideological, it eventually reached was the fusion of statist and, to some extent at least, *völkisch* strands embodied in the *Staatspartei* of 1930. Perhaps one cannot dub this party as "Fascist." However, in its glorification of a super-interest national idealism, its emphasis upon *Volksgemeinschaft,* its call for "strong personalities" to fill positions of leadership, and its glorification of youthful vitality, the *Staatspartei* program embodied at the very least some of the salient points of Fascist ideology. Again, this brings up a crucial point; *viz.,* are the Marxists correct when they assume that, if not Fascism in all cases, then at least a form of "functional statism," is the logical result of the playing-out of contradictions inherent in bourgeois, capitalistic society? To be sure, as social and economic thinkers such as Max Weber, Gustav Stolper, and more recently Ralf Dahrendorf, have pointed out, both German capitalism in particular and German bourgeois society in general, because of the relative lateness of the first and immaturity of the second, had a well-established tradition of seeking to avoid competition and conflict. Thus, one would suppose, the "corporatist," or "functional statist," or, if one wants, the "Fascist" solution was implicit in German intellectual and political history from the beginning.

However, this in no way obviates the possibility that, even in nations with more well-established traditions of competition and political conflict, the example provided by the German Democratic party might well find parallels as such nations undergo periods of tension and divisiveness which either are unprecedented or are viewed as such by citizens and elected leaders. At any rate, it is an open question.

BIBLIOGRAPHY

PRIMARY SOURCES

A. Unpublished Materials

1. Deutsche Demokratische Partei materials in Preussisches Geheimes Staatsarchiv, Berlin.
2. Deutsche Demokratische Partei materials in Bundesarchiv, Koblenz.
3. Deutsche Demokratische Partei materials in Institut für Zeitgeschichte, München.
4. Heussarchiv, Stuttgart.
5. Nachlass Dietrich, Bundesarchiv, Koblenz.
6. Nachlass Koch-Weser, Bundesarchiv, Koblenz.
7. Nachlass Külz, Bundesarchiv, Koblenz.
8. Nachlass Luppe, Bundesarchiv, Koblenz.
9. Nachlass Meinecke, Preussiches Geheimes Staatsarchiv, Berlin.
10. Nachlass Schiffer, Bundesarchiv, Koblenz.

B. Published Materials

BÄUMER, GERTRUD. 1928. *Grundlagen Demokratische Politik* (Karlsruhe).
—— 1930. *Sinn und Formen geistiger Führung* (Berlin).
—— 1919. *Bericht Über die Verhandlungen der Parteitags der Deutschen Demokratischen Partei* (Berlin).
BREITSCHEID, RUDOLF, and AUGUST WEBER. 1932. *Wider Den Nationalsozialismus* (Berlin).
DOHNA, GRAF ZU, and WILLY HELLPACH. 1927. *Die Krisis des deutschen Parlamentarismus* (Karlsruhe).
ERKELENZ, ANTON. 1926. *Moderne Sozialpolitik* (Berlin).
—— 1928. *Zehn Jahre deutsche Republik* (Berlin).
GESSLER, OTTO. 1958. *Reichswehrpolitik in der Weimarer Zeit* (Stuttgart).
HELLPACH, WILLY. 1944. *Einführung in die Volkerpsychologie* (2nd newly rev. ed., Stuttgart).
—— 1939. *Mensch und Volk der Grosstadt* (Stuttgart).
—— 1928. *Politische Prognose für Deutschland* (Berlin).
HEUSS, THEODOR. 1963. *Erinnerungen: 1905–1933* (Tübingen).
—— 1960. *Friedrich Naumann und die deutsche Demokratie* (Wiesbaden).
—— 1937. *Friedrich Naumann: der Mann, das Werk, die Zeit* (Stuttgart).
—— 1932. *Hitlers Weg* (Berlin).
—— 1955. *Preludes to Life; Early Memoirs*, translated from the German by Michael Bullock (London).
—— 1926. *Statt und Volk: Betrachtungen über Wirtschaft, Politik, und Kultur* (Berlin).
KOCH-WESER, ERICH. 1933. *Und dennoch aufwärts!* (Berlin).
LEMMER, ERNST. 1968. *Manches war doch anders* (Frankfurt-am-Main).
MAHRAUN, ARTUR. 1928. *Das Jungdeutsche Manifest* (2nd ed., Berlin).
MEINECKE, FRIEDRICH. 1962. *Ausgewählter Briefwechsel*, edited by Ludwig Dehio (Stuttgart).
—— 1949. *Die deutsche Katastrophe* (Vierte Auflage, Wiesbaden).
—— 1949. *Erinnerungen, Vol. II, Strassburg, Freiburg, Berlin* (Stuttgart).
—— 1919. *Nach der Revolution* (München).
—— 1958. *Politische Schriften und Reden*, edited by Georg Kotowski (Darmstadt).
—— 1907. *Weltbürgertum und Nationalstaat* (München).
NAUMANN, FRIEDRICH. 1916. *Central Europe*, translated from the German by C. Meredith (London).
—— 1904. *Demokratie und Kaisertum* (3rd ed., Berlin).
—— 1962. *Werke*, ed. Theodor Schieder (Köln/Opladen).
RANKE, LEOPOLD VON. 1924. *Politische Gespräch*, introduction by Friedrich Meinecke (München).
RATHENAU, WALTHER. 1929. *Politische Briefe* (Dresden).
—— 1965. *Schriften*, selected and introduced by Arnold Harttung et al. (Berlin).
—— 1912. *Zur Kritik der Zeit* (Berlin).
STEPHAN, WERNER. 1931. "Zur Sociologie der Nationalsozialistischen Deutschen Arbeiterpartei." *Zeitschrift für Politik* 20.
STOLPER, GUSTAV. 1929. *Die Wirtschaftlich-soziale Weltanschauung der Demokratie* (Berlin).
TROELTSCH, ERNST. 1966. *Spektator Briefe: Aufsätze über die deutsche Revolution und die Weltpolitik 1918/1922* (new ed. 1924, Darmstadt).
Verhandlungen des Reichstages. Stenographische Berichte. 1920–1933.
Verhandlungen der verfassunggebenden deutschen Nationalversammlung. 1919–1920.
WEBER, MAX. 1958. *From Max Weber: Essays in Sociology*, translated, edited and with an introduction by H. H. Gerth and C. Wright Mills (New York).
—— 1958. *Gesammelte Politische Schriften* (2nd ed., newly edited by Johannes Winckelmann, Tübingen).
WOLFF, THEODOR. 1936. *Through Two Decades*, translated from the German by E. W. Dickes (London).

C. Periodicals and Newspapers

Berliner Tageblatt
Blätter der Staatspartei
Das demokratische Deutschland
Der Demokrat
Die Hilfe
Frankfurter Zeitung
Mitteilungen der deutschen Staatspartei

SECONDARY SOURCES

A. Articles

CHANADY, ATTILA. 1967. "Anton Erkelenz und Erich Koch-Weser: A Portrait of two German Democrats." *Historical Studies: Australia and New Zealand* 12.
—— 1968. "The Dissolution of the German Democratic Party." *American Historical Review* 73, 5.
—— 1972. "Erich Koch-Weser and the Weimar Republic." *Canadian Journal of History* 7.
FRYE, BRUCE B. 1967. "A Letter from Max Weber." *Journal of Modern History* 39, 2.
—— 1968. "The German Democratic Party: 1918–1930." *Western Political Quarterly* 16.
JONES, LARRY EUGENE. 1972. "'The Dying Middle': Weimar Germany and the Fragmentation of Bourgeois Politics." *Central European History* 5, 1.
PAUCKER, ARNOLD, ed. 1968. Searchlight on the Decline of the Weimar Republic: The Diaries of Ernst Feder." *Yearbook* XIII of the Leo Baeck Institute.
PORTNER, ERNST. 1965. "Der Ansatz zur demokratischen Massenpartei im deutschen Linksliberalismus." *Vierteljahrsehft für Zeitgeschichte* 13, 2.
—— 1969. "Koch-Weser zur politischen Situation im Februar, 1919." *Vierteljahrshefte für Zeitgeschichte* 17, 1.
—— 1966. "Koch-Wesers Verfassungsentwurf von 1942." *Vierteljahrshefte für Zeitgeschichte* 14, 2.

B. Books

Allen, William S. 1965. *The Nazi Seizure of Power: The Experiences of a Single German Town 1918–1933* (Chicago).

Behrendt, Armin. 1968. *Wilhelm Külz: aus dem Leben eines Suchenden* (Berlin).

Bergstrasser, Ludwig. 1960. *Geschichte der Politischen Parteien in Deutschland* (10th ed., München).

Bracher, Karl D. 1957. *Die Auflösung der Weimarer Republick* (Stuttgart).

Dahrendorf, Ralf. 1967. *Society and Democracy in Germany* (New York).

Deak, Istvan. 1968. *Weimar Germany's Left-wing Intellectuals: Die Weltbühne. A Political History of the Weltbühne and its Circle* (Berkeley).

Eyck, Erich. 1962. *A History of the Weimar Republic*, translated by Harlan P. Hanson, Jr., Robert G. L. Waite (2 v., Cambridge).

Fischer, Fritz. 1967. *Germany's Aims in the First World War* (New York).

Halperin, S. William. 1965. *Germany Tried Democracy: A Political History of the Reich from 1918 to 1932* (New York).

Hartenstein, Wolfgang. 1962. *Die Anfänge der Deutschen Volkspartei: 1918–1920* (Düsseldorf).

Heckart, Beverly. 1974. *From Bassermann to Bebel. The Grand Bloc's Quest for Reform in the Kaiserreich, 1900–1914* (New Haven and London).

Hornung, Klaus. 1958. *Der Jungdeutsche Orden* (Düsseldorf).

Hunt, Richard N. 1964. *German Social Democracy: 1918–1933* (New Haven).

Iggers, Georg G. 1968. *The German Conception of History: The National Tradition of Historical Thought from Herder to the Present* (Middletown).

Klemperer, Klemens von. 1957. *Germany's New Conservatism: Its History and Dilemma in the Twentieth Century* (Princeton).

Kosok, Paul. 1933. *Modern Germany: A Study of Conflicting Loyalties* (Chicago).

Krieger, Leonard. 1957. *The German Idea of Freedom: History of a Political Tradition* (Boston).

Levy, Richard S. 1975. *The Downfall of the Anti-Semitic Political Parties in Imperial Germany* (New Haven and London).

Liptzen, Solomon. 1961. *Germany's Stepchildren* (New York.

Matthias, Eric, and Rudolf Morsey, eds. 1960. *Das Ende der Parteien 1933* (Düsseldorf).

Milatz, Alfred. 1965. *Wähler und Wahlen in der Weimarer Republik* (Bonn).

Mohler, Armin. 1950. *Die Konservative Revolution in Deutschland: 1918–1932* (Stuttgart).

Mosse, George L. 1964. *The Crisis of German Ideology: Intellectual Origins of the Third Reich* (New York).

—— (ed.) 1968. *Nazi Culture* (New York).

Mosse, Werner E., Arnold Paucker, ed. 1965. *Entscheidungsjahr 1932: zur Judenfrage in der Endphase der Weimarer Republik* (Tübingen).

Neumann, Sigmund. 1965. *Die Parteien in der Weimarer Republik* (Stuttgart).

Nohlen, Dieter, ed. 1969. *Die Wahl der Parlament und anderer Staatsorgane: Ein Handbuch* (Berlin).

Pikart, Eberhard. 1967. *Theodor Heuss, der Mann, das Werk, die Zeit: eine Ausstellung* (Stuttgart).

Pinson, Koppel S. 1965. *Modern Germany* (15th printing, New York).

Pulzer, Peter G. J. 1964. *The Rise of Political Anti-Semitism in Germany and Austria* (New York).

Ryder, A. J. 1967. *The German Revolution of 1918: A Study of German Socialism in War and Revolt* (Cambridge).

Saloman, Felix. 1926. *Die deutsche Parteiprogramme* (Leipzig).

Schieder, Theodor. 1962. *The State and Society in Our Time*, translated by C. A. M. Sym (London).

Schoenbaum, David. 1967. *Hitler's Social Revolution: Class and Status in Nazi Germany, 1933–1939* (New York).

Schorske, Carl. 1965. *German Social Democracy 1905–1917: The Development of the Great Schism* (New York).

Schriftenreihe der Friedrich Naumann Stiftung zur Politik und Zeitgeschichte. 1966. *Geschichte des deutschen Liberalismus* (Köln und Oplaten).

Schwabe, Klaus. 1969. *Wissenschaft und Kriegsmoral: Die deutschen Hochschullehrer und die politischen Grundfragen des Ersten Weltkrieges* (Göttingen, Zürich, Frankfurt).

Schwarz, Gotthart. 1968. *Theodor Wolff und das Berliner Tageblatt* (Tübingen).

Sontheimer, Kurt. 1962. *Antidemokratisches Denken in der Weimarer Republik. Die politischen Ideen des deutschen Nationalismus zwischen 1918 und 1933* (München).

Stampfer, Friedrich. 1947. *Die Vierzehn Jahre der Ersten Deutschen Republik* (3rd ed., Hamburg).

Stern, Fritz. 1965. *The Politics of Cultural Despair: A Study in the Rise of the Germanic Ideology* (New York).

Treue, Wolfgang. 1954. *Deutsche Parteiprogramme, 1861–1954* (Göttingen).

Turner, Henry Ashby, Jr. 1965. *Stresemann and the Politics of the Weimar Republic* (Princeton).

Ziegler, Wilhelm. 1932. *Die deutsche Nationalversammlung 1919/1920 und ihr Verfassungswerk* (Berlin).

INDEX

"Abegg Affair," 92 fn.
Ablass, Bruno, 23, 27
Africa, 95
Allen, W. S., 84
Allied Reparations Ultimatum, see "German Democratic party"
Anschütz, Gerhard, 14 fn.
Anti-Semitism, 5, 6, 12, 53, 71, 72, 74, 75, 79; see "German Democratic party"; 87, 95, 99, 100, 106, 107, 109, 110
Austria, 20–21, 26–27, 33

Bassermann, Ernst, 11
Bauer, Otto, 26, 38
Bauernbund, 91, 110
Bäumer, Gertrud, 5, 6, 19, 20, 21, 23, 31, 37, 38, 39, 40, 57, 58, 62–64; political romanticism of, 63, 66, 68, 71, 72, 73, 75, 79, 100, 101, 103, 109; attitudes towards parliamentarianism and pluralism, 63–64, 65, 100, 107; 75, 76, 82, 84, 97–98, 99, 100–104, 106, 107, 109, 110
Bavaria, 18, 22; attempted Nazi *Putsch* in, 45, 46, 87, 110.
Bavarian People's party (BVP), 52
Bebel, August, 11
Belgium, 45
Below, Georg von, 11
Bergstrasser, Ludwig, 41
Berliner Tageblatt, 8, 13, 16, 17, 58, 65, 72, 81, 82, 84, 85
Bernhard, George, 65
Bernhardi, General Friedrich von, 8
Bernstorff, Count Johann-Heinrich von, 31, 32, 47
Bethmann-Hollweg, Theobald von, 9, 15
Bismarck, Otto von, 17, 18, 21, 29, 37, 50, 54, 92, 108
Boeckel, Otto, 86
Böhme, Karl, 81
Bollinger, Heno, 59
Bonhoeffer, Dietrich, 111
Bourgeoisie, political position and attitudes of, 9, 10, 16, 21, 26, 29, 31, 37, 39, 42, 45, 47, 48, 59, 67, 70, 107, 108, 110, 111, 112
Bracher, Karl Dietrich, 5
Braun, Otto, 50
Breitscheid, Rudolf, 92
Brüning, Heinrich, 69, 76, 98
Brunner, Constantin (*né* Leo Wertheimer), 80
Brunner, Herr, 83
Bruno, Giordano, 103
Bülow Bloc, 11
Bürgerliche Demokratie (Austria), 83
Burke, Edmund, 79
Burschenschaft, 21, 27

Campe, Dr. von, 42
Catholicism, 11, 12, 50, 52, 83, 84, 91, 92, 94, 95
Cauer, Friedrich, 29, 30
Centralverein deutscher Staatsbürger Jüdischen Glaubens, 84, 85

Centre Party, 11, 14, 18, 25, 38, 43, 46, 49, 50, 52, 57, 65, 67, 69, 104, 109
Chamberlain, Houston Stewart, 93
Christlicher Volksdienst, 91
Church Issue, 21, 25, 33
Clauss, Max, 91
Cohn, Oskar, 23
Colsmann, Andreas, 69
Communist Party (KPD); see also "Spartacists"; 37, 45, 47, 50, 53, 54, 60, 61, 62, 69, 70, 82, 85, 89, 105, 110
Conservative party, 11, 12, 80, 86
Corwegh, Robert, 48, 49, 50–51, 65, 67, 72
Czechoslovakia, 19

Dahlmann, Friedrich, 108
Dahrendorf, Ralf, 5, 8 fn., 112
Dante, 100
Dawes Plan, 47
Deak, Istvan, 71 fn.
Deines, Herr, 81
Delbrück, Hans, 28
Democratic Club, 92
Demokratische Studentenbund, 49
Dernburg, Bernhard, 22, 23, 50
Deutsch-völkische Schutz und Trutz Bund, 81
Diels, Rudolf, 92, 99
Dietrich, Hermann, 6, 16, 61, 66, 67, 69, 76, 78, 81, 83, 85, 91, 98
Dohna, Graf zu, 62
Dolchstosslegende, 22, 60
Dühring, Eugen, 88

Ebert, Friedrich, 18, 49
Economic Policy, DDP (1929), 67–69
Eisner, Kurt, 18, 87
Elections; January 19, 1919, 18; June 6, 1920, 39; May 4, 1924, 47, 88; December 7, 1924, 47, 88; March 28, 1925, 50; April 23, 1925, 50; May 20, 1928, 62, 65, 88; September 14, 1930, 70, 78, 85; *Länder* elections: Braunschweig, 1927, 88; Saxony, Lippe, 1929, 88; Württemberg, 1932, 91
Erdmannsdorffer, H. G., 40
Erfurt Synthesis (1891), 10, 26, 108
Erkelenz, Anton, 6, 23, 26, 29, 30, 31, 34, 36, 37, 40, 42, 43, 44, 46, 49, 52, 53, 56–57, 58, 59, 64–65, 66, 68, 72, 73, 74, 76, 79, 97, 105, 106, 109, 111
Ermächtigungsgesetz, (1933), 87, 98
Erzberger, Matthias, 25
Eyck, Erich, 54, 57, 61

Factory Council Law (1920), 36–37, 110
Falk, Bernard, 19, 20, 25
Fascism, 64, 72, 74, 85, 87, 88, 89, 92, 94, 99, 112
Feder, Ernst, 6, 58, 65, 85, 92
Feder, Gottfried, 94
Fehrenbach, Konstantin, 38, 52
Fichte, Johann Gottlieb, 17, 25, 28, 30, 43, 57, 93, 100, 103, 107
Fink, Rabbi Daniel, 103 fn.

Fischbeck, Otto, 31
Fischer, Fritz, 13
Fischer, Hermann, 8, 16, 29, 31, 32, 40, 58, 66, 69, 76, 79
Flag Issue (1919), 20–21, 26–27, 28, 78; (1926), 53, 105, 110
France, 19, 45
Frankfurt Assembly (1848), 24, 107
Frankfurter, Richard, 31, 58, 59, 65
Frankfurter Zeitung, 81, 82
Freck, George, 83
Frederick the Great, 110
Freemasons, 84
Freicorps, 82
French Revolution (1789), 107
Freund, Leo A., 42
Friedländer, Adele, 71
Fromm, Eric, 101
Frye, Bruce, 81

Galileo, 103
Geiger, Theodor, 96
Gerland, Heinrich, 30, 80 fn.
German Democratic party (DDP), 5, 7, 9, 15; first electoral call of, 16; role in writing Weimar Constitution, 17–21, 23–25, 26–29; see "Parliamentary Government/Pluralism"; 19, 21, 22, 23; vote on Versailles Treaty, 26, 110; vote on Weimar Constitution, 29, 30; first party congress, 30–32; party program of, 32–33, 34; position on Factory Council Law, 36–37, 110; reaction to Kapp Putsch, 38–39, 40, 41; on reparations issue, 43, 44, 45, 46, 110; see "League of Nations"; 46; see "Elections"; 49; see *"Parteitag"*; 52, 53, 54, 56, 57, 58, 60; see "*Panzerschiffe A* Controversy"; 65, 66, 67; see "Economic policy, DDP (1929)"; 70; see "Political romanticism"; 74, 75; becomes *Staatspartei*, 75–79; attitudes towards anti-Semitism and Jews, 79–87; reaction to Nazism, 87–100; 98, 99, 100, 104, 105, 106, 109, 110, 111, 112
German National People's party (DNVP), 19, 28, 29, 37, 38, 40, 45, 46, 47, 48, 49, 52, 53, 54, 56, 57, 60 fn., 65, 69, 70, 78, 80, 88, 89, 90, 91, 97, 99, 110, 111 fn.
German People's party (DVP), 7, 15, 17, 19, 27, 29, 31, 34, 39, 40, 42, 44, 46, 47, 49, 52, 54, 57, 58, 60 fn., 65, 67, 70, 72, 73, 75, 76, 80, 88, 89, 90, 99, 111 fn.
Gessler, Otto, 6, 12, 36, 44, 48, 49, 55, 56, 57, 60, 65, 67, 81, 82, 84, 99, 106, 109, 110
Goebbels, Paul Josef, 97
Goepel, Kurt, 79
Göring, Hermann, 92
Gothein, George, 32, 37, 38
Graff, Herr, 85
Graf Spee, 60
Great Britain, 10, 25, 37, 53, 55, 105, 107
Gröner, General Wilhelm, 60, 61
Grund, Bernhard, 40

115

Grundrechte, 17, 23–25
Guérard, Theodor von, 67
Gutmann, Frau, 85

Haas, Ludwig, 16, 27, 43, 46, 48, 49, 57, 60–61
Hamm, Eduard, 47
Hammes, Peter, 35
Hansa Bund, 16, 29, 34, 66, 69, 76
Hartenstein, Wolfgang, 15 fn., 35 fn., 39
Hartmann, Ludo M., 20
Hartung, Arnold, 103 fn.
Hasse, Colonel (later General) Otto von, 49
Haussmann, Conrad, 6, 8, 23, 25–26, 28
Heckart, Beverly, 11 fn.
Hegel, Georg Wilhelm Friedrich, 17, 48, 105, 108
Heine, Wolfgang, 26
Hellpach, Willy, 50, 52, 62, 66, 79, 83, 91, 92 fn., 93
Hermann, Alfred, 22, 24, 25
Heuss, Theodor, 6, 8 fn., 9, 11, 12, 13, 16, 23, 30, 36, 40–41, 42, 43, 44, 46, 52, 53, 55–56, 57, 58, 64, 65, 66, 67, 70, 78, 80, 81, 84, 86, 87, 88, 90, 91, 92, 93–96, 97, 98, 104, 108, 109, 111, 112
Himmler, Heinrich, 84
Hindenburg, General (and President) Paul von, 50, 52, 53, 54, 69, 88, 97
Hirsch-Duncker Trade Union Movement, 6, 23
Historicism, 7, 8, 90, 108
Hitler, Adolf, 18, 85, 87, 88, 89, 90, 91, 93, 94, 95, 96, 97, 98, 99, 111
Hohzollern Dynasty, 36, 73
Hopf, Albert, 91
Hugenberg, Alfred, 88
Humboldt, Wilhelm von, 30, 33, 108
Hummel, Herman, 59
Hutter, Josef, 89

Iggers, Georg G., 92 fn.
Imperialism, 50, 108
Independent Socialist party (USPD), 23, 25, 29, 37, 43
Italy, 75, 87, 88, 89, 92, 99

Jaeger, Helmut, 73
Jarres, Karl, 50
Jews, 6, 12, 22, 32, 36, 48, 57, 60, 65–66, 72, 73, 74; see "German Democratic party"; 95, 97, 98, 99, 102, 103, 106, 109, 110, 111
Jones, Larry Eugene, 60 fn., 111 fn.
Jungdeutsche Orden, 7, 43, 65, 66, 67, 72, 73, 74–75, 84, 85, 99, 103, 111

Kaas, Msr. Ludwig, 98
Kahr, Gustav von, 87, 93
Kapp *Putsch,* 36, 38–39, 41, 82
Kauffmann, Robert, 31
Kennedy, John F., 28 fn.
Kerr, Alfred, 86
Kneisel, R., 73
Koch-Weser, Erich, 5, 6, 12, 21–22, 23, 25, 27, 28, 31, 38, 39, 40, 45, 46, 47, 48, 49, 52, 53, 54, 57, 58, 61, 65, 66, 67; increasing bitterness towards parliamentary government, 67, 69, 70, 104, 106; 73, 74, 75, 76, 78, 80, 82, 83, 84, 85, 87, 89, 98, 99, 100, 104–107, 109, 110

Köhler, Dr., 31
Kohn, Rabbi, 12
Kreissau Kreis, 111
Krieger, Leonard, 8 fn.
Kriegsrohstoffabteilung, 7
Kulturkampf, 18
Külz, Wilhelm, 7, 9, 34, 47, 50, 57, 85, 89, 97, 99, 100

Labor party (Great Britain), 105
Lachmann, Hans, 81
Lagarde, Paul de, 72
Landahl, Heinrich, 72, 98
Landbund, 110
Landsberg, Otto, 26
Lasker, Eduard, 108
Lassalle, Ferdinand, 93, 95
League of German Students, 12
League of Nations, 21, 26, 30, 50, 53, 110
Legien, Karl, 40
Leipziger Volkszeitung, 84
Lemmer, Ernst, 57, 59–60, 61–62, 71, 72, 76, 98, 110
Lenal, Walter, 12 fn.
Leo XIII, 94, 95
Levy, Richard S., 12 fn.
Liberale Vereinigung, 58, 65
Lindeiner-Wildau, Hans von, 67
Liptzin, Solomon, 80 fn.
Locarno, Treaty of, 50, 110
Loeball, Friedrich von, 54
Ludendorff, General Erich, 50, 60, 88
Ludwig I (Bavaria), 107
Lueger, Karl, 93
Luppe, Hermann, 7
Luther, Hans, 47, 48, 49, 52, 53–54
Lüttwitz, General Walther von, 38

Mahraun, Artur, 7, 73, 74, 75, 78, 84, 101
Maier, Reinhold, 91 fn., 98
Manchester Guardian, 56
Mann, Heinrich, 59, 102
Marx, Karl, 88
Marx, Wilhelm, 46, 47, 50, 57
Meinecke, Friedrich, 5, 7, 8, 9, 10, 11, 12, 13, 14, 15, 16, 18, 21, 22, 24 fn., 28, 35, 36, 40, 41, 43, 44, 46, 48, 49, 53, 55, 65, 67, 71, 75, 78, 79, 80, 82, 87, 89–90, 91, 93 fn., 97, 98, 105, 106, 108, 109, 111
Meyer, Oscar, 69, 85
Mills, C. Wright, 36
Mitteleuropa Concept, 13, 19
Moeller van den Bruck, Arthur, 40
Mohler, Armin, 7
Mommsen, Wilhelm, 55, 59
Mosse, George L., 5, 8 fn., 40 fn., 74, 105 fn.
Mosse, Rudolf, 81, 82, 84
Mosse, Werner E., 84 fn.
Mossisch, Ernst, 84
Mück, Friedrich, 66, 81, 86
Muhle, Hans, 84
Müller, Adam, 93
Müller, Hermann, 61, 62, 67, 69
Mussolini, Benito, 63, 74, 75, 85, 88, 90, 99, 101

Napoleon I, 25, 107
Napoleon III, 25
National Liberal party, 7, 8, 9, 10, 11, 12, 14, 15, 16

National Social Union, 7, 8, 9
Naumann, Friedrich, 5, 7, 8, 9, 10, 11, 12, 13, 14, 15, 16, 17, 18, 19, 20, 22; *Grundrechte* proposal of, 23–24; political romanticism of, 24, 25; 27, 32, 36, 37, 39, 43, 48, 56, 64, 79, 93, 95, 98, 100, 101, 103, 106, 108, 109, 112
Nazism, 5, 6, 45, 47, 48, 53, 60, 65, 69, 70, 74, 78, 84, 85, 86; see "German Democratic party"; 102, 105, 110, 111
Neumann, Sigmund, 70 fn., 105 fn., 112
"New Conservatism," 63, 86
New York Commercial, 56
Nietzsche, Friedrich, 94
Noske, Gustav, 36, 82
Nuschke, Otto, 31, 40, 91

Oeser, Rudolf, 30
Oranienburg Concentration Camp, 8
Organization Consul, 7
Osthilfe, 89

Pabst, Major Waldemar, 38
Panzerschiff A Controversy, 60–62, 67, 70, 110
Pareto Vilfredo, 90, 93, 94
Parliamentary Government/Pluralism, 5, 6, 10, 14, 19, 21, 22, 25, 27, 28, 29, 35, 36, 38, 39, 40, 41, 42, 44–45, 46, 47–48, 49, 50–51, 52, 53, 54–56, 60, 61, 62, 74–76, 76, 78, 79, 83, 94, 95–96, 97: see "Bäumer, Gertrud"; 65, 66; "Koch-Weser, Erich"; 70, 76–79, 105, 108–109, 110, 111, 112
Parteiausschuss, 6, 7
Parteitag, 6; DDP *Parteitag,* 1924, 47; DDP *Parteitag,* 1925, 51–52; DDP *Parteitag,* 1927, 58–59; DDP *Parteitag,* 1929, 67–69; DDP/Staatspartei *Parteitag,* 1930, 78–79
Parteivorstand, 6
Paucker, Arnold, 84 fn., 92 fn.
Payer, Friedrich von, 7, 8, 16, 26, 38, 39
"Peace Resolution" (July 19, 1917), 14
Petersen, Carl, 7, 27, 31, 32, 40, 44, 78, 79
Phoebus Film Corporation scandal, 60
Pikart, Eberhard, 99
Pois, Robert, 13 fn., 21 fn., 24 fn., 80 fn.
Poland, 16, 19, 22, 29, 43 fn., 56, 60, 61, 75
Political Romanticism, 5; see "Naumann, Friedrich"; see "Bäumer, Gertrud"; 63, 70–79, 83, 89, 91, 92, 93, 101, 109, 110
Portner, Ernst, 34 fn.
Preuss, Hugo, 7, 14 fn., 16, 17, 18, 20, 21, 22, 23, 24, 25, 26, 30, 112
Princes, expropriation of property of, 53, 54, 70, 91, 110
Progressive party, 8, 9, 10, 11, 12, 13, 14, 15, 16, 20, 34, 35
Pross, Harry, 105 fn.
Proudhon, Pierre Joseph, 93
Pulzer, Peter C., 12 fn.

Quarck, Max, 25
Quidde, Ludwig, 7, 25, 26, 27, 56, 76, 84

Radikaldemokratische Partei, 7, 76, 84 fn.
Ranke, Leopold von, 9, 10, 13, 14, 41, 112
Rathenau, Emil, 7

Rathenau, Walther, 7, 9, 12, 13, 15, 16, 34, 35, 36, 41, 43 fn., 44, 45, 54, 79, 80, 82, 103, 108
Reichsbank, 7
Reichswehr, 49, 56–57, 60, 82, 106, 110
Reinhold, Peter, 59
Rentenmark, 7
Rhineland Separatism, 19, 81
Richter, Eugen, 8, 29, 45, 95, 108
Richthofen, Hartmann Freiherr von, 25, 32, 65
Ringer, Fritz, 99
Ritter, Gerhard, 111 fn.
Röhm, Ernst, 95
Rönneburg, Heinrich, 85
Rosenberg, Alfred, 94, 95
Rote Kapelle, 111
Ruhr, Occupation of, 45, 46
Russia, 13, 15, 56, 110
Ryder, A. J., 10 fn.

Saxony, crushing of Communists in, 45, 46, 87, 110
Schacht, Hjalmar Horace Greeley, 7, 16, 91
Scheidemann, Philip, 26, 56, 110
Schiele, Martin, 38
Schiffer, Eugen, 7, 9, 16, 26, 28, 38, 47
Schleicher, General Kurt von, 49, 97
Schleswig-Holstein, proposed DDP/DVP combining in, 40
Schmerz, I. S., 85
Schmitt, Carl, 105
Schneider, Gustav, 59, 60, 69, 110
Schoenbaum, David, 40 fn.
Scholl, Hans and Sophie, 111
Scholz, Ernst, 7, 76
Schönerer, Georg von, 93
School issue, 20, 21, 28–29, 30, 33, 77, 101, 105
Schreiber, Georg, 65
Schücking, Walther, 7, 41
Schultze, Rainer-Olaf, 48
Schund und Schmutzgesetz, 8, 57–58, 60, 63 fn., 65, 66, 70, 82, 100, 110
Schwabe, Klaus, 13, 14 fn.
Schwarz, Gotthard, 14, 22, 28
Seeckt, General Hans von, 49
Simon, Kurt, 81
Sismondi, Jean Charles, 94
Sklarek brothers (Leo, Max, Willy) scandal, 86

Snowden, Philip, 25
Social Democrats, 7, 10, 11, 12, 14, 16, 18, 19, 21, 22, 25, 26, 29, 30, 31, 32, 34, 35, 36, 38, 40, 42, 43, 45, 46, 48, 49, 50, 52, 53, 54, 56, 57, 58, 60, 61, 62, 65, 66, 67, 68, 69, 70, 82, 84, 91, 92, 97, 98, 108, 109, 110
Sombart, Werner, 14
Sommer, Paul, 30
Sonnenberg, Max Liebermann von, 86
Sorel, Georges, 90, 93, 94
South Tyrol, 75, 88, 89
Spann, Othmar, 93
Spartacists, 16, 23
Spengler, Oswald, 93
Staatspartei, 6, 7, 23, 43, 70, 74, 75, 76; manifesto of, 76–77; 78, 79, 84, 85, 87, 89, 90, 91, 92, 93, 97, 98, 99, 105, 106, 109, 110, 111, 112
Stahlhelm, 57
Stalin, Joseph, 101
Stegerwald, Adam, 40, 67
Stein, Baron vom, 108
Stephan, Werner, 88, 90, 91
Stern, Fritz, 5, 40 fn.
Stöcker, Adolf, 8, 12, 95
Stolper, Gustav, 7, 67–69, 89, 112
Strasser brothers (Gregor and Otto), 95
Stresemann, Gustav, 7, 11, 15, 17, 31, 38, 45, 46, 47, 49, 81, 110
Stubmann, Peter 58, 65, 66

Tantzen, Theodor, 66
Thalheim, Carl C., 91
Thälmann, Ernst, 50
Tivoli program (1892), 12, 80
Treitschke, Heinrich von, 8, 72
Treviranus, Gottfried, 78
Troeltsch, Ernst, 7, 14 fn., 15, 45
Turner, Henry Ashby, 15 fn.

Ullstein, Hermann, 81, 82, 84
United States, 28 fn., 31, 50, 52, 77
Urdang, George, 80
Uth, Frau, 59

Vaterlandspartei, 12, 13, 14
Versailles Peace Conference and Treaty of, 7, 25–27, 32, 41, 43, 50, 60, 78, 90, 93, 97, 110
Viereck, Peter, 5

Vogel, Bernhard, 48
Völkischer Beobachter, 45
Volkskonservativen, 67
Volksnationalen, 67, 75, 84
Vorwärts! 56
Vossische Zeitung 81, 82

Wachhorst de Wente, Friedrich, 40, 65
Wagner, Richard, 93, 103
Waldstein, Felix, 37
Wandervogel Movement, 71, 79
Wassermann, Herr, 82
Weber, Alfred, 16, 111
Weber, August, 7, 92, 93
Weber, Max, 5, 7, 8, 9, 14, 16, 21, 35, 36, 37, 39, 48, 81, 96, 101, 102, 108, 112
Wedekind, Franz, 102
Weil, Bruno, 84
Weimar Constitution, 7, 17; see "German Democratic party"; 25, 29, 30, 34, 37, 41, 45, 53, 54, 62, 79, 104, 112
Weitling, Wilhelm, 88, 93
Wels, Otto, 61
Weltbühne, 71
Westarp, Count Kuno von, 78
Wieland, Philip, 82
Wiener, P. B., 84
Wilhelm II, 10, 15, 54, 108
Wilson, Woodrow, 19, 32, 35
Winschuh, Josef, 76
Wirth, Josef, 7, 9, 44, 67
Wirtschaftspartei, 6, 48, 50, 51, 58, 60 fn., 65, 70, 99, 110
Wittelsbach Dynasty, 36
Wolf, Kurt, 48, 49, 50–51, 65, 72
Wolff, Theodor, 8, 13, 14, 16, 25, 57, 58, 65, 85, 99
Working class, 8, 11, 16, 20, 31, 33, 34, 40 fn., 45, 47, 56, 60, 67, 68, 70, 90, 110
World War I, 12, 16, 18, 22, 24, 26, 39, 41, 47, 74, 112
World War II, 68
Würzburger, Karl, 39

Young Democrats, 69, 71, 74
Young Plan, 76

Zeitlin, Herr, 85
Ziegler, Wilhelm, 19 fn., 21 fn., 23 fn.
Zionism, 82, 94
Zöphel, George, 23

MEMOIRS

OF THE

AMERICAN PHILOSOPHICAL SOCIETY

Roman Construction in Italy from Nerva through the Antonines. MARION E. BLAKE and DORIS TAYLOR BISHOP.
Vol. 96. xx, 328 pp., 36 pls., 17 plans, 1973. $15.00.

The Life of Arthur Young, 1741–1820. JOHN G. GAZLEY.
Vol. 97. xviii, 727 pp., 23 figs., 1973. $10.00.

Medical Men at the Siege of Boston, April, 1775–April, 1776: Problems of the Massachusetts and Continental Armies. PHILIP CASH.
Vol. 98. xiv, 185 pp., 11 figs., 1973. Paper. $3.00.

Crucial American Elections. ARTHUR S. LINK et al.
Vol. 99. x, 77 pp., 1973. $3.00.

John Beckley: Zealous Partisan in a Nation Divided. EDMUND BERKELEY and DOROTHY SMITH BERKELEY.
Vol. 100. xvi, 312 pp., 6 figs., 1973. $6.00.

Peter Tudebode: Historia de Hierosolymitano Itinere. JOHN HUGH HILL and LAURITA L. HILL.
Vol. 101. xii, 137 pp., 2 maps, 1974. $5.00.

Benjamin Franklin's Philadelphia Printing: A Descriptive Bibliography. C. WILLIAM MILLER.
Vol. 102. xc, 583 pp., illus., 1974. $40.00.

The Anschluss Movement in Austria and Germany, 1918–1919, and the Paris Peace Conference. ALFRED D. LOW.
Vol. 103. xiv, 495 pp., 4 figs., 4 maps, 1974. Paper. $8.00.

Studies in Pre-Vesalian Anatomy: Biography, Translations, Documents. L. R. LIND.
Vol. 104. xiv, 344 pp., 54 figs., 1975. $18.00.

A Kind of Power: The Shakespeare–Dickens Analogy. ALFRED B. HARBAGE. Jayne Lectures for 1974.
Vol. 105. x, 78 pp., 1975. $4.00.

A Venetian Family and Its Fortune, 1500–1900: The Donà and the Conservation of Their Wealth. JAMES C. DAVIS.
Vol. 106. xvi, 189 pp., 18 figs., 1975. $6.50.

Academica: Plato, Philip of Opus, and the Pseudo-Platonic Epinomis. LEONARDO TARÁN.
Vol. 107. viii, 417 pp., 1975. $20.00.

The Roman Catholic Church and the Creation of the Modern Irish State, 1878–1886. EMMET LARKIN.
Vol. 108. xiv, 412 pp., 2 figs., 1 map, 1975. Paper. $7.50.

Science and the Ante-Bellum American College. STANLEY M. GURALNICK.
Vol. 109. xiv, 227 pp., 1975. Paper. $5.00.

Hilary Abner Herbert: A Southerner Returns to the Union. HUGH B. HAMMETT.
Vol. 110. xvi, 264 pp., 20 figs., 1976. Paper. $5.00.

Census of the Exact Sciences in Sanskrit. Series A, Volume 3. DAVID PINGREE.
Vol. 111. vi, 208 pp., 1976. Paper. $15.00.

TRANSACTIONS
OF THE
AMERICAN PHILOSOPHICAL SOCIETY

The Sacred Officials of the Eleusinian Mysteries. KEVIN CLINTON.
Vol. 64, pt. 3, 143 pp., 17 figs., 1974. $12.00.

Mappae Clavicula: A Little Key to the World of Medieval Techniques. CYRIL STANLEY SMITH and JOHN G. HAWTHORNE.
Vol. 64, pt. 4, 128 pp., 1 fig. (color), 40 pls., 1974. $7.00.

Benjamin Rush: Philosopher of the Revolution. DONALD J. D'ELIA.
Vol. 64, pt. 5, 113 pp., 1974. $5.00.

Ritual Structure and Language Structure of the Todas. MURRAY B. EMENEAU.
Vol. 64, pt. 6, 103 pp., 1974. $6.00.

Gears from the Greeks: The Antikythera Mechanism—A Calendar Computer from *ca.* 80 B.C. DEREK DE SOLLA PRICE.
Vol. 64, pt. 7, 70 pp., 45 figs., 1974. $5.00.

The Imperial Library in Southern Sung China, 1127-1279: A Study of the Organization and Operation of the Scholarly Agencies of the Central Government. JOHN H. WINKELMAN.
Vol. 64, pt. 8, 61 pp., 8 figs., 1974. $5.00.

The Czechoslovak Heresy and Schism: The Emergence of a National Czechoslovak Church. LUDVIK NEMEC.
Vol. 65, pt. 1, 78 pp., 1975. $6.00.

Distractions of Peace During War: The Lloyd George Government's Reactions to Woodrow Wilson, December, 1916-November, 1918. STERLING J. KERNEK.
Vol. 65, pt. 2, 117 pp., 1975. $6.00.

Classification and Development of North American Indian Cultures: A Statistical Analysis of the Driver-Massey Sample. HAROLD E. DRIVER and JAMES L. COFFIN.
Vol. 65, pt. 3, 120 pp., 12 figs., 5 maps, 1975. $7.00.

The Flight of Birds. CRAWFORD H. GREENEWALT.
Vol. 65, pt. 4, 67 pp., 41 figs., 1 pl., 1975. $7.00.

A Guide to Francis Galton's English Men of Science. VICTOR L. HILTS.
Vol. 65, pt. 5, 85 pp., 6 figs., 1975. $5.00.

Justice in Medieval Russia: Muscovite Judgment Charters (*Pravye Gramoty*) of the Fifteenth and Sixteenth Centuries. ANN M. KLEIMOLA.
Vol. 65, pt. 6, 93 pp., 1975. $5.00.

The Sculpture of Taras. JOSEPH COLEMAN CARTER.
Vol. 65, pt. 7, 196 pp., 72 pls., 2 maps, 1975. $18.00.

The Franciscans in South Germany, 1400-1530: Reform and Revolution. PAUL L. NYHUS.
Vol. 65, pt. 8, 47 pp., 1975. $3.00.

The German Center Party, 1890-1906. JOHN K. ZEENDER.
Vol. 66, pt. 1, 125 pp., 2 figs., 1976. $7.50.

Perugia, 1260-1340: Conflict and Change in a Medieval Italian Urban Society. SARAH RUBIN BLANSHEI.
Vol. 66, pt. 2, 128 pp., 2 maps, 1976. $8.50.

Crystals and Compounds: Molecular Structure and Composition in Nineteenth-century French Science. SEYMOUR H. MAUSKOPF.
Vol. 66, pt. 3, 82 pp., 4 figs., 1976. $4.50.

What Is an Ecosystem?

MAKE A CONNECTION
Many kinds of plants and animals live around a coral reef. How do you think the plants and animals affect one another and the things around them?

FIND OUT ABOUT
- the living and nonliving parts of ecosystems
- Earth's different ecosystems

VOCABULARY

environment, p. 4
ecosystem, p. 4
organism, p. 4
biotic, p. 4
abiotic, p. 4
system, p. 5
diversity, p. 5
species, p. 5
population, p. 5
community, p. 5

Parts of an Ecosystem

Imagine you are a frog living at a pond. Flies, lily pads, and water are part of your environment. An **environment** is all the physical things and conditions that surround a living thing.

All the living and nonliving things in one place make up an **ecosystem**. A pond is a freshwater ecosystem. It has living things, or **organisms**, such as animals and plants. The living things in an ecosystem are called **biotic** factors. The pond also has nonliving things, such as water, sunlight, soil, and air. The nonliving things in an ecosystem are called **abiotic** factors.

An ecosystem also includes the interactions among the biotic and abiotic factors. When things interact, they affect one another. For example, beavers interact with water, land, and plants when they build dams.

A frog, a lily pad, and water are all part of a freshwater ecosystem. So are their interactions. ▶

▲ Mallard ducks might be one of the bird species at a pond.

▲ All the painted turtles at a pond make up the painted turtle population.

An ecosystem is a kind of system. A **system** is a group of parts that work together, forming a whole. There is a balance among the factors in an ecosystem. What happens when one factor changes? Other factors will probably be affected.

One ecosystem can support a great variety, or **diversity**, of organisms. Scientists often use these three words to talk about the organisms in an ecosystem.

- **species** Organisms of the same kind belong to the same species. Mallard ducks are one species of birds. Great blue herons are another.
- **population** All the members of one species living in one place make up a population. A pond may be home to a population of 12 painted turtles.
- **community** All the different populations living together in one place make up a community. A pond community can include populations of many different species of animals and plants.

✓ Tell about the two kinds of factors in an ecosystem. Give an example of each.

Ecosystems Around the World

Our planet has many kinds of ecosystems. Some are very large. Others are very small. Some ecosystems have hot and dry weather. Others are cold and snowy.

We can group Earth's ecosystems into several large types. These are often called biomes. Ecosystems in a biome may have a similar climate. *Climate* is the average weather in a place over many years. The ecosystems in a biome may also have similar kinds of soil, plants, and animals.

Living things are found almost everywhere on Earth. Different kinds of living things are found in different places. In each kind of environment, some plants and animals thrive. Their parts or behaviors help them live well in that place. Other organisms do not thrive there but can stay alive. Still other organisms cannot live there at all.

✓ What are some ways ecosystems can be different?

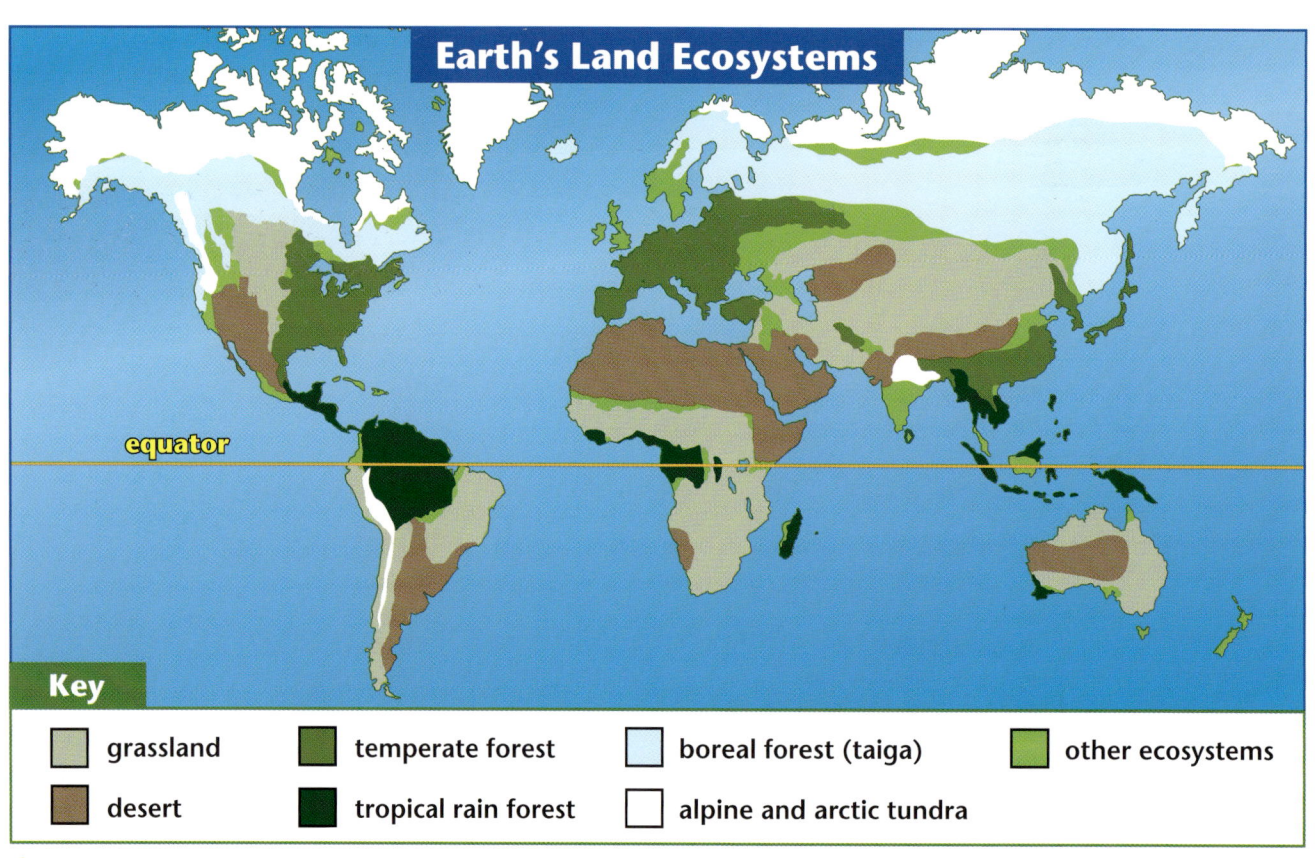

Earth's Land Ecosystems

Key:
- grassland
- desert
- temperate forest
- tropical rain forest
- boreal forest (taiga)
- alpine and arctic tundra
- other ecosystems

▲ This map shows some of Earth's major land ecosystems.

A Closer Look at Some Ecosystems

freshwater

lakes, ponds, rivers, streams
examples of organisms: algae, water plants, beavers, ducks, fish, frogs, insects, turtles

marine

oceans, their shores, estuaries, salt marshes
examples of organisms: seaweed, corals, dolphins, fish, sharks, shellfish, squid, sea stars, whales

desert

very little rain
examples of organisms: cacti, short grasses, coyotes, grasshoppers, lizards, owls, snakes

temperate forest

a medium amount of rain
seasonal weather changes
examples of organisms: mosses, oak and maple trees, shrubs, bears, birds, deer, rabbits

REFLECT ON READING
Before reading, you previewed photographs, captions, and other book features. Which features most helped you understand the different kinds of ecosystems? Tell how the features helped you.

APPLY SCIENCE CONCEPTS
Think about the abiotic and biotic factors in the place where you live. List as many as you can. Then make a picture or collage showing them.

Build Reading Skills
Main Idea and Details

The **main idea** of a paragraph or part of a book is the most important point. **Details** give more information about the main idea.

As you read page 12, look for the main idea about consumers.

TIPS

The topic sentence tells the main idea of a paragraph. It is often the first sentence in the paragraph. To find the main idea, ask, "What is this paragraph mostly about?"

Details may answer Who, What, When, Where, Why, and How questions about the main idea. Details can be

- examples
- descriptions
- reasons
- other facts

A concept web can help you keep track of the main idea and details.

How Do Parts of an Ecosystem Interact?

MAKE A CONNECTION
Sunlight is a very important nonliving part of most ecosystems. How do you think sunlight affects the living things in an ecosystem?

FIND OUT ABOUT
- the needs of living things
- producers, consumers, and decomposers
- symbiotic relationships between organisms
- competition among living things for resources

VOCABULARY

habitat, p. 10	**predator**, p. 12
producer, p. 11	**prey**, p. 12
photosynthesis, p. 11	**scavenger**, p. 12
consumer, p. 12	**decomposer**, p. 13
herbivore, p. 12	**symbiosis**, p. 14
carnivore, p. 12	**competition**, p. 15
omnivore, p. 12	

Needs of Living Things

All organisms need certain things to stay alive.

Needs of Plants
- air
- water
- light
- nutrients, such as minerals
- space to live

Needs of Animals
- air
- water
- food
- shelter
- space to live

Resources are things that an organism can use to meet its needs. An organism depends on resources in its habitat. A **habitat** is the place in nature where an organism lives.

Nonliving things can be resources. Soil is one example. Many plants get water and nutrients from soil. Animals that live in burrows get shelter from soil.

Living things can be resources, too. Many animals depend on plants for food and shelter. For example, some birds eat berries and make nests from twigs.

Plants also depend on animals. Some plants depend on bees to carry pollen from flower to flower. This helps the plants make seeds. Plants are also helped when animals carry their seeds to new places. This can happen when seeds stick to an animal's fur.

✓ List five main things a prairie dog needs to stay alive.

Prairie dogs use the soil for shelter. ▼

Bees are an important resource for some plants. Bees carry pollen from flower to flower. ▼

◀ Plants are producers. They use air, water, and energy from sunlight to make their own food.

Producers, Consumers, and Decomposers

Food has stored energy. Organisms use the energy in food to live and grow. We can group organisms by the way they get food. An organism can be a producer, a consumer, or a decomposer.

Producers

Producers are organisms that make their own food. Green plants are producers. They use carbon dioxide gas from the air, energy from sunlight, and water from the soil to make food. The way plants make food is called **photosynthesis**.

Producers are very important to the animals in an ecosystem. Animals depend on producers such as plants for food. Some animals eat plants. Other animals eat animals that have eaten plants. Producers also give off oxygen. Oxygen is a gas that animals need to breathe.

Consumers

Animals cannot make their own food as most plants do. Animals are consumers. **Consumers** are living things that eat, or consume, other living things. Consumers get energy from their food. They also get nutrients such as vitamins and minerals. There are three main kinds of consumers.

1. **Herbivores** eat only plants.
2. **Carnivores** eat only animals.
3. **Omnivores** eat both plants and animals.

A consumer that hunts and eats other animals is called a **predator**. The animals that a predator hunts and eats are called **prey**.

Consumers help keep an ecosystem in balance. They do this by eating other living things. This helps keep the populations in a community from getting too large.

Consumers

herbivore

A koala is a herbivore. Koalas eat mostly eucalyptus leaves. Deer, cows, and grasshoppers are other herbivores.

carnivore

A great white shark is a carnivore. Great white sharks hunt and eat fish, seals, sea lions, and even small whales. Wolves, lions, and snakes are other carnivores.

Some carnivores are **scavengers**. They eat animals that are already dead. Vultures and shrimp are scavengers.

Decomposers

Decomposers are organisms that break down dead plants and animals to get food. Earthworms and insects are decomposers. So are fungi, such as mushrooms. Bacteria are decomposers, too. You may think of bacteria as harmful germs. But most bacteria are helpful to other living things.

Decomposers break down dead plants and animals into nutrients. A decomposer uses some of the nutrients itself for energy and growth. The rest go into the soil, where plants can use them.

✓ Why are producers important to consumers in an ecosystem?

omnivore

A black bear is an omnivore. Some black bears eat berries in the summer and nuts in the fall. Then they eat ants and bees in the spring. Raccoons, blue jays, and most people are also omnivores.

Decomposers

earthworm

fungi

Earthworms and fungi are decomposers.

Symbiosis

Organisms of two different species sometimes have a special relationship. The relationship helps one or both of the organisms meet its needs. This kind of relationship is known as **symbiosis**.

One kind of symbiotic relationship helps both organisms. A cleaner shrimp eats bacteria and dead skin from the teeth and body of a fish. The cleaner shrimp gets food. The fish stays clean.

A second kind of symbiotic relationship helps one organism and does not affect the other. An orchid plant might grow high in a rain forest tree. The orchid gets sunlight. The tree is not helped or harmed.

A third kind of symbiotic relationship helps one organism but harms the other. Some wasps lay their eggs on caterpillars. When the eggs hatch, the young wasps eat the caterpillar. This helps the wasps but kills the caterpillar.

✓ What is a symbiotic relationship? Give one example.

A cleaner shrimp cleaning a fish is an example of symbiosis. ▼

An orchid living high in a tree is another example of symbiosis. ▼

Competition

A kind of struggle can happen among living things that share resources. Suppose both bears and birds eat from the same berry patch. There might not be enough berries for all the animals. The struggle for resources is called **competition**. Organisms often compete for things such as food and water. Competition can take place among members of the same species. Or competition can happen among different species.

The number of living things in an ecosystem depends on the amount of resources. Sometimes there are plenty of resources. So there is not as much competition. Populations might grow. But when populations get larger, there is more competition. This can make populations stop growing or get smaller.

✓ **What is competition? Why does it happen?**

Giraffes compete with one another for leaves to eat. They also compete with other kinds of animals for food. ▶

REFLECT ON READING
Make a concept web like the one on page 8. Use it to keep track of ideas about consumers. Put the main idea in the middle. Add details, such as examples.

APPLY SCIENCE CONCEPTS
Think about some resources from nature that you used today. Write about them in your science notebook. Give examples of both nonliving and living resources.

Build Reading Skills
How to Read Diagrams

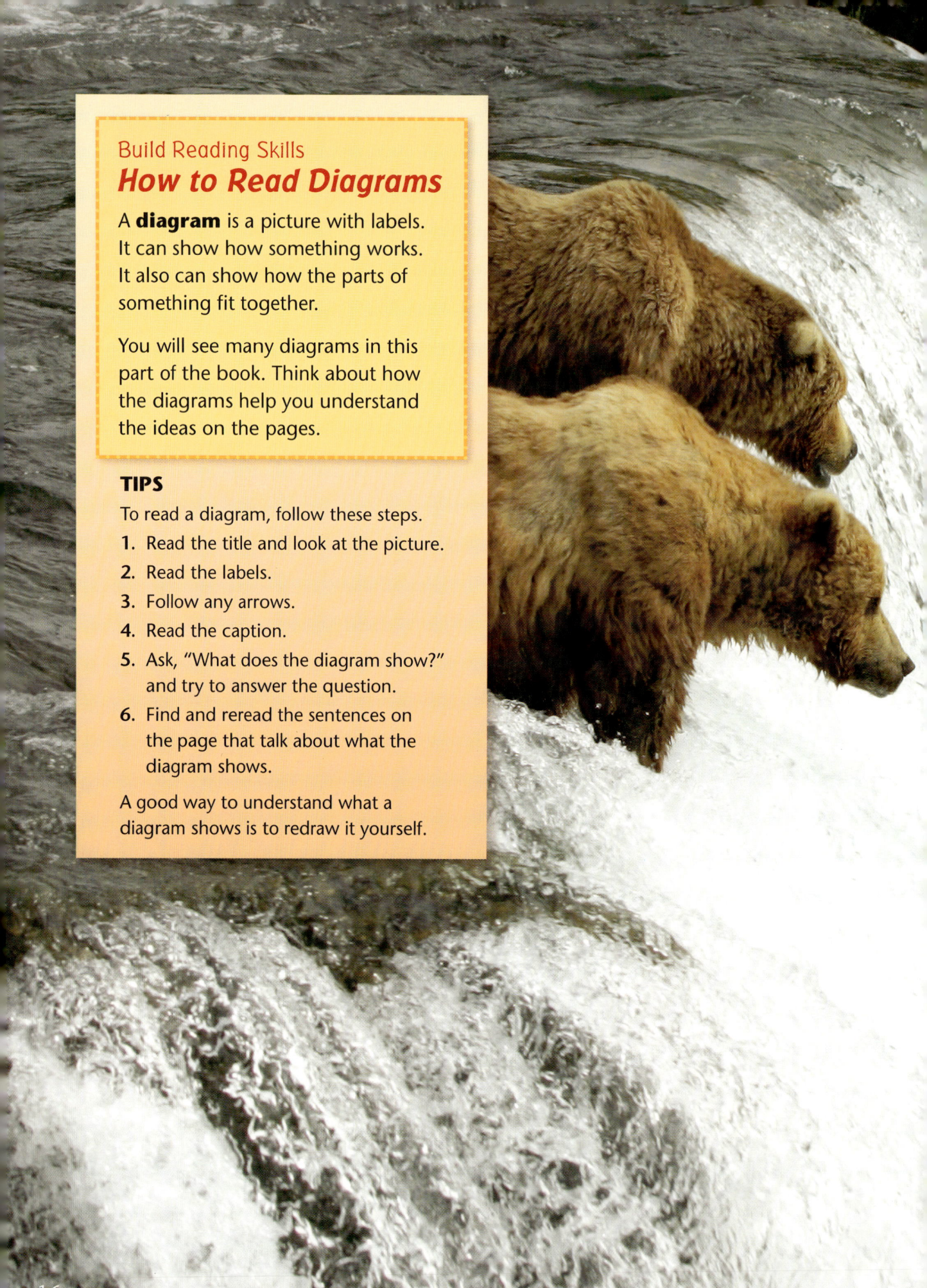

A **diagram** is a picture with labels. It can show how something works. It also can show how the parts of something fit together.

You will see many diagrams in this part of the book. Think about how the diagrams help you understand the ideas on the pages.

TIPS

To read a diagram, follow these steps.
1. Read the title and look at the picture.
2. Read the labels.
3. Follow any arrows.
4. Read the caption.
5. Ask, "What does the diagram show?" and try to answer the question.
6. Find and reread the sentences on the page that talk about what the diagram shows.

A good way to understand what a diagram shows is to redraw it yourself.

How Do Energy and Matter Move Through Ecosystems?

MAKE A CONNECTION

Plants and animals need energy in order to live and grow. The bear that eats this fish will get energy from it. Where do you think the energy in the fish came from?

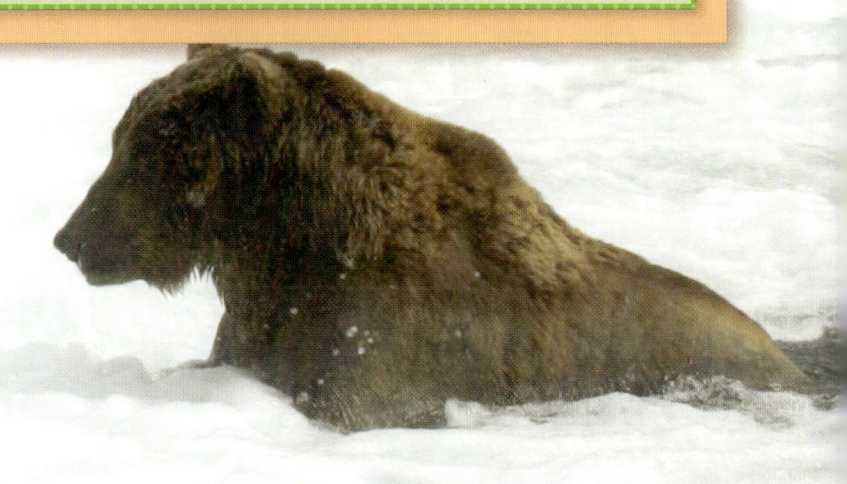

FIND OUT ABOUT
- food chains, food webs, and energy pyramids
- how matter is recycled in ecosystems

VOCABULARY

ecologist, p. 18
food chain, p. 18
food web, p. 20
niche, p. 21
energy pyramid, p. 22

Energy in Ecosystems

Food Chains

Ecologists study ecosystems. They look at how energy moves from one living thing to another in a community. Living things get energy from their food.

A **food chain** is a series of organisms that depend on one another for food. A food chain diagram shows the path that the energy in food takes as it is passed from one organism to another. Most communities have many different food chains.

A food chain diagram shows the path that the energy in food takes as it is passed from one organism to another. ▼

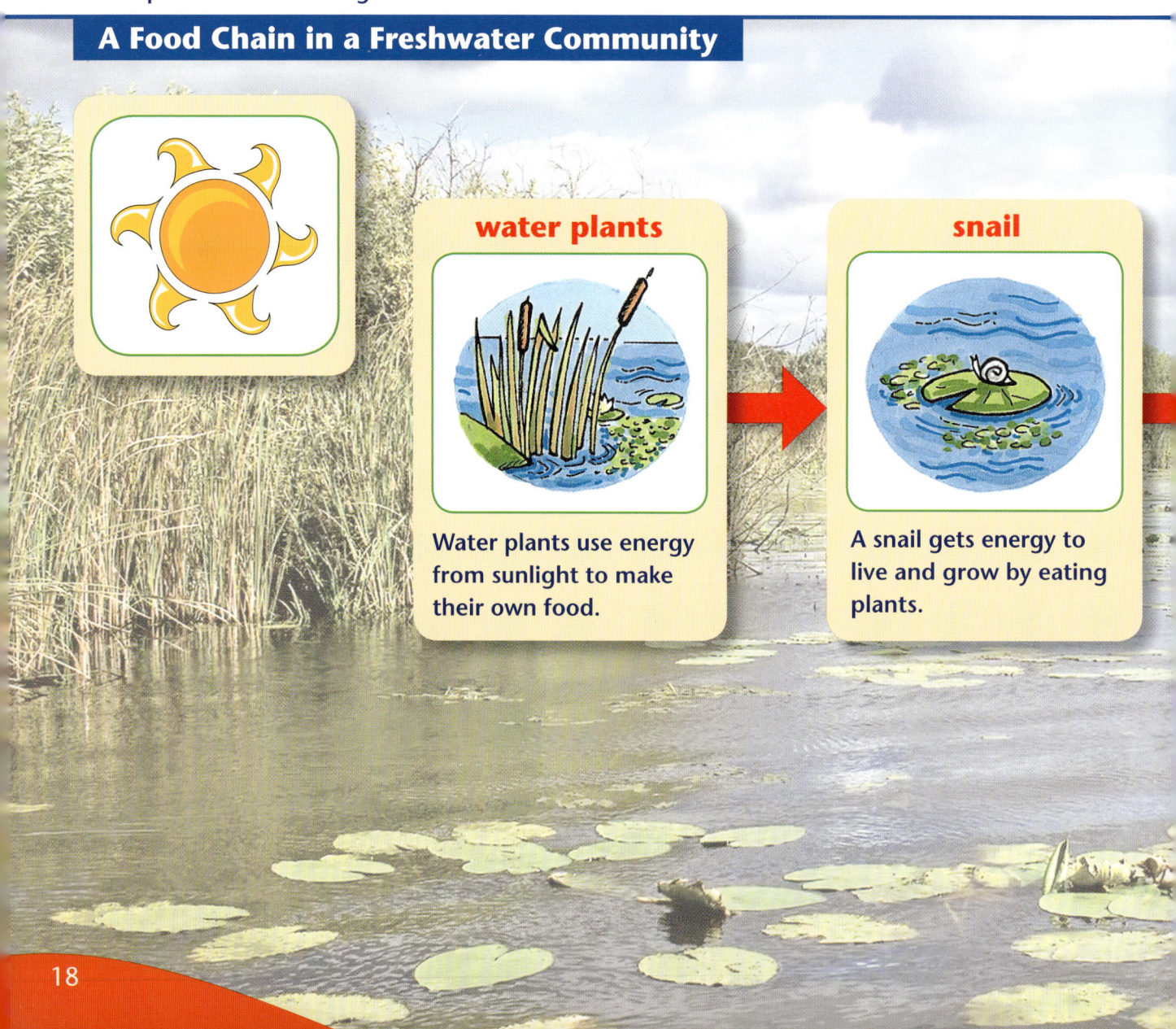

A Food Chain in a Freshwater Community

water plants

Water plants use energy from sunlight to make their own food.

snail

A snail gets energy to live and grow by eating plants.

Let's look at one food chain in a freshwater community. A water plant gets energy from sunlight. The plant uses the energy to make its own food. Suppose a snail then eats the plant. The energy stored in the plant goes into the snail. Next, a fish eats the snail and gets the energy. Finally, a heron eats the fish. Where did the energy in the heron's food first come from? The answer is the Sun. The Sun is the energy source for almost all food chains.

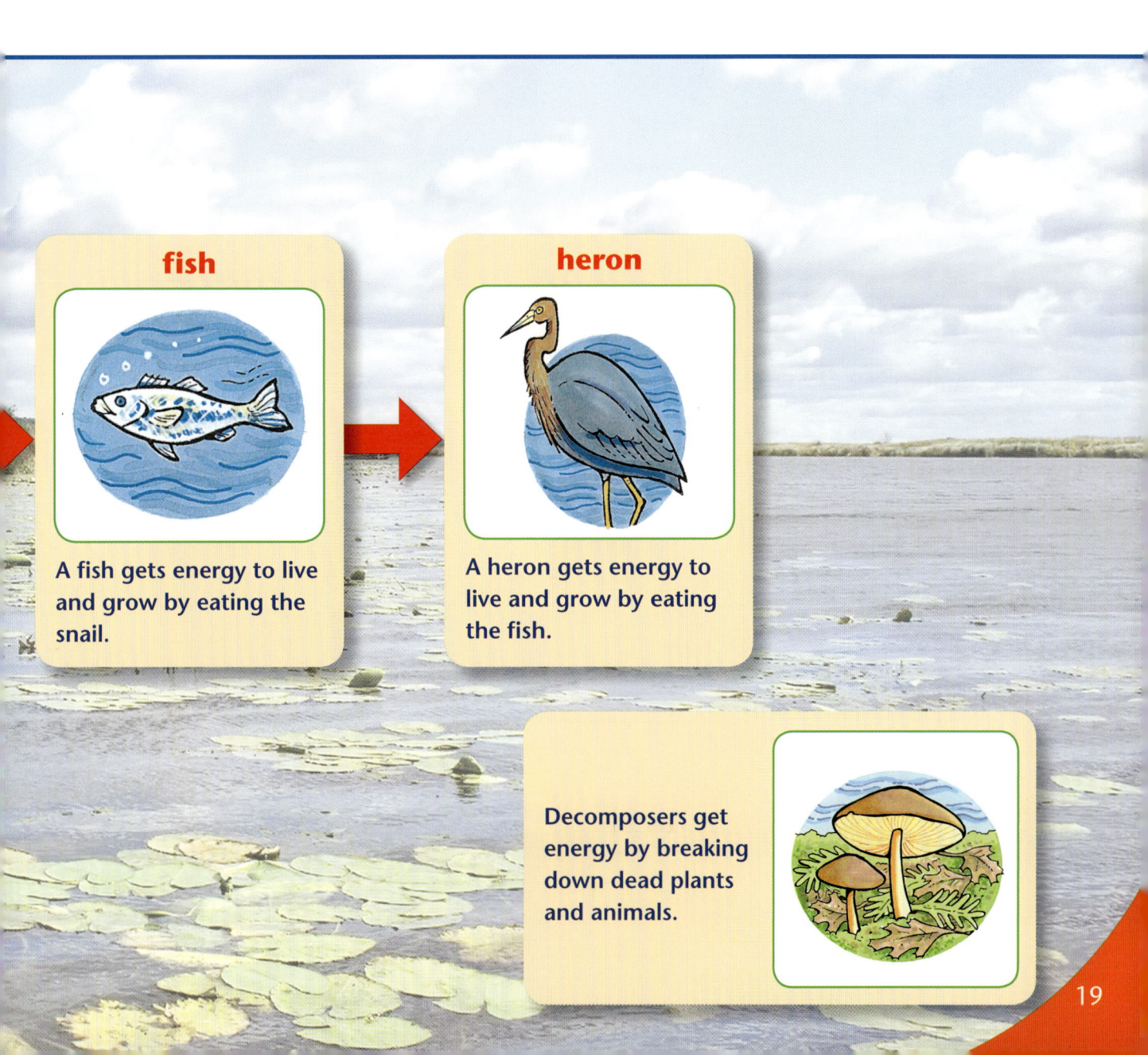

fish

heron

A fish gets energy to live and grow by eating the snail.

A heron gets energy to live and grow by eating the fish.

Decomposers get energy by breaking down dead plants and animals.

Food Webs

Plants and animals can be part of more than one food chain. The different food chains in a community can connect and overlap. The connected food chains form a **food web**.

Look at the food web diagram. These plants and animals live in a boreal forest ecosystem. The diagram shows how some of their food chains connect. Find the vole in the diagram. Voles eat grasses, seeds, and berries. How many

This food web diagram shows some of the food chains in a community. ▼

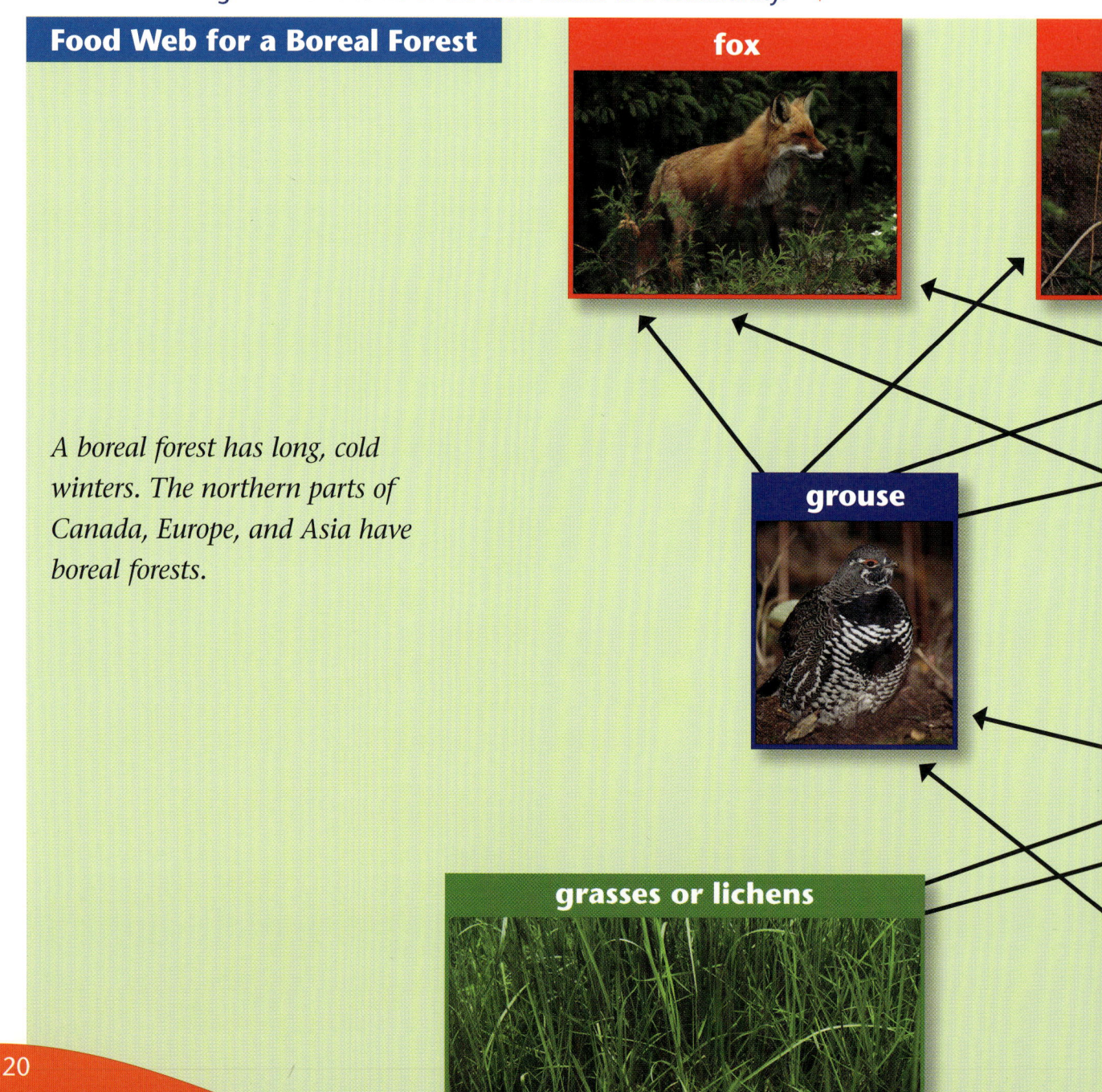

Food Web for a Boreal Forest

fox

A boreal forest has long, cold winters. The northern parts of Canada, Europe, and Asia have boreal forests.

grouse

grasses or lichens

arrows point from the vole to other animals? Those arrows show that voles are eaten by foxes, owls, lynxes, and pine martens. Suppose a disease kills many voles in this community. The animals that eat voles might have to eat more hares, grouse, or red squirrels instead.

Every organism in a habitat has its own role, or **niche**. A food web can tell us things about an organism's niche. Part of a squirrel's niche might be to eat seeds and berries and to become food for an owl or a pine marten.

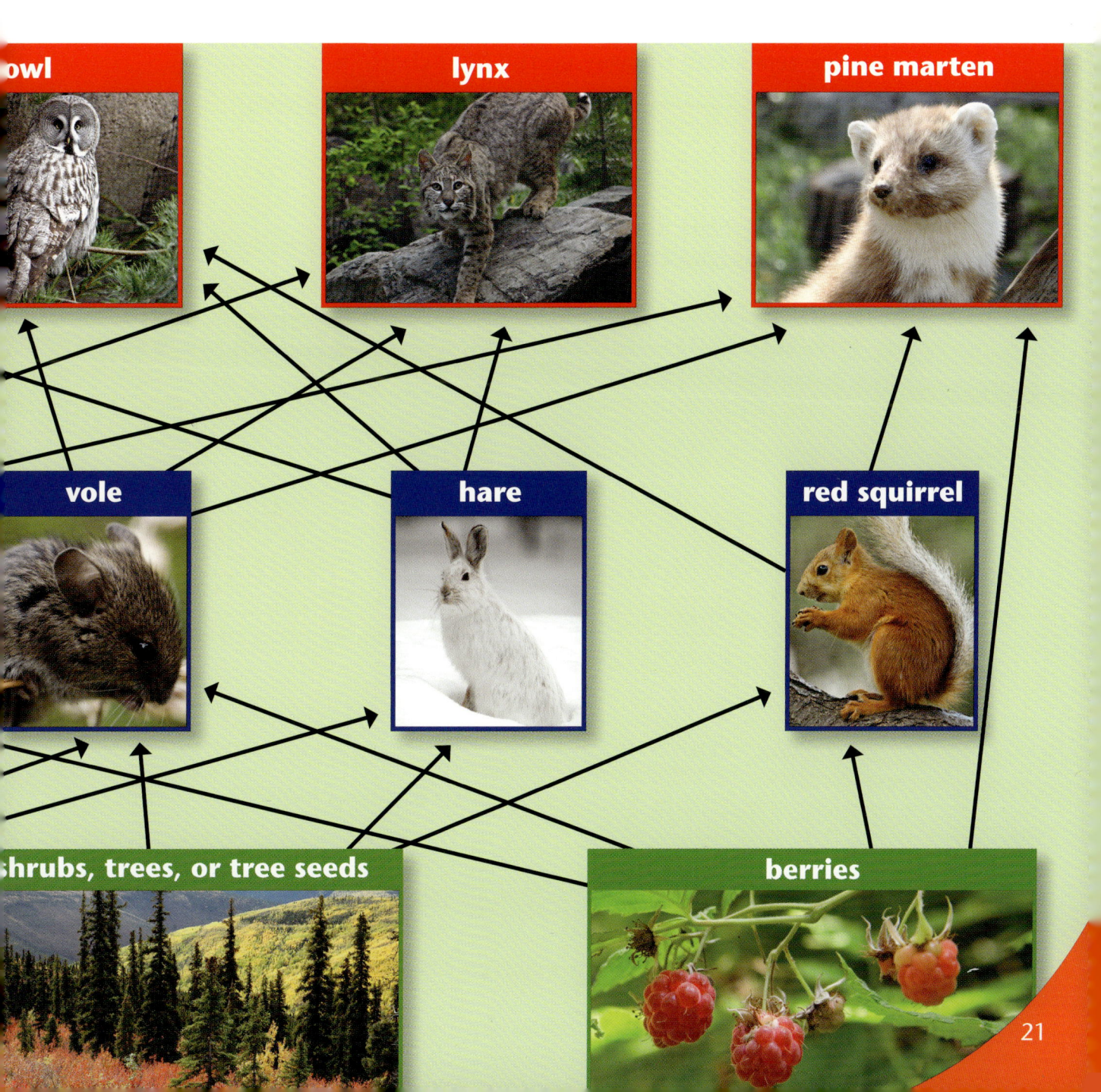

Energy Pyramids

Each organism in a food chain gets energy from its food. The organism uses up most of that energy to live and grow. Only the energy the organism does not use is passed to the next member of the food chain.

An **energy pyramid** diagram shows the amount of energy moving through a food chain. Look at the bottom level first. Producers use up most of the energy they get from the Sun. The small amount left over is passed to consumers in the next level up. Those consumers must eat many producers to get the energy they need. This pattern repeats all the way up the food chain. It takes many organisms at the bottom to support just a few at the top.

✓ What does an energy pyramid diagram show?

An energy pyramid diagram shows the amount of energy moving through a food chain. Energy moves from the producers at the bottom to the consumers above. ▼

Energy Pyramid for a Desert Food Chain

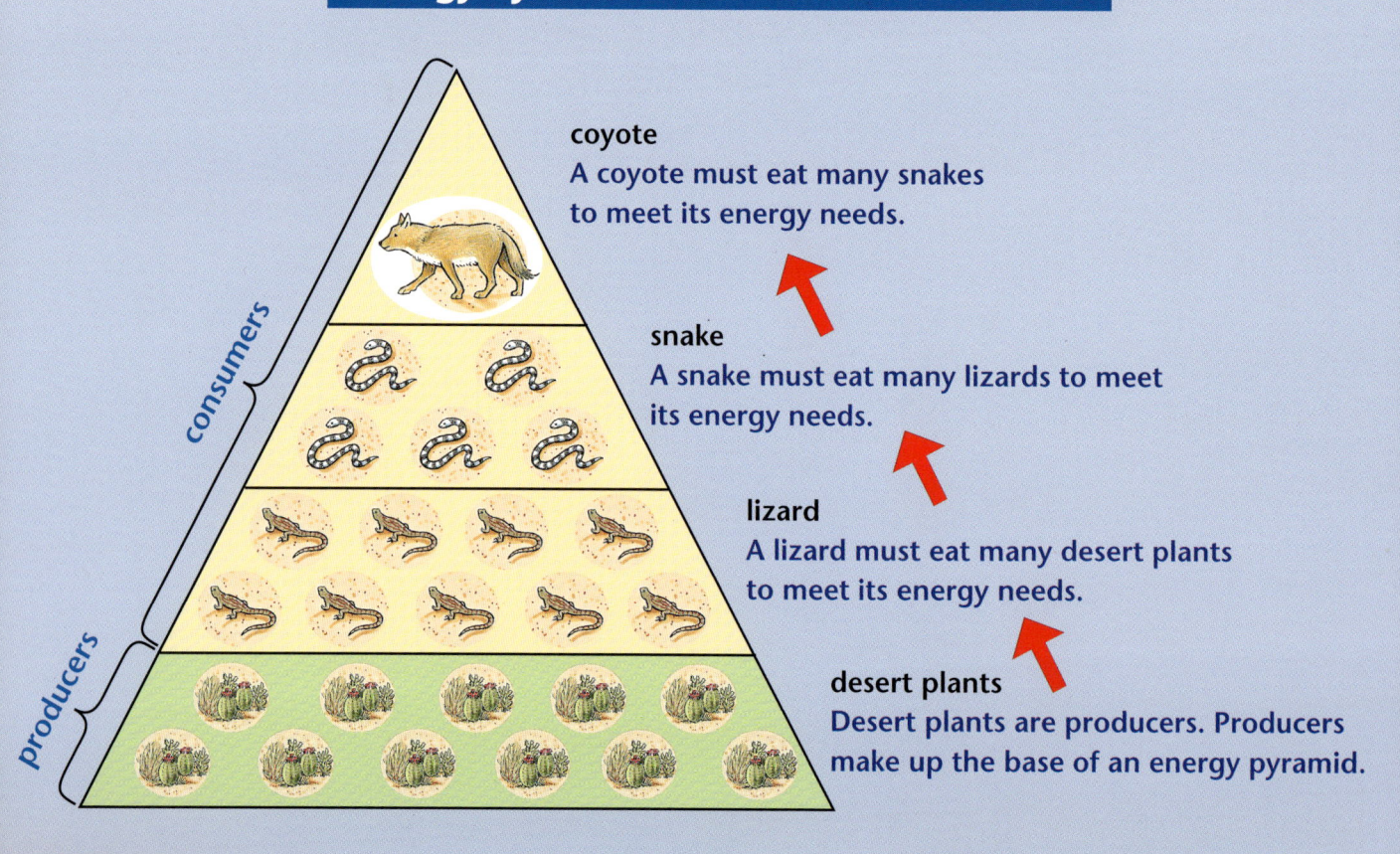

coyote
A coyote must eat many snakes to meet its energy needs.

snake
A snake must eat many lizards to meet its energy needs.

lizard
A lizard must eat many desert plants to meet its energy needs.

desert plants
Desert plants are producers. Producers make up the base of an energy pyramid.

22

Matter in Ecosystems

Energy is always moving through ecosystems. Matter moves through ecosystems, too. Matter is anything that takes up space and has mass. Nitrogen is one kind of matter. Nitrogen gas makes up most of the air. Nitrogen also is a nutrient that living things need in order to grow.

Nitrogen moves in a cycle. First, it moves from the air into the soil. Next, it moves into living things. Then, it moves back into the soil. Finally, it moves back into the air. The cycle continues.

✓ How does nitrogen move in a cycle through an ecosystem?

Cycles of Matter: Nitrogen

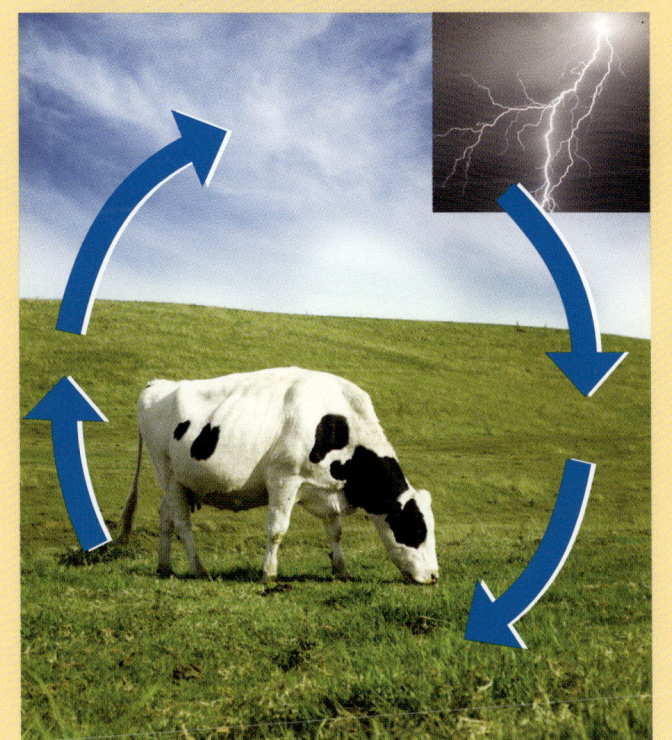

Lightning changes nitrogen gas in the air into a form of nitrogen that plants can use. Rain carries it into the soil.

Some *bacteria in the soil* change nitrogen gas into forms of nitrogen that plants can use.

Plants take in nitrogen from the soil.

Animals take in nitrogen by eating plants or by eating animals that eat plants.

Some *bacteria in the soil* change nitrogen in soil into nitrogen gas. It becomes part of the air.

Animal wastes and decomposing material release nitrogen into the soil.

REFLECT ON READING

Suppose a mouse eats some grass seeds. Then a cat eats the mouse. Make a food chain diagram showing these organisms. Show where the energy in the food chain first comes from.

APPLY SCIENCE CONCEPTS

Think of one food you ate for lunch this week. Write a paragraph about the path the energy in the food took on its way to your plate.

Glossary

abiotic (ay-bye-AH-tik) nonliving **(4)**

biotic (bye-AH-tik) living **(4)**

carnivore (KAHR-nuh-vor) a consumer that eats only animals **(12)**

community (kuh-MYOO-nuh-tee) all the different populations of organisms living together in one place **(5)**

competition (kom-puh-TISH-uhn) the struggle among living things that share the same resources such as sources of food, water, or shelter **(15)**

consumer (kuhn-SOO-mur) a living thing that cannot make its own food and must get energy by eating other living things; animals are consumers **(12)**

decomposer (dee-kuhm-POH-zur) a living thing that gets energy by breaking down the remains of dead plants and animals; fungi (such as mushrooms), bacteria, and some animals (such as insects and earthworms) are decomposers **(13)**

diversity (duh-VUR-suh-tee) variety **(5)**

ecologist (ee-KAH-luh-jist) a scientist who studies ecosystems **(18)**

ecosystem (EE-koh-sis-tuhm) all the living and nonliving things in one place and all their interactions; examples are grassland, desert, rain forest, and freshwater ecosystems **(4)**

energy pyramid (EN-ur-jee PIR-uh-mid) a diagram that shows the amount of energy moving through a food chain **(22)**

environment (en-VYE-ruhn-muhnt) all the physical things and conditions, such as soil, air, climate, plants, and animals, that surround a living thing **(4)**

food chain (FOOD CHAYN) a series of organisms that depend on one another for food; energy is passed from one organism to another in a food chain **(18)**

food web (FOOD WEB) the connected food chains in a community **(20)**

habitat (HAB-i-tat) the place in nature that is home to a living thing **(10)**

herbivore (HUR-buh-vor) a consumer that eats only plants **(12)**

niche (NICH) the role of a living thing in its habitat; includes where an organism lives, what it eats or takes in from its surroundings, and how it affects the other living and nonliving things in its habitat **(21)**

omnivore (OM-nuh-vor) a consumer that eats both plants and animals **(12)**

organism (OR-guh-niz-uhm) a living thing such as a plant or an animal **(4)**

photosynthesis (foh-toh-SIN-thuh-sis) the process by which a producer such as a plant makes its own food **(11)**

population (pop-yuh-LAY-shuhn) all the members of one species living in a place **(5)**

predator (PRED-uh-tur) an animal that hunts and eats other animals **(12)**

prey (PRAY) an animal that is hunted and eaten by a predator **(12)**

producer (pruh-DOO-sur) a living thing that makes its own food and serves as food for consumers; most plants are producers **(11)**

scavenger (SKAV-uhn-jur) a consumer that eats animals that are already dead **(12)**

species (SPEE-sheez) a group made up of all the living things of the same kind; mallard ducks and great blue herons are two different species of birds **(5)**

symbiosis (sim-bye-OH-sis) a relationship between two living things of different species that helps at least one of them meet its needs **(14)**

system (SIS-tuhm) a group of parts that work together, forming a whole **(5)**